Your Journey to Love

ANGELIC RECIPES FOR CREATING AND EXPERIENCING HEAVEN ON EARTH

BONNIE ANN LEWIS

SWAN
SELF-AWARENESS
CENTRE

PUBLISHED BY
Swan Self-Awareness Centre, Inc.
P.O. Box 151447
Austin, Texas 78715
www.swanselfawarenesscentre.com
www.bonnieannlewis.com

© 2010 by Bonnie Ann Lewis

All rights reserved. No part of this book may be reproduced in any form or by any means without written permission from the author. For excerpts or permissions to use any material from this book, contact the Swan Self-Awareness Centre, Inc. All quotes throughout this book that do not have author after are by Bonnie Ann Lewis. These quotes may be used in their entirety, including credit to author without written permission.

The information in this book is for personal growth purposes only. It is meant to be used in conjunction with, not in place of any necessary healthcare treatment. The author's intention is to offer information to assist you in establishing a healthy well-being. The author nor the publisher assume any responsibility for how you choose to use this information.

First Printing: May 2010

Library of Congress Control Number: 2009927123

ISBN-13: 978-0-9818698-4-1
ISBN-10: 0-9818698-4-X

Printed in China by Everbest Printing Co. through
Four Colour Imports, Ltd., Louisville, Kentucky

Visionary and cover art by Eva M. Sakmar-Sullivan
Book design by Jill Lynn Design
Edited by Carolyn Porter, D. Div.
Author photography by Bill Bastas

This book is lovingly dedicated to all of humanity.

FROM MY HEART TO YOURS . . .
My purpose for writing this book is to share with you
this angelic wisdom in the hope that it will lead you back
to the truth of who you are and why you are here.
My prayer is that the angelic guidance you receive from this
book fills your heart with love, your path with light, and
reflects to you the truths within your soul as it has mine.
May these pages reflect to you the beauty within
yourself so you can let your light shine.
My dream is that this divine guide paves the way
for you to create a life you will love and experience
heaven here on earth with love, grace and ease.

Love and Angel Blessings to you,
—Bonnie

ON ANGELS' WINGS

May the love within these pages embrace you like your angels' wings.

May this book be your guide and friend on your journey to love.

May it bring you the support, inspiration, encouragement,

Motivation, nourishment, empowerment and most of all,

The love that you desire, deserve and require

To succeed and fulfill your life's mission.

May you enjoy your journey to love . . . on angels' wings!

Gratitude and Blessings

This book is a collaboration of the essence of many on earth and many in spirit. I feel honored to be a part of this circle of love that is assisting humanity in evolving to our divine nature, and guiding the transformation taking place on our planet so we may all embrace the energy of our new earth. Unconditional love is the energy that creates heaven here on earth: love, peace, unity, abundance and freedom.

I contribute much of my success and richness in my life to God and my "friends in high places," my angels, the archangels, ascended masters and my guides for they have paved my way. It is amazing what we can accomplish when we invite these beings of light into our lives and allow God to express through us. I am grateful for all the support, guidance, inspiration, encouragement, nurturing and infinite love I receive as I continue fulfilling my life's mission.

My sincere gratitude to all who supported me on my journey to love, guiding me as I learned to spread my wings and fly while keeping my feet on the ground! Words can only scratch the surface of describing how all of your presence has touched my life. If you experience a fraction of what you have given me, you will be infinitely rich.

John Lewis, my wonderful husband, for your infinite love and support while I wrote this book, for believing in me when I doubted myself and for holding my hand and my heart with compassion as I created my life anew. Your gentle loving nature gives me the freedom to spread my wings and fly. I am blessed to have you as my partner to walk hand in hand and heart to heart with through life.

My precious children, Rebecca and Joshua, for you have both taught me the true meaning of unconditional love. I feel very blessed for you are both God's greatest gift to me. I'm glad you chose me to guide you through life.

Paulette Daubresse, my mom, for giving me the gift of life, and for always being there for me. You were my rock through many challenging experiences in my life. You taught me that beyond the rain there is always a rainbow waiting to shine. Your spirit lives on within me.

Doreen Virtue, it is beyond words the impact your teachings have had on my life. They have been an answer to many of my prayers and I am ever so grateful for your beautiful presence.

Louise Hay, for your teachings have touched my heart and enriched my life. They have been a part of my life since I was a teenager and have followed and guided me to where I am today. You are a divine model and inspiration for all.

Peter Sterling, for your beautiful *Harp Magic,* that has been so much a part of this book, my life and my spiritual awakening. It has touched my heart and soul.

Karen Hutchins, for your contribution to this book and for all the hours you listened to me, laughed with me, cried with me and held my hand as I worked through some of the most traumatic experiences of my life. Your guidance has been a blessing beyond words. I treasure our friendship.

Carolyn Porter, for paving my way in bringing this book to life, and for your teachings and inspiration in helping me to overcome my fear of speaking my truth, and most of all your friendship.

Christina Green, for your love, support and inspiration as I brought to life the angelic meditations in this book, and most of all for your loving essence and friendship.

Jill Anderson, for your beautiful design work that gave this book character and life. Thank you for your expertise, creativity and for making sure this book was all that I dreamed it to be.

Bekah Saylor, at Four Colour Print Group, for your expertise, efficiency and suggestions that contributed to the creation of this beautiful book.

Eva Sakmar-Sullivan, for your beautiful artwork that portrays the essence of God, and colored this book with love. You have an incredible vision for our new earth that is reflected in your art. Bless you for your amazing talents that are such a gift to this world. I am blessed to know you.

With love and gratitude from the bottom of my heart, and the depths of my soul to all who contributed to my journey to love and this book. I am so blessed!

Table of Contents

Preface... 11
Introduction: You Are the Creator of Your Own Life............ 17

PART I: AWAKENING TO LOVE

CHAPTER 1	The Awakening	33
CHAPTER 2	Self-Awareness	54
CHAPTER 3	Aspects of You	69
CHAPTER 4	The Mind, Body and Spirit Connection	147
CHAPTER 5	Your Spiritual Team	164
CHAPTER 6	Reflections	233

PART II: THE POWER OF LOVE

CHAPTER 7	Unconditional Love	272
CHAPTER 8	Creating Loving, Fulfilling Relationships	305
CHAPTER 9	Getting to the Heart of the Matter	364
CHAPTER 10	Freedom................................	399

PART III: CREATING WITH LOVE

CHAPTER 11	Co-Creating.............................	427
CHAPTER 12	Creating Your Divine Life...................	441
CONCLUSION	Creating Heaven on Earth	496

PART IV: GIFTS OF LOVE

Blessings and Congratulations 518
Angelic Exercises 520
Angelic Tools by Bonnie Ann Lewis 522
Connections... 523
About the Cover/Divine Inspirations 524
Afterword 526
About the Author 528
Your Journey to Love Daily Practices 530

Preface

I was born on the east coast and lived in Swansea, Massachusetts until age two, at which time we moved to Michigan where I grew up. The two gifts I carry with me from the east coast are my love of the ocean and swans. I have always loved flowers, animals, rocks and crystals and being out in nature. As a child, I felt things very deeply. At some point I put a big shell around me to protect myself from the harshness of earth energies. I closed off my true feelings so I could not get hurt and people could not get too close. I spent a lot of time tuned into the spiritual realms, interacting with all the angels and fairies. This is where I found much comfort, felt so much love, and it was very familiar to me. My favorite thing to do was to be outside at the park swinging and singing. This gave me a sense of freedom. I also enjoyed playing the organ and singing. During my childhood, my creativity was in full swing. I remember I would draw pictures, write stories and see visions of what I knew my life was to be, not realizing what I was doing nor the power of those activities. My childhood dreams for when I grew up were to be a mom, (I have always loved children and began babysitting at a very young age), a veterinarian or a teacher.

As a teenager my aspirations were to be a writer of poems and stories about life experiences to help and inspire others. When I was in high school I remember hearing about others fighting after school and I would get this sick feeling in the pit of my stomach. It hurt me to see this. I was concerned someone would approach me and I did not want to fight as I am a peacemaker. Fortunately, I was not one to follow the crowd so I never attracted those experiences. I also believe my angels were around me protecting me, although at that time I was not consciously aware of them. At age 17, I saw for the first time a homeless person sleeping on the doorstep of a downtown store. A feeling of sadness came over me and I thought nobody should have to live like that. When I moved to Austin, I saw more homeless people and began giving to them and sending them angels and love. In my later teens, I began reading metaphysical books by Louise Hay and books on reincarnation. These books really spoke to me. I did not resonate with the fear-based beliefs I was seeing in society although I sure collected my share of these along the way. I always believed everyone deserved and could have all that they desired and that there was plenty to go around for all of us.

As a young adult I took some beginning psychology classes. Oftentimes when I would go to public places such as the grocery store, I'd be standing in line and the people next to me would tell me about their personal life. I would offer a few inspirational words and go on my merry way. People I knew would come to me for advice and what I said made them feel better. This brought me joy knowing I had helped them. I later came to understand these words of wisdom came through me not from me. They were an example of God expressing through me. I have always had a passion for helping others, making things better, and I knew there had to be a better way of life for all than what I was seeing, and I was determined to find it. Looking back I understand how these passions have shaped who I am and have led me to where I am today. I knew I was here to make a difference in the world, but I was not sure to what extent or how to make that happen. I had many visions and dreams, and I knew so clearly what I desired my life to be, but I did not know how to achieve those aspirations. Like many of us, as I grew up I disconnected from these spiritual truths.

PREFACE

I recall searching for answers to what life was really about. At that time, I did not realize that all the answers were inside of me. I recall my sisters and friends saying, "You always get what you want." I really did accomplish my goals but felt like something was missing; I did not feel fulfilled. I felt like there had to be more to life than what I was experiencing. I came to realize I was trying to make my life what I wanted it to be from the outside in instead of the inside out and some of my experiences and relationships did not reflect my true desires. What I did not understand was why earth life did not reflect what I was seeing as truth in the spiritual realms. This was both confusing and frustrating to me as I thought what I saw in the spiritual realm is how life should be. I have come to understand that spirit shows us the ideal, giving us the opportunity to manifest it into form, and that God's will for us is the same as our higher self's will. I'd like to expand on this idea a step further as I share with you the description of heaven and earth that I read in the book *The Revealing Word* by Charles Filmore. It states, "Heaven and earth are two states of mind, the ideal and the manifestation. According to Revelation 21:1 we are to have new ideals with manifestations in the earth to correspond. God visioned two planes of consciousness, the heaven and the earth, or more properly, "the heavens and the earth." One is the realm of pure ideas; the other, of thought forms. Heaven is the orderly realization of divine ideas. Earth is the manifestation of these ideas."

This is not a religious book, but rather a non-denominational, spiritual guide for living, presenting universal wisdom. I'd like to share with you a description of spirituality that resonates with me. It came from an article written in the Hay House Present Moments Newsletter, April 2006, *The Creative Healing Force* by Eve A. Wood, M.D. Dr. Wood states, "I have come to believe, beyond any shadow of a doubt, that spirituality is the cornerstone of mental and physical health—but I want to be absolutely clear about what I mean when I say spirituality. To my mind, spirituality is a sense of meaning and purpose, and an ability to see what is possible in the world. It is an awareness of and a respect for one's inner wisdom. It is a receptiveness and an openness to the love, potential, and healing power in the universe. That said, spirituality does not necessarily have to involve organized religion. Many people are extremely religious, but they may not be spiritual; others are extraordinarily spiritual, but have no affiliation to a church, temple, or a congregation."

Many people lose sight of these spiritual truths due to religious beliefs and traditions. Throughout this book I refer to our creator as God, to reflect my own beliefs. I encourage you to use whatever label fits your beliefs. Everyone has their own definition, perception and relationship with God. I believe there are many paths to God and I encourage you to choose the path that speaks to your heart. The definition of God that resonates with me I quote here from *Divine Guidance* by Doreen Virtue, "God is all loving, all knowing and everywhere. We possess these qualities. God is pure love, pure light and pure intelligence. Every gift we could ever desire is produced from this source."

This divine guide is a reflection of how I brought these spiritual truths into my earth experience with the assistance of the angelic realm. It encompasses angelic guidance and ancient wisdom reflecting what I refer to as angelic wisdom. The ancient wisdom (meaning teachings from the past coming forth to help us now) within these pages came to and through me from a group of benevolent beings sent and guided by Jesus who I know as Comaneeshea, meaning common essence. It came to me that it reflects the Essenes way of life and the teachings of Jesus. These are lessons in love from the Dead Sea Scrolls. I've come to know these benevolent beings as the angels, archangels, and ascended masters as they assisted me in bringing forth this wisdom and implementing these principles of love into my life. I consider them my "friends in high places" as they are always there for me and available 24/7. They are my behind the scenes God team. They are always there to listen and bring to me whatever I ask for in a way that is for the highest good of myself and all concerned. They send an infinite flow of unconditional love when I am afraid. I am always safe in their embrace. They bring me clarity when I am confused. They help me connect with my true self and bring forth the truths within my soul, and they gently guide me back on my path when I lose my way. I communicate with them throughout my day and miracles continue to be a part of my life experience. This book is an example of these blessings. The angels want us to experience love, peace, joy and abundance in our lives and they are here to assist us in accomplishing that. Inviting the angels into your life will expedite your healing and transform your life in miraculous ways!

Along my journey, I have been touched by the teachings and tools by some divine spiritual teachers and leaders who have lit my path. The most prominent being Doreen Virtue, Louise L. Hay, Neal Donald Walsh, Ted Andrews, and Peter Sterling. I am truly blessed! I am very grateful for these teachings as they have led me to a greater understanding of myself and the oneness with all of life that has enriched my life tremendously. These angelic recipes are a compilation of my expertise as an ANGEL THERAPY PRACTITIONER ® (ATP®) and Spiritual Teacher, my own personal experiences and most importantly, divine guidance. The angelic wisdom within came to me as an answer to my prayers when I was facing some challenges and experiencing unsatisfying circumstances in my own life. Since then I have been applying these angelic principles along with angelic tools to my own life and in my Angel Therapy® practice, therefore gathering angelic recipes along the way. Angel Therapy® is a non-denominational method of spiritual healing that involves working with the angelic realm. I live, love and teach these principles for they have become a divine way of living for me. My vision is for all to experience on the earth plane that which I see in the spiritual realm . . . oneness, unconditional love and abundance of good for all. In other words, heaven here on earth: love, peace, unity, abundance and freedom. My passion is to teach these principles of unconditional love so we may all create and experience heaven here on earth. I feel so blessed to be the messenger and model for the angelic wisdom within this book. May it open your eyes and your heart and pave your way to creating a life you will love!

Introduction

You are the creator of your own life and a co-creator of this universe with source—God/Angels/Spirit. Everything you experience in your life you have created consciously or unconsciously and have chosen to experience before you incarnated in this lifetime. On a soul level, while still in the spiritual realm, along with your angels and guides, you have chosen your lessons. Spirit creates conditions necessary for us to learn these chosen lessons. Before you incarnated into this lifetime you chose the time of your birth and the time you will leave this earth. Everyone in your life you have chosen to reflect to you what you came here to learn through experience. You chose your parents, siblings, partners, friends, acquaintances, co-workers, experiences and yes, your body. So . . . love them all!

We are all one in spirit, however, due to our soul's personal path and choice of free will, we have different life experiences in human form. While some things that happen in life remain a mystery, we create our personal experience by the way we allow it to affect us and the way we choose to respond or react to situations or circumstances. What we think, say and do creates our personal experiences. What others think, say and do creates their personal experiences. We do not create for others. Others do not create for us. However, what we do does have an impact on everyone and on our planet, for in spirit we are all interconnected. Others can help, guide, give advice, inspire and empower us, however, we are the only ones who can create our life. We all deserve and have the power to create and experience all that we desire in our lives, for that is our birthright. This includes who we desire to be, items we desire to acquire, relationships we desire to share, and that which we desire to do and experience. In order to create your life, you must first remember who you are, why you are here, and what you desire your life to be. This wisdom resides within you. You have all that is required to fulfill your life's mission. The angelic recipes in this book will guide your way in retrieving this wisdom and creating a life that reflects the truths within your soul.

Although we are the creators of our own lives, we sometimes find ourselves in unsatisfying circumstances. It is essential not to blame ourself or others for what we are experiencing, for we all do the best that we can with the awareness and knowledge we have in that moment. Instead, we can choose to put the energy into re-creating the situation to reflect what we do desire to experience. Remember, the experiences we have are showing us our thoughts and beliefs at that time. This is a vast universe and there is plenty of everything we all need and desire to go around. All that is required is our willingness to re-connect to the infinite source of the universe where abundance is available to all of us and allow ourselves to receive these gifts.

When things do not work in our life, it is not because God is not listening or answering our prayers, it is because we have disconnected from our God-self, true self, higher self, whatever label you choose to use. We are all individual expressions of God. We remain exactly as God created us—perfect, whole and complete. The ego was created from our belief that we are separate from God and others. God does not create fear and violence, human thoughts and behaviors do. God did not bring us here to struggle and suffer, yet so many in this human experience we call life are experiencing fear, pain, and struggle. It doesn't have to be that way. These are man-made beliefs and we can change them. God brought us here to learn and grow in love, to love ourselves and others, to utilize our spiritual gifts and experience the material blessings earth life offers. There is a great need for healing within ourselves and on our planet earth. My definition of healing means removing the veils of illusion and judgments that prevent us from being our true selves, experiencing fulfillment and receiving abundance of all our desires. Healing releases the darkness and brings in the love and light. You may feel much lighter with the progression of this book. As we create love, peace, and transform discord to harmony in our own lives, it has a ripple affect and will be reflected in our world. This book will guide your way.

WHY THIS BOOK?

Our world is undergoing a miraculous transformation at this time. With this transformation, humanity is evolving and a planetary transformation is taking place. As this shift occurs, our world of fear and violence will end and the birth our new earth will begin, reflecting a world of love and peace. Due to this transformation there are many shifts and changes occurring on a personal and global level. While this transformation is taking us in a positive direction, many are experiencing turmoil in their life due to fears such as feeling unloved, unsafe and lack. These fears are a reflection of the fear-based consciousness and illusions of society. These experiences are being presented giving us the opportunity to let go of the old fear-based beliefs, systems and energy individually and globally, so we can bring in and embrace the new energy of unconditional love.

Unconditional love is the power to re-creating our lives, society and the creation of heaven here on earth. The beliefs of society are being transformed as humanity evolves. As we all awaken to love and accept responsibility to create anew the beliefs of society to love and peace, fear and violence will subside. As we all believe in oneness, wholeness and the power of love, we will love ourself and one another unconditionally and create with love. As we all take the gift of reflections from others and life itself and use them to look within to heal ourself, this contributes to creating heaven on earth. The emerging energy of unconditional love brings us greater awareness and the opportunity to heal ourselves and our planet. What a blessing to be a part of this transformation that will make our world a brighter place. Together we can make this happen, beginning with ourself. We all have the power and opportunity to make a difference by expressing acts of love. We also have an abundance of light beings such as the angels, archangels and ascended masters to assist us with these endeavors. All we must do is ask.

We can all create and experience heaven on earth just by changing the way we perceive, project and interact with the world. As we open our hearts, our minds and practice unconditional love, we will see God in all people and all things and we will experience heaven on earth right now. There are many paths to God. We must follow the path that resonates with us and honor the paths of others. We have all chosen to be on earth at this time and be a part of this transformation as one big human family. We all have an important mission to fulfill here on earth. We are all working toward the same goal: to love and be loved unconditionally. The universal purpose we all have is to love ourselves and one another unconditionally, and to allow God to express through us. As we align with truth and integrity and go with the ebb and flow of life, we can experience love, grace and ease during this process. Applying the angelic recipes in this divine guide for living will ensure a positive experience for all. Now is the time to close the doors to fear and open our hearts and minds to love. We must come from a higher consciousness to remove these illusions of fear so we can all live the life God intended for us to live—a life of love, peace, unity, abundance and freedom. As we each do our part heaven on earth is created!

WHO CAN BENEFIT FROM THIS BOOK?

This guidebook is for anyone who desires to awaken to their inherent nature to heal from within and create a life that reflects their heart's desires and the truths within their soul. If you desire to: simplify your life and live a healthy, balanced, fulfilling lifestyle; experience an abundance of good in all areas of your life; have the desire to experience your dreams; have a passion to make this world a brighter place and would like clarity, guidance and direction on how to do that, then this book is for you. This empowering guide to love is for those who desire to experience heaven here on earth and the magic that inviting the angels into your life brings.

BLESSINGS OF THIS BOOK

This enlightening book brings out the simplicity of the spiritual laws of the universe. It's presentation that there are no coincidences, accidents or mistakes, only lessons reflected from our soul that help us evolve puts a positive spin on the lessons life brings. Its light-hearted approach inspires you to focus on the beauty within yourself, the blessings each experience brings, and follow your heart so you can experience true joy. It brings clarity to the questions for which many seek guidance and what I refer to as the *wonders of life*: Who am I? Why am I here? How do I make my life what I desire it to be? There are many shifts and changes that occur as our lives come into alignment with our truths. This empowering book reminds you of the powerful being you are. It brings to your awareness your internal resources that I refer to as *treasures of your soul*, so that you can heal yourself and create all that your heart desires, utilizing your God-given gifts. Each section will bring you to a deeper understanding of yourself and oneness with all of life as you maneuver through this interactive, fun-filled, soul-searching expedition!

Part I, the appetizer illuminates your life through self-awareness. It introduces the principles of self-awareness and presents the *treasures of your soul* you will be utilizing throughout this book to create a life you will love. It will take you on an intimate journey in which you will explore your relationship with yourself as you remember your true identity, gain clarity to all aspects of yourself, and the importance they play in the creation of your life. You will dig deep within your soul to: uncover your desires, dreams, passions and life's purpose; gain insight through the reflections of the universe and your relationship with others to help you evolve; understand how you attract people and experiences into your life; learn to communicate intuitively with your body so you can give your body what it needs and desires on all levels; explore and discover how your dreams can bring clarity to your life by learning to retrieve, record and interpret their messages; increase your awareness about how uniting with other kingdoms such as animals and crystals can promote healing and enrich your life; and experience the miracles as you learn how to ask for and receive messages from spiritual beings including angels, archangels, ascended masters, fairies, spirit guides and animal spirits to assist you in your life. This part defines the awakening process so as you go through it you can awaken with love, grace and ease. As you awaken to the truth of who you are, you will experience the infinite blessings love brings!

Part II, the main course guides you to experience the power of love in action. It presents the characteristics of unconditional love, and provides the angelic recipes that give your soul the nourishment and nurturing necessary for healing to take place. It will take you on a magical journey to love that will empower you to: love, accept, respect, forgive, have compassion and gratitude for yourself and others; how to resolve conflict with love, release judgments and create fulfilling, empowering relationships, including attracting a soul mate and creating a divine love partnership. It offers natural comfort for the soul with angelic recipes for getting to the heart of the matter by healing the child within including: releasing fears and healing unhealthy behaviors, physical conditions and most importantly, how to let love be the foundation of your life. It reflects how the power of love enriches your relationship with money to promote financial abundance and freedom. You may experience many feelings on your venture through these chapters. Some may make you laugh and others may make you cry. Whatever those feelings are, let them come alive. Love is the source from which all good flows and makes the impossible possible. Embrace the magic of love and celebrate the freedom that brings as you step out of fear and into love!

Part III, the dessert, will empower you to experience the sweetness of life. It contains step-by-step angelic recipes to create with love and bring your dreams to life through manifestation with the assistance of the angelic, ascended master and elemental realms. These recipes will show you how to integrate both your physical and spiritual self to create balance and harmony, as you live your life on purpose while receiving support from the universe for all your endeavors. You will learn how to implement these angelic recipes into your life so you can experience all that your heart desires. This includes: creating your divine life, career and your sacred space. The conclusion is a reflection of and a vision for our new earth and will guide you in doing your part in the creation of heaven here on earth. Your creativity will be activated as you bring your dreams to life from the inside out. As you create with love, you love your desires into existence. Enjoy the magic of manifesting as you create and experience a life you will love!

Part IV presents a gathering of the gifts that were born from unconditional love. It encompasses angelic exercises, angelic tools, connections, divine inspirations, and *Your Journey to Love Daily Practices.*

This divine guide for living reflects how to experience the best of both worlds—living as a spiritual being and experiencing the material blessings earth life offers. It will pave your way to balancing your spiritual nature with your earth experience. The angelic guidance within will lead the way in learning your life lessons with love, and opening the gates to your soul as it brings forth the wisdom and truths that reside within. These angelic recipes will guide you to love. They will warm your heart with messages of love, inspire you with food for thought and support you with nourishment for your soul along the way. This book is a reflection of my journey to love and a true example of the angels in action in my life. It demonstrates how opening to love can transform a painful experience to a miraculous, joyful outcome. My experiences focus on what is relevant to the teachings in this book and are not in chronological order. As an empath, I understand how one can easily absorb energy. Therefore, I have shared the highlights leaving out much of the heart-wrenching details for my intention is to share the wisdom not instill fear. I share with you my angelic experiences so you may recognize divine guidance. This all-encompassing guide to enlightenment is filled with angelic wisdom, exercises, meditations, affirmative prayers and angelic tools that will empower you and enrich your life!

INTRODUCTION

HOW TO USE THIS GUIDE

Throughout this transformational guide, we will cover a lot of distance on your journey to love, so remember to take time to rest and play as you explore along the way. The distance we travel will be a priceless experience that will benefit you throughout your life. It is best to implement these principles into your life gradually. This guidebook can be used as part of your daily practice by holding it up to your heart and intuitively opening it up to a page. Whatever pages you are guided to will contain what you need to focus on and the guidance you need at that time. This guidance manual is one you'll want to keep at your fingertips as you will refer to it again and again.

After reading this book, you will continue your transformation throughout your life's journey and receive infinite blessings from applying these angelic principles and tools to your life. I encourage you to use these angelic recipes as a guide and season them to serve you so they reflect the truths and desires within your soul. It has been my experience that when something resonates with me, it is truth for me. Always remember, you are the creator of your own life. You have a choice as to what you desire to experience. You have all the answers and knowledge within you regarding your life's mission. This divine guide will assist you in retrieving this wisdom and guide your way as you create the life of your dreams. May you embrace the blessings and enjoy whatever this experience holds for you. I look forward to sharing many angelic experiences with you as I guide you in implementing these angelic recipes into your own life through this book, my workshops, coaching and other angelic tools. Within the pages of *Your Journey to Love*, you will find the voice of an experienced, compassionate friend. I share with you these angelic recipes to guide you in creating a life you will love!

GUARDIAN ANGELS
Celebrating the Divine Protection that is there for each and every one of us.

GUARDIAN ANGELS

We wish you much love, peace, joy, happiness, and freedom
as your soul continues to evolve through your experiences of this earth school.
May this book bring you comfort in knowing you
are always safe, secure and loved.
May it be your companion as you embark on this expedition to enlightenment.
May you know you always have friends who love
you and are holding your hand.

—Your Guardian Angels

PART I

Awakening to Love

UNCONDITIONAL LOVE

Love is food for the soul and the main ingredient in the recipe of life.
Love connects you to all of life and is the energy of creation.
Love is the highest vibration of energy that exists.
Love is your natural state of being . . . divine consciousness.
Love is the source from which all good flows.

Unconditional love has no restrictions, no stipulations,
but it does have boundaries.
To love unconditionally means to accept, respect and
forgive yourself and others as is without judgment
or criticism, but rather with compassion,
And to honor and give gratitude
for all that we each bring to this world.

Love is choice of free will.
When you chose love, you will experience
the infinite blessings love brings.
Love guides, it does not force.
Love is your true power.

Love is the ability to desire that only good
Comes to everyone including yourself.
The more love you give away, the more love you receive.
Love is having an open heart, open mind and open arms.
Love is to be in a state of gratitude and embrace all
the blessings that exist within and around you.

Love is the key to your soul.
Love is the power that heals and creates all that your heart desires.
Love is the answer to all questions, the solution to all challenges and
the cure for all ailments.

Love is the gateway for experiencing heaven on earth.
Love is the greatest power and gift on earth that
you can give to yourself and share with others.
Love is who you are!

—*Bonnie Ann Lewis*

5TH ELEMENT—LOVE
Celebrating that of all there is; Earth, Wind, Fire and Water . . . "Love" is all there is.

CHAPTER 1
The Awakening

The Awakening Process

"Awaken to your inner beauty and power . . . Love."

A spiritual awakening is remembering our innate spiritual nature, recognizing the divinity within and our oneness with God and all of life. It is a process of remembering who we are, why we are here, and utilizing our natural resources, spiritual gifts and talents to create our lives and be of service. The awakening process is a transformation of seeing beyond the illusions of fear and the shadows to your truth and true self. It brings the shadows to the light so that you can heal them and move beyond the limitations they have created in your life. It is a process of releasing the fear, and old beliefs that no longer serve you and creating new beliefs that reflect your desires. As you do this, you see clearly the truths within, healing of your inner child takes place, and you return to your natural state of love which empowers you to reach your souls' greatest potential and enjoy your life. You can then manifest all that you desire to experience on your earth journey as you fulfill your life's mission.

Everyone experiences this process a little differently, depending on their own personal growth, path, and their level of awareness at that time. Some awaken slowly while others experience a more abrupt awakening. For some the awakening process is not always the most pleasant as sometimes it takes a "crisis" in their lives to wake up. For those of you who feel like you are in the middle of a crisis or have experienced one, this book of wisdom will guide your way in putting your life back together the way you desire it to be. Sometimes when you are in the middle of a crisis your life feels like it is falling apart, when in truth it is actually coming together. The old is leaving your life making room for the new. This allows those things that are not in integrity with your intentions to fall away.

During my awakening process, I did not completely understand what was happening, which led to some painful experiences. Looking back and reflecting upon these experiences has brought me great clarity and blessings which I am sharing with you, in hopes that it will light your path and pave your way for a smoother road. My prayer is that the angelic recipes in this book guide you to awaken with grace and ease so that where others have stumbled, you may soar. Although I share with you my experiences and angelic wisdom, as always I invite you to follow your heart as to what feels right to you, and be open to whatever this experience holds for you as you embrace the blessings it brings. Throughout this book, you will be reflecting upon the principles of unconditional love and applying them to your life. Love is who we are and we know this at birth, however, as we grow up we forget this truth due to our life experiences.

The awakening process increases your self-awareness. Only by awakening to the truth of who you are, your spiritual nature, can you become free from experiencing the illusions of pain, suffering, struggle and separation that are created by fear that stand in the way of your truths and expressing your divine nature. When you allow the angels to assist you, this process occurs with love, grace and ease. We all have something unique to share with the world. As you awaken to who you are and why you are here, you contribute to making this world a better place.

Changes That May Occur During Your Awakening Process

I'm sharing with you the changes you may possibly encounter during this process so if they do occur, you will know what to do and seek assistance if need be. I recommend seeking assistance from professionals such as a spiritual practitioner, naturopath, osteopath, chiropractor or acupuncturist. These types of professionals offer a more natural approach to healing and are generally more aware of humanity evolving and the awakening process at this time than the mainstream medical field. These are changes that I have experienced personally or observed professionally in my Angel Therapy® practice.

- ♥ The awakening process stimulates and opens up your inner senses, also referred to as your intuitive or psychic abilities, awakens your creativity, opens your heart, expands your consciousness which increases your awareness while stimulating your universal mind. In addition this increases the well-being, performance and condition of your physical body and brings your upper and lower chakras along with your mind, body and spirit into alignment. Know that the spiritual awakening process affects you as a whole: mentally, physically, emotionally and spiritually, and it is important to support the physical body along the way, for this is the vehicle that is going to get you to where you are going as you fulfill your life's mission.

💜 Throughout your spiritual awakening, you will be shifting vibrations and adjusting to the different frequencies, for as the fears are released your consciousness expands. As your consciousness expands, your vibration will increase, expanding your light body. As your light body expands and your inner senses open up you may become more sensitive to lower energy, foods, chemicals, smells, drugs and noises. You may have some reactions to these things as this is your body's way of telling you it is not complimentary to you anymore. As this spiritual expansion occurs you will be adjusting to new levels of consciousness and you will be learning how to be connected to the earth plane and spiritual realms simultaneously. This is the process of your masculine and feminine energy coming into unison. There may be times your energy feels a little off balance. Staying grounded and engaging in meditation will help you during this process.

💜 As your crown chakra opens, your consciousness expands and you evolve. You may have many ideas, inspirations and much information coming to you. This is called downloading. If it feels overwhelming or seems to be coming too quickly, ask the angels to slow it down. It takes time for your body to adjust to these higher vibrations of energy. When you awaken too quickly, you can become off balance. When you do it gradually, you experience grace and ease. Sometimes during this downloading process you can become ungrounded meaning your spirit is not completely in your body. If you feel overwhelmed, scattered, confused, or forgetful, these are indicators of imbalance and a need for grounding. Each download that occurs allows your body to expand the amount of energy it can hold. In time, you will learn what your capacity level is. This is a time to reflect rather than take action. Record the information you receive during these downloads for you will act on these ideas when you are clear about what you desire to do with them. If there are things you do not write down, know that is okay. Your heart remembers everything that is of importance to you. As you think about parts of it, it will trigger the rest of it. You can also ask Archangel Zadkiel to help you remember that which is essential. As your consciousness expands, you will have many opportunities presented to you and you may feel the desire to do everything. It is essential to pay attention to where and how you are choosing to utilize your energy and keep it focused in the direction you desire to go. In the beginning you may do certain things but as you continue to evolve, you will choose to do those things that you are most passionate about.

- As your heart chakra opens you will experience oneness and the interconnectedness of us all. You may feel like everything relates to you. It is important to discern what relates to you and is about you and what does not. You may feel passionate about improving worldly situations as you recognize your oneness with all of life.

- As your sacral chakra opens up, it stimulates your creativity so you may feel passionate about life, certain activities or helping people. Direct this energy in positive ways by doing creative projects such as writing, painting, singing, playing music, or in whatever creative channels your heart desires to express. You may want to volunteer for a cause that speaks to your heart.

- When you become aware of your life's purpose you may be very excited about it but with it may come many fears as you step into your own power. A wise spiritual teacher once told me, "The bigger the purpose, the greater the fears." The goal is to overcome the fears so you can fulfill your life's mission. You may have thoughts and fears surface that you've never been consciously aware of before. It may seem as if you are going backwards as you begin to create more positive thought patterns and the negative ones come to the surface. Be kind and gentle with yourself and know this is part of the process of releasing the fears that surface, in order to lift your vibration to a higher level.

When I first became aware of the power of my thoughts and began to make changes, and the negative thoughts would surface, I was concerned those thoughts would create that situation in my life. The angels gave me a great metaphor to use when this occurs. They said, *"When these thoughts come forth you can treat them as dine in or take out. You can choose to feed and entertain them by giving attention to them or you can choose to just acknowledge them and let them go."* I have come to understand that thoughts can only manifest if we put energy into them. Floating thoughts alone without any emotion, continuous attention or action will not manifest into physical form. This metaphor brought much peace for me.

♥ As you go through this process, you may experience the feeling that you are living in two realities, and you feel one way one day and differently the next day. This is because you are shedding the shadows and becoming your true self, and sometimes you may find the ego arguing with your true self. Once you begin to see beyond the veils of illusion, you will begin to vibrate at a higher frequency. The illusion will subside and you will feel more confident about making decisions in your life. As your inner child begins to heal from past experiences and childhood issues, many feelings and emotions will come up for you. This is a natural part of the releasing process so allow yourself to feel however you feel and know this too shall pass. Journaling is a great way to allow these feelings and emotions free expression, and in the process will release them so that you will feel better.

- ♥ Sometimes as one goes through the awakening process, they do things that may not always make sense to those around them. This is because they are shedding their old ways and coming into alignment with their truths to reflect the person they are becoming. People often misunderstand, question and judge the choices they make when they do not reflect the person they have always been. It takes time for others to recognize and adjust to the new person they have become. Many shifts and changes occur during this process. It is best not to make any major life decisions until you are clear about what you desire.

- ♥ As you learn and grow, your vibration increases, and sometimes you outgrow old relationships, or there may be a shift in current relationships. Oftentimes those people who were a part of your life in the past, stay stuck in perceiving you as you were then and continue to treat you in that manner. When this occurs it is a time for you to choose not to participate in that energy. If you do this, you are choosing to move beyond it, living in the present rather than the past. These people may or may not catch up with you and that's okay. Choose to be where you are despite their lack of awareness about the true you.

- ♥ During the awakening process we go through what is called a life review in which we reflect upon our life—where we've been, where we are now, and where we desire to go. It presents the opportunity to let go of those old patterns and beliefs, experiences, situations, or relationships in our lives that no longer serve us and keep that which we desire to have in our life. It often brings greater awareness and insights about our life's purpose, gifts and talents. It presents a clean slate to begin our life anew and create it as we desire it to be.

♥ Some have a spiritual experience, epiphany or near-death experience that triggers their awakening and healing process. A near death experience (NDE) is when our spirit transcends out of our body and visits the afterlife. This is different than an out-of-body experience (such as during sleep or meditation when we journey out of our body for a short time, visit different spiritual realms, and then return). What we are actually doing at this time is shifting dimensions in consciousness. In a NDE we dis-connect from our physical body and the earth plane. A NDE happens suddenly. It is not something we plan or expect. There are many situations and circumstances that can lead to a NDE. Although there are similarities that occur during a NDE, I believe everyone has their own personal experience which can vary from those reported. Many report a miraculous healing after returning to the earth plane, while others are traumatized and afraid to talk about it because they do not understand what occurred or have the words to explain it. None the less, these are life altering experiences and talking with someone who is spiritually aware and evolved can be very beneficial to help one understand what is necessary for their soul's growth so they can move forward.

I have observed the spirit world as a medium in my Angel Therapy® Practice in addition to my own personal NDE which was triggered by a medical condition. During a NDE we go through a life review with our full spiritual team present. We are shown our past, present and possible future. We are given the choice to transition into the afterlife or stay on earth. What kept going through my mind during this time was my children and how I wanted to be there for them. I felt the angels around me and I asked them to bring me back into my body so I could be here with my children, and fulfill my mission. While in the spiritual world I saw so much light and angels everywhere. I felt so much love and complete oneness with everyone and all of life. I felt such a sense of compassion, an open heart and open mind. This experience reminded me of how I felt as a child when I would visit the spiritual realms. It helped me recall the truths within my soul bringing more clarity and insights relating to my life's purpose, claim the gifts that I brought in at birth and confirmed my sense of knowing that I am to be a part of leading humanity in the creation of heaven here on earth by sharing these teachings. I believe we can all awaken to these truths with grace and ease without going through a NDE, which is reflected in this divine guide for living.

Although my "tour" of the afterlife was beautiful, adjusting back to earth life was challenging and became a long healing process for me. Due to the trauma that occurred afterwards, I had tremendous fears that took me quite some time to overcome. All of my spiritual senses were open at this time so earth energy felt very harsh to me. I wanted to just stay at home where I felt safe. I read in *Angels 101* by Doreen Virtue that people who have had NDE's have extra guardian angels. I found this to be very comforting and became aware of my additional guardian angels presence. Quite a shift in energy occurs and it takes time to re-adjust to the earth plane. It is essential to allow your body the time to heal from a NDE. Although this experience was traumatic for me, I know it was all part of my releasing and learning process that my soul chose to experience, and that it would be invaluable in lighting the path for others.

Self-Care During the Awakening Process

The greatest challenges for many in the awakening process are staying grounded, balancing the energy that is coming through you as your vibration increases, and protecting yourself from feeling the discomfort attached to lower energies. The following recipe will enrich your experience.

- ♥ **Balance** is essential to ensuring a positive experience during this process. Because your body is undergoing so many changes during this transformation, it can create imbalances in your energy. To stay balanced, be sure to participate in both physical activities and your spiritual practices, giving attention to both the physical and spiritual aspects of yourself as you are adjusting to being in both dimensions simultaneously. These things will help support your physical body as this spiritual expansion occurs to assure this will be a pleasant and joyful experience that enriches your life.

- ♥ **Staying grounded** means staying connected to the earth plane while your spiritual awareness increases. There are many ways to stay grounded. You can walk barefoot in the grass, hug a tree, use grounding essential oils or do grounding visualizations. You can also massage grounding oil into the bottom of your feet in the center or at the top of your feet between your toes. Participate in many earthy activities such as spending time in nature, dancing, gardening, walking, bike riding, hiking, swimming, playing sports, and so on. This keeps you connected to mother earth. Eating foods that come from the earth such as white potatoes, sweet potatoes, green beans, carrots, beets, broccoli, and cauliflower also help with staying grounded. We can become ungrounded when we are stressed, afraid or in pain. This is our body's way of dis-associating from what we are experiencing.

I like the example Sonia Choquette gave in the Hay House Present Moment Newsletter, April 2006, in an article *Connecting with Earth Spirits*. She states, "Connecting with the earth is known as 'getting grounded'; a term that's casually tossed about, but rarely fully understood to be the act of allowing our spirit to be nurtured by mother earth. If you really want to feel some psychic support, hug a tree. The spirits of trees are so powerful that they act like amplifiers for your psychic sensibilities. Connecting with their energy will pull your awareness deep into the spirit world quickly, enhancing your ability to connect with higher-frequency entities such as your guides and angels. You will become clearer, more grounded and emotionally more peaceful. Tapping into the flowers brings your subtle awareness forward to connect with that flower and plant fairies and has an immense capacity to heal, and restore balance by reweaving the emotional body."

ANGELIC TOOLS:

♥ Grounding oil by Soleil's Influence (This can be purchased online at www.energywithin.net.)

GROUNDING VISUALIZATION

This visualization helps to keep you grounded, creating a balance between heaven and earth.

- Visualize yourself outside wherever you desire to be, standing in your bare feet.

- Imagine roots emerging from the bottom of your feet into the soil beneath you.

- As you breathe deeply, feel your feet sinking into the dirt touching a rock deep in the earth.

- Now visualize a golden ray of light coming from heaven going down through your body into the earth below.

- Where this golden light extends above your head reaching into the etherical sphere, see a white spray of light like rain expanding into the universe.

- Ask your angels to help you stay grounded on the earth plane while keeping your thoughts focused on love.

- Affirm: I AM simultaneously connected to the earth and the heavens in balance. And so it is!

NOTE: This visualization is found on *Your Journey to Love Daily Practices* CD included with this book.

♥ **Stay centered** in your natural state of love as that will keep your masculine and feminine energies balanced and prevent you from being affected by what is going on around you. The more centered you are, the less effect stress will have on you.

CENTERING VISUALIZATION

This visualization is designed to help you stay centered in your natural state of love even when there is chaos around you. It will also help to balance the masculine and feminine energy within you. You can do this in whatever position is comfortable for you.

- I invite you to cross your hands and place them over the center of your chest, and take four deep breaths.

- With each breath, breathe in love, and with each exhale release anything that is not of love.

- Repeat after me, "Dear Angels, please help me to stay centered in my natural state of love. Please guide my thoughts, words and actions to reflect love. Thank you!"

- Affirm: I AM centered in my natural state of love. I AM calm, peaceful and at ease. My masculine and feminine energies are in perfect balance. And so it is!

> NOTE: This visualization is found on *Your Journey to Love Daily Practices* CD included with this book.

💜 **Retreat a bit** as you reflect upon your experiences but do not seclude yourself. Find some like-minded people or a spiritual based support group to talk to as your body goes through these shifts and changes.

💜 **Ask your angels to protect you** from lower energies and your own emotions, and refrain from getting caught up in the drama of other people's lives.

💜 **Surround yourself with positive, supportive people.** Stay away from negative people and situations.

💜 **Exercise** regularly as this releases stress and keeps your energy high.

- ♥ **Meditate** to quiet your mind, calm your emotions and help you stay centered. While in this meditative state, messages come through as it opens you up to receive universal wisdom.

- ♥ **Acupuncture** can help tremendously in balancing your energy and giving your body a tune-up by integrating the mind, body and spirit.

- ♥ **Massage** is beneficial for relaxation. A hot stone massage is especially beneficial in connecting with mother earth.

- ♥ **Read spiritual material** to increase your awareness and understanding of what is occurring.

- ♥ **Clear your chakras** regularly.

- ♥ **Listen to music** that helps you feel calm, peaceful, centered or inspired.

- ♥ **Wear or bring crystals** into your environment for they help with grounding, protection, balance and empowerment.

- ♥ **Stay in close communication with your angels and guides** during this process for they will guide your way. Your inner guidance is your greatest resource.

- ♥ **Purify your body of chemicals.** We all have different things that are not complimentary to our bodies and chemicals affect each of us a little differently. Our bodies are naturally organic meaning free from chemicals. If you feel you are having a sensitivity or reaction to a medication, consult your healthcare provider before discontinuing. When releasing chemicals from your body, it is helpful to drink a lot of water with a few drops of juice from a fresh organic lemon to help your body release it as lemon is a natural cleanser for the body.

- 💜 **Cranial Sacral adjustments** are helpful in balancing your energy and aligning all aspects of self. Osteopaths provide this type of service.

- 💜 **Spend time in nature** as this brings you back to your natural state of love.

- 💜 **Make changes gradually** to ensure a pleasant journey as your life shifts to reflect your truths.

- 💜 **Talking to practitioners** with a spiritual approach is very helpful.

- 💜 **Drink plenty of water and eat healthy.** As your inner senses begin to open up, you will find more energy begins to move through you. Due to the amount of energy your body is using, you will need to drink a great amount of water and eat more frequently to give your body extra nourishment. Eating as much healthy, fresh, organic fruits and vegetables while getting enough protein at this time is also essential. This will support your physical body as this spiritual expansion occurs.

NOURISHMENT FOR YOUR SOUL: Honor both your humanness and your true self without judgment, and embrace the shadows as your true self emerges. You can honor your shadows by allowing them to come forth to the light, thank them for the lessons they brought, and let them go. When you honor both, you experience the blessings each aspect presents.

FOOD FOR THOUGHT: I honor and nurture both my spiritual and physical self.

ANGELIC TOOLS:
- 💜 *Angelic Reflections I: Awakening* CD by Bonnie Ann Lewis
- 💜 *Chakra Clearing* audio by Doreen Virtue
- 💜 Angelic Music by Peter Sterling: *Harp Magic, Angels Gift* or *Heart and Soul*

Illusions

Illusions are merely a state of mind created by fear and formed by society's beliefs. They reflect thinking, feeling and acting as if we are separate and take us out of our natural state of love. The results of these fears are unpleasant experiences, physical conditions, unhealthy behaviors and addictions. Although our goal is to stay in our natural state of love, there will be times in our life we will experience these illusions. However, we can lessen the impact they have on our life and the length of time in which we are in that state of disconnection, discomfort or dis-ease (this refers to dis-harmony or ailment of the body) by transforming them into love. As we transform them into love, we can move beyond the blockages and limitations they create. Illusions appear to be true because we accept them as truth. By changing our beliefs, we can choose what we accept as truth. The angels can help us to see things from a higher perspective which helps us move beyond the limitations these fears have created.

These illusions have a very important purpose. They reflect to us what is in our subconscious mind and give us the opportunity to bring them to the light so healing can occur. When we bring these shadows to the light, we become aware of them and they lose their power so that they no longer control our lives. The key is to honor both aspects, our true self and the shadows by acknowledging them, detaching from them and choosing to stay centered in our natural state of love to further our growth and awareness. These fear-based illusions vibrate at a lower vibration of energy. I am referring to this as dense energy. Our higher self vibrates at a higher level. I am referring to this as heavenly energy. Our purpose on this earth is for our soul to evolve. Our soul evolves by transforming this dense energy into heavenly energy. As this occurs it increases our light body and vibration. There are different levels of vibrations between heaven and earth. This vibration fluctuates depending on our perception of our experiences. Our thoughts and beliefs determine these vibrations. We attract to ourselves experiences that reflect our vibration of energy at that time. As we evolve, we move to the higher vibration of love which creates heaven here on earth.

Illusions of Society

SOCIETY

Society is what we've created it to be.
We can create anew if we do not like what we see.
Re-creation begins with each one of us.
Taking responsibility for oneself is a must,
For the energy we put out affects us all.
Let's create with love and learn to trust,
The universe will provide all our desires and needs,
As we create a world of love and peace.

—*Bonnie Ann Lewis*

Everyone wants to be loved and experience fulfillment and abundance in their life but many are looking in the wrong places to fulfill these needs and desires. They are looking to outside sources rather than within themselves due to the lack of understanding of who they are. Society has created a belief that if I'm like everyone else, then I'm okay. If I'm not like everyone else then there must be something "wrong" with me. The result of this is that we lose sight of who we truly are and live our life for others rather than ourselves. When we live our lives for others, we depend on others to provide us with our needs and desires. When these needs and desires are not met, we experience feelings of fear such as scarcity, abandonment and resentment. Some become frustrated and angry which causes them to use manipulative behavior to control others so they can get what they need and want. This creates violence. In truth we can have what we desire through manifestation instead of manipulation. When we come to the awareness that there is enough to go around for everyone, we know the need for jealousy, envy, competition, greed and behaviors such as manipulation and control that many feel they need to use to get what they want, or the necessity they feel to take what they want from others at anyone's expense, no longer exists.

Many strive to be "perfect," to meet the expectations of others, or pretend to be someone they are not in order to fit in. In truth, when we are our own unique self, everyone benefits. We can then reach our greatest potential and live a fulfilling and enjoyable life, accomplishing what we came here to do. There are certain characteristics as humans we experience and there are certain similarities as spiritual beings we have and exhibit, however, we are all unique in our own way. When we are not loved and accepted, we turn to addictions to fill those voids and ease the pain rather than looking within to meet those needs naturally. We are all equal human beings and deserve the love, acceptance and respect we desire. We must first recognize these within ourself in order to attract it into our lives. This book will guide you to be and honor the uniqueness within yourself and others.

Many believe their outer appearance is more important than their inner state of being. There is so much focus in our society on the external about what makes us beautiful. The media is filled with all these things that signify beauty and what we can do to be more "beautiful." In truth beauty comes from within and our outer appearance is a reflection of our inner state of being. Many are going through the motions of living rather than really participating in the fullness of life and living purposefully due to fear and the lack of awareness of why they are here in the first place. Many believe they are just here taking what life hands them, settling for less than they desire, feeling frustration and pain from life's struggles and feeling like a victim. They believe that they do not have a choice or do not deserve better. The truth of the matter is that we all have a choice, the ability and power to create all that we require and desire to fulfill our life's mission. The knowledge lies within each and every one of us. We just need to be educated on how to retrieve this information and implement it into our lives, and this divine guide will help you do that.

While we are growing up, we base our self-worth on the approval and reactions of others. We are taught to please others in order to be loved and accepted. We behave, make choices and take actions based on others reactions rather than our own inner knowing. Our beliefs are formed from the opinions of others rather than our own truths. Many times we are criticized and judged for being who we are. Consequently, we learn at an early age to disregard our own feelings and perceptions and respond in a way that gives us the reaction we desire from others. This is the way we have been conditioned to behave and believe due to the beliefs of society. As adults we have the opportunity to let go of these old beliefs that we inherited along the way and create new ones that reflect our own truths. Each generation gains more knowledge and awareness which gives us the opportunity to create and enjoy a healthier, more fulfilling lifestyle. Therefore, It is essential that we all take responsibility for, rather than blame our parents or others for the experiences in our life.

Society's belief that more is better, bigger is better, faster is better, etc. desensitizes people. It creates competition and the need to do whatever it takes to achieve these goals even if it is at the expense of others. Many are forced to overwork to meet the material demands and do not have time to do the things that bring them pleasure and enjoyment in their life. It also puts people in situations where they are continuously doing so that being doesn't exist. It is essential to have balance in our life between our spiritual practices and our physical activities in order to experience a healthy lifestyle and sense of well-being. In this materialistic world, it is very easy to get caught up in the material things and lose sight of our purpose for being here and who we really are. The key is to be our true self and focus on our purpose while enjoying and experiencing the material blessings this earth life offers. It's time to get back to the basics of life. This book offers the principles to create this balance in your life.

Society is like this due to a lack of love and awareness. The wonderful thing about society is that we can have a powerful impact and re-create it to reflect the way we desire to live by first beginning to change ourselves. We all contribute to the creation of society. Therefore, we are the only ones who can re-create it if we so desire. The more people remember the powerful beings they are and realize they are the creator of their own life and co-creators of the universe, the more people will be empowered, fulfilled and experience abundance in love, health, wealth and freedom. As a result our world will be a much more loving, peaceful and joyful place to be because that is the energy that we will all be creating.

Moving Beyond the Illusions

"In the apparent challenges that we face, there is always beauty to appreciate."

At this time, our society is beginning to move beyond the fear-based consciousness which reflects illusions of fear that take us out of our natural state of being, which is love. None of us are victims of any person, circumstances or life itself. We are powerful divine beings with the choice of free will to change our life and our world. As the thinning of the veil occurs we can see beyond the illusions of fear. It is love that sets us free!

The job of our true self is to remove the fearful thinking and shine through despite the fears. When we get in touch with our true self, we attract and create around us what our heart and soul desires. Everything in life is a reflection of where we focus our attention. Love is who we are; fear is what we learn. Our purpose on earth is to release the fear, open our hearts and minds to giving and receiving love, so we can experience more love in our lives. This is the true meaning of life. Although we all experience the illusions of earth life, the angelic recipes in this book will ensure a more pleasant journey as you step out of fear and into love!

CHAPTER 2

Self-Awareness

Illuminate Your Life Through Self-Awareness

"Who looks outside, dreams; who looks inside, awakes."
—CARL GUSTAV JUNG

We are all creators of our own lives and co-creators of the universe with God. Love is our natural state of being and the main ingredient in creating our life. Many times we look for love and fulfillment from other people or outside sources, however, these gifts reside within each of us. Our relationships with others as well as our experiences are an important part of life. They reflect to us the truths within our souls and the lessons we came here to learn as they are mirrors of what is going on within us. Although relationships can bring us much joy or pain, they are not our source of love, fulfillment or happiness—we are. It all begins within us. As we begin to make changes from within, we will begin to see changes in our outer experiences. Within us exists a wealth of knowledge, the power and all of the essential ingredients and natural resources to create a life of love and peace. These birthrights are available to us so we can fulfill our life's mission. All that is required is that we look within, retrieve this knowledge and apply it to our life. Our angels are here to assist us with that just for the asking.

It is through our own awareness that we see our God-self and realize that God is one with us and we are one with God, and that we were created in the image and likeness of God. Therefore, everything that God created is our birthright and can be created with love. God intended for us to live according to the universal laws. In order to do this we must understand these universal laws and reconnect to our natural state of love.

Self-awareness uncovers the veils of illusion that block us from our natural state of being for in truth, we are already perfect, whole and complete. In order to heal these illusions of fear, we must bring our shadow self to the light with unconditional love. Once we are aware of the aspects of ourself, we have the ability to modify or change the illusions if we so desire. We may wish to do this if they do not reflect the person we desire to be or the experiences we desire to have. The amazing thing about self-awareness is that as the issues are brought forward to our conscious mind, they increase our awareness and give us the opportunity to re-create differently if we so desire.

Self-awareness brings us the gift of understanding our relationship with ourself, others and the universe. Everything exists within the universe. Since we are all part of this universe, everything in the universe is our birthright and can be ours if we choose it for ourselves. When we understand our relationship to the universe, we realize we can create anything we need and desire through this connection. Rather than expect it to come from outside sources, we have the power to have all our needs and desires met through manifestation. Although God brings our desires through outside sources, they begin within. When we create from within and take the actions we are guided to take, our needs, desires and dreams will manifest into form and be a part of our earth experience. My definition of manifesting or co-creating, is utilizing our internal resources while we work with God and the universal laws to create our desired experience. God gave us the power of free will and the ability to create all that we desire, a physical body to take action and bring it to form, and the angels to guide our way.

What is Self-Awareness?

"Self-awareness is not a destination. It is a continuous journey to be explored, embraced, enjoyed and shared with others."

Self-awareness means to consciously know, be and love all aspects of ourself on all levels of our existence—mental, physical, emotional and spiritual. It is a continuous journey, not a destination. The outcome of our journey depends on our ability to overcome the illusions of fear and to allow love to be the foundation of our life. It is through the principles of self-awareness that we communicate with our soul to bring this information forward so that we can live our life with purpose through our service to others. It is through our service to others that we expand this energy which is love. It is also through our service to others that the universe provides for and supports us.

Life is a continuous journey and every step we take brings us more awareness. Each experience is part of the journey and contributes to our growth and evolvement. We are all spiritual beings having a human experience. We all came here to learn, grow and evolve. We do this from our experiences and interactions with others. If we did not have these lessons to learn we would not be here at this time.

Why Self-Awareness?

"The more aware you become, the more you can do, be and experience."

You are the creator of your own life and a co-creator of the universe with God. It is your relationship with yourself that attracts your experiences and relationships into your life, for they are merely reflections of what's inside. They provide you with the opportunities to learn, grow and evolve.

You are a treasure chest that contains all of the truths, answers, information and knowledge for your earth's journey, referred to as life, that will lead you to success and inner happiness. These treasures just need to be retrieved and utilized. Self-awareness holds the key that opens that treasure chest and the key to your natural state of being which is love. It is through self-awareness that you can heal the illusions of fear that prevent you from being in your natural state of unconditional love, experiencing fulfillment and receiving abundance of all your desires!

"It is through self-awareness that you can heal yourself and create all that your heart desires."

The Gifts of Self-Awareness

"Only where the heart is can the treasure be found." —J.M. BARRIE

Through the process of self-awareness, we gain clarity to the *wonders of life:* Who am I? Why am I here? How do I make my life what I desire it to be? I believe it is a very valuable process that will bring great clarity and blessings to each of our lives. When you understand yourself, you will then understand others, your connection to all of life and the universal laws.

When you open your heart and mind and awaken to your inner beauty, your true self, you open up to receive the universal gifts that come from the infinite source in which everything begins and exists... love. For love is the key that opens all doors and is the energy that creates peace, unity, abundance, freedom, joy, inner happiness and success. You deserve to experience all of these gifts for love is who you are!

"When you know yourself, you hold the keys to life."

The Pre-requisites for Self-Awareness

- ♥ Your willingness to accept responsibility for yourself and your life.
- ♥ Being flexible and open to change.
- ♥ Being honest with yourself.
- ♥ Getting in touch with your true power.
- ♥ Having an open mind and open heart.

NOURISHMENT FOR YOUR SOUL: Self-awareness is a commitment to yourself to understand, learn and remember as much as you can about yourself. The benefits are worth the investment.

FOOD FOR THOUGHT: Everyday my self-awareness increases, enriching my life experience.

Responsibility

Responsibility is the ability to choose your thoughts and creations you desire. It also means the ability to respond. Taking responsibility keeps you in your power. When you are consciously aware of your own thoughts, you can choose to respond rather than react. When you react, you give all your power away and you feel like a victim rather than the powerful being that you are. When you respond, you take responsibility for the thoughts you think, the words you speak and the actions you take. Then you will feel good about the divine person you are.

- ♥ We are responsible for ourselves, our lives and our experiences. Others are responsible for themselves, their life and their experiences.

- ♥ Have the courage to take responsibility for your life instead of blaming others, and you will experience the greatest blessings.

- ♥ Taking responsibility gives you the opportunity to make choices, take actions and create that which you desire to experience. This is very powerful and brings great joy.

NOURISHMENT FOR YOUR SOUL: When you understand you are the creator of all your experiences, you realize it is impossible to blame anyone else for the experiences in your life. When you take responsibility for your life and allow others to take responsibility for theirs, you will experience much peace and serenity.

FOOD FOR THOUGHT: I take responsibility for my own life and allow others to take responsibility for theirs.

Flexibility to Change

Be flexible enough to change, adjust, experiment and try something new. When you are flexible you create opportunities, and more doors will open up for you, inviting greater success.

♥ Being flexible is opening your mind and heart to greater possibilities.

♥ Change is the opportunity for new experiences. You can change the future in a moment just by a thought or action. Change has a domino effect. When you take one step toward change, it sets in motion for other changes to occur.

♥ The initial step to changing undesirable characteristics of yourself and circumstances in your life is becoming aware of them.

♥ Change does not have to be painful or fearful. It is how you perceive it to be. When you resist change, you struggle and feel stuck. When you welcome change, things just flow and you will have positive experiences.

NOURISHMENT FOR YOUR SOUL: Be excited about change knowing that only good will come your way.

FOOD FOR THOUGHT: I welcome and embrace change with ease and excitement, knowing that only good comes my way.

What is True Power?

"True power comes from knowing who you are, what you want and trusting spirit to guide your way."

- ♥ Love is your true power. Use the energy within you in a loving way.

- ♥ Be in touch with your intuition. Utilize your God-given gifts and talents.

- ♥ Have the desire and determination to do something.

- ♥ Make changes that reflect the truth within your soul.

- ♥ Utilize the *treasures of your soul* and work with the universal laws to create your life.

- ♥ Fulfill both your needs and desires and be of service to others.

- ♥ Be in control of and change your own thoughts, words, actions and behaviors to create your desired outcome.

- ♥ Being in your own power encourages others to do the same.

NOURISHMENT FOR YOUR SOUL: *"Activate Your Power . . . Choose Love!"*—Bonnie Ann Lewis

FOOD FOR THOUGHT: I AM lovingly powerful. I have a powerful loving impact on this world.

DO IT ANYWAY

People are often unreasonable, illogical and self-centered;
Forgive them anyway.

If you are kind, people may accuse you of selfish, ulterior motives;
Be kind anyway.

If you are successful, you will win some
false friends and some true enemies;
Succeed anyway.

If you are honest and frank, people may cheat you;
Be honest and frank anyway.

What you spend years building, someone could destroy overnight;
Build anyway.

If you find serenity and happiness, they may be jealous;
Be happy anyway.

The good you do today, people will forget tomorrow,
Do good anyway.

Give the world the best you have, and it may never be enough;
Give the world the best you've got . . . anyway.

You see, in the final analysis, it is between you and God,
It never was between you and them anyway.

—Mother Teresa

"R" Methods to Self-Awareness

Here I introduce the process we utilize to bring about awareness. It is very simplistic and useful in bringing clarity to many issues. I will be referring to this process throughout this entire book because it is the foundation for creating your life.

- ♥ **Remember/Recall:** the truths of your soul.

- ♥ **Recognition:** become aware of where this originated from. Does it belong to me?

- ♥ **Release:** let go of what no longer serves or belongs to you. What you acknowledge and let go of no longer exists in your energy field so you will not attract it or have to experience it.

- ♥ **Replace:** put in or fill those spaces with what you desire. Affirmations, inner dialogue, and changing beliefs are all good tools to use.

- ♥ **Reflect/Review:** this is a time to go within to connect with the truths within your soul, free from outer influences. This is a great time to take a mental inventory and review your life to see if it reflects your desires.

- ♥ **Retreat/Relax/Renew:** take time and just be, nurture and give to yourself so you will be available to give to others. Activities that are great to participate in at this time are meditation, rest, spend time in nature, take classes, read books, nurture and pamper yourself, take sea salt baths, detoxify your body, and do things that bring you joy. It is essential to your well-being to take time to relax and renew your spirit. When you do this you are more peaceful and productive when you get back into the flow of life.

- ♥ **Respond/React:** be in the moment, respond to life, react with love.

- ♥ **Receive:** to take in or gracefully accept with gratitude, that which the universe and others give to you. The blessings life offers are there, you just need to open up your heart and mind to receive these gifts.

- ♥ **Realize/Reality:** recognize or become aware of the nature of your existence, your state of being.

- ♥ **Retrieve:** bring forth from within, connecting with your flame from God.

- ♥ **Resonate/Relate:** know or feel what rings true for you. When something speaks to your heart, that is truth for you.

- ♥ **Repeat/Recite:** continuously to create a new belief.

- ♥ **Responsibility:** being accountable for your own experiences, thoughts, feelings, emotions and your own life.

- ♥ **Rewards:** accept infinite blessings of love, an abundance of vibrant health, wealth, greater awareness, divine consciousness, fulfilling relationships, pleasurable experiences, opportunities and relationships, freedom, success and inner happiness.

- ♥ **Reasoning:** get to the core of an issue and what you believe.

- ♥ **Record:** write down to keep a log of your progress or journey.

NOURISHMENT FOR YOUR SOUL: Self-awareness is one of the most important aspects of your life's journey. Everything begins with you, therefore it is essential to identify who you are, why you are here, and what your desires are, in order to create the life you desire to live so that you can become all that you came here to be. It's that simple!

SELF-AWARENESS

FOOD FOR THOUGHT: *"Everything in life is a gift that increases my self-awareness."* —Bonnie Ann Lewis

Who Am I?

"When you look at yourself through the eyes of other's you'll never be quite right. When you look at yourself through the eyes of God, you are exactly as you are meant to be . . . perfect."

—LYNN LABUDA

You are a magnificent, energetic, spiritual being in a physical form, with a soul purpose, having a human experience. Your physical body is the vehicle in which your soul encompasses to evolve. Your soul has come to this earth in physical form to learn and grow through experiences in order to heal from the illusions taken on from past experiences in this lifetime or others. This will help you get back to your natural state of being in which you were created—love, truth and divinity. Each individual soul has unique qualities and talents and will evolve through different experiences on this earth journey. Your unique talents and gifts are what you will utilize to fulfill your life's mission. It is through your life's purpose that you contribute to the evolution and healing of this planet, by serving others while at the same time fulfilling yourself. When you are fulfilling your life's purpose, you will feel alive to the joys of living and experience inner happiness, attracting success along the way.

The spiritual aspect of ourselves is our non-physical, energy body. We are all sparks of God. Within each of us are all the answers to our life. At birth we know this but as we grow we forget due to earth experiences and outer influences that take us out of our natural state. Our spiritual nature is our connection to God, the universe, others and all of life. When we are in our natural state of being we feel connected and experience fulfillment and abundance in our life. Our soul is on a journey to return to self, our natural state of love and oneness with all of life. It is by choice that we live in accordance with the universal laws of love, and by choosing to do so we experience the benefits of God's gifts of love, peace, unity, abundance and freedom. When we are in our natural state of love, we open ourselves up to the flow of divine love. It moves through us and becomes God in action. When we do this, we become a model and messenger of God. We live our life on purpose by choosing to follow God's divine plan for us and the spiritual laws of the universe.

EXERCISE: WHO AM I QUESTIONNAIRE

The questionnaire that follows will help you determine what areas of your life to focus on to increase your self-awareness and the areas of your life that require more love and healing to take place. Answer each question honestly and use your answers as a guide to reflect upon. Remember to give yourself recognition for where you presently are.

Do I . . .

1. Recognize my beliefs free from outside influences? Beliefs are thoughts that feel true to you. By recognizing your own beliefs, free from others influences, it will help you determine if you are experiencing what reflects your heart's desire or someone else's.

2. Have beliefs that reflect what I desire to experience?

3. Know what my desires are?

SELF-AWARENESS

4. Know what my life's purpose or mission is?

5. Recognize that I have the power within me to make my life what I desire it to be?

6. Take responsibility for myself and allow others to take responsibility for their life?

7. Love myself for who I am right now?

Am I . . .

1. In touch with my feelings? Being in touch with your feelings is understanding, accepting and being honest about them without judgment. When you recognize how you feel, you can change anything by changing your thoughts.

2. Aware of the energy I'm putting out into the universe through my self-expression (words and actions)?

3. Communicating and expressing myself with truth and integrity? (Am I saying what I really mean? Am I asking for what I want?)

4. Being true to myself, living my life for me by making choices and taking action based on my own truths and desires?

5. Allowing my true essence to shine?

6. Following my own inner knowing regardless of the opinions or actions of others?

7. Pretending to be someone I'm not in order to be loved and accepted? (Afraid others will reject me if I'm not who they think I should be).

8. Struggling to be perfect? (if only I were . . .thin, successful, beautiful, rich, blonde, and so on, I'd be perfect and everyone would love me).

9. Feeling overwhelmed and burned out trying to meet the expectations of everyone else?

Methods to explore that can increase your self-awareness and give more insights about who you are and what your life's mission is.

- ♥ Astrology and Numerology: www.astrology-numerology.com (determines your life path number)
- ♥ Identifying your Totem Animals
- ♥ Questionnaire in the book *Earth Angels* by Doreen Virtue (to determine what realm(s) you fit into)
- ♥ Aura Reading
- ♥ Past Life Regressions
- ♥ *Colors and Numbers* by Louise L. Hay (to determine your most powerful days and what is in store for the year ahead)
- ♥ Akashic Record Reading or accessing your own Akashic Records

NOURISHMENT FOR YOUR SOUL: Remember . . . you are a beautiful person inside and out who deserves all the happiness and joy you desire. Always, follow your heart; it will guide your way! As you express the love that you are, that is exactly what you will attract and experience.

FOOD FOR THOUGHT: I AM beautiful inside and out. I AM perfect exactly as I AM. I live my life according to my heart's desires.

ANGELIC TOOLS:

- ♥ *Angelic Reflections I–IV,* Meditation CD's by Bonnie Ann Lewis
- ♥ *Lightworker's Way* by Doreen Virtue
- ♥ *Earth Angels* and *Realms of the Earth Angels* by Doreen Virtue
- ♥ *Colors and Numbers* by Louise L. Hay

CHAPTER 3
Aspects of You

The aspects of you as a whole include: mental, physical, spiritual and emotional selves. We will discuss these parts of yourself throughout this book. It is essential to maintain all aspects of yourself to ensure a healthy well-being.

Mind

"When your mind is in a relaxed and peaceful state, you see clearly and will have all of the answers. Make your mind a home of love."

Our mind is a very complex mechanism. But for the purpose of this book, we are going to simplify it and focus on that which is relevant for our understanding of the concepts presented in this book. We are going to discuss the conscious, subconscious and universal mind, and how they work together. Our mind is a very powerful tool that helps us focus on our desires so we can bring them into our life. Our mind controls our entire being, and plants the seeds for all of our creations. Although we have only one mind, within our mind exists two states of being, love and fear. Love is the reflection of our true self. Fear is a reflection of the veils of illusion. Let's discuss these two states of consciousness for a moment. We already know our true self is love-based and the ego is fear-based. Our ego is merely a state of mind formed by fears and the beliefs of society. Society believes in fear, pain and struggle as it suffers in a life of lack and illness. It believes in the need to be right. It is also impulsive in quest for an adrenaline rush, is defiant, creates loneliness, wants immediate gratification and changes its mind continuously. Society puts limits on what you can do and often says you haven't done enough. It believes in separateness rather than connection, oneness or unity.

When we are in our natural state of love we are centered and free from outside influences and from the illusions that are the result of fear, for love is who we are! When our mind is in a state of love, we will attract and experience love in our lives. On the contrary, if our mind is in a state of fear, we will attract unpleasant experiences for ourselves.

- ♥ **Conscious Mind:** is where we perceive, reason, judge and reject. Through its function, we are aware of our power to think and free will to choose. Perception is the way we view a situation, person or experience. Our experiences will reflect whatever we perceive them to be.

NOURISHMENT FOR YOUR SOUL: *"It's not what you look at that matters, it's what you see."*—Henry David Thoreau

- ♥ **Subconscious Mind:** does not reason or judge. It does not know what is truth or what is not. It accepts whatever thoughts we give it. Our subconscious mind controls all our bodily functions and stores beliefs and past memories.

NOURISHMENT FOR YOUR SOUL: It is essential to be aware of what is going into your subconscious mind so that it reflects what you desire to experience.

FOOD FOR THOUGHT: I fill my mind with thoughts that reflect my hearts desire, planting seeds of love.

♥ **Universal Mind:** is our connection to God. It is our divine consciousness, our infinite source and resources. It is a realization that we are in alignment with the universal forces and oneness with all of life. God exists in each and every one of us.

NOURISHMENT FOR YOUR SOUL: *"As your awareness expands, so will your experience."* —Bonnie Ann Lewis

FOOD FOR THOUGHT: My mind is filled with divine wisdom.

HOW THEY WORK TOGETHER

Your universal mind connects you to all of creation and stimulates divine ideas. Your subconscious mind controls your body and your conscious mind creates your reality. Your conscious mind is a reflection of and operates under the guide of your subconscious mind. Your conscious mind takes any beliefs or ideas from your subconscious mind and takes the steps to create it in your life. The process in which your subconscious mind transfers thoughts and beliefs to your conscious mind is called awareness. Most of us utilize our conscious mind (rational) in our everyday life, due to the lack of knowledge about the power of our subconscious mind. Our conscious mind has limits. Our subconscious and universal mind are infinite.

Let's use gossip as an example. Your subconscious mind does not reason or judge, therefore it cannot separate thoughts that you may have directed toward another. When you gossip, your subconscious mind stores those thoughts and brings them forward to manifest in your life. Your subconscious mind also operates under heredity patterns, (the transferring of characteristics and beliefs from parents to offspring). So as children, when you continuously hear something, it becomes a belief which is stored in your subconscious mind. This relates to comments, teachings, music, TV, violence, etc. without you even realizing it. Then your subconscious mind goes to work to create it in your life. The goal is to become aware of what is in your subconscious mind, let go of what does not serve you, and then fill your subconscious mind with all the good that you desire which is here for you to experience.

NOURISHMENT FOR YOUR SOUL: Think of your mind in relation to a one-story house. Your conscious mind is the main floor where all activity takes place. Your subconscious mind is the attic where you store memories from past experiences and beliefs, where it is dark, and where you are unaware of what is stored away in there. Your universal mind is your connection to God and all of life, where there is always light. Your spirit is the energy within your house that directs the flow.

FOOD FOR THOUGHT: I AM a divine centre for love, peace, unity, abundance and freedom.

ANGELIC TOOLS:
- ♥ *You Can Heal Your Life* by Louise L. Hay
- ♥ *I Can Do It Affirmation Cards* by Louise L. Hay
- ♥ *Healing With the Angels* by Doreen Virtue (There are affirmations in back of book.)
- ♥ *Angelic Music* by Peter Sterling. (Angelic music keeps you in a higher state of consciousness, shifting your thoughts to love and peace.)

JOURNEY TO YOUR INNER SANCTUARY AND BEYOND MEDITATION

This meditation will guide you to your inner sanctuary and beyond where you can just be and receive the healing energy your body requires, the nurturing your soul desires, and clarity that will light your path. Each time you do this meditation you will gain more clarity regarding your life's path. So lets begin!

- I invite you to close your eyes, and just relax.

- Take four deep breaths and as you breathe in, breathe in love. As you breathe out, release any worries or concerns you may have. With each breath go deeper and deeper into that space of relaxation.

- Visualize your flame of divine white light in the center of your being. This is the spark within you that God created.

- Ask your angels to take you to your inner sanctuary, the place where you feel safe, secure and loved, a quiet place away from outer influences where you can just be. Just allow the angels to guide you to that inner sanctuary, without trying to control it or question it; just go with the flow.

- Pause.

- At this time, I invite you to create a symbol in your mind that will give you direct access to your inner sanctuary. Anytime you visualize this symbol it will take you directly to this space.

- Now we are going to move beyond your inner sanctuary and enter the universal sanctuary.

- In front of you is a beautiful green meadow filled with vibrant, fragrant, beautiful flowers. Take a moment to smell these fresh, sweet fragrances and to admire their vibrant colors. Explore your surroundings, and become aware of a plush red velvet chair with gold trim placed in the middle of this beautiful green meadow.

- I invite you to sit in this chair. Close your eyes. Relax and breathe deeply.

- Repeat after me, "Dear Angels, please send me healing energy that will benefit me at this time, and help me connect with and feel the divine love, light and wisdom that exists within me." Take a few moments to embrace this energy.

- Pause while you retrieve this information.

- Now explore your surroundings. Further into the meadow lies a beautiful pond of crystal clear sparkling water with a waterfall flowing into it. I invite you to take yourself there and submerge yourself into this pond.

- Repeat after me, "Dear Angels, please cleanse from my body, being and mind, conscious and unconscious and cellular memory that which no longer serves me."

- Now emerge from the water. The sun is shining down upon you filling your body with divine energy. Feel the warmth of the sun on your skin. See the sunlight reflect off the water shining light into your eyes. Touch your heart and feel the divine presence within.

- Once again observe your surroundings. Just ahead of you lies a path of light. Invite your angels to walk this path with you. Repeat after me, "Dear Angels, please bring me clarity about where I am going. Help me to walk this path with confidence and courage." Follow this lighted path making mental notes of what you see, feel, hear and know as you walk this path.

- Pause while you retrieve this information.

- Know you are a powerful child of God and that everything you require and desire to walk your path and fulfill your mission is inside of you and available to you now. Ask your angels to transform all fear into love as you joyfully walk your path letting your light shine. Thank your angels for their assistance.

- Bring yourself back to center, to your spark of divine light and affirm: I AM a loving child of God. I AM powerful and loving. I choose to share my gifts and talents and I have a powerful loving impact on this world. I let my light shine bright. Bring yourself back into your body and into this room. Open your eyes and record anything you want to capture from this experience.

May you always feel the angelic presence that exists within you as you walk your path with love and light!

NOTE: This meditation is found on my *Angelic Reflections I: Awakening* CD.

Thoughts and Beliefs

Our thoughts, words and actions determine our experiences. However, it all begins with a thought. Our thoughts are a reflection of our beliefs and create our feelings and emotions which create our behaviors, actions and essentially our outer experiences. Therefore, what we focus our thoughts on is what we create for ourselves, and contributes to the creation of our global consciousness. Since our thoughts create our feelings and emotions they also create physical conditions. All thoughts are either love-based or fear-based. Love represents God consciousness; fear represents the illusion. We always have a choice to choose love. The wonderful thing about thoughts is that if we do not like what we are experiencing in our life, we can change it from within by changing our thoughts. This creates new beliefs which are reflected in our feelings and emotions, which in turn attract and change our outer experiences. It's a chain reaction; they all impact the other.

A belief is an accepted opinion, something we claim as truth for ourselves. Beliefs are created by repetitive thoughts, therefore our thoughts are a reflection of and create our beliefs. They are stored in our subconscious mind. Many times these beliefs come from previous programming or experiences that have been projected onto us growing up yet do not ring true for us any longer. While growing up we unconsciously take on the beliefs from others opinions and the influences in our lives. As we learn, grow and become more aware of our own truths, we have the opportunity to keep what feels true to us and release what does not serve a purpose in our life anymore. Everything we see, hear and read has an impact on our lives.

When our thoughts are in our conscious mind we are aware and have control over them. When they are in our subconscious mind they become beliefs, and we do not have control over them because most often we are unaware of them. However, we can become aware of them by observing our thoughts. We can also put thoughts into our subconscious mind to create beliefs that reflect what we do desire to experience to replace the old beliefs. Our subconscious mind will then begin sending thoughts to our conscious mind to create these experiences in our life. When we become aware of our thoughts, we control them rather than our thoughts controlling us.

Changing beliefs is very simple. All we must do is make the choice to change the way we think. However, it takes patience, persistence and repetition for the mind to create new beliefs. As we begin to create new thought patterns we may notice unsatisfying or undesirable thoughts surfacing. This is to be expected as our mind is similar to a computer which accepts what we put into it and saves it until we replace it with something else. It is then recycled. The same happens with our thoughts. As they are replaced with new ones, they come out transformed to reflect what we desire. These surfacing thoughts are attached to patterns of old beliefs and they give us the opportunity to see what beliefs are in our subconscious mind so that we can change them to reflect what's in our hearts. When we acknowledge them without judgment and thank them for coming forth to show us what is in our subconscious mind, we can then let them go with ease. When you become aware of beliefs that are undesirable or do not serve you anymore, you can change them very easily with affirmations. We will discuss how to create effective affirmations later in this chapter.

NOURISHMENT FOR YOUR SOUL: *"Whether you think that you can, or that you can't, you are usually right."* —Henry Ford

FOOD FOR THOUGHT: I choose only loving thoughts.

EXERCISE: DISCOVERING YOUR BELIEFS

Below are seven steps to discovering your beliefs, releasing beliefs from outer influences, and replacing them with new beliefs that reflect your truth.

1. **Record:** take inventory of your beliefs. To do this pay attention to what thought patterns come up when you think about money, relationships, yourself, making a living, changes or whatever topic you want to reflect upon.

2. **Recognize:** which beliefs belong to you and which came from outer influences, such as the beliefs of society or what someone said to you. Put an "M" next to yours, and an "O" next to others. If you have negative thought patterns or feelings that surface around a subject or issue, it is an indication those did not come from within but rather from outer influences. If you have positive thought patterns and feelings that surface, this is an indication it is your belief. The beliefs that do not resonate, relate or ring true to you are ones you collected as you were growing up.

3. **Reflect:** on why you believe this to be true. This will help recognize which are yours and which are others. For example: If growing up one of your parents always said, "You can't always have everything or "Money doesn't grow on trees," is that something you believe is true?

4. **Remember/Recall:** where the belief came from. Send this person love energetically and then release the belief.

5. **Release:** the beliefs that are not true for you by saying, "I release you and set you free for you are not truth for me."

6. **Replace:** create new beliefs that reflect your truth with affirmations.

7. **Reward:** you will attract that which you believe in and desire, instead of the beliefs of others. Your subconscious mind stores your beliefs and your conscious mind takes steps to create them in your life. You can be true to yourself and others because you know what is true for you and you can live by these truths.

Practice: Make a list of five thoughts related to the area of your life you would like to focus on. This will give you a clue as to the beliefs that you have regarding this subject. Then observe these thoughts and see if they reflect what you desire to experience. If they do not, then you can begin to change this belief by creating an affirmation that reflects what you do desire to experience.

Example: Thought Pattern: I'd love to be an artist, but I can't make a living doing that. "O" This most likely came from outer influences since it is something you are passionate about. Without that influence, you would have thoughts about how good it would make you feel to be an artist and have an abundance of creative ideas rather than feeling disappointed because you did not believe you could make a living as an artist. Affirmation: I AM a successful artist and the universe supports all my endeavors.

NOURISHMENT FOR YOUR SOUL: It is essential for your well-being to create thought patterns to reflect your desires, for this creates new beliefs. What you focus on is what you will attract.

FOOD FOR THOUGHT: My thoughts and beliefs reflect what I desire to experience.

ANGELIC TOOLS:
♥ *Dissolving Barriers* audio by Louise L. Hay

Focusing Your Thoughts

FOCUS

Focus your thoughts on what it is you desire,
Whether it's who you want to be, do or acquire,
For the thoughts you think will come alive,
Reflecting what resides inside.

—*Bonnie Ann Lewis*

- ♥ Focus is the ability to keep your energy going in the direction you desire to go despite challenges or outer influences.

- ♥ What you focus on is what you will create. If you focus thoughts on love, you will create and experience love in all areas of your life. On the contrary, if you focus on thoughts of fear, that is exactly what you will experience as you block what you do want. The reason this is true is that your subconscious mind doesn't know whether it is something you desire or not. It only knows to create what is continuously repeated within.

- ♥ Focus on your strengths and what is divine, not what you perceive as "wrong" or shortcomings. This redirects your energy toward achieving your goals.

- ♥ Focusing frees your mind to move into deeper states of consciousness in order to bring about that which you desire.

NOURISHMENT FOR YOUR SOUL: Sometimes it can be difficult to focus on a goal, desire or dream when you have no idea how you will get there. At this stage it is important to follow divine guidance and have faith and trust. Know there is a lot going on behind the scenes that you may not be aware of. Continue focusing on your desires.

FOOD FOR THOUGHT: I keep my thoughts focused on that which I choose to experience.

This message came to me when I was feeling overwhelmed due to all the facets of my life's purpose.

MESSAGES OF LOVE:

> *Dear Child,*
>
> *Finish one project before you go on to another. You have many creative ideas. Write them down and when it's time you will have all the details to move forward. When you focus on one project at a time, the energy is all encompassed and intensifies. With this intensity comes fruition. Move forward one day at a time at a steady pace. You are being supported in whatever you choose to do. Some of the ideas you have will come forth later. However, the seeds are being planted and these ideas will be nurtured along the way. Bits and pieces of information will continue to come. Allow it to flow. You will know when it is time to move forward. Allow inspirations to come and do not get caught up in the "time" thing and become overwhelmed. Know and trust you are being guided and all is in divine order. You are a pure true channel. Trust, trust, trust in God and yourself.*
>
> *—The Angels*

Physical Body

Your body is the outer expression of and a reflection of the health of your soul. Your physical body is an incredible vessel of energy filled with knowledge and wisdom. It is the vehicle in which your soul uses to evolve through experience. Your body is an amazing instrument that takes you where you desire and direct it to go. It is filled with energy that will help you accomplish your life mission. It is your choice of what type of fuel you put into your body. You can fuel it with love or with fear. Being aware of what you put into your body is essential to staying in your natural state as much as possible. What you put into your body is what you get out of it, and its performance depends on how you maintain it. If you do not take care of your body appropriately, you will experience dis-ease in your life. When you take care of your body and give it the nurturing and nourishment in needs, it will perform at its best so you can accomplish what you came here to do.

Ways to Care for Your Physical Body

It is very important for you to nourish, nurture and treat your body with respect so it will function at its greatest potential.

- ♥ Consume healthy food and beverages.
- ♥ Exercise regularly. Choose exercise that makes you feel good as this will serve you the best. If you participate in exercise that you dread, it defeats the purpose.
- ♥ Get adequate rest. It is essential to take the time to rest and refuel your energy.
- ♥ Listen to your body; tune into what it needs.

- ♥ Eliminate the chemicals from your body.
- ♥ Recharge your energy with *Rainbows of Love Activation*.

NOURISHMENT FOR YOUR SOUL: Rainbow energy is essential for our well-being. We get rainbow energy from the rays of the sun. When we do not get enough of this energy, it affects our energy levels and our mood. *Rainbows of Love Activation* invokes this energy.

FOOD FOR THOUGHT: I AM slim, trim, fit and beautiful. I exercise in ways that bring me joy. I AM vibrantly healthy and full of life.

ANGELIC TOOLS:
- ♥ *Angel Medicine* by Doreen Virtue
- ♥ *Your Journey to Love Daily Practices* CD by Bonnie Ann Lewis (included with book)

RAINBOWS OF LOVE ACTIVATION

This visualization is designed to activate the rainbow light that your body needs to be vibrantly healthy and full of life. It will keep you energized, re-vitalized and filled with universal energy. I recommend doing this outdoors.

- Stand in an upright position facing the sun with your arms extending out into the air toward the heavens, palms facing upward.
- As you take your first deep breath, visualize rainbow light coming from the sun, entering your body through your crown chakra at the top of your head.
- As you take your second breath, feel this exuberant energy filling your whole body.
- With your third breath, see it extending down through the bottom of your feet entering into the earth.

- As you take your fourth breath, visualize this rainbow light coming up from the earth into your body and expanding out into the universe from your heart and your hands.

- Affirm: Thank you universe for this vibrant energy that re-vitalizes and nourishes me instantly.

> NOTE: This activation is found on *Your Journey to Love Daily Practices CD* included with this book

---

Eating Healthy to Support Your Body and Energize You

As your spiritual senses are heightened your body becomes more sensitive to foods and chemicals. All foods have different vibrations. When your vibration increases, your body can no longer tolerate foods of lower vibration and you may exhibit reactions or allergies to foods that are not complimentary to your body. Lower vibrational foods that contain chemicals such as processed foods, sugar, caffeine and alcohol take a lot of energy to digest and leave you feeling tired and unmotivated. They also alter your moods and take you out of touch with your body's natural state of love. When you eat foods that have a higher vibration, such as raw fruits and vegetables, the greater your energy level will be and the better you will feel since it takes much less energy for your body to process foods that are more like your natural state. When you eat healthy, it gives you the energy and motivation to do what you desire.

♥ Drink lots of natural spring bottled or filtered water, and fresh organic juices and beverages. We have a water dispenser in our home and have spring water delivered in 5-gallon jugs. This investment helps the environment by reducing the amount of recycling that occurs with individual bottles, saving on recycling costs.

♥ Eat as much raw, organic vegetables, fresh fruits and foods as possible. Be sure to eat a good balance of healthy protein.

♥ If you eat dairy products choose organic. If you eat meat or poultry choose organic or that which is from animals that are grass-fed and free roaming. Bless and thank the animal for the nourishment it provides for your body.

♥ Stay away from processed foods, fast food, foods high in sugar, foods containing caffeine, alcohol, artificial sweeteners and food colorings.

♥ Choose foods that support and balance your chakras. To do this, pick foods that have the same color as the chakra that needs extra support. You can also refer to the *Chakra Tune-up Chart* by Elizabeth Blackburn for foods that support each chakra.

♥ Put love into your food while preparing it and before eating it. With your intention and visualization, you can transform the energy by saying, "I bless this food and ask that it nourish my body in a divine way. Thank you! Amen."

♥ At times when you eat on the run or in a restaurant, before eating your food, ask the angels to transform the energy in the food you are eating to divine energy. Visualize it surrounded by white light. This increases the vibration of the food.

NOURISHMENT FOR YOUR SOUL: It is not just what you eat that determines your weight, health or level of energy. It is what you believe about what you eat that affects you as well. When you eat something, do you have thoughts that it will give you vibrant health and energy or do you feel guilty or afraid of what it may do to your body? As you change your beliefs about what you eat, your body will change what it desires to eat. It is essential to feel good about what you eat. When you recite the following affirmation, you will find yourself choosing healthy foods that nourish your body.

FOOD FOR THOUGHT: Everything I eat brings me vibrant health and energy.

ANGELIC TOOLS:
- ♥ *Eating in the Light* by Doreen Virtue
- ♥ *Chakra Tune-up Chart* by Elizabeth Blackburn

The Organic Shift

Our bodies are naturally organic, meaning as is from nature. Organic food is free from chemicals, pesticides, fertilizers and additives that are harmful to our body. Organic foods are grown in soil that is conditioned in a way that supports the growth of the food without using chemicals. Organic body products are made with all-natural ingredients such as flowers, plants, herbs, oils etc. instead of chemicals. Organic meat comes from animals that live healthy free roaming lives, and are raised on healthy grass fed diets that are free from injected synthetic hormones or antibiotics. Think about this in relation to your body. What that animal consumed is what is going into and nourishing your body. The quality of the animals' life is the energy you will be absorbing. When you consume meat from healthy animals that had a healthy life, you will experience a greater sense of well-being. Alternative medicine is made with natural ingredients from nature such as berries, plants, vegetables etc. rather than manufactured ingredients containing chemicals.

The biggest concern I hear from people about switching to organic foods and products is that it is more expensive. While this is a valid concern, I invite you to embrace an idea with me. Your health is the most important aspect of your life for without it you can not do what you came here to do. A contributing factor to our health conditions is related to the lifestyle we live as a society and the chemicals we are being exposed to and putting into our bodies. As we become educated about what affects our body, establish healthy eating habits and live a healthier lifestyle we will all experience a greater sense of well-being and live healthier lives. Organic food has a higher vibration and provides a greater quality of nutrition for your body. I invite you to consider the money spent as an investment in the quality of your life and the benefits it has on our planet. Organic food and products are more complimentary to your body and contribute to the healing of our land, the purification of our bodies of water and protects us from chemical exposure. While for many organic is perceived as a luxury, it is becoming a way of life. As we all adopt the organic method of living and support these businesses, the costs will be more affordable. If you desire to switch to an organic way of life, you can ask your angels to provide you with the money to do so.

The most important part of choosing foods and personal products that are complimentary to your body is reading the labels. Organic products will have ingredients that you recognize and can read. A good rule of thumb to follow is if you do not know what the ingredients are, do not buy it. When you go to the store, you can ask your angels to guide you to what your body needs. You can also hold the item in your hand or put it up to your heart and tune into your body. Take a deep breath and ask, "Is this what I need?" Listen for a reply. You may feel a sensation such as warmth, which indicates a yes. You may feel nauseated which indicates a no or your body doesn't need it. You may hear yes or no or just have a sense of knowing. Eliminating chemicals from my body has made an amazing difference in how I feel, has given me a greater sense of well-being, and is a healthier way of living. While removing chemicals from your environment can be done right away, it is best to eliminate chemicals from your body and adjust your diet gradually to ensure a smooth transition. This recipe will guide you to an organic way of life with grace and ease.

- ♥ Switch to eating all organic foods, dairy and meat in place of eating chocolate, sugar and processed foods. (Instead of throwing out the food that is currently in your pantry, give it to the homeless, a soup kitchen or another organization in need.)

- ♥ Switch to fresh organic juices or herbal teas in place of caffeinated beverages such as coffee and sodas. (When eliminating caffeine products, reduce the amount you consume a little each day until you have eliminated it completely. This will lessen the withdraw symptoms that can occur.)

- ♥ Switch to vegan cheeses and substitutes in place of dairy.

- ♥ Switch to a high protein diet in place of meat. (Eggs are not dairy and they are a great source of protein.) Although my desire is to eliminate meat altogether, this is still a goal in progress for me. My challenge has been getting enough protein. So eating small amounts of chicken, fish and beef occasionally is more compatible to my body at this time. I listen to my body as to what it needs each day and that's what I eat.

- ♥ Switch to homeopathic or herbal over-the-counter remedies. Do not go off or change any medications without consulting your healthcare practitioner. (Healthcare providers that specialize in oriental medicine, an osteopath, or a naturopath that practices alternative therapies can guide you.)

- ♥ Switch to organic personal care items such as shampoo, lotion, toothpaste, deodorant etc. According to AlphaZelle, a company that offers all natural products, here are the most popular chemicals to watch out for when choosing your personal care products: Propylene, Ethylene and Butylene Glycol, Sodium Lauryl Sulfate (SLS) and Sodium Laureth Sulfate (SLES), DEA (diethanolamine), MEA (monoethanolamine) and TEA (triethanoloamine), Polyethylene Glycol (PEG), Sodium Hydroxide, Triclosan, DMDM and Urea (imidazolidnyl), Parabens, Alcohol, Isopropyl (SD-40), Mineral Oil, FD and C Color Pigments and fragrances. For more information, you can visit their website at www.alphazelle.com.

- ♥ Switch to all natural environmentally safe household cleaning supplies to eliminate chemicals from your environment. (My cleaning ladies use earth-friendly products that I provide.)

- ♥ Switch your pest and lawn services to ones that use organic, chemical free products. You can also ask the angels to keep your home free from bugs and insects and visualize a white barrier around your home and windows. (Since I have done this there have only been a few rare occasions where it was necessary to use any pest control inside our home.)

NOURISHMENT FOR YOUR SOUL: Using organic products is beneficial to your body and also our environment.

FOOD FOR THOUGHT: I choose to live an organic life. I experience a healthy well-being and contribute to creating a healthier earth for us all.

ANGELIC TOOLS:
- *Eating in the Light* by Doreen Virtue
- *The Art of Raw Living Food* by Doreen Virtue and Jenny Ross
- *Recipes for a Small Planet* by Ellen Buchman Ewald
- *Diet for a Small Planet* by Frances Moore Lappe'

All my life I have been sensitive to prescription as well as over-the-counter medication and chemicals, and have had reactions to them, some more severe than others. After all of my senses opened up, my sensitivities increased. During my first pregnancy, I developed a thyroid condition. After the birth of my daughter it was recommended that I have radioactive iodine treatment to dissolve my thyroid. Although I felt reluctant about doing this, it was the best method of treatment at that time and I was told if I did not have the treatment it could affect the development of my next child. Since I knew I was going to have one more child, I chose to do it. This treatment dissolved my thyroid and I was placed on a thyroid replacement hormone. A few years later I gave birth to my healthy son. For this I am blessed and grateful!

Several years later I was under a lot of stress, my thyroid levels were fluctuating and I was feeling fatigued. So in addition to my thyroid replacement, I was given an additional medication that was supposed to help balance out my thyroid hormones. Instead I began to exhibit symptoms as if I was on speed. It was like my body was continuously on the gas pedal. I had racing thoughts, I was irritable, anxious and extremely nauseous, which made me feel dis-oriented. I felt out of control and like someone else was in my body. I was not eating or sleeping regularly and my weight declined. I had lost touch with reality and stopped taking my thyroid medication. Since I do not have a thyroid my body went into thyroid shock and began to shut down, and I nearly died. When I was taken to the emergency room because I felt like I was dying, I was mis-diagnosed and over medicated due to my symptoms, and my developed psychic abilities. Although I tried to tell them what was going on was thyroid related, they wouldn't listen. I do not place blame on any of the medical professionals who treated me as I believe everyone did the best that they could with the knowledge and understanding they had at that time. I believe that God works through all people and the treatment they provided for me in the emergency room saved my life. For this I am forever grateful! However, the label that was placed upon me followed me everywhere and was a challenge to detach from.

Prior to this experience, I had a mind of my own and was not affected too much by the opinions of others. Due to the judgments that were placed upon me during this experience and the trauma that occurred, my self-confidence was shattered and the opinions of others became prevalent in my life. I felt guilty for how it affected those around me especially my children. I felt hurt, mis-understood and I blamed and judged myself. I did not understand why I had chosen, let alone how I created this experience. This left me with the desire to get to the truth of this experience so I could be at peace and go on with my life. I did not settle for the label that was placed upon me. Instead, I chose to take responsibility for myself, my life and go within and get to the source of this experience. I asked for angelic assistance, reflected upon what my lessons in this experience were and began creating my life anew, using the principles this book presents.

After much research, observation from some divine medical professionals I was guided to, the teachings of Doreen Virtue, and the guidance from the angelic realm, we later came to understand the medication I was given was not complimentary to my body and had an adverse affect on me causing a thyroid imbalance and exhibiting similar symptoms in which the label placed upon me exhibits. For me being on that medication seemed similar to what one experiences when on street drugs or intoxicated. Although I have never taken street drugs or drank alcohol, I believe I experienced first hand what that feels like while on that medication. The blessing in this experience gave me the opportunity to understand how chemicals can affect our sensitive bodies and how dis-connected one feels. These sensitivities are part of humanity evolving and are often unrecognized or dismissed. One of my doctors said, "You are just too sensitive and a perfect example of the failure of that medication." Although many amazing things occurred along the way, here I share with you two experiences that confirmed this truth that brought much peace and resolution for me.

One night before I went to bed, I was working with my Archangel Oracle Cards by Doreen Virtue. I had asked for guidance that would bring me peace about this experience. I pulled two cards, both were Archangel Raziel. One was Spiritual Understanding and the other was Take Back Your Power. I invited Archangel Raziel into my dreams that night. The next day, I woke up and couldn't breathe through my nose. As always, I went to *You Can Heal Your Life* book, by Louise L. Hay, recited my affirmations and called on Archangel Raphael to assist me in performing a healing on myself. I also took some homeopathic remedies. These are things I do when I begin to feel any ailment coming on and it usually never manifests fully, but this time nothing seemed to work. In an attempt to open up my nasal passages, I went to the drug store and purchased an over-the-counter medicine. I took this medication and at three in the morning I woke up, felt anxious, and I was nauseous. I tried to go back to sleep but my mind was racing. It came to me this medication has a stimulant in it and I was having a similar reaction, but not as intense, that I had with the prescription medication I was sensitive to. I heard the angels say, "Go talk to a pharmacist." So I did and he confirmed it does have a stimulant in it. The next day my nose cleared up and I heard this was about honoring my self-worth by trusting my sense of knowing.

Soon after this experience I received a flyer with some products I had ordered for my healing center from New Leaf Distributing. The flyer was promoting a book called *The Thyroid Solution* by Ridha Arem, M.D. A sense of peace came over me and I heard the angels say, "order it." So I did and it brought so much clarity, confirmation and blessings for me. I have gained a greater understanding of the thyroid function, how essential it is to the body and the impact it has on the body as a whole. I've also learned what I can do to support my body to experience a healthy well-being. One day as I finished my meditation I went to the closet to get something and when I got there I did not remember what I went there to get. As I was thinking about why I was there, I looked up and *The Thyroid Solution* caught my eye. At that moment I chuckled knowing the angels had guided me there. I came out of the closet and sat down on the floor. I held the book up to my heart and a warm feeling came over me. I felt Archangel Raphael's presence around me and I asked him to guide me to the pages that contained the information that I needed at this time. The first page I opened to was a listing of all the recommended daily nutrition allowances to support the thyroid. The second page I went to had guidelines on foods to eat that contribute to supporting the thyroid. As I was reading, I heard that it would be beneficial for me to use nutritional supplements in addition to the replacement hormone for optimal health and well-being. While the thyroid substitute replaces the thyroid hormone, it does not give the body the nourishment that a healthy thyroid produces. The third page I was guided to had information about a nutritional supplement called ThyroLife Optima, created by Dr. Arem himself that is specifically formulated with all the multi-vitamins needed for people with thyroid conditions. To learn more about ThyroLife, visit www.thyrolife.com. The fourth page I was guided to entailed Dr. Arem talking about how oftentimes thyroid conditions are overlooked or mistaken for other conditions because of the complexity of symptoms which affect the body and mind. *The Thyroid Solution* is filled with so much wisdom and guidance on understanding the function, treatment, and self-care for thyroid conditions. This book presents the medical expertise and natural approaches to maintaining optimal health for people with thyroid conditions and has been a Godsend for me.

I felt drawn to my archangel cards once again. I asked, "What other messages related to these experiences do you have for me." I pulled one card. It was the Sensitivity card with a message from Archangel Haniel. Then I heard, *"You are seeing the truth in this situation. Trust your sense of knowing, let it go and be at peace."* I knew these experiences took place so that I would trust the guidance I was receiving and the messages my body was giving me. I have come to understand my body's way of talking to me when something does not agree with it or is not right for me often comes through my stomach. Our stomach is our power center, the center of our sense of knowing or intuition. For me, nausea is the physical sensation that occurs. Although not the most pleasant feeling, I've come to listen to my body and reflect upon its message. In hind site, had I recognized this, I would have had some very different experiences. It took me a long time to work through the emotions attached to the trauma and come to peace with all of this. For me, forgiving everyone else was the easy part however forgiving myself was my true challenge. I have to say there were times I felt confused and doubted my own sense of knowing, and thought maybe there was some truth in the label that was placed upon me, but in my heart I knew that was not truth for me. The challenge for me was listening to my inner guidance despite what some of the doctors were saying as I have a great respect and appreciation for their gifts. I have come to recognize and honor my own sensitivities and I am very selective about what goes into my body. I have found that consulting with healthcare providers who are open to alternative therapies and natural remedies has been very beneficial for me due to these sensitivities. In situations where traditional medication is necessary, I ask that the dosage be very minimal and I detoxify my body afterwards. I feel very blessed for the angels and my support system who guided me in getting to the truth of this experience. I am forever grateful for their continuous love, support, expertise and willingness to listen to the guidance I received from the angelic realm throughout my healing process. I am forever grateful for the wisdom within this book that guided me in creating my life anew. The angels said this was part of being a pioneer so I could assist others during this transformational time on the planet. I later came to know this experience was a reflection of some past life karma that I brought into this lifetime to balance.

Your Spiritual Self

"You have a beautiful spirit. In order to see it you must look within."
—THE ANGELS

You are much more than just your physical body. You are a spiritual being in a physical body having a human experience. Your spiritual self is that aspect of you which exists, but you do not physically see. It consists of your soul, your mind and your energy, also known as spirit. Your soul is the non-physical part of yourself, the spark within you which God created. It is the core of your being, your center, the true essence of who you are, and why you are here. It is the part of you that has traveled from lifetime to lifetime evolving from experiences. It has all the answers you will ever need. It holds all the seeds of your desires, beliefs, truths and your life's purpose. Your heart is the communicator between your soul and your physical existence.

Spirit is the life force that brings about what your soul desires. It is the power, passion and the motivation to bring your dreams to life. Your heart is the expression of and the doorway to your soul. Your soul is the individuality of who you are, your I AM presence. Spirit is the energy of your soul in which we are all connected as one. It is also known as your breath of life, your energy source and the home of your personal power, and your creativity. The vibration of spirit is love, the energy of God and creation, the highest vibration that exists. God is the source in which everything begins and exists. It is your spirit that connects you to the universal mind, the infinite supply of abundance in your life, God.

Your mind is the director of all activity in your life. Your higher self is the wisdom of your soul, your divine mind. Your higher self has a larger plan for your life than you can consciously comprehend, and every experience will fit together like a puzzle. It will give you knowledge and value in some way even though you may not always be able to see the big picture in that moment. As you connect to your higher self the bigger picture will begin to unfold. Part of the job of your higher self is to keep you safe and progressive in your life, and to guide you in fulfilling your life's purpose. It is the part of yourself that is wise beyond your years. It always knows and wants what is best for you. It is your inner guidance that puts you in the right place at the right time. Fear not about moving forward for everything you do and every step you take is part of your journey here. There really is no "wrong" choice. You will experience what is necessary for your soul to grow. No matter what road you take, it will be right for your learning experience. However, some roads present a smoother path. It is up to you to decide which road you desire to take. Choosing love always presents a more joyous journey. As your spiritual awareness expands, your vibration increases and your light body is activated. *Activating Your Light Body Invocation* will assist with this process.

ACTIVATING YOUR LIGHT BODY INVOCATION

This visualization expands and activates your light body by releasing lower energy, invoking more light into your body, raising your vibration. The more light you contain within you, the higher your vibration is, and the more loving experiences you will attract.

- Ask your angels to surround you in their divine white light and to remove from your body, being, thought forms (conscious, unconscious and cellular memory) that which no longer serve you.

- Below your feet is a blanket of white light.

- Visualize this blanket going up your body collecting everything that is to be released. As you do so, affirm: I release that which no longer serves me.

- As the blanket reaches the top of your head, pull the corners of the blanket together and give it to your angels to transform into light.

- Ask the angels to refill those spaces with their divine white light. Then visualize a ray of white light coming down through the top of your head and filling your whole body.

- Affirm: I AM a powerful loving being of light on this earth and I let my light shine! And so it is!

NOTE: This activation is found on *Your Journey to Love Daily Practices* CD included with this book.

Universal Birthrights

As spiritual beings, we all have access to these universal birthrights. I believe God brought us here to experience an abundance of love, peace, vibrant health, wealth, and support to fulfill our life's mission, to live a plentiful life filled with divine experiences, opportunities and relationships. We all deserve and have the ability to choose and create all that we desire to experience in our lives. This is our birthright.

IT IS OUR BIRTHRIGHT TO:

- ♥ Receive what is required to fulfill our life's mission. Be supported by the universe in all ways: financially, physically, mentally, spiritually and emotionally.

- ♥ Create and experience our desires and dreams.

- ♥ Feel nurtured, safe, and valued.

- ♥ Experience and acquire all that we desire.

- ♥ Express who we are freely without judgment. Speak our truth.

- ♥ Free will to choose and make decisions that honor what we desire.

- ♥ Draw boundaries and say "no."

- ♥ Love and be loved unconditionally.

- ♥ Expand our personal relationship with God and connect to infinite wisdom.

- ♥ Experience success and inner happiness according to our own definition.

- ♥ Use our gifts and talents to be of service to others.

NOURISHMENT FOR YOUR SOUL: Anything which stems from love is your birthright. You will experience these blessings when you are in your natural state of love.

FOOD FOR THOUGHT: I embrace and give gratitude for the blessings of my birthright.

ANGELIC TOOLS:

♥ *Songs of the Spirit* music CD by Karen Drucker. (This beautiful music is affirmative and is a reflection of the divinity within each of us.)

Free Will

As spiritual beings we have the choice of free will which gives us the power within to create what we desire to experience. At the beginning of your life, you were given a source of energy. Your lifetime offers you the opportunity to use and express your energy any way you choose. It is your divine right to have all that is required and desired to fulfill your life's mission according to your heart's desires, so that you can serve others in this evolutionary process we call life. Free will gives you the opportunity to create your life and choose your experiences, the people you interact with in your life, how you express yourself and what you do with your life. Spirit is always there to support and assist you in achieving what you desire to experience. When you make your own choices, you are living your life by your inner guidance and direction rather than leaving your life up to chance. Whether you make these choices based on the influences of others or on your own, you are still responsible for your actions and creations. Just because someone else makes a choice does not mean you have to follow. What may be right for them is not necessarily right for you, or vice versa. You know what is best for you.

How to Know if Something Is Right for You

Your body always knows the truth. As you listen to the wisdom within, it brings greater awareness and will guide your way. This recipe will guide you in making choices that are appropriate for you and honor who you are and what you desire.

- 💜 When reflecting upon a choice, tune into how you feel. Do you feel content and confident or do you feel nauseous or a knot in your stomach? When something is right for you, there is a sense of knowing and calmness even if you are feeling butterflies in your stomach. When you feel anxious, afraid, etc., that is an indication something is not right or needs further exploration.

- 💜 When you question if something is right for you, this is a sign for you to obtain more clarity or information, or that purification or healing may need to take place.

- 💜 Place your hands over your heart, take a few deep breaths, and focus on whatever you are contemplating. Ask your angels if this is right for you. If it is, you will feel warmth coming from your heart.

- 💜 Follow what your heart desires as it knows the truths of your soul.

When something crosses your path, here are some important questions to ask yourself prior to making choices that support what you desire to experience: Is this something that is of my heart?, Is this choice going to bring me closer to fulfilling my life's purpose?, Is this something I feel excited and passionate about doing?, Do I feel calm with a sense of knowing?, Do I have the desire to do it now?, Are the doors open for me to take action?, Does this choice feel right to me and give me a sense of peace?

If you can honestly answer these questions with a "Yes," then that is right for you. If you cannot then there is more for you to investigate. There may be a blockage, the timing may be off, or it's just not right for you. Know that when you follow your heart and the outcome is different than you expected, that does not mean you made an incorrect choice. It simply means that you followed your intuition and the outcome was what it needed to be for the highest good of yourself and all concerned. When you honor your feelings, it is then you can make choices that create positive outcomes.

NOURISHMENT FOR YOUR SOUL: When you listen to your body, it will guide your way to making choices that are right for you. You do not need to justify yourself to anyone, but you may need to explain yourself in certain instances so people understand what you mean.

FOOD FOR THOUGHT: I listen to the wisdom within my body. I utilize my free will for the good of all.

Treasures of Your Soul

Treasures of your soul are God-given inner tools you can utilize to heal yourself and create all that your heart desires. These internal gifts guide you through life. You will be utilizing these natural senses, natural resources, and natural rhythms of the universe throughout this book.

Natural Senses

"It is through science that we prove, but through intuition that we discover."
—HENRY POINCARE

Our natural senses, also known as intuitive or psychic abilities, are the ways in which we communicate with God, our angels, other spiritual beings, and access universal wisdom. These inner senses are what we utilize to tune into the truths within our soul. We can use them to view our own aura to bring us information about our life's purpose and what we are experiencing in our lives right now. They can also be used to be of service to others. As children our senses were open, however, many of us were very sensitive to the energies around us. We often heard what was not being said, felt things deeply and saw things that scared us. Some may have expressed these abilities and were told "oh, it's just your imagination!" Others may have been considered weird when they portrayed these abilities. In order to protect ourselves we closed down these senses. As adults, we are learning to re-open these natural gifts from God that are meant to guide us through life. Reflecting back upon my life, I can see a glimpse of these abilities being present but not understood on a conscious level. Although we can utilize these inner senses to receive the divine messages from God, the angelic realm and other spiritual beings on our own, sometimes we need confirmation or clarity if we are too close to a situation to see it clearly. It can be helpful to receive guidance from another person who's psychic abilities are developed.

- **Claircognizance:** means clear knowing. This is when you receive messages that come as complete ideas, thoughts or great inspirations. You just know things but you do not know how you know. Many people refer to this as intuition. People who are claircognizant bring forth ancient wisdom. Many times you know what people are going to say before they say it.

    When your claircognizance opens up, you may become more sensitive to the electromagnetic field (EMF) from the computer if you spend a lot of time in front of it. Should this occur, ask the angels to protect you from the EMF rays before working on your computer. Visualize a white screen of protection between you and your computer. Take time to go outside and take some deep breaths. This will help to clear your mind and rejuvenates you so you can continue on with your computer activities. Placing a salt lamp next to your computer is beneficial as it neutralizes the energy. You can also place a piece of an obsidian crystal next to your computer to absorb any negativity coming from your computer. Sitting back a bit from your computer lessens the intensity of the rays and the effect it has on you.

    Throughout my life, there were many times when I would be having a conversation with a person, and I would already know what they were going to say and know when they were telling the truth. At times I doubted myself thinking I was reading more into it than was there. In truth, I was reading between the lines. The angels told me to trust these impressions as they will guide me through life. Looking back I see if I had listened to these I would have had much different experiences.

- **Clairvoyance:** means clear spiritual vision. This is when you receive messages in your mind's eye as visions, pictures, symbols, and sometimes scenes like a mini movie. You use your clairvoyance to see your past for healing, the present for possibilities, and the future for creating. Sometimes the visions you receive can be symbolic rather than actual occurrences.

When your clairvoyance opens up you may begin to see visions of the future and of past lives. It can be somewhat tricky in determining whether it is future or past, but in time you will gain more clarity by the type of visions you receive. Paying attention to the surroundings of these visions and how they relate to your life now is helpful in understanding them. If you need clarity on whether it is past or future, ask your angels. When my clairvoyance first opened up, I began seeing visions and receiving information that did not relate to this lifetime, but I had such strong feelings of connectedness. I later came to understand they were past lives that I was seeing and remembering, ones that I had shared with people who I came in contact with in this lifetime. It was the remembering of past events and the recognition of kindred spirits.

♥ **Clairaudience:** means clear hearing. This is when you receive messages as sounds or voices inside your head or just outside your ear. It sounds as if someone else is talking to you.

When your clairaudience opens up your ears may become very sensitive to sounds and loud noises. This allows you to clearly hear the voice of spirit. Some people hear ringing in their ears or high pitched sounds. This is the angels trying to get your attention or downloading information. If it is not at a comfortable level for you, ask your angels to lower the volume, and they will.

Clairaudience is one of my strongest channels for receiving divine guidance. Therefore, when I am in places that are loud, I place a shield (I refer to these as my spiritual earmuffs) over my ears to protect them. I do this by visualizing a white fluffy earmuff over each ear. This reduces the sensitivity so I'm less affected by the outside noise but still allows me to hear divine guidance.

ANGELIC TOOLS:

♥ *How to Hear Your Angels* by Doreen Virtue

♥ **Clairsentience:** means clear feelings. This is when you receive messages by feeling physical sensations such as chills, gut feelings, smells or even tastes. People with clairsentient abilities are empathic and pick up energy. As your clairsentience opens up, you will feel other people's energy and emotions, the energy in buildings, or planetary energy. This can make you feel like you are on an emotional roller coaster and not know why if you absorb this energy. It is essential to shield yourself from absorbing this energy, clear yourself from any energy you have picked up and discern what is yours and what is not.

SHIELDING

Shielding is protecting the energy field around you from absorbing lower vibrations of energy. When lower vibrations of energy are absorbed, it lowers your vibration. Shielding is essential when your clairsentience is open. It allows you to have these abilities but to be able to function in the world without being pulled into the drama of other people's lives or the fear-based illusions of society. I recommend shielding yourself first thing in the morning before you get out of bed and throughout your day whenever necessary with the following exercise.

SHIELDS OF LOVE ACTIVATION

This activation protects you from taking on the energy of a lower vibration and the emotions of others. It is best to do this exercise first thing in the morning and then throughout your day as needed.

- Invite in your angels by repeating after me, "Dear Angels, please surround me in your protective shield of divine white light. Please protect me from taking on any lower energy or the emotions of others. Help me to know what is mine and what is not. Thank you!"

- Visualize your angels' wings surrounding your body with a ray of white light and embracing you with love as a ray of pink light.

- Now visualize a ray of purple light surrounding your body giving you spiritual clarity, protection and raising your vibration.

- Now visualize a ray of green light surrounding your body for physical healing and protection.

- Affirm: I AM surrounded with shields of love and protected at all times. I know what is mine and what is not. And so it is!

NOTE: This activation is found on *Your Journey to Love Daily Practices* CD included with this book.

DISCERNING WHAT IS YOURS AND WHAT IS NOT

When you feel a physical sensation, it is essential to determine whether it is for you or not so you know what action to take. If you do not know, ask your angels whether it is yours or not. You may receive clairsentient messages about other people showing you their intentions or about a particular situation. Usually when it is someone else's and you set the intention to allow it to move through you, the sensation goes away. If it does not then ask for further guidance from your angels on what it refers to and what action you are to take. If it is not yours, it is essential to allow it to move through you rather than absorb it.

NOURISHMENT FOR YOUR SOUL: Everyday ask your angels to help you to know what is yours and what is not.

OBSERVING NOT ABSORBING

When we absorb other people's energy it can make us feel emotionally drained, exhausted or have feelings that we do not understand or relate to us. We may feel like everything is about us. If you feel this way it is an indication that it is time to clear yourself from energy that you've picked up along the way that does not belong to you. When you feel energy coming into your space and you know it is not yours, set the intention to release it and allow it to move through you. If need be, remove yourself from the situation or person. Go outside or to the rest room; release the energy and put up your shields!

NOURISHMENT FOR YOUR SOUL: It is important when you release things from your body to replace them with white light or that which you desire. If you do not intentionally refill them with what you desire, they will refill with whatever may come along. When you are clairsentient, it is essential that the releasing and shielding exercises become part of your daily practice to ensure a healthy well-being for yourself.

ANGELIC TOOLS:

 Your Journey to Love Daily Practices CD included with this book

RELEASING VISUALIZATION

This visualization is designed to release any energy you have absorbed when you become aware of it and clear your energy field so you attract higher vibrations of energy. It can be done instantly anytime you feel yourself picking up lower energy or the emotions of others..

- I invite you to repeat after me: "Dear Angels, Archangel Michael, and Ascended Master El Moyra, please assist me with this releasing process, and clear my energy field so I may attract high vibrations of energy. Thank you!"

- Visualize the energy that you absorbed wherever it is in your body. See it come together forming a ball.

- Visualize this ball going out your dominant hand into the universe, knowing as it leaves your hand it is transformed instantly with the divine white light of your angels.

- Take a moment to visualize your body filling up with white light to refill those spaces where that lower energy has left.

- Affirm: I release that which does not serve me with grace and ease. I attract high vibrations of energy. And so it is!

NOTE: This visualization is found on *Your Journey to Love Daily Practices CD* included with this book.

I have to admit when my clairsentience opened up as an adult it felt like a burden rather than a blessing. I have found it to be the most challenging of all the abilities to have. In the beginning, I did not realize I was clairsentient but felt emotionally overloaded. There was a part of me that wanted to just stay at home and withdraw from others where it was safe, because I felt things so deeply. If I went any place where there were lots of people, I felt overwhelmed and could not wait to get out of there. During movies I began feeling nauseated because I could feel the emotions of the actors. When I would listen to the radio, if a sad song came on I could feel the pain in the song. I have never been one to read the newspaper or watch the news because I could not stand to hear about or see anything related to violence. I would get a heavy feeling in the pit of my stomach. Most of my life, it was challenging for me to be in crowds or large groups of people and I did not understand why. I later recognized it was because I was clairsentient and would feel the emotions of others. Thank God for the teachings of Doreen Virtue, I came to understand this ability. I learned to discern what was mine and what was not, how to protect and clear myself, and became comfortable with being so open. It was then I was able to see it as the gift it truly is, the gift of compassion and an open heart. I am very selective about what I expose myself to because with all of my senses open, I am very sensitive—in a good way.

Being empathic, I began to feel other people's energy and I would receive impressions about them that I would just brush off. I would doubt myself, thinking I was judging them. I'd think to myself, I just need to see the light in that person. The angels said, *"When you receive impressions about others, honor it, and do not question it. When receiving this information, you are not judging, you are simply observing their energy."* These impressions we receive about others can help us see who they are showing up as, if they are in integrity or not, and gives us the opportunity to choose whether we want to participate in that energy or not. This is being aware of their intentions and integrity. While we are all children of God and are love, not everyone chooses, has the awareness, or is in a place to show up as the love that they are in that moment.

Everybody has the ability to utilize these inner senses. Some people have more developed senses than others. Using these abilities does not make you special or gifted as they are a natural part of who you are. Generally you have two out of the four channels which are the strongest. It has been my experience, the more you utilize these abilities, the stronger they become, and you will begin to receive messages through all channels simultaneously. When I first began utilizing my

ASPECTS OF YOU

psychic abilities it felt like something I "did." As these intuitive abilities developed, I realized they are part of who I am and my daily life, and feel very natural. I have invited the angels into my life and communicate with them throughout my day. I now feel this angelic presence with me all the time. I feel the angels speaking through me and guiding my actions most of the time. As a human, I occasionally get in my own way. Once I get out of the way life is much more peaceful, joyful, fulfilling and miracles happen!

NOURISHMENT FOR YOUR SOUL: *"Listen to your intuition. It will tell you everything you need to know."* —Anthony J. D'Angelo

FOOD FOR THOUGHT: I utilize my inner senses to guide me through life. I AM one with God. I AM connected to universal wisdom. I AM open and receptive to messages of love and light.

AWAKENING YOUR SPIRITUAL SENSES INVOCATION

This invocation attunes your mind to universal oneness and allows divine wisdom to enter in ways you are most receptive to. I recommend reciting this invocation before beginning any of the meditations.

- I invite you to close your eyes, focus on the music and take three or four deep breaths.
- Visualize your flame of divinity sparkling within the center of your being.
- Repeat after me, "Dear Angels, please surround me in your divine white light. Dear Archangel Michael, please come to me and help me release any fears or doubts I may have about receiving angelic guidance."
- Take a moment to see yourself surrounded by Archangel Michael's cobalt blue energy. Feel this energy around you giving you a sense of courage and confidence.
- With your intentions, you can open up all of your spiritual senses by saying, "Dear Angels, Archangel Raziel and Archangel Haniel, please

open up my inner senses so I can receive your messages clearly. I AM open and receptive to receiving this divine guidance in whatever way you bring it to me so I can understand it. Thank you!"

- Let's affirm: Angelic guidance flows to me with clarity, grace and ease. I AM an open channel for divine messages. One love, one love, one love.

- Your inner senses are now open so that you can receive divine guidance.

May you be enlightened by the messages that you receive. Blessings to you!

NOTE: This meditation is found on my *Angelic Reflections I: Awakening* CD

Your Aura

Your intuitive abilities can also be used to read your own aura. Your aura is the energy field that exists around your body and exhibits your vibration of energy. This energy field shows your true nature and intentions. You can learn a great deal about yourself and others by this field of energy that surrounds all of us. Within your auric field exists rays and blotches of color. Each color has a specific meaning. Some colors within your aura stay the same and others change according to your thoughts, feelings and emotions. When your inner senses are open you can read your own aura and the auras of others. Below is a meditation so you can read your own aura and find out more about yourself and your life's purpose by interpreting the meaning of the colors you see.

AURA MEDITATION

This meditation is designed to help you read your own aura as this will bring clues to your life's mission. Before you begin you may want to get a piece of white paper and in the center draw an outline of your head and shoulders. After the meditation you will record the colors you receive on it. If you'd like, you can even use colored pencils or crayons to draw it as you saw it. When you are finished with this meditation, refer to the color chart to identify what these colors represent.

- I invite you to close your eyes. Focus on the music, allowing your mind to clear and just be.
- Take three or four deep breaths. As you breathe in, breathe in love, and as you breathe out, release any doubts or fears you may have about seeing your aura clearly.
- Now visualize your flame of divine white light shining bright in the center of your being.
- Continue breathing and with each breath, see your flame of white light expand throughout your body.
- With another deep breath, see it expand into your aura.
- Visualize yourself looking into a large mirror in front of you.
- Focus your attention on the area around your head and shoulders. Notice the colors that are in your aura. You may see them, hear a color, think a color or just know what colors are there. You may notice larger shades of color or just splotches of color.
- Trust whatever information you receive.
- Pause while you retrieve this information.
- Now I invite you to thank your angels for their assistance, open your eyes, and record your colors on your paper.

May this valuable knowledge guide you toward your life's purpose. Love and Light!

NOTE: This meditation is found on my *Angelic Reflections I: Awakening* CD

AURA COLOR GUIDE

These are large shells of color that go over your head and shoulders and represent your life's purpose. Generally they stay the same. Look for individual colors and ask the angels about specific fields. You may see different forms due to your choice of free will.

- 💚 **Emerald Green:** Healer of physical body on one-on-one basis (traditional or alternative).
- 💚 **Seafoam Green, Turquoise, Aqua:** Healer/Teacher-someone who has healing effect or teaches about healing with groups. Examples: counselors, speakers, writers, healing center, people who work with emotions.
- 💙 **Light Blue:** Communicators—they deliver messages. Examples: school teachers, musicians, artists, researcher, supporter, acting, photographer, dancers, feng shui, media, journalist.
- 💜 **Rainbow Stripes (tight band of stripes):** Energy worker. Examples: reiki healing, pranic healing, chakra work, physical therapy, chiropractic, massage.

These are blotches of color that change according to moods and thoughts.

- ❤️ **Bright Red:** money issues, financial insecurities.
- ❤️ **Dark Red/Maroon:** anger issues.
- 💜 **Violet Red:** clairaudient (hears spirit) and will use with life's work.
- 💙 **Dark Blue:** natural clairvoyant, will use with life's work.
- 🧡 **Orange:** moving to new home, want to travel.
- 💛 **Yellow:** do not like or feeling trapped in job.
- 💚 **Emerald Green:** going through physical healing.
- 💚 **Lime Green, Pea Green:** not being truthful with self or others, rationalize something to make it okay.

ASPECTS OF YOU

- 💙 **Light Blue:** communicators, writers, messengers, and talkative people.
- 💗 **Pink, Fuchsia:** love, very passionate.
- 💜 **Purple:** far along spiritual path, life's purpose includes spirituality, you do a lot of meditation or prayer.
- 💙 **Royal, Cobalt Blue:** Archangel Michael is present with you.
- 🤍 **White:** angelic energy.
- 🩶 **Silver:** pregnant or new idea, new part of life.
- 💛 **Metallic Gold:** Jesus, the great teacher, Christ energy.
- 🩶 **Gray:** depression.
- 🖤 **Greasy:** too many dairy products.
- 🖤 **Black:** can be any of the following, ask your angels which it relates to: unhealed grief, fear, substance abuse, build-up of toxic emotions, resentment, guilt, unforgiveness, self-doubt, dis-ease or injury.
- 💜 **Blackish Purple:** flip-flop between spiritual and material.
- 🤎 **Brown:** student.
- 🩶 **Smoky Aura:** indicates that person smokes too much, sometimes looks like clouds.

This guide was created from my notes taken during
ATP® training with Doreen Virtue.

Natural Resources

- 💜 **Affirmations** are positive, powerful statements (stated as if they already exist and are repeated frequently) used to create new thought patterns and beliefs so that you can attract into your life that which you desire. Affirmations are statements that reflect your desires. By repeating affirmations, you are stating them as truth for you. I was first introduced to affirmations in my teens by Louise L. Hay's books, *Heal Your Body* and *The Power is Within You*. I have and continue to receive infinite blessings in my life by using affirmations.

WHY DO AFFIRMATIONS WORK?

When a statement is repetitively heard it becomes part of your belief system. It is then stored in your subconscious mind. Your subconscious mind then sends thoughts to your conscious mind. The conscious mind begins to take steps to make this happen or bring it about in your life. You attract and experience that which you focus on. If you can create it in your mind, you can manifest it into the physical world as your reality.

STEPS FOR CREATING YOUR OWN SUCCESSFUL AFFIRMATIONS

1. Create them in already present sense, like it already exists in your life now, such as I AM _____, I now have _____, I AM now experiencing _____. (I AM is the most powerful way to begin an affirmation as this is your inner power, your I AM Presence).

2. State the affirmation to reflect your desire.

3. Allow them to come alive—put some feeling into them by imagining what it feels like to experience your desire.

4. Give gratitude for your desire as if it were already present in your life.

5. Repetition is essential. Say or review as often as possible. It takes 28 days to become part of your belief system. As you affirm them, ask your angels to make it so. Beyond 28 days, continue affirmations as you are guided or until what you desire comes into your life experience.

WHAT AFFIRMATIONS CAN BE USED FOR:

1. Creating anything you desire to acquire, achieve or experience.
2. Creating positive changes in your life.
3. Bringing forth characteristics you desire in yourself.
4. Re-creating beliefs to reflect the truth within your soul.
5. Inspiring and empowering you to reach goals.
6. Healing your body.
7. Changing unhealthy thought patterns.

HOW TO USE AFFIRMATIONS

1. Practice writing them or put on a 3×5 card and place them where you can visually review them throughout your day.
2. Memorize and repeat in sets of three (sometimes I do this while driving or waiting in line at the grocery store, etc.).
3. Repeat them by speaking in a mirror (this is very powerful).
4. Record them on a tape recorder and listen to them every night before you go to bed. (If you fall asleep that is okay. You will still benefit because they are going into your subconscious mind.)
5. Surround yourself with them by making posters or signs and put them on the wall, mirror, or cupboards.
6. Create imagery with them.
7. Another way to utilize affirmations is to create affirmative goals. Here are a few examples of an affirmative goal: I AM successful in all that I do. Everything that I direct my attention to and touch turns to gold.

ANGELS AND AFFIRMATIONS

It generally takes 28 days to create a new thought pattern, however, it has been my experience that using affirmations with the assistance from the angels is very powerful, and I begin to see a shift immediately. I do this by reciting the affirmation and asking the angels to remove the patterns in me that created that condition, and to make this affirmation effective now. I affirm: And so it is! Then I thank them.

BENEFITS OF AFFIRMATIONS

Affirmations are a powerful method to create what you desire, for what you focus on you attract, and what you believe you experience. I AM is a very powerful statement and will shape your experiences to reflect your desires. You will be amazed at how your life will begin to transform when using affirmations.

SOURCES OF AFFIRMATIONS

In addition to creating your own, there are infinite affirmations available to you from some magnificent spiritual teachers such as Louise L. Hay, Doreen Virtue and many others. You can also create an affirmation tape for yourself by using all of the affirmations from the Food for Thought section of this book. I encourage you to choose affirmations that reflect your desires and truths within your soul. At first they may not seem real, however, the more you repeat them and add some feeling to them, the sooner they will become your reality and part of your life experience.

NOURISHMENT FOR YOUR SOUL: As you change and your life shifts, and your new desires evolve, you will want to change your affirmations to reflect your new desires. I encourage you to keep a journal of your affirmations so you can refer back to them when necessary. If you do not know what to do, create an affirmation that states what you desire and see the opportunities that begin to appear.

FOOD FOR THOUGHT: Everything begins with a thought. Plant the seeds of love! I affirm and experience that which I desire in my life now.

ANGELIC TOOLS:

- *You Can Heal Your Life* gift edition book by Louise L. Hay. I highly recommend reading this book as it is full of affirmations for healing and changing everything you can imagine about yourself or your life. It is filled with so much inspiration and love, and provides a whole new outlook on life.

- **Visualizations** are inner visions in which you see in your mind's eye what you desire to experience. When you can see it in your inner world, it will come to fruition in your outer experience.

NOURISHMENT FOR YOUR SOUL: Your mind is like a camera. It takes a picture of what you are experiencing. If you are looking through the camera lens and do not like the picture you are viewing, you can change the picture by adjusting your thoughts and the vision in your mind's eye to reflect your desires.

FOOD FOR THOUGHT: I create the pictures in my mind's eye that reflect what I desire to experience.

- **Imagery** is a creative method used to create a physical image that reflects your desires. It brings the energy of your desires into your physical reality so they can come to form in your physical experience. Imagery is part of the nurturing process of bringing your dreams to life and must be visited often to be effective. As you focus on your imagery you are making room in your mind to receive your desires and setting the intentions to experience them. This keeps the energy moving in the direction of your desires. As you take the necessary steps toward your desires, they will become a part of your physical experience. Imagination is a divine gift in which you can build mental images to create any situation you desire. It is where you begin to create all your desires. You can build your desires without stopping to count the cost because there is no limitation in your imagination. It is the passions within your heart that sparks the magic of your imagination. Create whatever your heart desires. Your possibilities are endless!

NOURISHMENT FOR YOUR SOUL: *"Imagination is the beginning of creation. You imagine what you desire; you will what you imagine; and at last you create what you will."*—George Bernard Shaw

FOOD FOR THOUGHT: I allow my imagination to express its true desires.

This method has been very powerful and successful for me. It always amazes me how these desires come to fruition. I did some imagery ten years ago that is now coming to fruition in my life. It has been my experience that when we create imagery boards, we are bringing forth wisdom from our soul of how we know our life is to be. This gets us motivated to take the steps toward these desires and sets into motion the energy for these to come into our life. Although I have seen this happen many times, I'd like to share with you an experience that supports this observation. Many years ago my former husband and I had bought a plot of land with the intention to build our dream home on it. I worked for two years designing this home on the computer. I labeled every room and collected pictures that reflected what I desired in the home, and created an imagery board. When the marriage ended, this home had not been built yet. I felt like my dreams of that home had been shattered so I put the plans and pictures away, forgot about them and let go of those dreams. Life went on and a few years later I remarried and my husband and I had a home built. Several years later I came across these plans and pictures and was amazed at the many characteristics that I included in that "dream home" were present in our home! What was even more amazing was that in the plans I had included an office and labeled it "John" as that was my former husband's name. My present husband's name is also John!

♥ **Meditation** is a method used to quiet your mind and just be in your natural state of love. It is also a time of listening to God and your angels. When in meditation, you are in touch with your higher self. This gives you access to universal wisdom, love and light. In this quiet state you can hear true wisdom and receive answers to the truths within your soul, free of any outside influences. I like to describe meditation as quieting your mind so you can hear your heart. There are many methods for meditating. However, there are two types of meditations, quiet and guided. Both are beneficial. Guided meditations are helpful for those just learning to meditate. They take you on journeys, and set the scene for a specific intention. There are guided meditations throughout this book that are designed to assist you in retrieving the truths within your soul. Quiet meditation is a time to reflect, to be quiet and listen to your inner guidance, God and your angels. When you are busy with your daily activities you are not always tuned into this guidance. When in meditation, you are in tune, in touch and aware of your higher self. During meditation you may receive visions, hear words, feel emotions, smell things, or even taste something. No matter what you experience, you will feel a sense of knowing, oftentimes referred to as intuition. The information you receive during your meditations are reflections of your true self and your soul's journey. In order for you to remember who you are, why you are here, what your desires are, guidance and direction on accomplishing your life's mission, you must first enter the silence to your own inner guidance and intelligence. Therefore, it is essential to meditate on a daily basis so you can retrieve the information from God and your angels.

💜 **Prayer** is communicating with God and the angels, asking for assistance, guidance and giving gratitude. The power of prayer is simply amazing. You can say prayers for yourself and say prayers for anyone who is in need of them. Affirmative prayer is also a powerful way to attract what you desire to experience in your life. What you do is create a prayer that affirms what you desire to experience and then at the end affirm: And so it is! This puts your direct intention into asking for assistance and affirming it to be true.

💜 **Journaling** is a method of writing used to express, get in touch with, and process your feelings, release emotions and is helpful in resolving conflict in relationships and forgiveness. It is a great tool to release that which no longer serves you and bring forth that which you do desire.

💜 **Intuitive/Automatic Writing** is a process used to communicate with God, your angels, your inner child and departed loved ones.

💜 **Creative/Affirmative Writing** is a very powerful method used to create what you desire to experience in your life through writing. You write in the first (as if writing yourself) or third person (as if someone else is writing about you) what you desire as if it is present in your life now. After you have written your story, light a candle and say to your angels: 'Dear Angels, these are my desires and dreams. Please guide me in bringing them to life." It is best not to tell them how to make it happen as this puts limits on what can occur. Instead be open to infinite possibilities for the universe to bring it to you. Thank your angels and affirm: And so it is!

💜 **Mirror Exercises** are a method used to look through your eyes into your soul. When you look into your soul you are in your true I AM presence and power. As you affirm the love that you are and have for yourself and what you desire, you are stating your intentions to experience it. This is a technique I learned from the teachings of Louise L. Hay and experience great blessings from using it!

NOURISHMENT FOR YOUR SOUL: Mirror exercises are powerful and healing. They improve self-love, self-confidence, self-image, and empower you to achieve your aspirations.

💜 **Breathing Exercises** open you up to the flow of divine love, light and wisdom. When you breathe deeply, you are allowing yourself to breathe in the fullness of life. When you are fearful, your breaths become shallow. When you feel empty inside, go out into nature and breathe, and feel yourself fill with spirit. When you breathe, you bring in spirit. The deeper and more often you breathe, the more spirit is present within you.

NOURISHMENT FOR YOUR SOUL: I refer to these as *treasures of your soul* because we are all born with these gifts. They are universal gifts you have been given to guide you through life. These are the tools and techniques for creating or manifesting. These are ancient tools; you just need to get back in touch with them, understand them, and utilize them to enhance your life.

FOOD FOR THOUGHT: I utilize the treasures of my soul to create a life that reflects all that my heart desires.

Natural Rhythms of the Universe

Creating is a natural rhythm of life, therefore we all have the power to create all that our heart desires. In order to do this, one must look within and connect to that natural state of love in which everything begins and exists, and choose what they desire to create. It has been my experience that following the natural rhythms of the universe allows us to learn from the past, be in the present, and create the future along the way. When we learn to go with the rhythms of life, we will experience a balanced life. When we go with the flow, we are living in the now, meaning the present. The universe provides us with everything we require and desire and it is available to us in advance. We just need to choose to tap into this flow.

When I became very clear about my life's purpose, I felt very passionate about participating in these activities that spoke to my heart. I must admit there were times I felt overwhelmed with all of the facets and wondered how I would ever accomplish all of them. I felt a sense of urgency. I wanted to do everything right away and I pushed myself to get things done, trying to make things happen right then. I learned that the force and feeling of being driven is fed by fear. On the bright side of that, when we are in our natural state of love, we go with the flow, we are clear and move forward at a steady pace, one moment at a time, accomplishing much more. When we go with the rhythms of the universe, we trust the process of life and we feed these ideas with love. When nurtured they will bloom. As we learn to live in balance, all unfolds in divine timing. When we go with the flow, we create a solid foundation and our project or endeavors have great success.

♥ **Creating/Co-creating/Manifesting:** We are the creators of our own lives. The process of creation takes both the physical and spiritual to create. The creative flow is God in action. As we work together with this creative flow, take action and allow life to unfold, we are co-creating. Manifesting is the process of bringing spiritual truths into physical form, utilizing the treasures of our soul and the natural laws of the universe. It is the ability to create what we desire from within without demands on how it will come to us, leaving all doors open and allowing the universe to bring it through whatever channel serves all. This prevents us from blocking any channels due to thoughts of limitation and keeps us open and receptive to receiving in all ways. The universe is an unlimited power that resides within and is available to all of us. We just need to tap into this power. We do this through meditation, or quieting our mind and listening to the messages within our soul, our internal wisdom and taking action on these ideas. Here are a few equations to clarify these processes.

$$\text{Passion (heart)} + \text{Imagination (mind)} = \text{Creativity}$$
$$\text{Energy (spirit)} + \text{Action (physical)} = \text{Co-Creation}$$
$$\text{Affirm} + \text{Visualize} + \text{Emotion} = \text{Manifestation}$$

♥ **Law of Magnetism or Attraction:** All thoughts have a vibration to them. We attract to us people and experiences that reflect our vibration at that time. This vibration fluctuates depending on our perception of these experiences. Our thoughts and beliefs determine these vibrations. We are all energy. Energy is magnetic. Therefore, the energy we put out is what comes back to us. As you send out love to others, love is what you will experience. This is an example of cause and effect.

- **Giving and Receiving:** To receive is to recognize in our consciousness as truth. The true meaning of giving is giving with an open heart without expecting anything in return. However, the way the universal law works is as we give we also receive. If we give out of obligation it defeats the purpose. The blessings we receive from giving are infinite. There are infinite ways in which we can give. This includes: money, time, energy, love, support, kind words, encouragement, a helping hand, a gesture such as a smile, a hug, gifts, etc. It does not matter in what way or how much or little that we give, what is important is that we give from our heart. Although many of the gifts we receive in life are priceless, money is just the earthly exchange for the services we provide in utilizing our gifts and talents in our service.

NOURISHMENT FOR YOUR SOUL: As you give from your heart, you receive in your hands. Give that which you desire to receive for the universal law states, as we give, we also receive. *"It's not how much we give but how much love we put in the giving."* —Mother Teresa

FOOD FOR THOUGHT: I always give with an open heart as this is the true gift through which blessings come.

- **Letting Go and Letting God:** is the process of believing and trusting in the power of something greater than you and allowing that energy to work in your life. When you surrender to God, you get out of your own way and things in your life flow.

NOURISHMENT FOR YOUR SOUL: When life seems like too much of a struggle, it is time to let go and let God so that the universe can bring forward your desires.

FOOD FOR THOUGHT: I let go with ease and allow God to guide my life. I now let go and let God create miracles in my life.

- ♥ **Flow/Grace/Ease:** is a state in which everything falls into place with ease and perfection. Grace means moving freely with ease and beauty. When we go with the flow we experience grace in our life.

NOURISHMENT FOR YOUR SOUL: When things are not flowing in your life and you feel frustrated, ask yourself, "Do I need to let go and let God? Am I trying to force things to happen rather than allowing things to happen? What blocks or resistance am I holding on inside? Am I too caught up in the outcome rather than focusing on my desires and allowing God to make it happen in a way that is for my highest good? Am I being too narrow-minded and putting limitations on the situation?" Call on your angels and ask them to help you release that which is preventing you from moving forward with grace and ease, and ask them to give you guidance on what you can do to create forward movement.

FOOD FOR THOUGHT: I choose to go with the flow and experience grace and ease in my life now. I AM in the flow of divine love, divine light and divine wisdom.

- ♥ **Synchronicity:** is the process in which the universe lines up opportunities to reflect our desires. Some examples are: being in the right place at the right time; running into certain people; things in your life falling into place and receiving signs or messages.

NOURISHMENT FOR YOUR SOUL: Allow things to take their natural course. Do not be so attached to the outcome that you miss the experience. Know that you are always where you are to be, at the perfect time, doing the perfect things with the perfect people for your soul's growth.

FOOD FOR THOUGHT: I flow with the natural rhythms of life and experience the blessings of synchronicity.

SYNCHRONICITY AND ANSWERED PRAYERS

There was a chain of events that led to my spiritual awakening. The most profound event was my introduction to the angels and the teachings of Doreen Virtue. This opened up a whole new world for me and has given me a sense of comfort, belonging and new meaning to my life. The angels have guided me each step of the way in healing and creating a life that reflects my true desires.

A window to my spiritual awakening opened when I was facing some challenges in my personal life and I had been praying for help. I had developed a rash on my right hand as the result of the emotional turmoil I was experiencing. I couldn't get it to go away and nothing seemed to heal it, including what the medical doctors prescribed. I was fairly new to Austin and I did not know many people, but I wanted to find a practitioner who could help by utilizing natural remedies. As I was having lunch one day I spotted a local metaphysical newspaper. I was so thrilled because I had been reading a metaphysical newspaper in Michigan for years that I loved called *PhenomenNEWS*. I even had it delivered to me in Texas so I could read it, and I distributed it to various locations so others could benefit from it as well. As I browsed through the Austin paper I saw an ad for Beth Carpenter, a Naturopathic Practitioner, and I knew I was to call her. I began seeing her on a regular basis to work through the emotional turmoil in my life that was creating the rash. After some time, she and I became friends and I began working for her part-time as a public relations director, since she is the author of the book, *Strength of the Spirit*. It is an incredible story about courage, faith and how she healed herself from cancer using alternative therapies.

The door to my spiritual awakening opened up when Beth asked me to help tend to her booth while she did intuitive readings at the Whole Life Expo here in Austin. In return, she gifted me with a ticket to see any one of the speakers who were there. She handed me the program guide and I opened it up to a lecture Doreen Virtue, was giving and I knew that was the one I was to attend. A feeling of excitement came over me. I had never heard of or seen Doreen Virtue before, in this lifetime anyway, but I felt a strong connection and had a sense of familiarity. As I stood in line with hundreds of other people for the doors to open for her lecture, I prayed to God that I would get in there. A few minutes later, one of the attendants came up and began talking to the person standing in front of me. I overheard the conversation and that person told the attendant she had a pass. The attendant told her to follow him. I said to the attendant, "I have a pass too." He asked me to follow him also. So I did and was seated in the first row! By the time the lecture started, the conference room was full. I was so grateful for my place there. I felt such a sense of peace, and what she presented during her lecture spoke directly to my heart. As I sat in this lecture, I knew my prayers had been answered and I felt a deep sense of gratitude. Something shifted for me that day and I felt like I was home.

During the lecture I received a flyer that she was going to be teaching a workshop on Connecting with Your Angels', in Dallas the following weekend. I immediately signed up and wrote out a check for the workshop. A few days later, as I drove to Richardson, Texas (which is near Dallas) where my sister lives, I listened to some of Doreen Virtue's books on tape. My sister watched my two children while I attended the workshop. What a turn my life took. At the workshop I bought several of her books, the first one being *The Lightworker's Way*. This book brought so much clarity about who I am and reflected to me my passion to help others and be a published author. The second book I had purchased from her workshop and read was *Indigo Children* by Lee Carroll and Jan Tober. This book has been a Godsend to me.

I began reading all of Doreen Virtue's books and as I read them I felt as if she was sitting next to me talking. I have never experienced this feeling before while reading a book. I attended all of her weekend workshops which were held near me. Then in July of 2001, I attended a Hawaiian healing retreat that Doreen Virtue manifested. It was held at the Hilton resort in Waikoloa Village on the big island of Kona. While I was there, it became very clear to me that I was to take her ANGEL THERAPY PRACTITIONER® Course that was coming up in February, which is my birth month. As a gift to myself, I took the ATP® training. What a transformational experience, filled with so many blessings! I later took my Spiritual Teacher's Training with Doreen Virtue. Her teachings have opened up so many doors in my life personally and professionally. I am ever so grateful for her teachings which have had such a miraculous impact on my life. These experiences have shown me the power of prayer, love and the magic of synchronicity that occurs when we open ourselves up to it.

♥ **Divine Timing:** is the process in which the universe aligns things to occur. Sometimes certain things must fall into place before others in order to create a solid foundation or the greatest outcome for the highest good of all concerned.

It is best to focus on what you desire rather than when you want it. When you focus on time, you put limits on your manifestations. It also distracts you from your intention. Just allow the universe to bring it to you in divine timing. Sometimes there are pieces to the puzzle that need to fall into place before other things can happen. There are many things happening behind the scene in the universe that you do not know about. This is the mystery of life. As you allow things to unfold, everything falls into place easily in divine timing. Always, things turn out better than you can imagine when you allow spirit to enter.

Sometimes we can be so serious and so used to being in control of everything in our lives that it can be a challenge to let go. It gives us a sense that things are falling apart when actually many times they are coming together. We run ourselves ragged thinking "If we could just do this, then that will happen." We push ourselves to work harder and accomplish more, when really what we need to do is relax a little, let go and have some fun. When having fun we find enjoyment and it is through our joy that we experience love. It is important to do our part but also essential to allow the universe to do its part. There have been times in my life in which I have tried to force things to happen only to find myself feeling frustrated with no results, but when I let go and gave it to God and the angels, things began to flow and I was open to receive.

In order to have your needs and desires met, you must first communicate to the universe what it is that you want and believe you deserve it in order for the universe to provide it for you. You must also be patient and give it time to align whatever is necessary to create your request in a way that is for the highest good of yourself and all concerned. When you make a request for something in your life and it doesn't happen, it may not be for your highest good or it may be answered in other ways. You must be willing to relax and go with the flow of life. When you are not relaxed but are tense and have negative thoughts about a situation, you block the channel for things to come to you. It can be disappointing when things do not go according to your plans. However, it has been my experience that things always work out for the best even though it may not be seen until later. Spirit knows the bigger picture. Maybe some other things need to fall into place first. Sometimes it is just a matter of divine timing for the universe is creating the best scenario according to your desires. That may not always coordinate with your "earth time," but the results are always worth waiting for!

♥ **Faith/Trust/Patience:** Faith is a sense of knowing that what you desire will come to you. With faith, you can transform unpleasant circumstances into new beginnings and opportunities. Faith is something that comes from within. As you look back and reflect upon the times you trusted and God came through, you will recognize faith. Trust is a sense of knowing the universe will provide for you and bring you what you desire. Also trust in yourself, knowing you have the capacity to create what you desire. Patience is a willingness to wait for things to unfold in your life. As we trust, we see faith in action. Know that the universe will bring to you all that you desire, but sometimes it takes time for things to come together for the highest good of all concerned. There are many things occurring in the universe of which you are not aware to bring forth your desires. You just need to trust and have faith that the universe is aligning things to bring your desires to fruition.

NOURISHMENT FOR YOUR SOUL: When you allow things to happen in your life in divine timing, you display patience due to your faith and trust in the process of life.

FOOD FOR THOUGHT: I trust myself, God and the process of life.

♥ **Change:** is a continuous process that occurs in our life. It is part of the evolving process and the catalyst that initiates forward movement in our life. Change is merely movement, a shift in energy, circumstances, situations and consciousness. Change has a domino effect. One change sets into motion another, therefore, how we react and adjust to change affects the way other changes occur. There are some changes that occur that are out of our control and others we experience by choice. Every day is a new day that presents changes. We can choose to welcome or resist these changes. For many the unknown can be scary so they fear change. Change does not have to be fearful or painful. Our experience with change is a reflection of how we perceive it to be. While change can take us out of our comfort zone, it is truly an opportunity to expand our horizons. It opens doors for new experiences and opportunities to come into our lives. If everything stayed the same, life would be monotonous, boring and stagnant. When things are not working for us that is a sign that something needs to change. Flexibility opens us up to accepting change with grace and ease. The more flexible we are, the easier it is to adjust to and flow with the changes that present themselves in our lives and in our world. The brighter side of change can present variety, excitement, and newness that can make us feel alive. As we focus on the good we embrace the blessings of change and thrive.

NOURISHMENT FOR YOUR SOUL:
Serenity Prayer

Dear God,

Please grant me the serenity to accept the things I cannot change; the courage to change the things I can; and the wisdom to know the difference."

—*Dr. Reinhold Niebuhr*

FOOD FOR THOUGHT: If you cannot change a situation, you can change your thoughts about the situation. This will create a more desirable experience for you. Change can be wonderful when you embrace the gifts. I embrace change with grace, ease and confidence.

♥ **Law of Opposites:** Opposites are a natural rhythm of life. The law of opposites states that everything in the universe has an opposite. Sometimes opposites repel and sometimes they attract and compliment each other. Sometimes we attract opposites because we see in that person what we desire to bring forth in ourself. Sometimes opposites attract for the purpose of overcoming adversity. Opposites help us determine what we desire and what we do not desire. It is the unification of the opposites that creates balance. There are infinite opposites. The following are some we will be addressing in this book.

Love/Fear • Physical/Spiritual • Light/Darkness

True Self/Shadow • Birth/Death or Endings/Beginnings

Conflict/Resolution • Male/Female • Flow/Stagnant

Open/Closed • Ease/Struggle • Action/Reflection

Desirable/Undesirable • Pleasant/Unpleasant

Anger/Passion • Giving/Receiving • Reflect/Express

Attach/Detach • Experience/Observe • Heaven/Earth • Being/Doing

NOURISHMENT FOR YOUR SOUL: Every situation has a positive and negative to it, every opportunity has advantages and disadvantages, every relationship has blessings and challenges, and every experience has lessons and gifts. The key is to focus on and experience the side of the spectrum that reflects your desires or meet in the middle where necessary to create balance.

FOOD FOR THOUGHT: I see opposites as a tool for spiritual growth and balance.

♥ **Balance and Harmony:** are also natural rhythms of life. Within our body exists a continuous movement of energy. It fluctuates according to our thoughts and emotions. Balance occurs when we have an even amount of energy distributed throughout our body, going in and out simultaneously in moderation. When we experience obstacles such as chemical exposure, fear, addictions or physical conditions in our life, our natural flow of energy is blocked and we become off balance. Karen Hutchins, a dear friend of mine who is a Psychotherapist and Shamanic Practitioner, specializes in trauma recovery. She explained to me that any time we feel dis-ease in any form, it is an indication that some aspect of us is out of balance.

Balance is essential for our well-being. It helps us unify all aspects of ourselves. Achieving balance is being aware of and having an equal flow of energy coming and going in our life and being conscious of what we need when we need it. Too much of anything can be overwhelming. Not enough of anything can leave us feeling unfulfilled. Moderation creates balance. Spider medicine helps teach balance of spirit and physical, male and female, and creative energy. This can be found in the book, *Animal Speaks* by Ted Andrews. When you are grounded while allowing your thoughts to focus on love, you are connected to the earth plane and in alignment with the energies of the spiritual realm simultaneously, and balance occurs. To enjoy life to the fullest, we must find the proper balance in our life. Balance creates harmony.

Harmony means to be in the flow of life, living in your natural state of love, allowing spirit to guide you, taking the necessary steps to make things happen and then allowing life to unfold. Being in harmony is being present in the moment and enjoying what you are doing when you are doing it. When you are in harmony, things occur in a very synchronistic way.

💜 **Death and Rebirth:** is a natural process of life that we continuously go through many times throughout our lifetime(s). It can represent endings and new beginnings, the death of the ego and birth of our true self, the death of a situation or transformation – the releasing of the old and making room for and embracing the new. It can also represent the death of the physical body. When a physical death does occur, that soul has chosen to exit the earth plane at that time and in that manner. It is not an ending for these souls but a new beginning. From this perspective the "cause" of death is irrelevant as that is just the way the physical body chose to leave the earth plane for the soul to continue on its journey. When we realize this truth, we no longer experience the fear of dying and we can truly live life to the fullest. In the book, *Home With God*, Neale Donald Walsh talks more about this process.

ANGELIC TOOLS:
💜 *Home With God* by Neale Donald Walsh

Experiences, Opportunities and Lessons

EXPERIENCES

"The thoughts we think and the words we speak create our experiences."
—LOUISE L. HAY

Our soul came to this earth school to learn and evolve through experiences. We do this through opportunities which are doorways to life, and relationships which are reflections to us. Everything in life is relevant to our soul's growth. We create our experiences through the thoughts we think, the words we speak and the actions we take. Our outer experiences and relationships reflect to us what is going on inside. In a relationship, each person has their own experience, for we are all unique. In other words, two people could be doing the same thing and have a different experience as the lesson and perception is different for each of them. Everything in life is energy. Because we are energetic beings and due to the law of attraction, what we give out comes back to us. We attract experiences, people, and situations according to our vibration. The highest vibration is love. We all came here to learn, grow, express and expand God's love on this journey called life. Some of us chose to have a personal purpose and others of us chose to have a personal and global mission.

We can only evolve from our own experiences, and from these experiences we come to an understanding or greater awareness. By sharing these experiences, we can help others evolve along their path. Our soul has memories from experiences and lessons that it carries from previous lifetimes. During this lifetime we may recall experiences from these other lifetimes. When we recall memories from past lives, we are retrieving parts of our soul. We may recognize people in our lives today who have been with us in these previous lifetimes and we may feel very connected to them. These are referred to as kindred spirits or soul mates. The term soul mate does not necessarily mean a romantic relationship. It simply means we recognize someone on a soul level because we have shared past lives together or incarnated as part of a specific soul group. These relationships can be a family member, friend, co-worker etc. and be the same or opposite sex. I'll discuss this topic further in chapter eight.

Every experience in our life is an opportunity for growth. It is most beneficial to take the wisdom from each experience and move on. Everyday is a new day and we are given the opportunity to choose love. God re-directs us, not punishes us. When we do not feel God's presence, we have disconnected. We must stay true to our heart about what we desire and choose to experience.

NOURISHMENT FOR YOUR SOUL: When you are in a situation that you are not enjoying or is not what you thought it would be, ask your angels to help you be open to whatever that experience holds for you.

FOOD FOR THOUGHT: I AM open and receptive to whatever this experience holds for me.

LESSONS

We all came to this earth school to learn lessons. There are no "coincidences," "mistakes" or "accidents," only lessons from our soul giving us an opportunity to grow and evolve. With these lessons we sometimes experience challenges and conflicts. They are nothing to be embarrassed about as they are an important part of life. They teach us how to come up with solutions and resolve the situation. What is most important is how we respond to these circumstances. As we face the challenges life brings, we can choose to see them as opportunities to grow rather than "problems," which will give us positive experiences. It's all in the way we perceive the situation. All lessons present the opportunity to love more.

As humans, we continue to repeat patterns until we become aware of them because it is familiar to us. These patterns lie within our subconscious mind and prevent us from accomplishing our goals or experiencing the outcomes we desire. Once we become aware of these patterns we can change them. When the belief that created the pattern has been changed, our experience will change. Our lessons will keep presenting themselves through different experiences or people in our lives until we learn them. Once we learn the lesson, it breaks the patterning and disengages the energy so we do not have to repeat it. It is no longer part of our experience. So it is much better to resolve things as they present themselves so we can put it behind us and move forward. Sometimes a lesson has many facets and we need several experiences to grasp and complete the full lesson. This is part of our learning experience here on earth. Regardless of what we do, we will learn the lessons we chose to learn prior to incarnating in this lifetime. We have chosen people and situations in our life to help us learn these lessons to evolve. However, we can choose to learn our lessons with love, grace and ease, or fear, pain and struggle.

NOURISHMENT FOR YOUR SOUL: When you take the blessing from each experience and leave the rest you are learning your lessons with love.

FOOD FOR THOUGHT: I choose to learn my lessons and grow with love.

OPPORTUNITIES

"If we are facing in the right direction, all we have to do is keep walking."
—BUDDHIST TEACHING

Your life is full of opportunities and experiences. What is important is that you choose those things that reflect your heart's desires. When an opportunity presents itself, instead of feeling embarrassed because you do not know something, choose to be glad for the opportunity to experience it and learn more about it. When presented with an opportunity ask yourself or your angels, "Is this an opportunity that I am to embrace?" Although you may not always know why at the time, know the step you are taking always has a purpose in the greater scheme of life, and take in the blessings of that experience. When you want something, take the steps toward that goal to make it happen rather than making excuses why you cannot have or accomplish it due to situations such as lack of money, time, and so on. Let go of unlimited thoughts, and take the steps that you can take now. When you put your energy into your desire by taking one step at a time, it brings your desire into form. It has been my experience that when you take the steps you can in the moment, you open up the channels to provide whatever it is you need next to proceed. The reason for this is to teach you to take one step at a time without skipping any so you can build a solid foundation for your endeavor. Each step will lead you to the next and bring you to a more knowledgeable place. When you walk through a new door, the door closes behind you and a new experience awaits you.

When doors are closed there is a reason. I have found through my own struggles with blockages, things not working, and feeling stuck, that trying to force things to happen rather than allowing them to unfold can actually block us from the very thing we desire to occur. When you let go and let God, miracles happen.

When you feel a sense of urgency, this is your angels telling you it's time to move forward. That doesn't mean to rush through. It means moving forward in the flow at a steady pace, one step at a time, to accomplish your goals. Be patient and aware of what is going on around you. When doors open it's time to walk through them. What is helpful is paying attention to what is in front of you each day and doing those activities that present themselves. The angels will guide your way. When it is time, the opportunities will present themselves to you. You do not "have" to do anything. Life presents you with opportunities, and you get to choose what you desire to participate in. When you follow this desire, your heart is leading the way. You can choose to do certain things because it will create the outcome you desire. Spirit doesn't force you to do things, punish or trick you. These are all acts of ego, not spirit. Spirit shows you possibilities and ideal outcomes and you get to choose what you desire to experience. Life is your friend not your enemy.

EXERCISE: OVERCOMING OBSTACLES

An obstacle is present when you feel stuck, immobilized, stagnant, confused, frustrated or feel like you are up against a roadblock and things are not coming together. In order to remove the obstacle, you must first identify what that obstacle is. When you are faced with these situations, here are some questions to reflect upon: Is this not happening due to divine timing? Is there an action I am to take at this time for this door to open and present itself? Am I blocking the flow in some way? Do I have fears that are preventing me from the opportunities beyond this door? Have I done my part and released it for spirit to enter? Here are some things you can do to help you.

1. Ask for angelic assistance by saying, "Dear Angels, please help me to see this obstacle clearly so I may release it from my experience. Thank you."
2. List the obstacle.
3. Reflect upon why it feels like an obstacle.
4. Figure out what steps you can take now toward moving beyond the obstacle and making your dream or goal happen.
5. Affirm the desire present in your life now.
6. Visualize an image of what you want to change and an image of what you desire. Place them side by side then shrink the one you do not want. Make the one you desire bigger and say, "Yes." This works because each time you think of the old belief it immediately

triggers your new belief. After repetition, the old will diminish and the new will expand.

7. Look for the doors that are open and proceed forward.

NOURISHMENT FOR YOUR SOUL: When you have taken the steps necessary to achieve your goal, ask for assistance from your heavenly helpers. Let it go, put it in God's hands, and allow things to unfold in divine timing. You can also call on Goddess Kali to remove the obstacles that are in the way of accomplishing your goals. Once you ask for her assistance, get out of the way and allow her to create miracles her way.

FOOD FOR THOUGHT: I overcome obstacles with grace, ease and simplicity. Obstacles are part of my past and I AM living my dreams.

EXERCISE: DOORWAYS OF DIRECTION AND OPPORTUNITIES

When you have several options or opportunities available to you, or many facets of your life are calling you, the following is a great exercise to do to gain clarity about each subject and what to focus on at this time. It allows you to focus on one thing at a time and bring forth information relating to that situation or opportunity.

1. On a piece of paper, draw doors and label them for each area of your life or each opportunity you would like clarity about.
2. Relax. Take three or four deep breaths.
3. Ask your angels to surround you and assist you in receiving clarity and truth in each situation.
4. Choose one door at a time and place your hand on top of the door. Ask, "What am I to know about this now?" or "What information do you have for me about this subject?"

5. Allow the information to come forth. After each doorway write down the information that you received, then continue on to the next doorway.
6. When you are finished, thank the angels for their assistance and decide what steps you are going to take.
7. Focus on the doors that are open to you and walk through each doorway with love, courage and confidence, and enjoy the blessings awaiting you!

Below are some examples for areas you can focus on in your life. You can also label the doors for specific situations.

NOURISHMENT FOR YOUR SOUL: Stepping stones get you to where you are going. Relax and take time to breathe, walk softly, and listen. Every step you take is a stepping stone for bringing your desires and dreams to life!

FOOD FOR THOUGHT: I welcome new experiences and walk through the doors of opportunity with confidence, courage and ease. I have many doors of opportunity to choose from and I walk through the doors that lead me to where I desire to go.

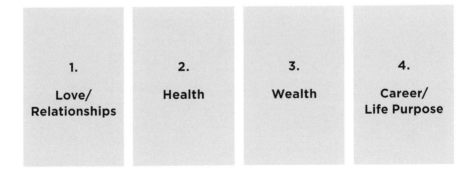

DOOR OF ETERNITY
Angel of Choice.

ASPECTS OF YOU

Your Emotional Self

Your emotional self, also known as your inner child is the part of you that matures, grows and evolves. In order for your inner child to mature, it must have its needs met. The basic needs of your inner child are love, nurturing, support, safety, security, praise, attention, opportunity to play, to be creative, and to express. Your emotional self includes your feelings and emotions.

Feelings are a gift. They are our inner guidance showing us what is going on within ourselves. They are signals that tell us when something is or is not right for us. We do not always listen to them or give them the attention they need due to outer influences. Many people have never really identified with their feelings because as a society we have been conditioned to ignore them to please others. Feelings are how our body communicates when we are either connected or disconnected from God. There are many varieties of feelings, however, they all stem from either love or fear-based thoughts. Since our feelings are a reflection of our thoughts, we can change our feelings by changing our thoughts and perception of the situation if they are not comfortable to us.

Emotions are energy in motion, the outward action from our feelings. In other words, our emotions are the expression of our feelings. Emotions themselves are neither right or wrong. It is the energy and behavior attached to them that make it a pleasant or unpleasant experience for us. Emotions can come from memories related to previous experiences, whether in this lifetime or another. These can be happy or unhappy memories. These memories create feelings and these feelings trigger our emotions. When we put energy into the past or future we get caught up in emotion, and it creates drama. If our emotions are not expressed, they may ignite unloving behavior, addictions or create various physical conditions. We will discuss this more deeply in Part II, The Power of Love. When we listen to, take responsibility for and understand our feelings and express them in healthy ways, we embrace the gifts feelings and emotions bring.

Getting in Touch with Your Feelings

In order to understand the messages your body is giving you, it is essential to get to the core of your feelings. This recipe will shine light on and guide you in getting in touch with your feelings so you can understand what they mean to you.

- ♥ Acknowledge and identify your feelings
- ♥ Honor your feelings without judgment.
- ♥ Look up your feelings in the book, *Feelings Buried Alive Never Die . . .* to discern what it means to you.
- ♥ Create an affirmation to change the thought pattern associated with the feeling.

NOURISHMENT FOR YOUR SOUL: Your feelings are valid, honor them.

FOOD FOR THOUGHT: I acknowledge, honor and understand my feelings and the messages they bring.

ANGELIC TOOLS:
- ♥ *Feelings Buried Alive Never Die . . .* by Karol K. Truman

Taking Responsibility for Your Feelings

Your feelings are about you, not about other people, therefore it is essential to take responsibility for your feelings rather than blame anyone else for the way you feel. This recipe will empower you to take responsibility for your feelings so you will feel good.

- Get to the core of what they mean to you.
- When people say things and your feelings are hurt, it is a time for you to reflect upon the reason why you feel hurt. This brings great healing. While some may say hurtful things because they are hurting, you can choose not to identify with those words or you can allow them to hurt you. When you allow others to seemingly "hurt" you, you become the victim. When you choose to go within and see what the truth is for you, you are then empowered and can respond in a loving way.
- We cannot control what others do but we can change our perception of the person or situation and the way that we respond to them. This changes our experience.
- Express them in a healthy way.

NOURISHMENT FOR YOUR SOUL: No one else can make you feel a certain way unless you allow them to.

FOOD FOR THOUGHT: I take responsibility for my feelings whatever they may be.

Healthy Ways to Express Your Feelings

Your feelings are meant to be expressed. If your feelings are bottled up inside, suppressed and never expressed, they begin to eat away at you and can lead to feelings of anxiety, depression or guilt that can manifest into unpleasant behaviors or physical conditions because that is their way of coming out. This recipe will guide you in expressing your feelings in a healthy way to create positive experiences for yourself.

- ♥ Get in touch with your feelings before you express them or respond to a situation.
- ♥ Write your feelings down in a journal. This helps you to process them more easily and brings clarity, greater awareness and peace of mind.
- ♥ Share your feelings with your angels or someone you trust.
- ♥ Express them in a constructive way. An example of this is: when you do_____, I feel _____ rather than you made me feel _____ because you did _____.
- ♥ Look in the mirror and talk about your feelings. When you are finished thank your body for the messages and send love to yourself.
- ♥ Do something creative that allows the feeling to come to life.

NOURISHMENT FOR YOUR SOUL: Expressing your feelings in healthy ways strengthens relationships and brings you freedom.

FOOD FOR THOUGHT: I express my feelings with love and integrity and I feel joy and peaceful.

CHAPTER 4

The Mind, Body and Spirit Connection

DIVINITY

Divinity is within each and every one of us.
It is a greater expression of who we are.
As we express this divine nature,
Our world is illuminated.

My mind is filled with divine wisdom.
My heart is filled with divine love.
My body is filled with divine light.
My life is filled with divine experiences,
opportunities and relationships,
For I am one with God, angels and all of life.
I am a divine being of love having a human experience,
And I allow my light to shine!

—Bonnie Ann Lewis

Aligning Your Mind, Body and Spirit

"Spirit is the life; mind is the builder; physical is the result." —EDGAR CAYCE

On a soul level we are all interconnected and exhibit similar characteristics, however on a physical level we are individual sparks of God and unique in our own way. We all have our unique talents and gifts to offer the world and we all contribute to creating our world by utilizing these gifts and talents in our service. What we do for ourselves, we do for others and vice versa. Just as we were all created in the image of God, we have the power and will to create our lives. We all have free will to choose that which we desire to experience. These are our birthrights.

The mind, body and spirit connection is the blending and aligning of all aspects of yourself. You are an important part of the universe. You are connected to the universal source of everything that exists, creation. Your soul is that part of you that came here to evolve through experience. Your spirit is the essence of who you are, the energy, the power that resides within to create. This is your female self. Your physical body takes the action that brings your creations to form. This is your male self. Everything begins in the spiritual realm before it comes to physical form. In order to create, you must unify the male and female aspects of yourself, your inner or spiritual being, and your physical body. Your mind is your choice of free will and the director of all this activity which initiates your bodily senses, your feelings and emotions, and spirit is the flow of divine love that exists within you. Your soul sends signals to your

THE MIND, BODY AND SPIRIT CONNECTION

physical body through your senses to communicate its needs and desires. By giving attention to these senses, they will guide you to the inner truths that exist within your soul. Your heart is the doorway to your soul.

When we understand the way our body functions as a whole, and our communication between our physical and spiritual self are clear, our mind and heart walk hand in hand and our needs and desires are fulfilled. We are connected to spirit and the infinite resources of the universe. We are in the flow of life, and we experience a life of love, peace, unity, abundance and freedom.

Example: Think of your whole being in relation to an airplane. Your mind is like the pilot of the airplane—it creates and directs your path through its thoughts. Your body, the airplane itself, is the physical vehicle that takes you from place to place. Your spirit is the power or fuel in your airplane that makes it fly. This is an airplane as a whole. Therefore it is important that all parts of the airplane are functioning properly to experience a successful flight. The same is true for you. All parts of yourself must function properly to ensure a healthy well-being.

Consequently, your soul has all the answers in which your mind connects to control your body. Your body must have power and direction in order to function. Just as the pilot cannot fly the plane without fuel, you cannot create and direct your path without your divine mind and energy (spirit). In other words, it is important for your mind, body, spirit and soul to be in alignment in order to experience a successful life. Therefore, it is essential to take responsibility for your body as a whole—mentally, physically, emotionally and spiritually, and create a comfortable state of balance in all areas of your life. When you understand yourself as a whole being and your communication between all aspects of yourself are clear, all of these aspects work together to perform at their best. Your needs are met, desires are fulfilled and you live a life of harmony and balance. Your chakra system regulates the synchronicity between all aspects of yourself. Synchronicity means you are allowing the energy of love to flow through you and you have the ability to create all that your heart desires. When synchronicity occurs, you are inspired. Inspired indicates you are "in spirit," connected to spirit so everything in your life works. People show up, relationships are harmonious, money flows and everything falls into place with grace and ease. This is the magic of spirit.

Our body, mind and spirit function together to create. Spirit (love) is the energy that creates. Our mind holds the power and choice of free will that directs and attracts our creations, and our physical body is the action that brings these creations to life. The communication between our soul and our physical body sometimes gets misinterpreted due to outside influences and interferences such as illusions of fear, the beliefs of others, and the busyness of our day to day lives. Therefore, we need to quiet our mind to reconnect to that divine communication between all aspects of ourselves, to connect to that inner wisdom, intelligence and truth within, our higher or God-self on a daily basis.

Many times what prevents us from moving forward and finding happiness in ourselves, in relationships, careers, health and money, are our fears and limited beliefs that we do not deserve good in our life. The truth of the matter is that we all deserve to be and acquire all that we desire. We all have the inner knowledge and opportunity to be happy and fulfilled. God's energetic vibration is love and divine consciousness, which is the highest vibration there is. The spirit within each of us speaks in the silence of our soul. It speaks with clarity, truth

THE MIND, BODY AND SPIRIT CONNECTION

and eternal wisdom. Our spirit is sustained by unlimited sources of divine love.

NOURISHMENT FOR YOUR SOUL: Nourish, nurture and pamper yourself with love. This will be the greatest investment you'll ever make. A healthy mind, body and spirit is a precious gift. Honor it with gratitude.

FOOD FOR THOUGHT: My mind, body and spirit are aligned with the divine.

Heart and Head Working Together

WHOLENESS

When you follow your heart,
Your soul will grow.
For it is love and light,
That makes you whole.
I am whole. I am whole.
The flow of love,
Runs through my soul.

—Bonnie Ann Lewis

Your heart and head working together as a team is important so that you can create what's in your heart, for this reflects your soul's desires. Tune into how you feel as to whether your heart or head is leading.

♥ When your heart is leading you, you will feel passionate, excited, motivated, alive and optimistic.

- ♥ When your head is leading, you may feel stressed, anxious, fearful, confused, or controlled.

- ♥ When they work together, your heart brings forth your desires, your mind focuses on the desires and your body takes action to fulfill your desires.

- ♥ Your heart and mind working together creates balance and harmony in your life.

- ♥ You are the keeper of your heart, mind, body and soul. You have all the power within to create your desires and heal yourself on all levels. When you utilize this God-given power, you will know things happen because you, along with God, made it happen. This is co-creation, the combining of the spiritual guidance and taking action in the physical to bring it to fruition. Spirit can give you all the guidance in the world, however, you must take action yourself to make it happen if you so desire. By doing so, you will reap the infinite rewards of watching your dreams grow, bloom, bear fruit and come to life!

NOURISHMENT FOR YOUR SOUL: When what you think, say, feel and do reflect what's in your heart, then your heart and head are working together.

FOOD FOR THOUGHT: My heart leads and my head follows. My heart and mind are now aligned with love.

ANGELIC TOOLS:

- ♥ *Angelic Reflections I: Awakening* CD by Bonnie Ann Lewis (Aligning Your Heart and Mind Meditation)

ALIGNING YOUR HEART AND MIND MEDITATION

This meditation is designed to bring your heart and mind into unison.

- I invite you to close your eyes and just relax, relax . . . relax.
- Take three or four deep breaths and as you breathe in, breathe in love. As you breath out, release any fears or concerns you may have.
- I invite you to visualize a silver thread extending down from the heavens entering the top of your head.
- Connected to this silver thread is a vibrant purple ball. This represents your divine mind.
- At the bottom of the purple ball the silver thread continues and is attached to an emerald green ball. This represents your heart.
- Visualize this silver thread between the purple and green balls getting shorter and shorter. As this occurs, the purple and green balls will become closer and closer together, and then they will merge.
- As they merge they will transform into divine white light, connecting your heart and mind.
- Now see this ray of light expand to where your heart and mind exist within your body, taking the shape of a vertical barbell.
- Think loving thoughts by repeating after me," I AM love, I AM love, I AM love."
- Take a moment to feel the love that exists within your heart.
- Take another moment to feel the joy and peace it brings to have your heart and mind filled with love.
- Affirm: My heart and mind are now aligned, reflecting the divine. And so it is!

Namaste'

NOTE: This meditation is found on my *Angelic Reflections I: Awakening* CD

YOUR JOURNEY TO LOVE

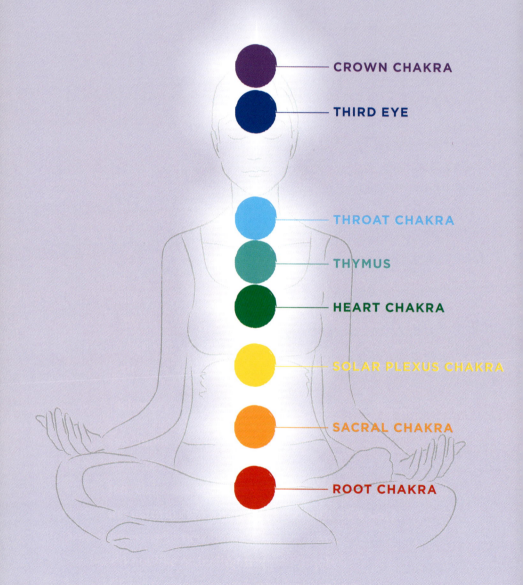

THE MIND, BODY AND SPIRIT CONNECTION

Chakras

Your body has many energy centers that exist within and transmit energy throughout your body. These energy centers are called chakras and they vibrate at different levels of intensity. Your vibration of energy is reflective of your thoughts. Their purpose is to regulate the inflow and outflow of your energy. You have many chakra centers throughout your body. For the purpose of this book, we will focus on seven major energy centers and one new evolving chakra. Your chakras are bridges or gateways between the spiritual and physical realms as they interact with the mind and body, and connect you with spirit. It is through these energy centers that you attract people and experiences into your life and connect with the divine. You can balance your energy by balancing your chakras. Each chakra is represented by a different color and relates to specific matters. There are also certain stones or crystals that support each chakra.

♥ The three lower chakras are concerned with earthly matters and regulate your physical power. They represent your relationship to the physical world. They are the root chakra, sacral chakra and solar plexus chakra.

FIRST: ROOT CHAKRA relates to your physical needs: money, security, and survival, career and home.
Location: base of spine
Color: red
Represents: grounding, balance and your connection to earth
Supporting Stones: Hematite, Obsidian, Smoky Quartz, Bloodstone and Red Jasper

SECOND: SACRAL CHAKRA relates to health and vitality, physical desires, appetite and addictions
Location: midway between navel and tailbone in pelvic area
Color: orange
Represents: creativity, sexuality and emotions
Supporting Stones: Coral, Orange Calcite and Carnelian

THIRD: SOLAR PLEXUS CHAKRA relates to fears, obsessions, personal power and control
Location: behind the navel
Color: yellow
Represents: personal power, intellect, will, control
Supporting Stones: Amber, Tigers Eye and Aragonite

💜 The Heart chakra is the center and unifies the upper and lower chakras. This is our connection to all of life.

FOURTH: HEART CHAKRA relates to love, compassion, forgiveness, relationships with self and others.
Location: in center of chest
Color: green, pink
Represents: healing, growth, clairsentience
Supporting Stones: Rose Quartz, Watermelon Tourmaline, Rhodochrosite, Peridot, Aventurine and Emerald

💜 The four upper chakras are concerned with spiritual matters. They regulate your internal power. They represent your relationship with yourself, your internal world, and your connection to spirit. They are the thymus chakra, throat chakra, third eye chakra and crown chakra.

THE MIND, BODY AND SPIRIT CONNECTION

I'd like to call your attention to a new emerging chakra. It is essential to activate this chakra to support you and increase your self-awareness. This chakra already exists but is emerging as humanity is evolving. It is called the thymus chakra and is sometimes referred to as the high heart chakra. It helps people understand and practice unconditional, universal love.

THYMUS: relates to authenticity, self-identity, self-discovery, self-awareness, universal love and compassion.
Location: between heart and throat
Color: blue-green/turquoise
Represents: inner peace, protection from chemicals and pollutants, soul connection, heightened awareness, infinity, universal love
Supporting Stones: Chrysocolla, Laboradite, Sodalite, and Turquoise

FIFTH: THROAT CHAKRA relates to creative expression, speaking your truth, and written and verbal communication.
Location: throat area between collar bones
Color: light blue
Represents: communication, self-expression, clairaudience
Supporting Stones: Angelite, Celestite, Kyanite, Larimar

SIXTH: THIRD EYE relates to spiritual sight and visions
Location: between eyebrows
Color: dark blue, indigo, with white and purple swirls
Represents: intuition, psychic vision, connection to higher self, clairvoyance
Supporting Stones: Azurite, Lapis Lazuli, Sugilite

SEVENTH: CROWN CHAKRA relates to realizing we are all one with God and others, allows in divine knowledge, and is a channel for wisdom, guidance and understanding to enter.
Location: inside top of head
Color: purple

Represents: spirituality, divine consciousness, inner peace, claircognizance, wisdom, universal connection

Supporting Stones: Amethyst, Clear Quartz, Fluorite, Moonstone

SUPPORTING YOUR CHAKRAS

When you first begin balancing your chakra, you will want to do this daily. In time, you will be able to listen to your body and know when it is time. When your chakras require clearing, you will feel tired, sluggish and your life will lack flow. There are many ways that are effective in clearing and balancing your chakras. What technique you use is not as important as doing it on a regular basis. I encourage you to use whatever method resonates with you. Here are some methods to clear and balance your chakras.

- Visualizations or Meditations
- Sound Therapy (music, tuning forks or bowls)
- Crystals
- Color Therapy or Chakra Oils

NOURISHMENT FOR YOUR SOUL: Clearing your chakras on a daily basis will enrich your days, and you will attract loving experiences.

FOOD FOR THOUGHT: I balance my chakras on a daily basis and I feel good.

ANGELIC TOOLS:
- *Angelic Reflections I: Awakening* CD by Bonnie Ann Lewis (Chakra Power Meditation)
- *Chakra Clearing* book and CD by Doreen Virtue
- Chakra Tune-up Chart by Elizabeth Blackburn
- Chakra Activation Oils by Soleil's Influence

CHAKRA POWER MEDITATION

This meditation is designed to clear, balance, and activate your chakras. It includes the new emerging thymus chakra which represents authenticity, self-awareness, self-discovery, self-expression and universal love.

- Let's invite in Archangel Metatron to assist you by saying, "Dear Archangel Metatron, please assist me in clearing, balancing and activating my chakras." You may recognize Archangel Metatron by his violet and seafoam green stripes of color.

- I invite you to close your eyes. Take three or four deep breaths and with each breath, allow your body to relax, relax, relax.

- Visualize a wand with a geometric shape attached coming from Archangel Metatron down through the top of your crown all the way down to your root chakra which is located at the base of your spine.

- Identify your root chakra as a red ball.

- As this geometric shape turns, visualize it removing any dirt or blockages from your root chakra, transforming them instantly.

- See your root chakra shining bright like a polished red ball and affirm: My root chakra is cleansed and balanced.

- As this geometric shape moves up your body to the area between your root chakra and your navel, it reaches your sacral chakra.

- Identify your sacral chakra as an orange ball.

- As this geometric shape turns, visualize it removing any dirt or blockages from your sacral chakra, transforming them instantly.

- See your sacral chakra shining like a bright polished orange ball and affirm: My sacral chakra is cleansed and balanced.

- As this geometric shape moves up your body to the area of your navel, it reaches your solar plexus chakra.

- Identify your solar plexus chakra as a yellow ball.

- As this geometric shape turns, visualize it removing any dirt or blockages from your solar plexus chakra, transforming them instantly.
- See your solar plexus shining bright like a polished yellow ball and affirm: My solar plexus chakra is cleansed and balanced.
- As this geometric shape moves up your body to the area in the center of your chest, it reaches your heart chakra.
- Identify your heart chakra as an emerald green ball.
- As this geometric shape turns, visualize it removing any dirt or blockages from your heart chakra, transforming them instantly.
- See your heart chakra shining bright like a polished emerald green ball and affirm: My heart chakra is cleansed and balanced.
- As this geometric shape moves up your body to the area between your heart and your throat chakra, it reaches your thymus chakra.
- Identify your thymus chakra as a turquoise ball.
- As this geometric shape turns, visualize it removing any dirt or blockages from your thymus chakra, transforming them instantly.
- See your thymus chakra shining bright like a polished turquoise ball and affirm: My thymus chakra is cleansed and balanced.
- As this geometric shape moves up your body to the area at the base of your neck, it reaches your throat chakra.
- Identify your throat chakra as a light blue ball.
- As this geometric shape turns, visualize it removing any dirt or blockages from your throat chakra, transforming them instantly.
- See your throat chakra shining like a polished light blue ball and affirm: My throat chakra is cleansed and balanced.
- As this geometric shape moves up your body to the area of your forehead between your eyebrows, it reaches your third eye chakra.

THE MIND, BODY AND SPIRIT CONNECTION

- Identify your third eye chakra as a dark blue ball.
- As this geometric shape turns, visualize it removing any dirt or blockages from your third eye chakra, transforming them instantly.
- See it shining brightly like a polished dark blue ball with sparkles of purple and white light and affirm: My third eye chakra is cleansed and balanced.
- As this geometric shape moves up your body to the area inside the top of your head, it reaches your crown chakra.
- Identify your crown chakra as a purple ball.
- As this geometric shape turns, visualize it removing any dirt or blockages from your crown chakra, transforming them instantly.
- See your crown chakra shining bright like a polished purple ball and affirm: My crown chakra is cleansed and balanced.
- Then mentally ask Archangel Metatron to activate your chakras with divine white energy.
- Visualize white light emerging from this geometric shape above your head, moving down through the top of your crown into your body, activating each chakra as it continues down your body and reaches the ground.
- Thank Archangel Metatron for his assistance.
- Affirm: My chakras are clear, balanced and activated with the light of God. And so it is!
- Your chakras are now aligned so that you may attract joyful, loving experiences throughout your day.

May you feel your true power as you lovingly impact those around you!

NOTE: This meditation is found on my *Angelic Reflections I: Awakening* CD

The Power of Color

Colors are an essential part of life as they stimulate, activate and heal us on many levels. Each color has a vibration. That vibration helps our body to heal, our spirit to soar and feeds our soul. When we bring color into our energy field, it lifts our vibration, allowing healing to occur as it enhances our life. There are many ways you can bring the vibration of colors into your body to support your chakras, body, mind and spirit. Here are some ways to incorporate colors into your life.

Foods you eat • Clothing • Crystals • Flowers
Visualization of colors • Bring colors into your environment
Candles • Art • Essential oils

SOUL COLORS

We all have what I refer to as soul colors. These are colors that really resonate with you and represent specific aspects of yourself. Although all colors have their own properties, soul colors have additional relevance and specific meaning for you. Soul colors are different from the chakra colors and aura colors although they may be present within your aura. You can have several soul colors. You may already be aware of these colors as they are oftentimes your favorite colors. Throughout your life your favorite colors may change according to the colors that you intuitively know you need at that time. However, these soul colors stay the same and are beneficial for you to have around you, and in your environment throughout your life, as their vibration nurtures and stimulates your souls growth.

Here is an example: For me, two of my soul colors are purple and green. As far back as I can remember as a child, my very favorite color has been purple. My birthstone is amethyst. For me, purple represents higher consciousness, spirituality and the divinity within. Green represents healing, nourishment and growth. I do not recall green being one of my favorite colors, however, whenever I enter my inner sanctuary, I always see a beautiful green meadow that brings me such a sense of refreshment and renewal. Interestingly enough, the Swan Self-Awareness Centre I am the founder of has a logo that consists of the colors purple and green. These colors represent spiritual healing. I did not become aware of my soul colors until several years after my logo was chosen. I love the amazing synchronicities that occur when we allow the angels to guide us!

EXERCISE: FINDING YOUR SOUL COLORS AND CREATING A PORTRAIT

To find out what your soul colors are, find a quiet place, go within and ask that these colors be shown to you. Then ask what their representation means specifically for you. After you become aware of your soul colors, take a picture of yourself and put it in the center of a white piece of paper or canvas. Then create a portrait of these colors around you using paint, crayons, markers, colored pencils, charcoals or whatever you desire. Place this portrait in a place where you will see it often. This will remind you what colors to keep around you. Each time you look at it, it will bring in the vibration of those colors. On the back, write the specific meaning these colors have for you so you will have it as a reference.

CHAPTER 5

Your Spiritual Team

We all have a spiritual team that guides us through life. They are around us waiting for us to ask for their assistance. Your spiritual team reminds and reflects to you your true self. Your spiritual team consists of many angels, archangels and other spiritual beings such as ascended masters, fairies, spirit guides, goddesses and saints. You also have earthly helpers such as the animal and crystal kingdoms which are available to assist you just for the asking. All your spiritual helpers work together to assist you in your life. They each have their own essence and duties so to speak. By becoming aware of their presence you can establish a connection and call on them for assistance.

The more you can work with your spiritual team, the more familiar you will become with who is around and guiding you, and you develop a personal relationship with them so you begin to easily recognize their presence and request their assistance. You use your inner senses to connect with all the different realms of your spiritual team. When you feel a presence around you and want to know who it is, you can ask them to identify themselves. They will tell you who they are as they want you to feel more connected to them so they can assist you. For example, an essential member of my spiritual team is Archangel Michael. When he shows up, I sometimes hear "Archangel Michael here." Other times I will see his cobalt blue energy. Sometimes I feel his presence and just know it is him. Sometimes I see him in full form.

This chapter will increase your awareness about you spiritual team so that you can experience the infinite blessings this inner connection brings. Throughout this chapter, I share some examples of my communications with these wonderful beings of light so you can recognize the voice of spirit and deepen your connection to them. These messages have brought me so much love, support, guidance, comfort, clarity, and confirmation. Know that you can receive these divine messages as well. May these inspiring messages of love bring clarity on your path, empower and encourage you to be the beautiful light that you are as they enlighten and enrich your life. May they help you feel the loving presence which is around you and available to assist you throughout your life.

The Angelic Realm

"Make yourself familiar with the angels, and behold them frequently in spirit; for without being seen, they are present with you." —ST. FRANCIS DE SALES

Angels are non-denominational messengers of love and light sent from God. They can guide, protect and help you to heal, love, create and experience all that your heart desires as you fulfill your life's mission. You have many angels around you to guide you throughout your day. There are different hierarchies of angels. There are guardian angels, archangels, universal angels, and the cherub angels. Angels are spiritual beings therefore they do not have physical bodies or wings per say, however, they do take on this form so that we humans can identify, recognize and feel more connected to them. What appears to us as wings are actually their auras. Many are androgynous, (a blending of male and female energy) although some do carry specific male or female energy. They are in a dimension where time and space do not exist. Angels are omnipresent so they can be everywhere simultaneously. The key is to receive their guidance and apply it to your life where time and space do exist. Angels have never been on earth in a physical body, since they are energy forms of love and light, however, they do take on human form to assist people when necessary. There is a term earth angels used to describe people who deliver messages from heaven to earth and have come to earth to help heal our planet while teaching heavenly principles. These people take on characteristics of angels but are not actual angels. To explore this topic more, I recommend the book, *Earth Angels* or *Earth Angel Realms* by Doreen Virtue.

Angelic assistance, guidance and messages are available to all of us. All that is required is for us to ask for heaven's help and open our hearts and minds to receive this divine love and wisdom. The angels help us retrieve the truths within our soul and reflect to us our true self. The more aware of the angels' presence, the more connected to God and the more centered we will feel. They help us to be in our natural state of love and express our unique self. The angels give me infinite unconditional love, support, guidance and inspiration. I am truly grateful for their presence in my life!

NOURISHMENT FOR YOUR SOUL: *"Inviting the angels into your life expedites your healing and transforms your life in miraculous ways."* —Bonnie Ann Lewis

FOOD FOR THOUGHT: I AM aware, open and receptive to the angelic presence that surrounds and guides me.

YOUR SPIRITUAL TEAM

ANGELIC TOOLS:
💜 *Angels 101* by Doreen Virtue
💜 *Healing with the Angels* by Doreen Virtue
💜 *Angel Medicine* by Doreen Virtue

Hierarchy of Angels

💜 **Guardian Angels** are with us from the time we are born until we make our transition from this lifetime. They help carry out God's will, protect and guide us through life. Guardian angels can be recognized with their large rounded wing span.

💜 **Universal Angels** are with us at difference times and come and go in our lives depending on what we need or what we ask assistance with. These angels take on different forms: A full form as we see them in pictures; a silhouette; flashes of colors; or a head view.

💜 **Cherub Angels,** also known as the romance angels, are the highest vibration of the angelic realm. They can be recognized by their clusters of flickering sparks of light.

💜 **Archangels** are the managers of the angels. They oversee the angelic realm and assist with more worldly matters. They give very action-oriented guidance and assist us in fulfilling our life's mission. An example of the distinction between angels and archangels is, angels give us nudges while the archangels gently push us forward. Throughout this book you will become more familiar with some of these archangels. The archangels often appear as colors. They can also be identified by the large pointed wing spans they portray. I'm going to introduce you to the archangels. To learn more about their essence and how they can assist you I recommend referring to the book, *Archangels and Ascended Masters* by Doreen Virtue, as it is a divine reference guide.

Archangel Ariel helps with manifesting and she oversees environmental issues, especially water. You can recognize her by her pale pink aura.

Archangel Azrael helps people cross over into the afterlife and he assists those on earth who are grieving the loss of their loved one. You can recognize him by his ivory aura.

Archangel Chamuel helps with bringing soul mates together and creating balance and harmony in relationships. He also assists with your careers, fulfilling your life's purpose and creating peace on our planet. You may recognize him by his pale green aura.

Archangel Gabriel is the messenger of God. She assists those who deliver messages such as writers, artists, musicians. She also helps with pregnancy until the child is born and Archangel Metatron takes over. She can also assist you in creating your website, brochures, and other marketing materials. You can recognize her by her copper aura.

Archangel Haniel assists with opening up your spiritual senses and she helps you to stay centered so you can experience grace and ease in your life. You can recognize her by her soft, gentle essence or bluish-white aura.

Archangel Jeremiel helps to release fears from past experiences and helps with emotional healing. He can assist you in understanding, interpreting and bringing forth the wisdom within your dreams. You may recognize him by his deep purple aura.

Archangel Jophiel helps to bring more beauty into your life by purifying your thoughts and assists you in being beautiful from the inside out. She has a friendly and positive essence. You can recognize her by her deep rose aura.

Archangel Metatron helps with clearing and balancing your chakras with geometric shapes. He also helps with raising children and assists those who work with children. You can recognize him by the violet and sea-foam green stripes of color of his aura.

Archangel Michael is a powerful protector and helps you release fears so you can fulfill your life's purpose. He transforms lower energy to light. He is also great with assisting you with computer issues. You can recognize him by his cobalt blue aura.

Archangel Raphael is the powerful healer. He can assist you with your healing process related to physical conditions, addictions and food cravings, and he guides healers who work with people and animals. You can recognize him by his emerald green aura.

Archangel Raziel helps with awakening all of your spiritual senses and assists with manifesting. You can recognize him by his rainbow aura.

Archangel Raguel helps with resolving conflicts and empowering you to be the light that you are. He also assists with divine order and makes sure that justice and fairness occur. You can recognize him by his sky blue aura.

Archangel Sandalphon has a very gentle essence and he delivers answers to your prayers. He also helps people who are associated with music. Oftentimes you will recognize his presence around you when you keep hearing repetitive songs in your mind. You can recognize him by his light turquoise aura.

Archangel Uriel is very gentle and helps with forgiveness of self and others. He shines light on situations so that you can see things from a higher perspective in order to facilitate healing. You can recognize him by his pale yellow aura.

Archangel Zadkiel helps with remembering things. He assists students and is great to call on when you are taking tests. You can ask for him to be present with your children at school every day. You can recognize him by his deep blue aura.

ANGELIC TOOLS:

- *Archangels and Ascended Masters* book and oracle cards by Doreen Virtue
- *Archangel Oracle Cards* by Doreen Virtue
- *The Romance Angels* audio by Doreen Virtue

INVOKING IN THE ANGELS

- Ask them for their presence and assistance.
- Listen to angelic music.
- Surround your environment with statues or pictures of angels to bring in their energy. Place them in the helpful people corner (according to the Bagua layout in Feng Shui) in your home or office.
- Invite the angels into your dreams.
- Communicate with them frequently.
- Light a candle and invite them in.
- Read books about angels as that opens you up to their energy and guidance.
- Do meditations that open you to the angels' presence so that the messages they have for you can come through.

NOURISHMENT FOR YOUR SOUL: I use Doreen Virtue's oracle card decks to bring in the energy of the beings of light who are helping me with specific issues at that time. I line them up across my window sill in my office or whatever area it relates to. It is amazing the power available to assist us and the miracles that occur just for us asking!

FOOD FOR THOUGHT: Thank you angels for assisting me along my journey.

ANGELIC TOOLS:
- *Angelic Reflections I–IV* Meditation CD's by Bonnie Ann Lewis
- *Angels Gift* or *Harp Magic* music CD's by Peter Sterling

A GATHERING OF ANGELS MEDITATION

This meditation is designed to help you become aware of and connect with your guardian angels and other angels around you. Throughout this meditation, pay attention to anything that comes to you. You may receive a vision, hear a name, think a thought or feel a physical sensation. Whatever you receive, know this is your angels responding to you. If at anytime during this meditation you do not receive an answer, take a deep breath, repeat the question mentally and be still . . .your response will follow. This meditation can be used over and over to connect with the many angels that are around you and come and go in your life.

- Now I invite you to close your eyes and clear your mind by focusing on the music.
- Take three or four deep breaths. As you breathe in, breathe in love, as you breathe out, release any worries or fears associated with connecting with your angels.
- With each breath, allow yourself to be in a state of relaxation.
- Now invite in your angels by repeating after me, "Dear Angels, please surround me in a bubble of white light."
- Visualize your angels' wings wrapped around you like a nice warm and cozy blanket.

- Feel the warmth, safety and outpouring of love coming from your angels' wings.

- You are safe, secure and loved.

- It is safe for you to connect with your angels.

- Bring your focus to the area above your left shoulder.

- Ask your guardian angels to connect with you by repeating after me silently, "Angels on my left side, please tell me your name or give me a sign or symbol so that I may recognize you. Please come forward and identify yourself so I may feel more connected to you. Please tell me what you are helping me with."

- Pause while you retrieve this information.

- Bring your focus to the area above your right shoulder.

- Ask your guardian angels to connect with you by repeating after me silently, "Angels on my right side, please tell me your name or give me a sign or symbol so that I may recognize you. Please come forward and identify yourself so I may feel more connected to you. Please tell me what you are helping me with."

- Pause while you retrieve this information.

- Bring your focus to the area above and around your head.

- Ask your angels to connect with you by repeating after me silently, "Angels that are around me, please tell me your name or give me a sign or symbol so that I may recognize you. Please come forward and identify yourself so I may feel more connected to you. Please tell me what you are helping me with."

- Pause while you retrieve this information.

- Thank the angels for coming forward and bringing you this information so that you can recognize and connect with them. You may want to take a few moments to record the information you received.

Enjoy the blessings this inner connection brings. Angel Blessings to you always!

NOTE: This meditation is found on my *Angelic Reflections I: Awakening* CD

Angelic Guidance

ANGEL LOVE

Angels of love,
So pure and bright,
Shine upon you day and night,
Guiding you through life,
So you may thrive.
Ask for their assistance,
And you will see,
Just how joyful life can be!

—*Bonnie Ann Lewis*

I'd like to explain to you the purpose of angelic guidance and what occurs. Angelic guidance is not about telling you what your life is going to be. It is about giving you the guidance that will help you create the life that you desire to live, for you are the creator of your own life and a co-creator of the universe with God. Understand that the angels bring you information. However, it is up to you to take responsibility, make choices and take action to make these things happen if that is what you desire, or change your course of action to prevent them from occurring if it is something you do not desire. Your future is your own responsibility, for you hold all the power within to choose and create what you desire to experience. Things change according to the actions you take so be sure to ask for guidance from your angels regularly. Following divine guidance will expedite your healing and transform your life in miraculous ways!

RECEPTIVITY

When we are in our natural state of love, we are most receptive to the angels' messages. Things that increase our receptivity to angelic guidance are:

practicing • meditation • being out in nature • chakra clearing listening to angelic music • purifying your body of chemicals

Those things that take us out of our natural state and are mood altering substances will reduce our receptivity to divine guidance such as:

caffeine • chocolate • sugar • alcohol • chemicals • processed foods • drugs

Discernment

There are times we all question and need validation for the divine messages we receive as we are connecting with our angels; that is part of our humanness. However, asking the angels for confirmation helps us to get clear and feel confident about the information we are receiving. The following recipe will help you recognize and trust the messages from your angels.

❤ Whenever you feel an inner sense that it is time to take better care of yourself, help someone else, have the desire to be of service or make a difference in this world, this is divine guidance from God and your angels.

❤ All guidance from the angels is very loving, supportive, and inspiring. It is always focused on healing, serving or improving. You will feel calm, safe, a sense of comfort, at ease, peaceful, excited, motivated or passionate. The angels' messages leave you feeling good with a sense of knowing. If you receive information when you are communicating with your angels on your own, in which you feel "forced" or "controlled" to do something, these are fear-based thoughts coming from your human interpretation—not divine guidance. The more you communicate with the angels, the stronger your connection will be. By communicating with the angels you allow God's love to be ever-present in your life, in your heart and in your mind.

♥ Sometimes we are guided to take certain steps and we do so with a certain outcome in mind, yet it turns out to be totally different than we expected. This doesn't mean we weren't divinely guided, it just means that the outcome is for the highest good of ourself and all concerned.

♥ Sometimes certain things happen and we wonder why our prayers are not being answered, or later we come to be grateful for what we believe were "unanswered" prayers, when in truth they were blessings in disguise and the angels answered our request with something greater.

NOURISHMENT FOR YOUR SOUL: Whenever I feel confused or stuck and need confirmation or clarity, I use whatever card deck by Doreen Virtue that I feel drawn to, and that always brings me clarity and confirmation.

ANGELIC TOOLS:
♥ *Divine Guidance* or *How to Hear Your Angels* by Doreen Virtue

BLESSINGS IN DISGUISE

We choose our lessons prior to our incarnation in order to help our soul evolve in this lifetime and lead the way for others. We also create our own experiences, consciously or unconsciously, but we may not always consciously understand why we have chosen these experiences and what the outcome will be. I'd like to share with you an experience of mine in which I questioned why I chose this experience, yet it turned out to be filled with blessings in disguise.

I was married to a man for nine years and gave birth to two children. I was a stay-at-home mom. After our divorce I had custody of our children and was able to keep the home we lived in. I had just taken my ATP® training and was planning to open my healing center and begin my Angel Therapy® practice. Due to the mis-diagnosis of a medical condition, I lost custody of my children. This resulted in me moving to Dallas to live with my sister so I could heal and get back on my feet, leaving my children behind in Austin with their dad. Being away from my children was the most heart-wrenching experience I had ever had. I missed them so much and I would cry to my mom on the phone and say, "Why did this happen? "Why do I have to be here in Dallas?" Although I felt very grateful that my sister gave me a home and took me under her wing while I got back on my feet, I felt so misplaced. I was devastated, shocked and numb and couldn't understand why I had chosen this experience.

When I moved to Dallas, I did not have a job or any money. I had attorney fees and bills to pay. My mom and dad, bless their hearts, paid all my bills for six months so I could have my medical coverage, keep my car and pay the attorney fees. This allowed me to have some visitation with my children. My sister Gina allowed me to live with her and paid for everything I needed along the way. She helped me get back on my feet until I could get a job. Due to the medication the doctor's had given me for a condition I did not even have, it took some time to get the dosage adjusted so I could even function. Although I tried to express to the doctors the medication they put me on made me feel "out of it," they would not listen to me. They just kept changing and adjusting it. I was told if I wanted to see my children I had to follow their treatment recommendations and take this medication.

My mom was my rock during all this time. I could not have done it without her. All said and done, I ended up owing my parents $20,000 and the attorneys were telling me it would cost me $30,000 to get my rights and custody of my children back. I desired to have a happy, fulfilling marriage, move back to Austin where my children were, and have them and my life back. I found myself having to rebuild my life. I did not know how all of this was going to happen but I had a sense of knowing it would. Others were telling me not to talk to the angels and to forget pursuing my career as an ANGEL THERAPY PRACTITONER® or I would lose my children for good. I prayed to the angels and asked them to please help and guide me to the doctors that could help me. When I moved back to Austin they guided me to a wonderful doctor who recognized I was on way too much medication and weaned me off slowly. This began my journey to feeling like my self again. I am forever grateful for her expertise, compassion, loving care, and her openness to the guidance I was receiving from my angels. Her presence in my life has gotten me where I am today. I stayed true to my heart and followed the angels' guidance that said I could have both my children and my career, and with the help of the angels, I have accomplished that!

While in Dallas, an opportunity opened up for a job through an agency but it was quite a drive from where I lived, so I decided not to pursue it. I heard the angels say, *"Go for the interview,"* so I did. It was a perfect situation because they only needed someone to fill-in for a short time as their assistant was on maternity leave. I only wanted short term since I was moving back to Austin. The angels guided me to this great job in a dental office that provided me with the money to move back to Austin within eight months. When I was in the process of moving back to Austin, I asked the angels to bring me a job that would support my children and myself, and provide an affordable two bedroom apartment in a good area close to my children. I asked them to bring this job to me right away so I did not have to keep traveling back and forth for interviews. Upon my request, the angels brought me my job. It was the very first job I interviewed for and the salary was exactly what I asked for. It was two miles from where my children lived with their dad. The dentist needed me to start right away so a friend of mine invited me to stay with her for a while until I found an apartment. Within one month, I was guided to an apartment that was just two miles away from my children and my job, and was affordable! I was so grateful because the rental fees for apartments in Austin were very high.

Prior to my NDE, I had been working on manifesting a divine love relationship. While in Dallas, I attended a few singles outings and joined the Sierra Club (a group of people who get together and participate in outdoor activities) just to get out, meet people, and socialize. I was feeling so secluded. About six weeks before moving to Austin, information about a singles luncheon crossed my path that was arranged by the Center for Spiritual Living, (a Science of Mind Church) and Unity Church of Dallas, where I had been attending regularly since I was in Dallas. I had planned to go and decided this would be my last outing with the singles. As it got closer, I was debating on whether I should go or not and I heard the angels say *"Go."* So I followed their guidance. During lunch I sat across the table from a man and we instantly felt a strong connection so we began talking. The conversation led us to talk about things we like to do. I had mentioned I loved to ice skate and had wanted to go skating at a rink that was inside a nearby mall. After lunch we went outside and continued talking. Both of us had that feeling we did not want to leave, we just wanted to be together. At the end of our conversation, he invited me to go ice skating with him. I knew I was going to be moving back to Austin because that is where my children were and was home to me. I was very upfront about it with him and we decided to just go out and enjoy each other's company and have fun. On our first date we spent the whole day together. We went out to lunch, went ice skating, out to dinner and to a movie, and we talked as if we had known each other forever, as if we were old friends catching up.

The next day I was going to watch a movie and the angels guided me to call him and invite him to join me. Although I was excited about the idea, my head kicked in and I have to admit I said to the angels, "You want me to what?" A few moments later I called him but received his voicemail, so I left a message. A short time later he returned my call and said he would like to join me. We watched the movie *Pretty Woman* with Julia Roberts and Richard Gere. In the movie, Richard Gere's character name is Mr. Lewis! As we sat next to one another watching the movie, a warm sense of comfort and peace came over me. From that day forth we spent every spare moment we had together. During our time together, we spent lots of time outdoors and would go to a park that was close to his apartment. I had been taking country western dance lessons and he joined me. He reflected so many of the characteristics I desired in a partner. The feelings I experience in his embrace are beyond what words can describe. His sweet, gentle essence spoke to my heart!

He helped me move back to Austin and he flew down every weekend to see me and my children. Two months after returning to Austin, we were engaged and he said that he would look for a job in Austin so he could be with me and my children. When he proposed to me we were at our favorite park. It was dark outside and as we walked down the path to a ridge that overlooked the river where he proposed, there were lightening bugs twinkling all over the place lighting up our path. It was like a magical wonderland! Neither of us had ever seen anything like it. We had been to that park many times and had never seen such a mass of these beautiful creatures!

During our engagement, I began teaching him how to manifest a job for himself in Austin, and we began manifesting the money to have our home built, pay off my parent's and pay an attorney to get my rights and custody of my children back. I wanted to change careers, leave the dental field and open my healing center so I could be of service as well as be home for my children after school. Together we prayed and utilized the principles in this book to bring these dreams to life.

A year later we were married at the Center for Spiritual Living in Dallas. Two months after that, the construction of our new home that was designed to accommodate the healing center was finished and we moved in. Three months later I began the journey to get my rights and children back. After a year of negotiating, going through some preliminary steps, and dealing with the doubts of the attorney representing us to accomplish our goals due to my spiritual practices, I was guided to change attorneys. I asked the angels to guide me to an attorney who supported my spiritual beliefs and could help me get my children back. Right away I was led to an attorney whom we did hire who supported my spiritual beliefs and felt strongly we could accomplish our goals and we began the process.

I left my job at the dental office and began my ATP® practice part-time so I could be home for my children after school. Although I had planned on having my children right away, the custody "battle" took two years. At the end of this time there was a lot of back and forth movement happening, but things weren't getting resolved. I was feeling frustrated and everyday that went by was one more day I would miss with my children. It hurt me inside to see my children going to daycare instead of being with me. I had attended the Goddess and Angels Workshop here in Austin that Doreen Virtue presented and I learned about Goddess Kali. Two days later I called on Goddess Kali and asked for her assistance. I asked her to take care of the situation and that the outcome be for the highest good of all concerned. I told her I was releasing this situation to her and letting it go so she could work her magic. I thanked her.

Two days before we were to go to court for the final hearing, we came to an agreement that is ideal for all of us. We share the children equally which gives them the opportunity to share healthy relationships with both parents. In addition we have equal rights as parents, allowing us both to have a voice in the way our children are raised. My prayer is that this arrangement nurtures our children so they grow up to be happy, healthy, balanced adults. I am deeply grateful to Goddess Kali for her assistance, and for Doreen Virtue teaching me about her.

Another answered prayer . . . for three and a half years my husband commuted back and forth to Dallas for work while actively searching for a job in Austin. The traveling back and forth was beyond old and we were both feeling very discouraged. We so much wanted to live together all the time and have a normal family life. We thought his job in Austin would happen rather quickly and questioned why it was taking so long. The angels told me the job would come through in November and to just be patient. So we held on to faith and trusted that the angels would come through as they always did. During this time, the company in which he was an executive merged with another company, and due to the investments he had acquired while working there, we received an abundance of money that allowed us to purchase our home, pay off my parent's and pay the attorney fees to get my rights and children back! In January of the following year my husband finally moved in with us and started his new job at a company here in Austin. He had gone through a series of six interviews that began in November! Our question of why it took so long for his job in Austin to manifest was another blessing in disguise.

My question for why I was in Dallas for that short time had been answered. This experience has shown me the blessings that unconditional love brings. My prayers for a divine love relationship were answered. The angels brought us together in Dallas—I found my partner, lover, companion, friend, and soul mate. I consider him and my children to be the greatest blessings in the biggest nightmare of my life—I am so blessed! My beloved husband John Lewis has supported me through my healing process, getting my children back, and fulfilling my dream of being home for them after school, all of the endeavors of the Swan Self-Awareness Centre, utilizing my gifts and talents through being of service and bringing forth my angelic tools. I am blessed to have his love and support. When we were bringing to life my *Angelic Reflection Meditation* CD's, we had so much fun. *Tides of Abundance* is my favorite CD as it encompasses each of us, reflects so much of the love that we share and our love of the ocean. My husband took the photos and we carry in our hearts wonderful memories of this angelic creation. We escape to the ocean anytime we have the opportunity. for this is a passion that we share.

I am doing what I love most and that is being a mom, wife and of service to humanity as a model and messenger of God's love by teaching angelic principles. I am sharing my angelic tools with the world, which are my contribution to enriching your life experience and creating heaven here on earth. My husband and I support one another on our individual paths and create our lives together utilizing the angelic wisdom and principles this book presents. Together we continue to nurture and manifest our divine love partnership that reflects both of our desires and is fulfilling and empowering as we walk hand in hand and heart to heart through life. We are ever so grateful for the angels' guidance and assistance in fulfilling our dreams. Time and time again our prayers have been answered in the most miraculous ways in which we could never have planned or foreseen, and our dreams continue to become a reality, delivered on angels' wings!

How Angels Can Guide and Assist You

Angelic assistance is always at your finger tips. You can ask the angels to help you with anything you can imagine or desire. There are infinite ways in which the angels can assist you in your life. Below are some examples.

- ♥ **Learn your lessons with love:** Focus your thoughts on love, speak loving words, and take loving actions.

- ♥ **Release fears:** Throughout my awakening process many fears came up for me. I called on the angels and Archangel Michael to be with me always and assist me in releasing the fears and feel safe, secure and loved. I invited Archangel Michael to be present in every room in my home. His presence brings me much comfort.

- ♥ **Forgiveness:** The angels and Archangel Uriel help us to forgive and see the blessings in all situations. I have asked the angels to help me to resolve conflicts with love, release resentment and frustration in relationships, and asked that they help me to see things from a higher perspective so I can open my heart to giving and receiving love to myself and others. It always amazes me the miraculous healings that occur.

- ♥ **Heal physical conditions, addictions and stop food cravings:** When I first began communicating with the angels I asked them to help me to stop my craving for chocolate. One day I had a taste for a candy bar. I took one bite and it did not taste good to me so I threw the rest away. That was the end of my chocolate cravings.

- ♥ **Help you find something:** When I first met my husband, we were running errands and as he was getting in the car, he put his wallet on the hood for a moment. He got back in the car and we continued on our way. As we approached a traffic light, the car next to us was honking their horn. I looked over and there was an elderly gentleman and lady in the car. I rolled down my window and they said, "Something flew off the top of your car back there. It looks like a wallet." We thanked them and I immediately called on the angels to assist us in retrieving it as we were on a busy four lane road with a median in the center, and traffic coming and going. My husband took the next turnaround as I looked for the wallet. As we were driving, I caught site of it on the other side of the median. In order to get to the wallet we needed to make another turn around. As my husband made the turn around and we came to where the wallet was in the middle of the street, there was not a car in sight. My husband got out and picked it up. It had been run over a few times but it was in one piece and everything was in it! We thanked the angels.

- ♥ **Protect you in your car:** Every time I get in a car I ask the angels to surround us in their divine white light and protect us all and the other drivers and keep us safe. I visualize a circle of angels surrounding the vehicle.

💜 **Bring guidance relating to your life's purpose:** this assists you in focusing on the truths of your soul so you can accomplish what you came here to do.

💜 **Directions:** The angels are great at getting you where you want to go. Since directions are not one of my greatest strengths, I'm always relying on the angels for their assistance. Every time I find my way to where I am going on time!

💜 **Making decisions:** that are for the highest good of yourself and all concerned.

💜 **Help achieve goals:** they give encouragement, motivation, a positive mindset and anything else you may need to succeed.

💜 **Assist you in creating your life:** and experiencing all that your heart desires. To feel love, be love and experience love in all that you do, for love is who you are.

💜 **During dream time:** Angels sometimes come into our dreams and help us heal by removing fear or sending us healing energy. They also bring us messages because we are more receptive then.

💜 **Guide your children:** I am always calling on Mother Mary, Archangel Metatron and Archangel Michael for assistance in guiding my children. I am so grateful for their love and support in this precious endeavor. Here are a few examples of the things I ask the angels to assist my children with. I ask them to protect and keep them safe, to bring them the teachers that will nurture their soul's growth and who are for their highest good, to help them have positive experiences and succeed in what they are doing, and to help them learn their lessons and grow with love, grace and ease. I also ask them to assist me in my parenting skills so I may guide them to grow and bloom with love, nurturing the soul's growth of each child.

- 💜 **Assist you with your shopping:** I ask them to guide me to the store that has what I'm looking for at the best price. I also ask that a checkout is available when I am ready.

- 💜 **Get a table at a restaurant:** In Austin on a weekend night, there is always a long wait to get in and seated, so on the way to the restaurant, I always ask the angels to have a table or booth available and ready for us in a quiet area. I also ask that we get served promptly and courteously.

- 💜 **Make the traffic flow:** I do not like to be in bumper-to-bumper traffic and I avoid it if at all possible. Fortunately, I work from home and set my own schedule so I can do this most of the time. However, the times I do drive in high traffic areas or during rush hour, I ask that the traffic be flowing. There have been times when I have approached a stand-still traffic jam and I asked the angels to make it flow. It worked!

- 💜 **You can send angels to help other people:** It is best to ask them to be with that person without telling them how to help, and allow them to help in whatever way that person is open and receptive to.

- 💜 **Help resolve issues:** When you are addressing a situation, require assistance or information that involves speaking with a representative. Ask your angels to help you get someone who is knowledgeable and can resolve the issue efficiently and give you accurate information. If you are placed on hold, ask that you receive assistance promptly.

- 💜 **Scheduling appointments or meetings:** Ask the angels to assist you in getting an appointment with who you desire at a time that is convenient for those involved. If it is something that requires immediate attention, ask that there is an opening for you right away. When you go to your appointments, ask your angels to help you so when you arrive you get in and out promptly.

- 💜 **Help you see the truth in a situation:** This is helpful in situations where you feel someone is not being honest with you. Just ask the angels to help you see the truth in the situation and that person's intention.

- 💜 **Angels often assist us through people:** They do this by sending people into our lives to help us or to share our journey with. When angelic encounters with others occur, it is a gift for all involved.

I communicate with the angels all day long and ask for their assistance, and more often than not, my days are very peaceful, enjoyable, productive and synchronistic. I'm going to share with you a funny request that I made to the angels to show you that it doesn't matter what you ask for. If it is something you desire or something that will make your life easier, better or more comfortable, your request is answered.

My Request: When we first moved into our newly built home, over a few week period, I saw three scorpions, which I had never seen before in my life. Although I do believe every encounter is holy and I know the animal kingdom brings us messages from heaven, when I saw these scorpions, I was so afraid that at first I did not recognize the blessing in the experience. I was upset that they were in my house as it is quite challenging to gently put them outside without harming them or getting stung! After I calmed down and came to my senses, I knew it was a message from the angels so I looked up scorpion in the book, *Animal Wise,* by Ted Andrews, and it was very relevant to what was going on in my life at that time. I thanked the angels and the scorpion for the message. Because I do not like bugs, spiders, insects, snakes, etc. in my space, I asked the angels to bring me these messages in a non-physical way.

Answered Prayers: About a week later I was working at my desk and I had asked the angels for a sign about something I was working on. A few minutes later I felt a sensation of a spider crawling up my leg. I felt very calm and I knew right away it was not a physical spider. I reached down and touched my leg and chuckled as there was no physical spider, but I knew it was a sign from the angels trying to get my attention. Then I got up and looked up the message in *Animal Speaks* by Ted Andrews, and it brought so much clarity in what I was doing. I thanked the angels for bringing the message to me in a non-physical way. This was a much better experience. Since then, the messages I have received from insects, snakes, etc. have come in a non-physical way such as a sensation, in a dream or outdoors. For this I am very grateful!

NOURISHMENT FOR YOUR SOUL: Asking for angelic assistance creates miraculous outcomes and divine experiences.

FOOD FOR THOUGHT: I remember to ask for angelic assistance throughout my day and I am experiencing the magic the angels bring.

ANGEL WHISPERS

Receiving Angelic Messages

Everyone has these abilities to receive angelic guidance; some are more developed than others. You receive angelic messages through your inner senses of claircognizance, clairvoyance, clairaudience and clairsentience, which we previously discussed in chapter three. Sometimes you receive messages through more than one sense simultaneously. The way the messages come through is not as relevant as the importance that you do receive them. Here I share some examples of how I have received angelic guidance through each channel to increase your understanding.

This is an example of my clairvoyant abilities. As a child I saw the angels all the time, but as I grew up, I moved away from seeing them. My first visual spiritual experience as an adult occurred after I went to a group meditation. After the meditation, we were all given sunflower seeds to plant wherever we wanted. At the time my former husband and I owned a piece of land alongside my parent's property out in the country, where we intended to build our dream home. I chose to plant the seeds on our land. My friend Zanna went with me. We got out of the van and it was pitch dark. We had a flashlight but it wouldn't work so I left the headlights of my van on. I scattered the seeds across our lot and we proceeded to my parent's lot. Just as we walked around the pond toward my parent's future home site, the headlights on the van went off. It was so dark I almost jumped out of my skin! I grabbed for Zanna and said, "Lets go back to the van." She was calm and replied "Its okay, just relax. Let's finish what we came here to do." We continued on to my parent's lot and all of a sudden I saw this large white light shaped like an angel over a large clump of trees between our properties. I was amazed but a little nervous I must admit. I asked the angel to protect the land, us and anyone who enters there. Then I thanked the angel and said good-bye. The white light moved and looked as if the angel was waving. It was quite an amazing experience! This made me feel so peaceful because I knew the angels were watching over all of us. It was also very clear to me the flashlight and van lights went out so I could see this angel!

This example that I'm going to share with you is a message I received through my clairsentience and clairaudience. This happened when I was a teenager. I had gone to a drug store and as I drove past the front of the store to go to a parking space, I noticed a black car with dark tinted windows and I suddenly felt a sick feeling in the pit of my stomach. I immediately heard a loud voice that said, "Get out of here." At the time I did not question it. I just left and as I drove out of the parking lot, the feeling in my stomach went away. To this day I do not know what was happening at that store, but I knew I was not to be a part of it. I believe this was a situation in which my angels intervened to protect me.

Here is an example of a clairaudient message. One day as I was drying my hair, I was reflecting upon the activities of my life's purpose and how it was all fitting together, and I was feeling grateful for how the angels were helping me. Then I heard the sound of a doorbell. I knew it was not the physical doorbell so I thought it was the angels letting me know they were around me. I thanked them. I continued to dry my hair and I heard the angels say, "Answer the door." I have learned to listen and not question these messages so I went to the front door and opened it. There on my doorstep was the biggest, most beautiful butterfly I had ever seen and beside it lay three eggs. This was very relevant to what I was reflecting upon. Each egg represented a facet of my purpose and brought with it a message related to that aspect. It always amazes me the blessings that occur when we listen to the angels' guidance.

This book is an example of my claircognizant abilities since much of the wisdom came through my mind and out my hands before I even understood what was occurring. I knew this wealth of knowledge was coming through me not from me. Thank God for the teachings of Doreen Virtue, I have come to understand I was channeling ancient wisdom. When I say channeling, I am referring to being open for divine wisdom to flow through me. When we are in our natural state of love, we are open to the flow of divine love, light, truth and universal wisdom.

Ways in Which Angels Bring Us Messages and Signs

The Angels bring us messages and signs in many ways. The more aware we become, the more receptive we are to these messages. It always amazes me the creative ways in which these messages appear. Angelic messages generally come in three's. It has been my experience when I ask for a sign, the sign that comes is usually crystal clear the first time. You will see this reflected in my experiences below. May they serve as a guide to help you recognize messages and signs from your angels.

♥ **Books / Classes / People:** For about six months, I continued to hear the words "Akashic Records." I had no idea what that meant so I asked the angels for clarity. I was guided to read a few books and do some research, but it did not seem to give me what I was looking for. So I continued asking for clarity. At the time I had my Angel Therapy® practice and I was receiving guidance to record

Let LOVE Be, an affirmative song that I had channeled from the angels four years earlier and had been singing to myself and my children without music. Then one day I was in a friend's office and I saw a flyer on her bulletin board for Akashic Records Training that Jodi Lovoi, an Akashic Record Consultant and Teacher was presenting. I knew immediately this was what I was to do. So I came home and talked to my husband about it and we decided to take it together.

During the class, I found out that Jodi was a singer/songwriter and we purchased her music CD, *Rhythms of Life* and love it! I shared with Jodi I was being guided to record a song and that the angels had given me the words and tune but I knew absolutely nothing about music. She gave me the name of Parrot Track Studio where she recorded her CD here in Austin and told me that the owner/producer, George Coyne, would take good care of me. She was right! I went to see him with a cassette of me singing the words to my song and he listened to it and then recommended a musician who could write the music and play piano. As I walked into the studio for the first time, Floyd Domino was playing on the piano and it sounded so beautiful to me. I had chills all over me. I said, "Oh, that is beautiful, what are you playing?" He replied, "That's your song!" He was so patient and perfect for what I needed. He told me to just sing it the way I knew and he would follow me. This was such a blessing.

Although I had the passion and desire to record this song, with it came some big fear. Because of my fear, there were times that I doubted I could sing in front of anyone so I wanted to have Jodi sing it. The angels told me I could choose to do that but this song was my baby since I chose to be the messenger for it, and it reflects my teachings. I knew this in my heart and I really did want to deliver the message this song presents. Jodi worked with me in the records along with the angels and helped me to overcome the fear about recording it. She also gave me some voice coaching and was the "ghost singer" guiding me as I recorded it. When I went into the studio to do the final vocals, I called on all the music angels and archangels to help me. I wore my Archangel Michael pendant created by Doreen Virtue, around my neck. I had a Archangel Sandalphon pendant in my pocket and crystals in my shirt. I felt so relaxed and the words just flowed. I could feel the angels surrounding me and singing through me. It was an amazing experience to bring this song to life, and the healing that took place throughout the process. I am so grateful!

After the Akashic Records class, I was working in my records regularly, utilizing the method Jodi had taught me. One day I was sitting in my healing center at the table where I conduct private Angel Readings and Therapy Sessions, and I had used the Akashic Records sacred prayer to open my records. I asked the angels for guidance about finding an artist to design the cover of the CD for my song. Just as I finished asking for guidance, I looked up at a print of a painting called *Healing of the Nature Kingdom* I had purchased seven years earlier, knowing I would put it up in my healing center when I opened it. My eyes went directly to the artist's signature—Eva Sakmar-Sullivan. She is a very gifted visionary artist and her paintings are absolutely divine! I knew I was to contact her and although I had my doubts of finding her and being able to afford the artwork, I followed the angels' guidance and looked her up on the internet. I found her website which is www.stardolphin.com and I contacted her. When I called her we really connected and she is the sweetest person, truly an angel on this earth. The angels had given me a vision of the cover so I painted a very rough draft with my watercolors so she could fabricate it. Then I sent it to her. She sketched a rough draft and faxed it to me. We made a few minor adjustments and she painted it. When I received it, it took my breath away. It was so beautiful! I could feel so much love in it. You can see the results of her beautiful painting on the cover of this book, and my CD, *Let LOVE Be*. The day I received the artwork from Eva, I also received Doreen Virtue's *Daily Guidance from Your Angels Oracle Cards* from my supplier. To my surprise four of these cards have Eva's artwork on them. That interconnectedness continues to amaze me. I feel very blessed to have been guided to all of these divine people. Many of Eva's beautiful paintings are encompassed in this book. I had been communicating with Eva over the phone for the last few years as I was bringing this book to life. I was blessed to finally meet her in person when I went to Pittsburgh for family matters prior to wrapping up this book. She lives very close to where we were staying. My daughter and I had a wonderful time touring the city with her as she took us to the sights that my daughter wanted to see. We are blessed to have her in our life.

Angels and the Akashic Records: The Akashic Records, also known as the book of life, is a vast library where all of the information of our soul's journey is recorded. There are record keepers in the Hall of Akashic Records that record all events from the past, present and possible future related to our soul's journey. Everyone and everything exists within the Akashic Records and all universal wisdom comes from the Akashic Records from all realms such as angels, ascended masters, goddesses, spirit guides, animals, etc. There are different methods of accessing the information in this book of life. When you have psychic readings, angel readings or Akashic Record readings, all the information from these readings is retrieved from these Akashic Records. When you enter this vast space, it expands according to your level of awareness, so each time you go there you receive more and more knowledge. Spirit gives us the ideal possible outcome as things are in that moment. Nothing is written in stone. Everything changes minute by minute due to the thoughts, choices and actions we make. When we access these records, we retrieve the truths within our soul.

- **Signs / Billboards:** At a time when I was struggling with my decision to let go of private sessions and classes for a while so I could bring this book to life, I had asked the angels to please bring me clarity that I was making the right decision. I was on my way home from The Angel Store with my daughter and the traffic was at a stand still and backed up for miles on the highway, so I got off on the closest exit with which I was not familiar. I asked the angels to guide me to familiar territory so I could find my way home. As I was driving down a road, I saw a building with large purple letters that said, "Life is in your hands." Then I heard the following message: *"You are making the right choice to focus on your writing at this time. You are very passionate about writing and it is a large part of your life's purpose."*

- **Songs:** One day as I was getting ready to go over to someone's house to discuss a situation, I was feeling very nervous. I had a bad feeling in the pit of my stomach and I was arguing with myself over what to do. So I asked the angels to help me to feel calm and peaceful and to bring me a sign as to whether I was to discuss this situation at this time. As I was driving over to this person's house, I felt Mother Mary's presence around me. I began hearing the words, *"Let it be . . . Let it be . . . Let it be . . . Yeah, Let it be . . . Speaking words of wisdom, Let it be.* The title of the song is *Let it Be* by the Beatles. So when I got to this person's house I did not bring up the issue, I just let it go, and the next day my cell phone rang and it was this person. I heard Mother Mary say, *"Now is the time to discuss this situation."*

I felt a sense of peace about it, so I did discuss it and the situation had a great outcome!

♥ **License Plates:** One day as I was driving down the road I was thinking about my life's purpose and I was feeling a little overwhelmed with all the facets, so I asked the angels for clarity on what to focus on right now. A few minutes later I stopped at a red light and as I looked to my left there was a car waiting in the turn lane. It had a license plate on it with big red bold letters WRITR. That was a clear sign to me to focus on my writing. I thanked the angels for the sign.

♥ **Bumper Stickers:** For several months I had been working through a situation in my life that required forgiveness. I felt like it continuously came up for me and there were many layers of the onion to peel, so to speak. One day while I was running some errands, I was thinking about my situation and felt like it was complete so I asked the angels for a sign to show me that the situation had been healed. Driving home, I stopped at a red light and the car in front of me had a bumper sticker that said, "Perfectly Forgiven!"

♥ **Numbers:** I went through a period when the angels were bringing me messages in numbers. I would see the same numbers repetitively on my clocks, cell phone and even signs. At first, the numbers 444 kept showing up on my cell phone. I referred to the book, *Angel Numbers*, by Lynette Brown and Doreen Virtue, to see what the message was and it says, "Thousands of angels surround you at this moment, loving you and supporting you. You have a very strong connection with the angelic realm and are an earth angel yourself. You have nothing to fear—all is well." Later I began seeing 333 on my clocks and cell phone. The meaning of this message according to *Angel Numbers* is, "You've merged with the ascended masters, and they are working with you day and night—on many levels. They love, guide and protect you in all ways." More recently, as I was wrapping up this book, I kept seeing the numbers 777 on addresses, street signs and license plates. According to the book *Angel Numbers*, this is the message: "Congratulations! You've listened well to your divine guidance and put this wisdom into fruitful action. You are now reaping the rewards. Your success is inspiring, and helping others, so please keep up the good work." When you see the same numbers or sequence of numbers repetitively, three times or more, pay attention as these are messages from your angels. To interpret what the angel messages are, I encourage you to use the following guides.

ANGELIC TOOLS:
- *Healing with the Angels* by Doreen Virtue
- *Angel Numbers* by Doreen Virtue and Lynette Brown
- *Angel Numbers 101* by Doreen Virtue

- **Symbols:** When my husband and I were considering building a home, we asked the angels for their guidance. When we found the location, I asked for confirmation and as I closed my eyes I saw a symbol of a light bulb. The angels' told me that light was a symbol to let me know we were making the right decision.

- **Sayings on Shirts:** As I finished up working on this book for the day and prepared to go to FedEX/Kinkos to pick up my business cards for the expo I was exhibiting in that weekend, I heard an angelic voice say, "It's time to go now." So I stopped what I was doing and I went to FedEX/Kinkos. While driving there, I wondered why it was so important for me to go right then. None the less, I followed the guidance. As I walked up to the service counter, the person in front of me was wearing a shirt with a saying on it by the famous philosopher Confucius: "If your plan is for 10 years, plant trees, if your plan is for 20 years, plant rice, and if your plan is for 100 years, educate children." This was very relevant to me as a large part of my life's purpose involves working with teens and children in addition to guiding adults in healing the child within.

💜 **Other ways:** After receiving guidance to begin teaching classes the following messages came. One of my clients was paying for their angel reading with a credit card and I was processing it. On the card it said emerge which means rise up or come forth. Later that same day my son came up to me and showed me a teddy bear that he had gotten and the bear had a gold t-shirt on it that said get out there!

NOURISHMENT FOR YOUR SOUL: The angels bring us messages and signs in ways that we can understand them.

FOOD FOR THOUGHT: I AM open to receiving divine messages.

How to Communicate With Your Angels

We communicate with the angels through our inner senses of claircognizance, clairvoyance, clairaudience and clairsentience. Your angels are always around you however, they respect your choice of free will so you must ask for their assistance in order for them to help you. The only exception to that is in an emergency situation. If it is not your time to go, they will intervene without your permission.

💜 Communicating with the angels is the same as communicating with God. When we pray, God answers our prayers by sending angels. Communicate with your angels as if you were talking to your best friend. You can address your angels by name or until you become familiar with them you can just think or say, "Angels, whoever can help me with this situation please do so," and they are there.

💜 There are simple ways to communicate with your angels. You can do this quietly in your mind, by speaking aloud, through writing, visualizing a picture of an angel and ask for help, imagine feeling the sensation of the angels wings wrapped around you like a cozy blanket, or you can use any of Doreen Virtue's oracle card decks to open up your connection with your angels or to bring clarity or confirmation to you. Each oracle card deck contains a guide book that shows you how to use them and gives a description of the message each card brings. You will feel drawn to the one that has the guidance you need at that time. You can also carry these guide books in your purse or pocket. This keeps the energy of these spiritual beings with you and you can receive guidance at any time, anywhere by asking a question and opening the book up to whatever page you are guided to.

💜 Your angels communicate with you by giving you repetitive, loving, supportive, guidance and messages. When you receive guidance that you do not understand ask for clarity, a sign, or ask them to bring it to you in another way.

💜 When asking for angelic assistance it is best to ask for what you desire rather than telling them how to do it. When you let the angels assist you, the outcome will happen for the highest good of yourself and all concerned.

💜 After asking for their assistance, thank them knowing it is already taken care of. Trust and have faith they will answer your requests.

If you find yourself getting in the way by worrying or trying to figure things out, immediately thank the angels for taking care of the details and let the fear go. This gets you out of the way so the angels can work their magic.

NOURISHMENT FOR YOUR SOUL: As you ask for the angels' help with clear requests and intentions, you will receive clear guidance.

FOOD FOR THOUGHT: I AM receiving clear guidance that enlightens my life.

EXERCISE: GOING WITHIN

This exercise is for communicating with your angels through intuitive writing. It can be used to bring guidance and clarity regarding any area of your life. You may receive the messages in pictures, symbols, words, feelings or thoughts. It doesn't matter how you receive the messages. What is important is that you do receive them. Do not be concerned with what you are writing, or how much you receive, just allow the information to flow and write until you are finished. You will receive what you need.

1. Write down a question at the top of your paper.
2. Close your eyes, relax, take three or four deep breaths and quiet your mind.
3. Ask your angels to surround you and bring information regarding your question.
4. Focus on your question by repeating it mentally three or four times.
5. When the guidance begins coming forward, open your eyes and write down everything you receive.
6. When you are done, go back and read it. You will be amazed at the information that comes through.
7. Thank your angels for their guidance.

YOUR SPIRITUAL TEAM

GUIDELINES

- ♥ If you find you are not receiving any messages, take a few more deep breaths and continue to focus on your question.

- ♥ Trust that the information that comes forth is from your angels for you have set your intention and requested their help.

- ♥ The dialogue from the angels is different than the way we talk. The angels usually refer to us as you, your, dear child, your name or another label that resonates with you. If what you wrote down is written in I, me or my text, this is not the angels, unless they give you affirmations, poems, songs, prayers or quotes. If you find yourself getting in the way, call on Archangel Michael to help you get out of the way so you can receive your angels' messages.

- ♥ You can also ask several questions about one subject, however, I encourage you to focus on one question at a time, receive your answer and move to the next one to ensure clarity. An example could be wanting to know about your career and asking several questions relating to this.

- ♥ It is helpful to play some soft music to help you relax as this opens you up for the guidance to flow. I recommend any music by Peter Sterling as this invokes the angels, but any instrumental music that makes you feel good, calm and peaceful is helpful.

Angelic Progress Reports

After using intuitive writing for quite some time, I began receiving what I call progress reports from my angels and guides when I used this method. These loving and empowering messages brought great clarity. They were the pat on the back, the courage, clarity, support, motivation and inspiration I needed at that time. I always feel so much love, peace and gratitude after receiving an angelic progress report. You too can ask your angels for a progress report. To do this, simply follow the going within exercise and ask your angels to bring you guidance regarding your progress instead of asking a specific question. Here I share a few of my progress reports to show you what they are.

This progress report came to me as encouragement while I was bringing my dreams to life, to keep me moving forward and to help me understand the manifestation process.

Dear Child,

You see things so clearly about what you desire. You can experience and create those dreams one step at a time. You tend to want to give up when things do not happen right away. Manifestation is a process of steps in the physical to bring it to fruition. Intuitively you know manifestation can happen instantly. This is part of your magical abilities for in the realm of spirit thoughts are instantaneous. On the physical plane, earth energy is much denser than in the spiritual realm. Therefore, it takes time to come to form due to action needed and the aligning of the forces and energy. You are very wise yet young at heart which gives you the passion, motivation and determination to succeed and bring your dreams to life.

You know as you continue to use your internal resources and follow our guidance, you will accomplish the dreams within your heart and they will fly, for all dreams have wings and they always learn to fly from within first, and then they will soar on the earth plane. Be sure to spend lots of time out in nature as this is important for you. It replen-

ishes your energy and prevents stagnancy, and keeps the mind clear so you can hear our messages of love from your heart. These are the pieces of the puzzle that needed to come together for you in understanding manifestation on a conscious level. Your greatest challenge is sticking with longer projects as you become discouraged. Know this is a lesson for you in believing in your dreams no matter how far away they seem, and learning patience. The journey it takes to get there will be worth the wait as you experience your life blooming one day at a time. Enjoy this journey and you will know the keys to the kingdom. You are being guided by Jesus.

This progress report came from Archangel Michael when I was feeling stuck, struggling with fears created from my past, and afraid to move forward.

Dear Child,

You are blocking the flow to the next step in your life's work. It is time to release the fears; they no longer serve you. You know in your heart what is truth. Make some choices as to what you desire to do. Stand your ground; believe in yourself. The time has come for you to move forward in full faith that you are not alone. You have many angelic beings and ascended masters around you helping you break free from the ties that bind you to the past. Know that when you commit yourself to achieving your goals and take one step forward each day, you will conquer those obstacles and break free to the flow of life. You are learning to balance right now. You are also learning how to productively spend your freedom. Do the things you love, spend more time in nature, and exercise regularly so the energy and passion will come forward. Make a choice for forward movement. Work on that which flows. Continue to meditate and visualize daily. Continue to give gratitude. That's all for now my child. Do rest and be at peace with your life.

The following progress report came to me as encouragement to shine my light while I was bringing to life my CDs and this book.

Dear Child,

You have grown into that beautiful swan. Your book has shown the way. Your journey to love has taken time. This is so you could build a solid foundation for your teachings which you are doing by finishing your book. Continue to move forward as you are to bring this gift to life. It will greatly benefit many. Focus on your angelic tools as these are much needed at this time on the planet. You are a powerful lightworker and manifestor. Keep your focus on love and remember to go at a steady pace. There is much energy flowing as you do your life's work. You are bringing much information from heaven to earth. Remember to stay grounded and you'll be just fine.

This project (book) has been a great one and there have been times you've questioned yourself, the purpose and validation of this divine endeavor. Have confidence and know all is in divine order right here and right now. When it all comes together you will see. Please trust and continue to move forward with love and gratitude in your heart as you are. You vibrate at such a high vibration as you are a master teacher (you bring forth much ancient wisdom) on this earth plane. Do not lower your light for others. Continue to let yourself shine regardless of the opinions of others. This has been a tough lesson for you as you all desire approval. You are beginning to understand that approval comes from within . . .keep going. Go forth in love and peace and pace yourself.

Nameste'

Angelic Principles to Live By

Here are some of the most valuable lessons I have learned from the angels.

♥ Stay centered in your natural state of love. If I am feeling afraid, I ask them to help me to feel safe, secure and loved so I can stay centered in my natural state of love. If my thoughts are going off on a tangent of "what if's," I ask the angels to guide my thoughts so I can focus on the good and create the outcome I desire to experience. I have found that when things happen, instead of going into fear mode, I just call on the angels and ask for assistance. Miraculous solutions always occur, creating positive experiences.

♥ Our part in life is to decide what we desire and leave the how and details up to God and the angels. We just need to be clear about our intentions, put it out there, give it to God, ask for guidance and be open to receiving and following divine guidance, for the angels will lead the way. The outcomes are miraculous and fulfilling. This is an example of co-creating, the spiritual and physical working together. The energy of spirit which is love and the action in the physical of the human make things happen. The term manifestation is the process of bringing the energy of thought to physical existence and experience. When we retrieve information from our soul, we become consciously aware. This gives us the opportunity to manifest that which we desire because we are all one with and expressions of God.

♥ It has been my experience that God's timing and our timing are not always the same. In the angelic realm there is no time or space. Our job is to receive angelic guidance and apply it to our life where time and space do exist. Much of my life I have been "ahead of the world." With this gift came feelings of anxiety, that I have so much to do by a certain "time." The angels have assured me that all is in divine order and that I am where I am to be, doing what I am to be doing at the perfect time for my soul's growth. They also assure me that I will accomplish everything I am to accomplish and they will guide my way. They said it is important to have balance in my life, to move forward at a steady pace, doing what is in front of me, going with the flow, and each project will be completed in divine timing. This has helped me to feel more at ease and go with the flow rather than feel stressed over what I needed to accomplish according to earth time. There have been times when I have done certain things I felt guided to do and saw visions of the outcome, but it did not manifest right away. This was confusing for me. I would question why I was guided to do this or if it was truly divine guidance. The angels told me those steps were for planting the seeds of what was coming next. We do not always know why we are guided to do certain things as we do not always see the big picture. Sometimes our outcome is completely different than what we expected, however, it is always for the highest good of ourselves and all concerned when we ask for and follow angelic guidance. Following the angels' guidance and trusting that all is in divine order has brought me much peace and infinite blessings.

MESSAGES OF LOVE:

I heard this message in answer to my question: "Why do I feel like I'm always ahead of the world?"

YOUR SPIRITUAL TEAM

Dear Child,

You are moving along in divine timing according to universal laws. Sometimes it feels as though you are ahead of the world because you are a pioneer for new thoughts. You also have the ability to see the future through spiritual vision. Continue to move forward at a steady pace. It is time for your gifts to come forth, for you to share your wisdom, knowledge, gifts and talents with the world.

- ♥ There are things in life that happen and we may or may not know the "why." It is just life happening and some things in life remain a mystery. It is best to let them go and start anew as each day is a new beginning.

- ♥ Always choose love and you will have a much better outcome. Love is the answer to all questions, the solution to all challenges, and the greatest blessing on earth.

- ♥ God is your source. Outside sources such as others or jobs are not your source. Be open to receiving what God gives to you in whatever way it comes.

- ♥ Follow your own inner guidance for this is your greatest resource.

- ♥ There are times when I have been doing my earth activities and I begin receiving messages related to other things. I find this happens most often when I'm driving. When this occurs, I ask the angels to hold my messages that pertain to things other than what I am doing and give them to me at another time when I can be fully present to receive them. It is okay to do this. The angels do not take offense to this. This is your choice and your life.

- ♥ If you receive information about someone, ask your angels for clarity on whether you are to share it with them or if it is only for your own knowledge. If you are guided to share it, it is best to ask the person if they want the guidance before giving it to them. Ask your angels to guide you in delivering that message with clarity and love.

NOURISHMENT FOR YOUR SOUL: The choice is always yours. If you make a choice that doesn't give you the experience you desire, you can choose again and re-create. Ask the angels for their assistance. They will deliver on wings of love. Be open to receiving and recognizing these blessings.

FOOD FOR THOUGHT: I allow the angels' magic to be ever present and create miracles in my life now.

Angelic Blessings for You

"Inviting the angels into your life expedites your healing and transforms your life in miraculous ways!"

I have experienced and continue to experience many miracles and blessings in my life by inviting the angels to be a part of it. Having experienced this divine connection, I can not imagine my life without them! As you read this book you may feel more connected to your angels. May you choose to invite them into your life by asking for their assistance so you may experience the blessings this inner connection brings. Below I share with you some angelic blessings that inspired and empowered me. May they do the same for you!

💜 May you always focus on the truths within your soul, for all that's required to fulfill your mission is within you.

- ♥ May you always follow your heart, for it will guide your way, as it is the doorway to your soul.

- ♥ You are a beautiful person inside and out. You deserve all the happiness and joy you desire.

- ♥ You have gifts and talents to share with others to make this world a brighter place. You are a bright light on this planet . . . Let it shine.

- ♥ May your life be filled with divine experiences, opportunities and relationships! As you express the love that you are, that is exactly what you will attract and experience.

- ♥ The universe supports you in all your endeavors.

- ♥ You are a powerful creator . . . Create with love and watch your dreams come to life!

- ♥ A job without love is work. A job with love becomes service.

- ♥ May you always see beyond the illusion the truth and blessings in all situations and experiences.

- ♥ May you always choose to learn your lessons with love.

- ♥ You only need to know what you desire; we will take care of the how. Do what presents itself each day and we will guide your way.

- ♥ As you get out of your own way and allow us to assist you, your dreams and desires will manifest more quickly.

NOURISHMENT FOR YOUR SOUL: May the angels' presence fill your heart with love, your path with light and your life with angelic experiences!

FOOD FOR THOUGHT: Love is the main ingredient in the recipe of life. May you always experience and enjoy the infinite blessings love brings!

HEALING WITH THE NATURE KINGDOM
Celebrating our connection with the other realms that are part of our planet.

Fairies

Fairies are part of the angelic realm. They are the guardian angels of plants and animals. They are also known as nature spirits or elemental realm. You will find them outdoors around flowers, plants, trees and near water. You will also find them indoors around plants and animals. The fairies want you to know they are real and here to assist you. The more you are aware and believe in fairies, the more they can help you and our planet. For those of you who are passionate about the environment and animals, I encourage you to increase your awareness by connecting and communicating with the fairies. They will bring you messages on what you can do to help the environment and animals, and they will bring you messages about nurturing your inner child and allowing your true self to emerge. Fairies also help with manifesting.

I have a strong connection to the fairies and I receive many messages from them. I spend a lot of time out in nature at the Botanical Gardens and Zilker Park on Lady Bird Lake here in Austin. To me, this is heaven on earth in Austin. When I visit the botanical gardens I often take my journal with me so I can record the messages from these loving, joyful, lively, playful beings. I have found their loving messages to be very healing and inspiring. Although I have received many messages, I share these examples with you so you may recognize the speech and beautiful essence of the fairies.

MESSAGES FROM THE FAIRIES

COLORS OF LOVE

"I love to think of nature as an unlimited broadcasting system through which God speaks to us every hour, if we will only tune in."
—GEORGE WASHINGTON CARVER

YOUR JOURNEY TO LOVE

One day I went to the botanical gardens and I took my camera and journal with me. It was springtime and the flowers were beginning to bloom. I was guided to take pictures of the flowers and channel a message from the fairies. I had the pictures developed, laminated them and put the messages on the back, then I hung them in my office where they bloomed into the colors of love! These pictures bring in the color so I can enjoy the beauty of these flowers all year long and feel the essence of the fairies. I invite you to enjoy these colors of love for yourself.

These purple and pink pansies are a reflection of the deep spiritual roots inside of you, expanding out into the universe with much love.

White represents the purity of your mind, intentions and the angelic energy which is embedded in your soul.

The pink represents the love in your heart and the fuchsia represents the passion you have in bringing this love forth in your teachings, books and workshops.

This purple Iris represents your uniqueness. The different shades of purple represent the levels of awareness your spirituality is taking on in your teachings. Adults are deeper, teens keep lighter, and children focus on love.

These two purple flowers are a reflection of you and your husband walking hand-in-hand and heart-to-heart in service with spirit as your guide. This is coming to fruition; just be patient.

These peach and orange flowers represent the creativity that is alive within you. Allow this creativity to blend with your work as there is much passion to explore. The peach brings peace of mind. You have much creativity, so share this in your teachings. Let your creativity loose and you will experience the blessing of your dreams blooming from the seeds you've planted and nurtured. The yellow represents the compassion you so freely give to others. Give this to yourself as well.

These red flowers represent the life force within you that is flowing and blooming to new heights, in which you will soon feel more secure. You will be standing on solid ground as you implement these new endeavors into your life and see how they bloom as a result of the pure loving heart that you have. It also represents your strength and tenacity. You are very strong, courageous and you have physical and spiritual support to bring your dreams to life. It also represents success. This is all your teen teachings.

CONNECTING WITH THE FAIRIES

You communicate with the fairies the same as you do the angels. When I am walking, I often feel drawn to certain flowers. I walk up to them, smell their sweet fragrances, admire their beauty and breathe deeply. As I do this the fairies begin talking to me.

NOURISHMENT FOR YOUR SOUL: The fairies assist us in being playful, care-free and joyful. They show us how to allow our free spirits to come alive.

FOOD FOR THOUGHT: I easily hear the sweet gentle messages the fairies bring.

ANGELIC TOOLS:
- *Healing with the Fairies* by Doreen Virtue
- *Fairies 101* by Doreen Virtue
- *Healing with the Fairies Oracle Cards* by Doreen Virtue

Ascended Masters

Ascended Masters are great teachers and healers who are in the spirit world. You can call on them for assistance. Many of them have been on earth. Although there are many, you may be familiar with these masters: Jesus, Moses, Mother Mary, Saint Germain, Yogananda and Quan Yin.

NOURISHMENT FOR YOUR SOUL: The ascended masters can help you create the outlines for your classes and workshops, write books and get your teachings out to the world. They can give you healing techniques and assist you in any creative invention or inspirational endeavor. All you must do is ask and invite them into your life.

FOOD FOR THOUGHT: I AM open and receptive to receiving guidance from the ascended masters. I have merged with these powerful teachers and healers to be of service and bring my dreams to life.

ANGELIC TOOLS:
- *Archangels and Ascended Masters* book by Doreen Virtue
- *Ascended Masters Oracle Cards* by Doreen Virtue

MESSAGES FROM ASCENDED MASTERS

This is a message I received about following my heart.

This is Saint Germaine. Keep up the good work my child and move forward with grace. Continue to let your light shine through you and onto others. You inspire others with your courage, strength, compassion and loving power. Stay true to you always no matter what you do. Always follow your heart. The time will come for you to travel.

This is a message I received after my NDE as I was working through some of the fear associated with that experience.

Dear Child,

This is ancient wisdom you bring forth. These teachings are meant to be told, taught, shared, modeled and experienced. These are the blessings life brings to all of you on earth, the gift of experiencing heaven as you go through earth school. You all came to earth for your soul to learn lessons, grow and evolve. You can do this without struggle, pain and hardships. I'm here to show you this can be done with love, joy and peace. Pace yourself. Embrace the gifts. When one moves too quickly you can become scattered and lose focus on what's important and miss the greatest blessings. Remember, earth life is to be lived, experienced and enjoyed and it's blessings to be embraced with all your heart, for this is what helps the soul to grow. When you learn to go with the rhythms of life you will experience a balanced life. Do not fear death my child as it is not physical death, it is only transformation. This is a change in consciousness and situations. You and your loved ones have much work to do on this earth plane. You chose to come together for a long duration of time to work out issues and be an example to help others on your planet earth to heal and thrive. Go from survive to thrive. You are on your way. You have shifted out of survival mode. It is time to rise, shine and thrive, one day at a time by just being you!

Much love to you dear child for walking in my footsteps in love rather than pain, for there is much more to gain. Continue to shine your light each and every day by choosing to walk in the light yourself. This is the most powerful way to teach others. Your writings will also teach these principles. The truths in the scrolls you already know, are lessons in love. Your intuitive interpretations of these are very clear. Allow fear to subside and bring them forth. You have everything you require and desire to do this. Remember to go within from time to time to reflect upon these truths so you can bring them forth in your physical experience. I am always with you. I, along with many other light beings, will guide your way. You are never alone. Your path is clear. Follow the light, use your heart as a guide, let go of pride and be the beautiful free spirit that you are.

 Jesus

This was a progress report I received from Saint Germaine.

Dear Child,

You are making great progress. Your focused intentions are bringing your dreams to life. Keep moving forward one step at a time as you are with grace and ease. We are beside you supporting all of your endeavors. Fear no more. There is much good in store for you in the future. With each step you take and complete, it frees you up to focus your energy on the next step. We know you have done much work this year bringing forth your divine gifts. We are glad to see you taking some time to rest, relax and rejuvenate so you will be ready to move forward once again with a sense of renewal and replenishment of your energy. That is all for now. Go in peace.

Goddesses

Goddesses are beings of light who are the feminine aspect of God. They help us to nurture and recognize the feminine within ourself and bring in this energy on our planet earth to create balance. They are powerful and can assist us with many endeavors in our life.

As I was completing this book, I felt blocked and stressed due to the amount of time I was spending in front of my computer. I asked Goddess Kali to come into my dreams and remove all obstacles, fears, or anything that was preventing me from moving forward and completing this book. I thanked her. I went to bed that night with my crystals on my bedside table that I was guided to put there. I woke up the next morning and felt a shift in my consciousness. As I sat down at the computer to write, a sense of peace came over me.

Here is the message I received from Goddess Kali.

Today is a new beginning. You've asked for help and it is done. All obstacles have been removed. The doors are open wide for you to move through. You just needed to be willing to let the past go and embrace the newness in your life. This you have done. Blessings to you for walking this path, and sharing it with others. You are powerful and you can complete this endeavor with grace and ease, one step at a time. Take time to rest in-between and go outside and get some fresh air. This will keep your mind clear and your heart open as you write, and prevent you from feeling drained from the computer rays.

Saints

Saints are divine spiritual helpers who can assist us in all areas of our lives. Although they are recognized most in the catholic religion, they are not a specific denomination and will help anyone who calls on them.

Message from Saint Mother Teresa

Dear Child,

Your teachings are to reach the world. They will touch the hearts of all who come before you. Know that I am with you as you reach out to the children of this earth. Blessed be, love to all.

Message from Saint Francis

Dear Child,

Your love for the animals on this earth runs deep in your soul, deeper than you recognize. I am with all who ask for my assistance in helping the animals on this planet. Spread the word, and this love you have for these animals.

ANGELIC TOOLS:
- *Goddesses and Angels* by Doreen Virtue
- *Saints and Angels Oracle Cards* by Doreen Virtue
- *Goddess Guidance Oracle Cards* by Doreen Virtue

Spirit Guides

Spirit Guides are humans who have been on earth but are now in spirit form. They are available to assist us in our lives. They spend a lot of their time helping on the earth plane but they do attend classes and participate in other activities in the afterlife. Although they are at your side always to help and guide you, they respect your choice of free will and will not interfere or make all your decisions for you as you need to learn things on your own. Spirit Guides can be, but are not always, departed loved ones, who have gone through training for this in the afterlife. Sometimes they are relatives that we did not even know in this lifetime. Spirit guides usually appear in clothing we recognize and appear to us the way they looked on earth so we can identify them.

Here are a few messages I received from my spirit guides.

This is a female spirit guide I know as Harmonica. She looks to be of Swedish origin and has a headband around her head with long blonde hair.

> *Dear Powerful Lightworker,*
>
> *I am here to help you create balance and harmony in your life as you go out into the world with your teachings. Go forth with full faith, all will unfold. Let go of any worries you have. Harmony brings joy to your soul.*

This message comes from a male spirit guide who is one of my teachers known to me as Hakishima. He is dark-skinned, big and muscular. He is part of the team who assisted me with this book.

> *Dear Wise One,*
>
> *I am here to help you move forward and take action steps. These action steps will lead you to your dreams. Dream big and enjoy your journey!*

YOUR SPIRITUAL TEAM

Earthly Helpers

Animal Spirits

Animals are of the earth and bring messages from God. They show you your innate nature and help to bring this out in you. Like other spiritual beings, they can assist you in healing and creating your life. You have a power animal and totem animals around you that are part of your spiritual team of helpers.

💜 **Power Animals** are a specific animal which comes in at birth and walks beside you so to speak, throughout your life, similar to a guardian angel. You blend with the energy that your power animal carries. For example, my power animal is the swan. In metaphysics and according to the book, *Animal Speaks* by Ted Andrews, the swan teaches us to awaken to our inner beauty and power which is love. As you realize your true self, you acquire the ability to bring your spiritual desires to physical form through manifestation. It also teaches you how to see the inner beauty within yourself and others regardless of outer appearances. When you are capable of this you become a magnet to others. Swan energy helps you blend the spiritual and physical to create all that your heart desires. It teaches the mysteries of song, poetry, music and art for these touch the child and beauty within. Swan medicine also teaches you how to move through life with grace and ease. Throughout this book you can see how these spiritual characteristics are reflected in who I am and what I teach. I remember reading in one of Doreen Virtue's books how the angels and swans shape-shift. What this means is that at certain times they take on the form of one an-

223

other. Knowing this brings greater awareness for me. The angels are of the heavens and the swan is of the earth. Together they help us move through life with love, grace and ease.

💜 **Totem Animals** are other animals that are around you throughout your life. You can usually recognize these animal spirits by paying attention to the ones you feel drawn to or keep showing up in your life. You can call on any animal spirit to assist you in your life. I have been blessed with the gift of connecting with and communicating telepathically with the animals since I was a child. I find the animals messages to be inspiring and empowering. Although I have had many, here are a few examples of these communications to assist you in recognizing the speech of the animal kingdom.

MESSAGES FROM THE ANIMAL KINGDOM

During the process of writing this book, I had put it away for a while. One day as I sat in my office looking out the window, I asked the angels for a sign on what to do with this book. A few minutes later an eagle flew across the front of my window and this was the message I received.

Persistence, Perseverance and Patience

You are able to see from a higher perspective when your emotions are in perspective rather than in the way. When emotions are high the fears rise, when emotions are calm life flows.

I came to you today,
To show a brighter way,
To accomplishing your dreams in stride.
See the broader picture by looking inside,
For that is where the truth does lie.

Not beyond the sky,
But in your hands and heart,
It's time to start writing again.
For every dream has wings,
and it's time to let them fly.

Inside is where the truth lies beyond the fear and pain,
When you look inside you can see the truth once again,
And your fears will subside.
Go in peace and love, and
Enjoy your earth life of divine living.

The following communications took place at the Botanical Gardens and Zilker Park in Austin.

MESSAGE FROM A SWAN

Dear Beautiful One,

Your gentleness and grace touch all you meet and your positive outlook inspires others. You've learned to move through life with grace, pacing yourself to create a solid foundation and success in all you do. You've stuck your neck out many times in life, feeling as though you fell. You did not fall, you grew taller and your neck gained more strength to move on and connect the physical with the spiritual. When you have a stiff neck, think about moving with grace, letting go of the rigidity. Visualize yourself as a swan and flowing with spirit. This will release tension and help the energy to continue to flow. Swan energy also helps you walk your talk and sing your song—your soul's song which you are doing now. It's time to share all your gifts and talents with others. Let your light shine. Swan also teaches the importance of moving with grace and greater awareness as you are an instrument for God's love. This love shines through you to others, and others are attracted to the light you project. Remember to give thanks for all of your blessings no matter how small they may seem.

This crystal I received as a gift from a client of mine. It appears to be a Clear Quartz Crystal with Amethyst in it. Here is the message I received.

This crystal will help you by preventing you from having a heavy heart but rather a light heart, as you do now. Know and remember God is working in your life and no matter what the situation, have a light heart free from any burdens, for you are a loving child of God.

Your life is filled with rainbows. These are the gifts of love, joy, peace and being in your own power. Prosperity and abundance is yours now. This crystal holds Christ-energy. When feeling low, use this crystal to recharge. Place it upon your heart and breathe deeply, then place it upon the crown of your head and breathe, bringing energy through your body.

The amethyst within represents your divine consciousness, spiritual protection and connection. Anytime you desire pull from the energy of this crystal and you will experience the gifts within its make-up. This is a symbol of your energy. Your connection to spirit is very strong. You are always protected by the angels, archangels and ascended masters, and your mind functions in a divine consciousness state.

NOURISHMENT FOR YOUR SOUL: It is essential that you clear your crystals often as they absorb energy. To do this place them in sand overnight, place them in the sun for at least 4 hours, place them outside during a good rain or run them under water for at least 20 minutes. (This can be done conserving water by placing them on the floor or shelf inside the shower when you take one.) For my jewelry, the sand method is most convenient for me. When I went to the ocean, I brought home a bucket of sand from the beach and I place my stones in there overnight so they are available to wear the next day. The big crystals I have throughout my home I use the sunshine or rain method.

FOOD FOR THOUGHT: I easily tune into the wisdom of the earth.

ANGELIC TOOLS:
- *Crystal Therapy* by Doreen Virtue
- *Love is in the Earth* by Melody

INVITING IN THE ANIMAL AND CRYSTAL KINGDOMS

Calling on the animal and crystal kingdoms can be very beneficial to bring in the energy we need in our lives. Here are ways to do this.

- Ask them to help you by saying, "Dear _____, I invite you into my energy field to assist me with this process, situation, relationship, etc. or ask them to unite with you."

- Bring animals into your environment by putting pictures or statues of them in the helpful people corner (according to the bagua layout in Feng Shui) in your home or office. Bring crystals into your environment by placing them wherever you feel guided.

- You can carry crystals in a pouch around your neck or wear jewelry made out of natural crystals.

- You can also wear pendants of the animals to keep their energy around you.

I wear jewelry that is intuitively designed and created for me by Karen Hutchings of Cicada Creations. I just tell her what I desire to bring into my energy field and she tunes in and creates beautiful pieces with all natural stones.

WAYS TO GIVE GRATITUDE FOR THEIR ASSISTANCE

Here are some suggestions on how to give back to the animals and crystal kingdoms for their assistance.

- ♥ Thank them for their messages and assistance.
- ♥ Support the environment. Keep our earth green and clean by picking up litter, recycling, and using environmentally safe products.
- ♥ Send healing energy to animals or places on earth.
- ♥ Support a cause that speaks to your heart.

NOURISHMENT FOR YOUR SOUL: These other kingdoms bring messages from heaven to earth. These are internal messages. Our job is to understand the message and apply it to our life.

FOOD FOR THOUGHT: I gratefully accept the assistance, support and guidance available from other kingdoms and realms.

EARTHBOUND SPIRITS

Earthbound spirits are not members of our spiritual team. When we are surrounded by our spiritual team, there is a sense of knowing that we are safe, secure and loved. If at any time you feel an energy around you that does not feel comfortable to you, ask it to leave and call on Archangel Michael for assistance. Sometimes we become aware of the energy of earthbound spirits who haven't realized they have crossed over yet. If this should occur, do not be afraid, just know you are to assist them. They are not here to harm you, they want love just like the rest of us. The way we can help them is to do it with love rather than go into fear.

EXERCISE: ESCORTING EARTHBOUND SPIRITS TO THE LIGHT

1. Call on your angels and ask them to surround you in their divine white light.
2. Call on Archangel Michael and ask him to escort this soul to the light.
3. Light a candle. When you light a candle, lower vibrations of energy will leave.
4. Ask what this soul needs from you.
5. Send it love (pink light) and say, "I release you to the light to continue your soul's journey."
6. Visualize it ascending into the light.
7. Thank it for removing its presence from your space.
8. Thank your angels and Archangel Michael for their assistance.

PEACE RAINBOW
Celebrating our individuality and diversity yet Oneness of All.

CHAPTER 6
Reflections

REFLECTIONS

When looking at others, what I see,

Are merely reflections of aspects of me.

Within the universe you'll see,

Life mirrors to you,

All that you are, all that you do.

—*Bonnie Ann Lewis*

We Are All One

As spiritual beings we are all one. Every living being is an individual expression of God and spirit is our link, therefore we are all reflections of one another. Spirit is the life force in all of us which connects us to the divine. Although we are all interconnected, we express ourselves individually as humans with our unique talents and gifts, making us individual expressions of God, creating our own experiences based on how we choose to use our energy. When we are in our natural state of love, we are all one.

Everyone and everything is relevant in this journey we call life for our soul's growth. There are no "accidents," "coincidences" or "mistakes," only lessons reflected from our soul that help us learn, grow and evolve. Our life is a reflection of our relationship with ourself. The universe mirrors back to us through our relationships and experiences beliefs, aspects of ourself or areas that require healing. I believe this is a gift because it brings to our awareness what we are focusing our thoughts on and creating, giving us the opportunity to continue on in the direction we are going or change our course of action if we so desire. It is whether or not we pay attention to these reflections that we experience the blessings of these universal gifts, which bring us greater awareness about ourself and enrich our lives.

There are internal and external reflections to guide us in our lives. These reflections come in repetitions of three or more. Internal reflections are clear direct messages from God. These internal messages reflect to us our true self and the truths within our soul. Messages from other realms such as angels, archangels, goddesses, saints, spirit guides, ascended masters, fairies and other kingdoms such as animals and crystals are internal messages, and help us connect with our God-self, bringing messages from heaven to earth. These we do not need to filter as they are divine messages that come directly from God. External reflections can come from other people, books, songs, classes, internet, and so on. Although God speaks through all people, when we receive reflections from outer sources, due to our humanness these reflections require filtering on our part. Filtering gives us the opportunity to take what feels right to us and leave what does not, and make choices or take actions that reflect the truths within our own souls. Our soul speaks to us through our heart. It has been my experience if something resonates with me, than it is truth for me. If it does not resonate with me, then it is not truth for me. Growing up, I thought there was only one "right" way to do everything and one truth for us all. As I have evolved, I have come to understand what's right or truth for one may not be right or truth for another. We can discern what our truth is by going within so we can make choices based on our heart's desire.

These reflections are a blessing in that they reflect to us the truths within our soul or the lessons we came here to learn. They all have the same purpose of guiding us and giving us the opportunity to love. The reflections we receive are not good or bad, they are simply reflections. When we are aware and see these reflections for what they are without judgment, we experience their greatest blessings. For example, if you are driving and someone cuts you off, send that person loving thoughts. Maybe they did not see you or maybe they are in a hurry for a good reason. Give them the benefit of the doubt. If someone is driving slowly in front of you, thank them for slowing you down as perhaps that prevented you from getting a ticket or having an accident. Always look for the lesson and the blessings in each experience and thank the universe for the reflections it brings to you. As you become more aware of the reflections being presented to you, you can make changes to attract more of those experiences or repel them. It all begins within you. When you make changes from within, you will begin to see the results in your outer experiences and relationships. The following reflections will guide you in recognizing and embracing the gifts of these universal reflections.

Reflections of Your True Self

BEAUTIFUL YOU
A playful, flamboyant ball of light,
Filled with love that shines so bright,
Delivering messages from heaven to earth,
Modeling God's love since your birth.

Enjoying life, as lessons come and go,
Honoring the truths of what you know,
Free from influences of the outer world,
Experiencing life's blessings as you twirl,
Through the changes that come forth,
The gold in your heart measures your worth.

Embracing the love that's all around you,
And continues to grow,
In light you will walk, in darkness you will glow,
For the truths of life you surely know.

Take these gifts and share with others,
By just being you.
Whatever you choose to do,
There is no rhythm or rhyme,
To do it a certain way,
Just allow your heart to lead,
As you serve and play.

Remember to add exercise, mediation,
Time to reflect and pray,
Taking time for you and others,
Along the way.
For this is what makes the heart sing,
And you will surely experience,
The blessings life brings.

We are with you all the way,
Guiding you day to day.
The key to life is to enjoy,
Whatever comes your way,
And give gratitude for the blessings,
In each and every day.

—The Angels

Being Your True Self

"Spirit put the stamp of individuality upon itself and called it you."
—DR. ERNEST HOLMES

Your true self is who you are, your spiritual self, the part of you God created free from outside influences. Unconditional love is the essence of your true self. When you remember your true self, it is then you are aware of your connection to the universal energy and infinite resources of the universe. When you connect with this energy, you vibrate at a higher frequency. When you vibrate at a higher frequency, you experience clarity and love. The higher your vibration is the greater your awareness. The angels reflect to you your true self and assist you in being in your natural state of love. When you are in your natural state of love, your true self is present and your communication between the spiritual and physical are clear. When you are being your true self, your thoughts, feelings, words and actions are conducive to one another. This means one facilitates the other and all reflect one another.

♥ As your true self emerges, you will be shedding the illusions of fear that are blocking your true self from being present. You can do this by recognizing the difference between these two states of consciousness, your ego and your true self. You can use your heart as a guide for when you follow your heart you are allowing your true self to be present. The "job" of your true self is to release the fearful beliefs and shine through despite the fears. As you do this, you get in touch with, show up as, and express your true self.

♥ When you first begin identifying with your true self, you may feel like a yo-yo, but as you continue to work on distinguishing the difference between the illusions and your true self, the more you will understand the difference. You may notice you flip back and forth between these two "roles of consciousness," or states of mind if you will as your true self and ego argue with one another. Once you became more aware of who you really are, then you will feel more centered and begin to notice you spend most of your time in your natural state of love, being your true self. Know this is part of the awakening process.

♥ As you show up as your true self, your heart will lead you and you will experience inner happiness and success in your life. The ego is part of our human experience at this time on earth. However, as we all awaken to our true selves, the ego will be a memory of our past. The key is to honor both your ego and your true self and you will receive the benefits that both present. To acknowledge and recognize the ego, say, "Thank you for your opinion, but I'm choosing to follow my heart."

NOURISHMENT FOR YOUR SOUL: Being yourself is the greatest gift you give to yourself, others and the world. Be your natural self, express yourself with love and let your light shine!

FOOD FOR THOUGHT: I awaken to my true self with grace and ease. I love who I am and what I do.

MESSAGES OF LOVE:
When my true self was emerging, fear came up for me. There was a part of me that just wanted to be what others considered "normal" instead of what seemed weird to them for exhibiting my spiritual gifts. This is the message I received from the angels.

Dear Child,

Do not try to be "main stream," for that is not being who you are. Your great strength and spiritual understanding is to be shared. Your purpose is to blend heaven and earth by bringing these heavenly principles forth in a balanced, practical way. This will play a part in the creation of heaven here on earth. That's what swan teaches, the blending of heaven and earth.

Just go with what flows. You will be supported in spirit and people will be receptive to your teachings as you are so very loving, which they feel. The way you live your life is an example to them and they will want to know what your "secrets" are to a life of love and a love like your relationship with your husband.

THE EMERGING OF YOUR TRUE SELF INVOCATION

This invocation is designed to assist you in letting go of the illusions as your true self emerges. It will empower you to connect with your true essence so you can show up as the powerful being you are.

- I invite you to close your eyes. Take three or four deep breaths.

- As you breathe in, breathe in love. As you breathe out, let go of any illusions or shadows that are blocking your true self from emerging.

- Now I invite you to visualize your flame of divine white light which exists within the center of your being. This is the flame of your true essence.

- As you focus on your flame of divinity, allow it to expand throughout your body, radiating out into your aura that surrounds your body.

- Repeat after me, "Dear Angels, please assist me in staying connected with my true power and distinguish the difference between my ego and my true self. Please guide me to stay centered in my natural state of love and to show up as my true self. Please guide my thoughts, words and actions to reflect love. Thank you!"

- Affirm: My true self is fully present and I allow my light to shine. And so it is!

- May you always feel the essence of your true self and allow it to shine! You are beautiful!

Namaste'

NOTE: This meditation is found on my *Angelic Reflections I: Awakening* CD

The following inspiration crossed my path and touched my heart so I'm passing it along to you.

BE WHO YOU TRULY ARE

My dear friends, we love you so very much. Know that you are indeed in a time on earth where there is much change. You are all sorting through yourselves, working to figure out who you are and who you are not. Just as many are sorting through debris and disrupted lives, you are sorting through the beliefs you have used to define yourselves, trying to figure out exactly what resonates with you and what does not.

Dear ones, we wish you would stop trying to be someone other than who you are! Do not try to imitate those you see in the media or on spiritual "pedestals." Do not seek to emulate those you admire at the expense of your own truth. Instead, we beseech you simply to be the reality of who you are truthfully in any given moment. If you are upset, grieving, or fearful about something, do not try to pretend you are not.

Own the emotions and decide upon what you must do or say with the greatest compassion for yourself and all involved. Perhaps you need to reach out for comfort. Do so. To be authentic at these times is to allow yourself to connect more deeply with life.

If you are overwhelmed with joy, abundance or love, do not tone yourselves down to make those around you comfortable! Be the joy that you are and celebrate your life with abundant gratitude.

To be as happy as you really are is to serve as an inspiration for life. Wear what makes you happy, not necessarily the latest whims of the industry. Spend your free time doing what you truly enjoy, not necessarily what others say you should.

To express your own unique spirit authentically is to color your world beautifully. Find a way to worship and talk to God in a way that helps you feel more connected. This could be within a religion, a group of like-minded people, alone in nature, or even in the solitude of a peaceful place in your own home. God is everywhere dear ones. Find the place and time that helps you realize the connection that is already there. Finding a real and authentic connection to the divine makes you an ambassador for peace.

Dear ones, each one of you is a sparkle of God's beautiful light. Each one of you is unique, beautiful, special and loved in your own right.

We challenge you this week to find a few things very unique about you and to own them, express them and take delight in them. At the same time we ask you to look into the eyes of another and celebrate their uniqueness. You are precious gems, dear ones, each one of you colored and faceted by God, by love itself. Be who you truly are. We love you so very much!

—The Angels
Channeled by unknown

FROM THE HEART OF GOD

Reflections of Your Heart and Soul

"Follow the dreams of your heart to remember your magnificent true self."

Your soul speaks to you through your heart as your heart is the doorway to your soul. Within your heart exists desires, dreams and passions waiting to come to life. They are pure potential seeking manifestation. These desires, dreams and passions are clues to direct you toward your purpose here on earth.

♥ The things you loved as a child, love to do now, or the things you've always dreamed of doing are all associated with what you are meant to do here. That is why you have a passion for them. Desire and passion are messages from your soul. Your uniqueness, individuality and strength can assist you in effectively fulfilling your life's mission. As you discover your talents, you can use them to guide you in the direction that you desire to go.

♥ You may have some passions you act upon that are there for a while in your life and then move on. They were simply stepping stones but you will have other passions that stay with you throughout your lifetime. Your talents, dreams and goals will grow and change with age. You deserve to be who you are, acquire all that you desire and experience your dreams as you fulfill your life's mission. Dreams are fulfilled with the presence of God. When you have desires, this is God talking to you. Desire means to want something with all your heart and with good intentions. Your intent must be that of truth, love, purity and for the highest good of all concerned, not based on selfish motives or at the expense of others.

♥ You have the power to be all that you desire to be, experience and acquire. You must first know what your desires are before the universe can fulfill these desires. When you connect to your true self, you uncover what your desires are. I encourage you to discover, explore, create and enjoy bringing these desires to life. The search for your desires begins!

NOURISHMENT FOR YOUR SOUL: *"He who cherishes a beautiful vision, a lofty ideal in his heart, will one day realize it."* —James Allen

FOOD FOR THOUGHT: *"Plant the seed of desire in your mind and it forms a nucleus with power to attract to itself everything needed for its fulfillment."* —Robert Collier

EXERCISE: EXPLORING YOUR DESIRES

This exercise will assist you in bringing forth the activities that are part of your life's purpose.

When you think back to when you were a child and reflect upon your desires, it can give you clues to your life's mission. As a child you are more in tune with your sense of knowing and more aware of what you came here to do. As you grow up and have life experiences, you tend to get distracted or disconnected due to outside influences. Here are some questions to reflect upon and record your answers.

1. What activities did you enjoy doing as a child?
2. What did you want to be when you grew up?
3. What were your interests or hobbies?
4. What did you dream about doing?

NOURISHMENT FOR YOUR SOUL: *"Remembering your past is the foundation for creating your future."* —Bonnie Ann Lewis

FOOD FOR THOUGHT: It is safe for me to remember my past and see my future clearly so that I can create it.

EXERCISE: CHARACTER DESIRES
I AM . . .

This exercise will help you to focus on your true characteristics, and claim them for yourself as your true self emerges. The characteristics that you desire in yourself are already there. They just need to be recognized so they become present as part of your physical reality and experience.

1. At the top of your paper write your name.
2. Then make a list of characteristics you desire in yourself and all you desire to become (it is helpful to think about the people who have characteristics you admire in them, or what people do for a living that you admire or inspires you, to help you with this exercise).
3. Go through each characteristic on your list and create an affirmation beginning with I AM _____. *I AM* is the most powerful way to start an affirmation as that is your individual inner power.
4. Look in the mirror, into your eyes, and recite these affirmations frequently.

Here is an example: I desire to be a published author. I AM passionate about helping others and it brings me great joy. I AM a successful published author.

NOURISHMENT FOR YOUR SOUL: You've just created some powerful affirmations for becoming who you desire to be. Enjoy the process as your true self emerges!

FOOD FOR THOUGHT: I have confidence in my performance and I AM the best that I can be.

EXERCISE: I DESIRE TO EXPERIENCE . . .

This exercise will bring forward fears or blockages that are preventing you from achieving your desires. It will also help you discern if it is a blockage or if it is just divine timing. For this exercise, you will need a red and green pen.

1. Make a statement of activities beginning with "I desire" that you enjoy or have always dreamed of doing, and why you like to do them or want to do them. Ask yourself, "How do I feel when I think about or do these?" and "What do these activities give me?"
2. Then go through each item and put a green check next to the activities that you feel you can do now.
3. Put a red check mark next to the ones you feel you cannot do in this moment and why.
4. Then, on all your desires, cross out I desire and write above, next to or below it an affirmative statement. Begin statements with I now have _____, I now experience _____, I AM _____, I now enjoy _____, I see _____, etc. By creating an affirmative statement, it shifts the energy and opens the flow for these desires to come into your life.

Here is an example: I desire to go bicycling. It gives me a sense of freedom and serenity. I am now enjoying my bicycling activities.

NOURISHMENT FOR YOUR SOUL: You have just created some affirmations you can use to manifest your desires.

FOOD FOR THOUGHT: I AM experiencing all that I desire to experience in every moment.

EXERCISE: I DESIRE TO ACQUIRE . . .

This exercise will assist you in bringing forth the items you require and desire as you fulfill your life's mission.

1. Make a list of items you desire to acquire, why you want them, and what that item will bring you. Be very honest with yourself. This will bring clarity to any underlying issues relating to your shadow versus true self, so that you can modify them if you so desire. If your reason for this desired item is for an outside purpose such as to impress someone else or make you feel important, then you will want to look at what is missing inside of you for which you feel this item will fill the void.
2. Go through your list and put a star by the ones you feel are out of your reach, and a star with a circle around it next to the ones you feel are within your reach.
3. Go through each one you feel is out of your reach and state why you think this.
4. Then create an affirmation that reflects the opposite of why you felt it was out of your reach. This helps shift the energy to remove obstacles.

NOURISHMENT FOR YOUR SOUL: You have just created some powerful affirmations to assist you in reaching for those stars!

FOOD FOR THOUGHT: My desires are present in my life now and I AM living my dreams.

Now that you have explored and discovered your desires, created affirmations to bring these desires and dreams to life, it is time to take action! On a clean piece of paper, make a list of the action steps you can take now toward each desire. You've just created a list of divine activities and goals for yourself to achieve these desires. Give thanks for these desires being present in your life now.

SEEDS OF LOVE

This meditation is designed to activate your personal power to bring your desires to life.

- I invite you to close your eyes and just relax, relax, relax.
- Take three or four deep breaths and as you breathe in, breathe in love, and as you breathe out, breathe out any fears or concerns you may have about bringing your dreams and desires to life.
- Now visualize a silver thread extending from the heavens, entering through your crown at the top of your head and extending down through the center of your body, connecting into the earth beneath your feet.
- Take a few minutes to focus on your dreams and desires.
- Pause.
- Feel the passion in your heart that feeds these dreams and desires. Just be in this space for a few moments.
- Pause.
- Now visualize a yellow ball in the center of your stomach where your belly button is; this is your power center. This yellow ball is filled with the seeds that you planted in your mind and feel within your heart. See this yellow ball move down the silver thread and into the earth beneath your feet. As this ball sinks into the earth, it is illuminated with white light and expands, scattering seeds throughout the earth.
- Now visualize these seeds taking root and see a plant sprouting from the ground. As it begins to grow from the seeds it forms a beautiful yellow flower.

- This yellow flower represents your personal power and the seeds you planted will continue to grow and bloom in your life.

- Feel the joy and gratitude of experiencing these dreams and desires now.

- Pause.

- Give thanks to the heavens and earth for their support.

- Affirm: All of my loving power is activated bringing my dreams and desires to life. And so it is!

May the seeds of love you planted continue to grow into beautiful experiences for you!

Namaste'

NOTE: This meditation is found on my *Angelic Reflections II: Tides of Abundance* CD

EXERCISE: EXPANDING YOUR DESIRES: DISCOVERING YOUR GIFTS, TALENTS AND LIFE'S MISSION

Now let's go another step further and reflect upon the jobs you've had in the past. The reason is that these jobs have given you skills and have been stepping stones to prepare you for the next steps of your life's mission.

1. What skills or talents have you developed throughout your life?
2. What jobs do you admire that people have?
3. What jobs have you had in the past?
4. What aspects of those jobs did you enjoy the most?
5. What were the blessings that you received from those jobs, the people you worked with, etc.?

NOURISHMENT FOR YOUR SOUL: No matter how much you disliked your previous jobs, they served a purpose in your life.

FOOD FOR THOUGHT: *"Find something you love to do and you will never have to work a day in your life."* —Harvey MacKay

---

OPENING THE GATES TO YOUR SOUL MEDITATION

This meditation is designed to help you release fears and retrieve information regarding your life's purpose through a process called automatic writing, so you can make it a part of your life experience. When you open the gates to your soul you become aware of what's inside waiting to come alive!

Before beginning, I recommend that you write down the following questions on a piece of paper or in your journal, allowing space in-between to record the information you receive. What is my purpose here? Do I have a global mission in addition to a personal mission? If so, what is it? What am I to know regarding my life's mission now? What action steps can I take now? After each question you will be given time to record your answers. When doing this meditation, do not be concerned with what you are writing or about how much or how little comes through, just allow it to flow and know you will receive what you need.

Let's begin.

- I invite you to close your eyes, clear your mind by focusing on the music.

- Take three or four deep breaths. With each breath allow yourself to feel more and more relaxed, relax . . . relax.

- Repeat after me, "Dear Angels and Archangel Michael, please help me to release any fears or blockages preventing me from knowing or fulfilling my life's purpose. Please open the gates to my soul and bring forth information that will bring clarity to what my purpose and mission is in this lifetime. Please bring it to me in a way that I can understand it clearly."

- Affirm: I AM open and receptive to receiving guidance regarding my life's purpose and I AM ready for it to come forth now. It is safe for me to know my life's purpose. It is safe for me to see the past, present and future clearly.

- All of the information needed to fulfill your life's mission is within you. Let's bring this wisdom forth.

- Now I invite you to focus on your first question by repeating silently three or four times, "What is my purpose here?"

- Remember to continue to breathe deeply, be still and listen. As soon as the information begins coming through, open your eyes and record everything you receive.

- Pause while you retrieve this information.

- Close your eyes. Take a few deep breaths. Let's proceed with your next question by repeating silently three or four times, "Do I have a global mission in addition to a personal mission? If so, what is it?"

- Be still and listen. As soon as the information begins coming through, open your eyes and record everything you receive.

- Pause while you retrieve this information.

- Close your eyes. Take a few deep breaths. Let's proceed with your next question by repeating silently three or four times, "What am I to know regarding my life's mission?"

- Be still and listen. As soon as the information begins coming through, open your eyes and record everything you receive.

- Pause while you retrieve this information.

- Once again close your eyes. Take a few deep breaths. Let's proceed with your next question by repeating silently three or four times, "What action steps can I take toward my life's mission now?"

- Be still and listen. As soon as the information begins coming through, open your eyes and record everything you receive.

- Pause while you retrieve this information.

- Now thank your angels and Archangel Michael for the information. When you go back and read it you will be amazed at the clarity that came through for you.

- Now ask for universal support by saying, "Dear Universe, please provide me with all that I desire and require to accomplish my life's mission, and support all of my endeavors." Send thanks to the universe, knowing all of your endeavors are divinely guided, supported and orchestrated.

May you always have clarity and universal support as you fulfill your life's mission. Love and Light!

NOTE: This meditation is found on my *Angelic Reflections I: Awakening* CD

Inner Happiness

WITHIN

To find inner happiness one must look within,
Communicating with your soul is where to begin,
To explore your desires, life's purpose and truths,
And discover the wonders of your youth.

—*Bonnie Ann Lewis*

Happiness comes from being in our natural state of love, therefore it comes from within and not from outside sources. Many look to others or material things to make them happy. We think if we have everything we want—the perfect job, home, car, relationships, money and so on we will be happy. Although others may bring much joy into our life or do things that make us feel happy, they are not the source of our happiness, we are. We are the only ones responsible for our inner happiness or unhappiness for that matter. It all begins within us.

In truth, when you love yourself, show up as the love that you are, and follow your passion and purpose, you will experience inner happiness. You must choose to be happy in the moment or happiness will always be one step ahead of you. When you are happy with what you have and where you are in the moment, you will know true happiness. When you are happy, your life experiences will reflect this happiness.

NOURISHMENT FOR YOUR SOUL: When your thoughts, feelings, words and actions are in alignment with each other, you will experience true happiness. Feel the essence of inner happiness flowing within you. Happiness is a state of mind. If you make happiness a priority now, you will always experience it. Happiness leads to your path of success.

FOOD FOR THOUGHT: I AM experiencing happiness in my life now.

EXERCISE: INNER HAPPINESS

Inner happiness has a different meaning to all of us. In order to achieve inner happiness, we must first recognize what it means to us. We achieve inner happiness through self-awareness and unconditional love. To determine what inner happiness means to you, reflect upon the following questions: What does inner happiness mean to me? What thoughts, visions and feelings come to me when I reflect upon inner happiness? Make a list of what you feel brings you inner happiness, and create affirmations to reflect this list. Use this as a guide to achieving inner happiness in your life.

Success

"When we invite love into our lives, the doors to success open wide."

Everyone wants to be successful. Due to fear we do not always take the steps we need to create success in our lives. When we become more in tune to our own desires, that inner voice inside of us, our intuition, we can overcome the fear that causes barriers to forward movement. What's most important is that we define and align with success according to our own definition. Here are a few quotes from others about success.

"Success is . . . the natural result (beauty) of man's co-creation with God."
—MARIANNE WILLIAMSON

"The key to success is to regularly represent your experience in ways that support you in producing even greater results for yourself and others."
—THOMAS KINKADE

"Those who succeed are committed to changing and being flexible until they create their desire or the life they desire to live."
—ANTHONY ROBBINS

NOURISHMENT FOR YOUR SOUL: Rather than using your energy worrying about how you are going to succeed, visualize yourself succeeding in everything you do and you will succeed.

FOOD FOR THOUGHT: I experience success and prosper every moment of my life.

EXERCISE: SUCCESS

Success has a different meaning to all of us. In order to create success in our lives, we must first recognize what it means to us. To determine what success means to you, reflect upon the following questions: What does success mean to me? What thoughts come to mind when I think of a successful person and a successful life? Make a list, create affirmations to reflect your list and use these as a guide in achieving success.

Reflections of Your Dreams

"All human beings are also dream beings. Dreaming ties all of mankind together." —BERNARD EDMONDS

Dreams are a great way to receive messages and bring clarity to your life. They are guideposts showing you where you are in your life and can serve several purposes. They may be progress reports, reflecting to you where you have been, where you are headed or what you need to do about a situation. They may show you what is in your subconscious mind so you can see what you are creating. They may show the communication between your true self and ego. They may also review daily events so you can process them, or they can help you work through fears and unresolved emotions. If you have fearful dreams or nightmares, this is your body's way of bringing these fears to your attention, resolving conflict, and releasing them so healing can occur.

When working with your dreams it is very helpful to use a dream journal and date each page since dreams sometimes come in pieces and your clarity may come over several consecutive nights. I like to think of interpreting dreams as putting together a puzzle. Each night you get a piece, so recording their meaning is helpful in putting the pieces together and seeing the whole picture. Interpreting your dreams can be a complex process. However, I am sharing with you the simplicity that the angels gave me in understanding my own dreams.

Inviting the Angels Into Your Dreams

Inviting the angels into your dreams brings great clarity and healing. When I first invited the angels into my dreams I just asked them to please bring me guidance through my dreams. I began having dreams and waking up several times throughout the night remembering them, but in the morning I would wake up tired and feel like I had traveled all night. So then I asked my angels to help me have a deep sleep, and bring me messages through my dreams that I would remember upon awakening in the morning. This worked much better! This was a lesson for me in being specific when asking for assistance. When you invite the angels into your dreams, you may wake up with a sense of knowing the angels were doing a healing on you and bringing you messages while you were sleeping.

- ♥ Write down a question(s) or subject you would like clarity on at the top of a piece of paper (focus on one subject at a time to ensure clarity).

- ♥ Before going to sleep, invite the angels into your dreams by asking them to bring to you the answer for whatever you want clarity on through your dreams, and to bring it clearly in a way that you can understand it and to help you remember these dreams upon awakening.

- ♥ Repeat the question three times in your mind or out loud and focus on this question as you fall asleep. You can even put the piece of paper with the question on it under your pillow or on your bedside table.

Recording Your Dreams

It is best to write your interpretation down as soon as you awaken for this is when they are the clearest and you will recall the most.

- ♥ Upon awakening, in one color ink, record everything you can remember about your dream even if it doesn't seem relevant or make sense. Make sure to record as much detail as possible.

- ♥ Then in a different color ink write what the dream means to you at that moment and what messages are within the dreams.

- ♥ Review your dream journal from time to time so that you can put the pieces together to create the whole puzzle.

- ♥ Thank the angels for helping you remember and interpret the messages within your dream.

NOURISHMENT FOR YOUR SOUL: Do not be too concerned if you do not remember your whole dream upon awakening, as it is recorded in your subconscious mind, and when you reflect upon parts of your dream, your subconscious mind replays the whole dream so you may recall more later. I have found when I re-read dreams at a later time, they sometimes bring more clarity to me of what the message of the dream is.

Guidelines on Interpreting Your Dreams

- ♥ The most important lesson I have learned from working with my dreams is that in interpreting them, it is best to go with what feels

USING VISUALIZATIONS

When you reflect upon your dream, instead of replaying it in your mind as it was, visualize it to be the way you desire it to be, or seeing the conflict resolved, the relationship healed, or whatever it is. Allow yourself to feel the joy of the situation being the way you desire it to be and feel a sense of peace knowing it is all taken care of. Ask your angels to intervene and to help you transform the fear into love, or assist you in manifesting your desired outcome. Thank your angels for their assistance.

USING CREATIVE WRITING METHOD

When you awaken, instead of recording your dream as it was, write down your dream the way you desire it to be. This creative writing process is very powerful and effective because it shifts your consciousness immediately.

NOURISHMENT FOR YOUR SOUL: Remembering and understanding your dreams will guide you through life. Working with dreams takes patience and persistence, however the outcome brings greater awareness and enlightenment.

FOOD FOR THOUGHT: I interpret and understand my dreams with clarity and ease.

Reflections from Your Body

Your body is also a mirror to you and communicates to you in many ways. Your thoughts are a reflection of your beliefs, your feelings are a reflection of your thoughts, and your emotions are a reflection of your feelings. Physical conditions are a reflection of your thoughts, feelings and emotions. When we have feelings and emotions these are messages from our inner child, and our body telling us what is going on inside of us. There are many feelings and emotions but they all stem from your state of mind and there are only two states of mind—love and fear. Your body communicates with you its needs and desires through your feelings, emotions, physical conditions, addictions, behaviors and even food cravings. When you view these reflections as messages without judgment and listen to what your body is trying to tell you, it will always bring greater awareness, healing and spiritual growth. Your body is a miraculous communicator filled with wisdom and is a powerful healer. All you need to do is take the time to listen to its messages and ask for assistance from God, and the angels and miracles will occur.

Our body also reacts to what we put into it. For example, if we eat something that doesn't agree with our body, we may have a reaction such as an upset stomach, or digestive ailments. If we put chemicals on our body that are not complimentary to it, our body may react with skin conditions such as a rash, hives or itching. If we put mood-altering substances into our body, it may react through behaviors. These are ways our body communicates with us to get our attention when something is not compatible to it or our emotional needs are not met.

Physical conditions, addictions and behaviors are nothing more than our body communicating with us to let us know of unfulfilled emotional needs. They are messages to show us areas of our lives that need attention and more love. They are not a part of who we are. They are created by fear and take us out of our natural state of love, making us feel disconnected from ourselves, life and God.

An addiction is any person or thing that one uses as a crutch to fill an emotional need, get through life, to help the pain go away, or to falsely make your life fulfilled. This is the way that society has been taught to fill the voids—from outer sources rather than within. You are the only one who can make your life fulfilled. The responsibility is yours. Addictions show up in many forms such as: alcohol, drugs, caffeine, nicotine, obsessions, food, etc., and they affect your body and life in unhealthy ways. They lessen your senses by blocking the receptivity of your body as well as your higher self, and cause you to disconnect from yourself, reality and life.

People often participate in these unhealthy behaviors to escape the pain of what they are experiencing in life, in order to feel comforted. Yes, it may take care of the pain temporarily, but it does not get to the core of the issue, and many times creates other unhealthy situations. A healthier way to fill these voids is to tune into the messages your body is giving you. These "voids" can be filled with love and healed naturally from within by getting to the heart of the matter. When you recognize the messages your body is giving you and understand the truth of the matter, the condition will heal itself. We will discuss this in Part II, The Power of Love, which will provide you with the angelic recipes to heal these unfulfilled emotional needs from the inside out by getting to the heart of the matter.

Reflections from Relationships

EVERY ENCOUNTER IS HOLY

"When you meet anyone, remember it is a holy encounter.
As you see him you will see yourself.
As you treat him you will treat yourself.
As you think of him you will think of yourself.
Never forget this, for in him you will find yourself or lose yourself."

—Course in Miracles

Every person who crosses our path we have chosen to be in our life and holds a gift for us. As energetic beings we attract people into our lives that mirror aspects of ourselves or because there was a soul contract made prior to our incarnation. On a soul level we are all interconnected, however, in our physical existence as humans, we have the choice of free will and we choose to show up and use our energy in different ways. The way you use your energy and the actions you take are about you. Others actions are about them. When others are hurtful, we can have compassion and choose to see beyond that behavior the light within them rather than judge them because underneath they are hurting when they act in hurtful ways. If we judge them, by putting energy into what they have done or play a part in their drama by seeing them as a victim, we are participating in creating more of that energy. This does not serve either person. As we detach without judgment from what they have done and see the good in them, we are reflecting back to them their true self so they can heal. This helps us all learn and grow with love. As we see past the personalities of other people to their true self we find ourself. When we judge them, we lose ourself.

The characteristics we see in others are mirrors of our own thoughts, feelings, emotions or beliefs. When you see characteristics in another that you admire, it is something that already exists within yourself that you recognize or desire to bring forth. You can create an affirmation to bring that characteristic forward into your life experience. Thank this person for the reflection if appropriate. If not, send gratitude energetically to them. When you see characteristics in another person that are undesirable, that push your buttons or trigger emotion within you, then this is an aspect of yourself that requires healing. When this occurs you can create an affirmation for the opposite of that so you can change that part of yourself that attracted and participates in that energy. As you change this within, your outer experiences will reflect these changes and you will no longer be affected by those people or attract those situations.

NOURISHMENT FOR YOUR SOUL: Everyone you meet has a gift for you. Look for that gift and you will always be blessed!

FOOD FOR THOUGHT:

I honor the place in you in which the entire universe dwells. I honor the place in you which is of love, truth, light and peace. When you are in that place in you, and I am in that place in me, we are one. And so it is! Amen.

— *Namaste' Greeting, Hindu form*

EXERCISE: RELATIONSHIP REFLECTIONS

Make a list of people in your life and what they are reflecting to you. Here are some questions to reflect upon to recognize what the gift is for you.

1. What is my lesson or responsibility with this person?

2. Is this person reflecting to me an aspect of myself that requires healing?
3. Is this person reflecting something I desire to change?
4. Is this person reflecting to me things I'd like to do, have or be?
5. Is this person reflecting to me how I do not want to be or what I do not want?
6. Is this person in my life so I can assist them along their path by sharing my wisdom?

NOURISHMENT FOR YOUR SOUL: When someone crosses our path it is relevant. Our job is to discern what relates and resonates with us and what does not.

FOOD FOR THOUGHT: I see and embrace the gifts from all of my interactions with others.

What's Yours, What's Not

When we have encounters with others due to a soul contract, sometimes we have similar vibrations and it is a pleasant encounter and sometimes it's like oil and vinegar, we just don't mix because our vibrations are different. When you have interactions with other people, not everything is about you or for you. Learning to discern what relates to you is essential for you to know where you are allowing your energy to be focused and what kind of energy you choose to participate in. When you are aware of your energy field it helps you to disconnect from the drama in other people's lives. As you do this, you take responsibility for your part in each situation and allow others to take responsibility for theirs. When you reflect to others it is essential to detach from the outcome, or any judgment, and allow them the freedom to do whatever they choose with the information. To clarify whether something is about you or not, here are some guidelines to follow.

- ♥ When something is happening in your life and you are having an experience or relating to a person, it is about you. When you see or hear something happening in another's life, that is part of their experience, not yours. You are simply an observer. When this happens, you have chosen to be an observer of that experience for a reason. Ask your angels for guidance on what your purpose is in that situation. This can simply be an opportunity for you to have compassion and send love to that person or situation without absorbing the energy. Instead, say to yourself, "I do not choose to experience this situation," or "That is not truth for me." Then ask your angels to release the energy associated with it. This allows you to observe without absorbing the energy and attracting that experience for yourself.

- ♥ The opinions of others are not about you, they are only their perception of who you are. Do not take it personally. However, if it bothers you or you have an emotional attachment to it then that part is about you and there is a lesson for you. Your job will be to reflect upon why it bothers you so healing can take place. For example, if someone says something to or about you that places judgment, you can choose to accept it as truth or not. Instead of identifying with it, mentally say to yourself, "That is not my truth." Affirm: I am loving and loved or whatever your truth is in that situation. What is most important is what you believe about yourself.

- ♥ When you see characteristics in another that you have no attachment to and are in a place of neutrality, then that is about them not you.

♥ When someone is behaving unkindly, realize it has nothing to do with you. If someone is angry with you that is an indication they are afraid or angry at themselves. When you let go of the need to take things personally, you detach from the emotions of fear, guilt, and blame of other people. When you detach with compassion from other peoples lessons, you allow them to be accountable for their experiences and you take responsibility for yours. You are not responsible for the feelings of others, their actions or experiences. It is a reflection of the way they feel inside. The way other individuals choose to express themselves and their experiences are about them, not you. If their behavior affects you, there is a lesson for you. If something is bothering another person, then that is a lesson for them. However, you are responsible for the way you treat them through your self-expression as that is what comes back to you.

NOURISHMENT FOR YOUR SOUL: The greatest gift you can give yourself and others is to take responsibility for what is yours and allow others to take accountability for what is theirs.

FOOD FOR THOUGHT: I clearly know what is mine and what is not. I take responsibility for my experiences and release feeling responsible for the experiences of others.

Reflections from Experiences

"Your outer experiences are a reflection of your inner state of being."

When we have experiences, we attract people and situations that reflect our thoughts, beliefs, feelings or emotions at that time. If we desire to have a different experience, we can change our thoughts which change our beliefs, our feelings and ultimately our experiences. When our experiences involve another person, it is essential to determine what is ours and what is theirs.

EXERCISE: EXPERIENCE REFLECTIONS

When you have an experience and you are not aware of what your lesson is, ask for clarity from your angels by saying, "What is my lesson in this experience?" "How can I apply it to my life to make me a better person?" Then be still and listen for their response. Make a list of experiences and what they are reflecting to you. This will show you what lessons you are learning at this time.

When you find yourself surrounded by loving people and experiences, this is a reflection that you are being and expressing the love that you are. On the contrary, if you find yourself surrounded by negative people or experiences, then you are focusing on fear. You can choose who you interact with. Pick your friends wisely who reflect what's in your heart. You can also choose what you desire to experience. It all begins with you. When you make changes from within, you will begin to see the results in your outer experiences and relationships.

NOURISHMENT FOR YOUR SOUL: As you become more aware of the reflections being presented to you, you can make changes to attract or repel them.

FOOD FOR THOUGHT: I give thanks for the reflections the universe provides. I express the love that I am and attract loving relationships and experiences.

REFLECTION

BLESSINGS LOVE BRINGS

These birthrights are a reflection of the blessings love brings. We will experience these blessings when we are in our natural state of love, for these are our birthrights and love is their source.

Acceptance • Respect • Compassion • Forgiveness • Gratitude

Love • Peace • Unity • Abundance of Good • Freedom

Choice of free will • Divinity • Creation • Infinity

Vibrant Health • Inner happiness • Success • Prosperity

Hope • Faith • Joy • Pleasure • Passion • Desire • Fulfillment

Courage • Strength • Confidence • Independence

Empowerment • Inspiration • Unity • Enlightenment

Knowledge • Wisdom • Truth • Clarity • Divine guidance

Balance • Harmony • Synchronicity • Flow • Change

Energetic • Motivation • Liveliness

Self-love • Self-awareness • Self-confidence • Self-esteem

FOOD FOR THOUGHT: I choose to experience these infinite blessings, for LOVE is who I AM!

PART II
The Power of Love

CHAPTER 7
Unconditional Love

POWER OF LOVE

There is a power within each of us,

A power greater than all of us.

There is one intelligence,

In which all answers, all solutions,

All creations and all healings come from.

Trust that this intelligence will provide,

All that you require and desire,

To fulfill your life's mission.

This power is LOVE.

The Source of this power is

God.

—*The Angels*

Love is what we all desire and require, for it is our natural state of being. However, in our society we have learned to respond to situations and make decisions based on the opinions of others and outside influences instead of the truths within, or out of fear instead of love. Fear is not a part of who we are, it is merely an illusion that is part of our earth experience and takes us out of our natural state of love. These illusions such as separateness, judgment, addiction, physical limitations, poverty, pain or struggle, are not created by love; they are the result of fear. They prevent us from being in our natural state of divine love, experiencing fulfillment and receiving abundance of all our desires. This section will guide you in transforming these fear-based illusions into love, and empower you to open your heart and mind to that flow of divine love and wisdom, so you can experience the infinite blessings life brings when you choose love instead of fear.

As humans we are all affected by the illusions of fear that take us out of our natural state of love. The good part about this is that we are all evolving, becoming more aware of and reconnecting to the love that we are as well as our own truths. In her book, A Return to Love, Marianne Williamson shares that although it seems there are many problems in life, there really is only one problem, and that is we walk away from love when the only solution is walking back to love. I like how this defines what happens in life so simplistically.

The one universal purpose we all share in being here on earth is to love ourselves and others, and allow God's love and light to express through us by being the love that we are. We all do this in our own unique way that nurtures our soul. The angels want you to feel love, be love and experience love in all you do, for love is who you are and what you require to thrive and accomplish all that you came here to do. When you are in your natural state of love, there is no room for fear. As you let love be the foundation of your life, you will experience the blessings unconditional love brings—love, peace, unity, abundance, and freedom. As we all activate, embrace and express this unconditional love, heaven on earth is created. True Power is unconditional love in action!

What Is Unconditional Love?

Unconditional love is the highest energetic vibration that exists; the essence of God—the energy of the universe, the expression of our spirit, the energy of our soul, and of creation. It is our natural state of being at birth, meaning from nature. Love is the thread that ties us all together, the connection between ourselves and all of life. It is a state of being in which we choose to be a part of the oneness with all of life giving and receiving love. It begins with each and every one of us. We all have a choice whether to participate in the vibration of love or fear. When God is present in our life we move from fear to love and really begin to live and experience joy. When we choose love, we love ourselves, and we are happy and fulfilled. When we are fulfilled, we express acts of love. When we express ourselves with love, we attract that love into our lives and it will be present in our outer experiences, opportunities and relationships. Since love is the true essence of life, the divine energy of the universe, and makes everything work, we can understand why everyone requires to be loved and love to thrive. The following angelic recipes for healing will guide you to experience an overflow of love in your life.

- ♥ Unconditional love means loving yourself and others completely without conditions, stipulations or limitations. It is the ability to know and be one with all of life and to desire that only good comes to all including oneself.

- ♥ Unconditional Love is the foundation for all our relationships beginning with ourself. It is the essence for creating and experiencing loving, fulfilling relationships.

- ♥ Although unconditional love is free from conditions, it does have boundaries. It allows us to honor ourselves and others without judgment.

- ♥ When we live our life with a loving attitude of gratitude, only good comes to us and effortlessly flows. Things work out for us with ease instead of struggle. The more loving we are, the smoother and more satisfying our life experience will be.

- ♥ When we are in our natural state of love, we can then be the best that we can be and reach our greatest potential.

- ♥ When in our natural state of love, we feel energetic, motivated and full of life. We expect the best outcomes, strive for and achieve excellence, focus on our desires with our mind and heart open to all the good available to us, and we are in a state of gratitude with the passion to be of service in life and experience joy.

- ♥ To love unconditionally means to accept, respect and forgive ourself and others as is without judgment or criticism and feel compassion and gratitude for all that we are, all that we have and the blessings life brings.

NOURISHMENT FOR YOUR SOUL: Love is the magic that makes life work. As we let love be the foundation of our life, we begin to heal ourself, our life and our relationships. It gives us the passion to build bridges instead of walls with all.

FOOD FOR THOUGHT: My life is overflowing with love. I give and receive love freely and unconditionally.

This flower of unconditional love has five heart-shaped petals connected in the center of the circle of life with the energy of love. Each petal represents an aspect of unconditional love and is an art within itself.

Recipe for Unconditional Love

4 Cups of Respect
4 Cups of Acceptance
4 Cups of Forgiveness
4 Cups of Compassion
4 Cups of Gratitude

Mix it all together with an abundance of love, season with gratitude, and you will experience the infinite blessings love brings! Share with all . . . Serves everyone it touches.

The Art of Acceptance

"Acceptance is loving the shadow as well as the light."
—JOHN ASHBROOK, PHENOMENEWS, AUGUST, 2000

- ♥ Acceptance means to give and receive approval to yourself and others without judgment.

- ♥ Acceptance is being at peace with a situation you do not have control over or can not change.

- ♥ Acceptance begins with you. This means accepting all aspects of yourself.

- ♥ Acceptance allows everyone to exist and learn at their own pace, for we are all unique and have our own rhythm.

- ♥ Accepting others for who they are doesn't mean you have to always agree with everything they say or do. It simply means you respect them enough to allow them to be themselves, and have their own opinion without criticism or judgment.

NOURISHMENT FOR YOUR SOUL: Acceptance and respect go hand in hand. You must be willing to accept in order to respect. When you begin to accept and respect yourself, others will do the same. That is acceptance in action!

FOOD FOR THOUGHT: I love and accept myself just as I am and others just as they are.

The Art of Respect

- ♥ Respect means to have consideration for yourself and others.
- ♥ Respecting yourself means standing up for what you know or believe with confidence and courage.
- ♥ Respecting yourself means setting boundaries about what you are willing to experience.
- ♥ Respect is honoring each other's differences even though you disagree. It is not necessary to justify or apologize for being who you are. Follow your own inner guidance, whether it is different from other's or not.
- ♥ Respecting others is being open to seeing things from a different perspective and honoring who they are and their space.

NOURISHMENT FOR YOUR SOUL: With acceptance and respect there is less competition, peer pressure, gossip, manipulation and the need to control and be controlled by others. That is respect in action!

FOOD FOR THOUGHT: I respect myself and others.

The Art of Compassion

- ♥ Compassion is the ability to see another's situation without judgment.
- ♥ Compassion means to put yourself in another's situation for a moment (observing, without absorbing), and see how you would feel if that were you. Be helpful if you can.
- ♥ To have compassion is to desire to help another who is in need or is hurting.

- 💜 Being compassionate means responding with love. Example: "I am sorry you are experiencing _____. I'll keep you in my prayers" or "I'll send you love or angels." "Is there anything I can do to help you?"
- 💜 Compassion is being sensitive to what another is going through without pitying them. When we pity them it enables them keeping them stuck. Instead we can empower them to move beyond the challenge they are experiencing by helping in whatever way we can.
- 💜 Compassion is thinking with your heart.

NOURISHMENT FOR YOUR SOUL: The art of compassion is to lend an ear, give a hug or a smile, offer words of comfort, hope, faith, encouragement, or wisdom to inspire or empower, not to pity. Reflect upon what would be helpful to you that another person could offer if you were in that situation. That is compassion in action!

FOOD FOR THOUGHT: I AM compassionate with myself and others.

The Art of Forgiveness

- 💜 Forgiveness is the ability to see things from a higher perspective and detach from it.
- 💜 Forgiveness means to let go of the energy attached such as hurt, anger, resentment, guilt, shame or blame associated with that person or experience. It means to choose not to participate in the energy which brings you discomfort any longer.
- 💜 Forgiveness opens your heart to give and receive love and the flow of abundance.
- 💜 Forgiveness is a strength and a gift you give to yourself.

♥ The ability to forgive is one of the greatest powers you have. When you forgive, you free yourself from someone else's power. When you do not forgive, you give your power to another. Forgiveness frees you from the ties that bind and gives you a sense of peace.

NOURISHMENT FOR YOUR SOUL: To forgive, you do not have to forgive the action or behavior, you are not saying what you did is okay, you are just releasing the emotions connected to that situation which causes you dis-harmony. You are forgiving the person for doing the best that they could with the awareness and knowledge that they had in that moment. That is forgiveness in action!

FOOD FOR THOUGHT: I forgive myself for anyone whom I may have mis-treated and I forgive anyone who may have mis-treated me.

EXERCISE: FORGIVING YOURSELF

We've all done things we wish we had done differently or hadn't done at all. We can't change the past but we can change the now. It is important to forgive yourself, move forward and make different choices that create a better outcome for yourself.

1. Ask your angels and Archangel Uriel to assist you in your forgiveness process.
2. Make a list of all the things you have done to others or to yourself that you choose to forgive.
3. Go through each situation and identify why you did this. This process will help you find what it is within yourself that you are missing or that requires healing.
4. Write down your feelings associated with these issues. As you write, allow these feelings to surface and let them go.
5. Go through the list and write how you could have done it differently.

6. Next to each item, write "I forgive myself" or "I forgive me." It would also be helpful to say this affirmation: I release the past with grace and ease. As I release the past, new, fresh and vital life enters me. The past is forgiven and forgotten. I am free in this moment." (these affirmations came from the book, *You Can Heal Your Life* by Louise L. Hay)
7. Now pat yourself on the back and praise yourself for forgiving. You deserve it.
8. Do something that you really enjoy or gift yourself with something you desire as a reward for accomplishing this forgiveness.

NOURISHMENT FOR YOUR SOUL: Forgiveness brings you freedom so you do not have to experience that issue, situation or circumstances in your life anymore.

FOOD FOR THOUGHT: I release all guilt, blame and shame from my past and childhood. I see my past as a learning experience without judgment and I create new and loving experiences for myself. I forgive myself with ease knowing I do my best in each moment.

EXERCISE: FORGIVING OTHERS

1. Write on a piece of paper all the people you choose to forgive who you feel have offended you or stepped over your boundaries without invitation, anyone toward whom you feel anger or resentment. Include people from your past and present as well as people who have passed on.
2. Next go through your list and write why forgiveness is in order.
3. Check your list again and think about the situation. Allow yourself to feel however you feel. Then take a deep breath and allow the emotion and attachment to that feeling go. Say, "Dear Angels and

Archangel Uriel, please release me from the energy attached to the issues and people who require forgiveness so we may all heal. I choose to release all resentments, anger, fears and hurts. Thank You!"

4. Picture these individuals surrounded by white light and bless them on their journey. As you do this say, "I forgive you." Then take your pen and write next to the person's name, "I forgive you. Thank you for this experience for it contributed to my spiritual growth."
5. Affirm: I love and forgive myself and others with grace and ease. I am at peace.
6. Thank all involved including yourself.
7. Burn the paper in the fireplace or a chiminea, (a freestanding, clay fireplace for outdoors) tear up and throw away, or shred this paper as this symbolizes letting them go. The weight is lifted off your shoulders. Your heart is open, free and full of love.

NOURISHMENT FOR YOUR SOUL: If you find it difficult to forgive some people on your list, let it be and try another time because you want to do this with sincerity, honesty and willingness. Reflecting on the following affirmations for a few days before you try forgiving those people again is helpful: I choose to forgive; I forgive myself and others with grace and ease. This will help release your resistance and set the intention of choosing to forgive. Forgiveness out of obligation creates resentment not forgiveness. Forgiveness takes an open heart and willingness to let go of the energy that is causing an unpleasant experience for you.

FOOD FOR THOUGHT: I lovingly forgive myself and others with ease.

ANGELIC TOOLS:
♥ *Forgiveness and Loving the Inner Child* audio by Louise L. Hay

The Art of Gratitude

Gratitude opens your heart and makes you feel good. The more you live in a state of gratitude, the more good you will attract into your life. When you give gratitude, you will enhance your life tremendously. Here are some suggestions to live with an attitude of gratitude.

- Gratitude is a state of being. It is feeling love for the blessings in your life.
- Focus on the good in all experiences, relationships and situations. The more you focus on good and give gratitude, the more good you will attract and experience.
- Every situation has blessings. Always reflect upon these blessings.
- Make a list of all that you are grateful for. It lifts your spirits and you will see your life transform right before your eyes.
- As you go through your day, give gratitude for the experiences, opportunities and people who have crossed your path. Remember to thank people for anything they have contributed to your life and the person you are today. This could be something they said, did or gave to you.
- Pat yourself on the back often for your accomplishments. Reward yourself when you accomplish your goals by doing something you really enjoy, buying an item you've wanted, or treating yourself to something special. You deserve it!
- At the end of every day take a few minutes to reflect upon the days blessings (you can do this mentally, verbally or write it down).
- Create a gratitude board that reflects all you are grateful for.
- Create affirmations that reflect gratitude and repeat them often.

💜 Open your heart and feel love for who you are, what you have, what you have accomplished or experienced, and the blessings in your life. You will truly be blessed with an attitude of gratitude!

NOURISHMENT FOR YOUR SOUL: When you live from an open heart and mind and focus on the blessings life brings, prosperity follows in infinite ways. That is gratitude in action!

FOOD FOR THOUGHT: I AM living in a state of gratitude. I give and receive love, joy and gratitude.

ANGELIC TOOLS:
💜 *Gratitude* by Louise L. Hay
💜 *Let LOVE Be* music CD by Bonnie Ann Lewis

GRATITUDE BLESSINGS

BLESSINGS

You've learned compassion . . . Use it.
You've learned acceptance . . . Choose it.
You've learned respect . . . Expect it.
You've learned gratitude . . . Feel it in your heart.
You know love . . . Share it.
Enjoy the blessings of unconditional love . . . You've earned it!

—*The Angels*

EXERCISE: COUNT YOUR BLESSINGS

Make a list of all the things you have in your life for which you are thankful. These can be material things, things about yourself, experiences, opportunities, goals, dreams you've accomplished, your health, family, friends and answered prayers. Remember to include gratitude for yourself, who you are, your body functioning properly, eating healthy food, your home, the beauty of the planet, lessons you've learned, all those people who have guided you on this earth plane, and your spiritual helpers. This list reflects your infinite blessings. Begin your list with I give thanks for or I am grateful for. You have just created some gratitude affirmations for yourself.

NOURISHMENT FOR YOUR SOUL: I recommend giving gratitude daily; however, it is beneficial to reflect upon and do a complete inventory on a monthly basis. This keeps the energy moving in a positive, abundant direction every month. The more you focus on your blessings, the more blessings come.

FOOD FOR THOUGHT: My life is filled with infinite blessings. I AM grateful!

Loving Yourself

"Self-love is the greatest gift you can give to yourself and this world."

The most important relationship we have is the relationship with ourself for this is the foundation for our life. When we love ourself, we express ourselves with love and we attract loving experiences, opportunities and relationships into our life. Loving yourself includes accepting and respecting yourself for who you are (not who others think you should be) and where you are at this time (not when you are thin, successful, etc.), having compassion and forgiving yourself when necessary, and expressing gratitude for all that you are and all that you do. This is self-love in action!

Loving yourself is about being and honoring your true self and expressing the love that you are. This includes being honest with yourself and willing to look at your perceived shortcomings while focusing on your strengths and divine characteristics. This is self-esteem in action!

When you let go of society's belief for the need to be perfect in order to be loved and accepted, you release the self-criticism and judgment that you bought into at one time or another in your life. This is self-respect in action!

We are all our own worst critics. It is essential to change your thought patterns and habits, and be gentle and kind with yourself. When you let go of these old beliefs and judgments you have placed upon yourself, you will feel confidence in yourself and your life. This is self-confidence in action!

When you believe you deserve what you desire in your life, you open yourself up to receive these desires into your life. Know that you deserve to have anything you desire in your life as long as it comes with good intentions and a loving honest heart. It is then you can set boundaries that reflect the values you choose for yourself. This is self-worth in action!

Love heals all areas of our lives—relationships, physical conditions, addictions, unhealthy behaviors and our relationship with money. It makes the impossible possible. Since we are all interconnected, when we love ourselves unconditionally, it is then we can truly love others and others will love us too. As we release the judgments and expectations we place upon ourselves and others we are all free. This is unconditional love in action!

Self-love is empowering and creates self-esteem, self-respect, self-worth and self-confidence. This is self-awareness in action!

EXERCISE: WHAT I LOVE ABOUT ME

1. Write down all that you love about yourself.
2. Include characteristics you admire in others as these reflect things within yourself.
3. In front of each characteristic, put I AM. You've just created some additional affirmations to be used to love yourself and bring forth those characteristics you desire to bring into your experience. These are great to repeat into the mirror and review often.
4. At the bottom of your paper write the affirmation: I love all of me just the way I am right now!

NOURISHMENT FOR YOUR SOUL: In order for you to be fully available to help others, you must first nurture yourself. When your needs and desires are met, you will feel loved, fulfilled, nurtured and free.

FOOD FOR THOUGHT: I love all that I AM and all that I do. I see myself and what I do through eyes of love. Love is the greatest gift I give to myself and others.

ANGELIC TOOLS:
- ♥ *Love Your Body* book, by Louise L. Hay
- ♥ *Self-Esteem Affirmation* audio by Louise L. Hay

Ways to Love and Nurture Yourself

When you put a lot of love into yourself, you are living your life at a higher vibration and you will experience a better quality of life. When you are a loving person, you attract similar people into your life who are also living at a higher vibration, for you are a magnet for what you give out. When you love yourself, you feel a sense of happiness and you attract success into your life.

♥ **Believe in yourself.**

♥ **Follow your heart and be true to yourself.** Your heart is the communication between your soul and your physical reality. Prior to coming into this earth life your soul makes choices to learn certain things and makes a commitment to achieve and do certain activities in this lifetime that will help you evolve. It is important for you to honor your soul's journey. You do this by being true to yourself, following your heart and taking steps that will continue to help you grow on a soul level. Your heart holds all the answers to your soul and will lead your way. That is why your desires come from your heart. Sometimes it may not seem like the right thing to do from another's perspective, but you know the truths of your soul. You are the only one who knows what is best for you. Move forward one thoughtful step at a time. Everyone has a different chime that makes them ring. They may not agree with your dream and that's okay. What's most important is that you follow your own heart, believe in your dreams and in yourself! When you follow your heart, you are making choices that are going to nurture your soul and contribute to its evolvement.

NOURISHMENT FOR YOUR SOUL: When you follow your heart, everyone wins because the energy of your heart is love and love is the energy of spirit. This is your connection to the universal source of creation. The power of love makes everything possible.

FOOD FOR THOUGHT: I AM true to me. I choose to follow my heart. I have confidence in my performance and I AM the best that I can be. I believe in me.

- ♥ **Speak up for yourself.** It is important to speak your truth with love regardless of the opinions or reactions of others, for their reactions and opinions are not about you, they are about them. When you live your life based on the beliefs of others, you will feel confused, afraid and change your mind constantly. This gives your power to others. But, when you create your own beliefs, it is then you can live in integrity and be at peace because you are in your own power, standing your ground.

- ♥ **Be honest with yourself; live with integrity.** When your beliefs, words and actions are in unison with each other, you are living in integrity.

NOURISHMENT FOR YOUR SOUL: People with integrity know their values and are both admired and remembered by others. *"You are in integrity when what you are doing on the outside matches what you are feeling on the inside."* —Alan Cohen

FOOD FOR THOUGHT: I AM honest with myself and I AM living with integrity.

- ♥ **Create healthy boundaries.** Boundaries are standards that you set for yourself and others to establish the value of yourself and your life. Establishing boundaries is important in choosing to let things into your life that you desire to experience. By setting boundaries you will acquire in your life those things, people, and experiences you choose and desire. It is essential for your well-being to set boundaries for others in relation to yourself. No one can do anything to you unless you let them. They can't take your power unless you give it to them. When you set boundaries, you are honoring your space and time so that you can bring into your life only that in which you desire to be, do, interact with, and acquire. This contributes to your happiness and the fulfillment of your life's purpose.

It is essential in life to create healthy boundaries for yourself and others. When you set boundaries for yourself, you are making your intentions clear to the universe for what you desire to experience. When you set boundaries in your relationships, you honor yourself and let people know what you are willing to experience in that relationship.

EXERCISE: CREATING BOUNDARIES

This boundary exercise is a great tool to set your intentions for what you desire to experience, and can be done for anything you desire in your life.

1. On a piece of paper draw a large circle or heart.
2. At the top of your paper write the topic for which you are setting boundaries.
3. Within the circle or heart list all the things you desire to experience, acquire or do as it relates to your subject.
4. Light a candle, and say a prayer asking the universe to bring these desires into your experience. Let these go by blowing them into the universe. Thank the universe for making them so, knowing the universe will take care of the details and how it will unfold. Affirm: And so it is!

NOURISHMENT FOR YOUR SOUL: By placing these things inside the circle you are setting the intention, and making them your focus so they can come to you as experience.

FOOD FOR THOUGHT: I set boundaries around what I desire to experience and watch them come to life.

♥ **Say "No" gracefully.** Sometimes one of the most difficult words to say is no. This is because we do not want to hurt someone's feelings or be rejected by them. It is really important to say no when something doesn't feel appropriate to you. If it does hurt another's feelings, then there is something within them that needs healing. They must take their own responsibility for that. Saying no to something that doesn't feel right to you is very different from doing something deliberately to hurt another. When you do not say no to something that is not right for you, you are living your life for others rather than yourself. When this happens everyone loses. One of the greatest gifts we give to ourself is saying "no" when something doesn't feel right to us.

Here are some suggested phrases you can use to say no gracefully. "No thank you, I do not choose to do that; This doesn't feel right to me and I'm going to honor that; That's not for me." Notice how your body feels when you ask yourself if something is appropriate for you. If it feels good, go for it! If it does not, be proud, stand tall, follow your intuition, and say no without guilt or embarrassment.

- ♥ **Walk away from situations that are not right for you.** When someone is doing something or saying something to you that you do not want to participate in, choose to walk away. Walking away is not a sign of weakness, it reflects strength. You are walking away because you are choosing not to participate in that energy or experience that situation. Therefore, you can walk away with your head held high because you are choosing a better experience for yourself. You are making choices that are appropriate for you.

NOURISHMENT FOR YOUR SOUL: When you make choices which reflect things that are fulfilling to you, you will create joyful experiences and live a fulfilling life. Love yourself enough to walk away from a situation that doesn't mirror your highest good or reflect your heart's desire.

FOOD FOR THOUGHT: *"Success is having the wisdom to say "no" when something is not appropriate for you."* —Author Unknown

- 💜 **Take responsibility for yourself and your life.**

- 💜 **Do things that bring you joy** and pleasure and make you feel good about yourself.

- 💜 **Find recognition from within,** instead of from others. If others do not understand you, that's okay.

- 💜 **Buy yourself a gift,** something you've been wanting.

- 💜 **Create affirmations that reflect the good that is within you.** When life reflects something I desire in my life, I create an affirmation to reflect this. I find this helpful in creating my own affirmations.

- 💜 **Talk lovingly to yourself in the mirror.**

- 💜 **Send loving thoughts to your body.** Surround yourself with love and light.

- 💜 **Consume healthy foods and beverages** that give you nourishment, support your body and energize you.

- 💜 **Surround yourself with beautiful things** or things that have meaning to you.

- 💜 **Gift yourself with flowers** as this brings life and color into your environment.

- 💜 **Pamper yourself** in whatever way that feels good to you and brings you joy.

- 💜 **Take time for yourself to do what you desire.**

- 💜 **Choose to spend time with people** who you resonate with and enjoy their company.

- 💜 **Be creative.** Draw, sing, dance, paint, write or any other creative endeavor you enjoy.

- 💜 **Go for walk out in nature**.

- 💜 **Listen to angelic or inspirational music.** You can even do some free-flowing dancing or body movement as this opens the flow of energy.

- 💜 **Listen to any CD's or read books on love,** self-enrichment, personal growth or inspirational topics.

- 💜 **Go to a museum** and view the art or go to a botanical gardens.

- 💜 **Read or write poetry** that is about love or inspires you.

- 💜 **Watch movies** that are heart warming, romantic or spiritual.

- 💜 **Dress in clothes that you feel good in.**

- 💜 **Bring a lot of color into your home** as this creates a heightened mood.

- 💜 **Get adequate exercise that you enjoy.**

- 💜 **Express yourself with love.**

- 💜 **Write love letter to your self.**

- 💜 **Give yourself the recognition you deserve.**

EXERCISE: A LOVE LETTER TO YOU

1. Write a love letter to yourself beginning with Dear and your name.
2. As you write this letter put as much love as you can into it. When you are finished sign it with an I Love You plus your name.
3. Put it in an envelope and review it when you are feeling down or need some encouragement or self-love. This will inspire you, lift your spirits, and help you to recognize all the good that is within you.
4. Affirm: I am the best that I can be. I love me! If you have a hard time doing this at first, think of it in relation to the love you have for a child, or your inner child.

EXERCISE: SELF-RECOGNITION

Oftentimes we are busy changing what we do not like and focusing on where we desire to go that we do not take the time to reflect upon all the good that we are and have accomplished so far. This exercise will give you the self-recognition you deserve!

1. Write down all your accomplishments.
2. After writing each accomplishment give yourself praise.
3. Take a moment to feel the joy and gratitude this recognition brings.
4. Review these accomplishments often. When you do this, it brings it to your awareness so you can feel good about yourself.

NOURISHMENT FOR YOUR SOUL: When you give yourself recognition, others will recognize your successes too.

FOOD FOR THOUGHT: I go within and recognize all my accomplishments.

Express Yourself with Love

EXPRESS

As you express, you experience.
You deserve to live the life you desire, whatever it may be,
All you have to do is ask, and be open to give and receive.
So the universe can for you provide,
The thoughts and dreams that reside inside.
Everything is first a thought, just like planting a seed,
The thoughts you give attention to are what you'll reap indeed.
Pay attention to your expression in everything you do,
For what you give out is coming back to you.

—The Angels

Self-expression is the process you use to get what is inside of you out to the world. It is how your soul communicates with others and the universe. As you express yourself, you move your inner thoughts, feelings and emotions to the outer world through your words and actions. This includes choices, attitude, behavior, body language and communication. Your self-expression is your communication between your inner state of being and your physical existence. Your soul communicates with you through your heart. Your heart is the doorway to your soul which is where your passion and desires reside. When your communication between your inner and outer selves is clear and true, it is then you are in balance and your inner creations come to form in the way that you desire. The transmission or communication between your soul and your physical body sometimes gets misinterpreted due to outside influences and the interference of illusions, fears, others beliefs and the busyness of your day to day life. Therefore, you need to quiet your mind to reflect and reconnect to that divine communication between all aspects of yourself. In order to connect to that inner wisdom, intelligence, and truth, you must go within. When you go within, you connect with your God-self.

The way you express yourself is vitally important as what you give out is what comes back to you as experience. Allow yourself to express yourself in a way that feels good to you without being self-conscious of what anyone else thinks. Due to the law of attraction and your choice of free will, whatever you choose to express creates your own experiences. However, it affects everyone around you. As you express yourself with love, this love permeates and everyone that is around you will feel this love.

Here I share a great description for expression that crossed my path. *"To express a thought is to give it life. The life of that one focused thought contains all possibilities as it evolves and spirals out from its point of focused expression. Whoever can bring a thought to a point of conscious expression can create their own universe by letting it go, setting it free, giving it life and allowing it to evolve and express its individuality. From its individuality springs infinite aspects of its own uniqueness so it goes on forever. The same way that God has done with each and every one of us!"* —John Ashbrook, *PhenomeNEWS*, Aug 2000.

When you love yourself, you express yourself with love. When you express yourself with love, you will attract love. You contribute to the well-being of this planet by expressing yourself with love. Your self-expression is a reflection of how you feel about yourself. So when you respond to someone with love that is a reflection of what you believe about yourself. Here are some guidelines for expressing yourself with love.

- 💜 **Think loving thoughts** about yourself and others.

- 💜 **Make loving choices** based on how you feel, using divine guidance, not the opinions or reactions of others.

- 💜 **Speak loving words with integrity.**

- ♥ **Respond to others and situations with love** instead of reacting with fear.

- ♥ **Be sure your heart and head are working together** with your heart leading, your head following.

- ♥ **Be sure your actions are a true reflection of your thoughts and feelings.** For example, do not walk around mad with your hands crossed and say, "I'm fine, everything is just fine." Sometimes we say one thing but really feel differently. This is like putting on your right blinker and turning left. It is contradictory to what is really happening and it confuses others. This creates conflicting beliefs for you because you are not being in integrity with yourself or clear to the universe on what you desire.

- ♥ **Take loving actions.** Be sure your actions are a true reflection of your thoughts and feelings. When you are lovingly direct, you are assertive instead of aggressive. Assertive means applying with love, aggression is reacting from fear and attacking. Society has taught that you have to be mean or rude to get what you want. In truth, when you communicate in a respectful way, then you will receive respectful responses.

NOURISHMENT FOR YOUR SOUL: Knowing your thoughts, choices and actions create your experiences, you can use this as a guide to create your desired life.

FOOD FOR THOUGHT: I AM lovingly direct. I express myself with love, grace and integrity. As I express myself with love, I attract loving relationships and experiences. I AM powerful and assert myself in a loving way.

Communicating with Love

"When you communicate with love, you will be heard."

An essential part of your self-expression is communication. Communication is the expression of your inner thoughts and feelings that takes into consideration other people's thoughts and feelings. It determines your relationship between yourself, others and the universe. Mis-communication occurs when people communicate but do not say what they truly mean. Sometimes you might speak from anger and words get thrown back and forth, then things are said you do not really mean. If someone says something that is hurtful to you, let them know it was hurtful and ask them if that was their intention. Sometimes communications are mis-interpreted on the giving and receiving end so this is a way to clarify ones intention and clear up any misunderstandings. When you communicate in a positive way, you are more likely to get the response that you desire. People do not always say what they mean or mean what they say for several reasons. Sometimes people are not truthful because they are afraid of being rejected. They are embarrassed about something they did or did not do, and to protect themselves or another, they cover up their true feelings to prevent from hurting the other person's feelings. When you lie to yourself, you lose. When you lie to others you are also lying to yourself so everyone loses. When you are truthful with yourself and others, you have nothing to fear or be embarrassed about so everyone wins. Honesty is always the best policy. Let the truth be known. Be honest with yourself and others. When you are honest with yourself, you live in integrity which gives you a sense of confidence and self-esteem. When you believe you are worthy of something, it becomes part of your life experience.

- 💜 **Say what you mean and mean what you say.** Be clear with your intentions.

- 💜 **Ask for what you want,** not what you do not want. Instead of telling someone what you do not want them to do, ask them to do what you do want them to do. Here are a few examples. If someone is yelling at you and you want them to talk, say, "Please talk to me." instead of "Do not yell at me." If you do not want someone to touch your things say, "Please leave my things be" Instead of "Do not touch my things." By asking for what you want, it encourages the other person to pay more attention and listen to what you are saying and you will more likely have your request honored.

- 💜 **Emphasize the positive.** Example: Instead of stating, "Love never fails," say, "Love always succeeds."

- 💜 **Listen.** Create a safe and nurturing environment for other people to open up to you. Listen attentively to what they are saying. Sometimes we are thinking about the next thing we are going to say or something else we are going to do that day and our full attention is not on what the person is saying. When we are in the moment and listen attentively, the lines of communication are open and all will benefit. This builds healthy relationships.

- 💜 **Respect the beliefs and feelings of others.** This doesn't mean you have to agree with what they say it just means you allow that person to have their beliefs and feelings without judgment, criticism or blame. Allow others the freedom to be who they are.

- **Let go of the need to be "right."** Oftentimes conversations occur in which individuals think they need to be "right." When communicating, it is not important who is wrong or right. What is important is that both or all people are respected for their opinions. That doesn't mean you both have to agree. It just means that both people respect each other for their differences and have the freedom to agree to disagree on that particular subject. In letting go of the need to be right all the time, you will experience peace of mind.

NOURISHMENT FOR YOUR SOUL: As you communicate with love, you will create an outcome that makes you feel good about yourself.

FOOD FOR THOUGHT: I speak my truth with joy, ease, confidence and integrity. I speak loving words that inspire others. Spirit speaks through me in all ways.

EMPOWERING SELF-TALK

Words are powerful! The dialog you have with yourself is very important because it contributes to the well-being of your self-esteem, self-confidence, self-worth and self-love. How do you respond to yourself when you do something you wish you had done differently? Do you criticize yourself with words such as, "How could I be so stupid, What's wrong with me, I'm such an idiot." or do you make up excuses such as "Oh, I'm having a bad day," or "I'm just a klutz." If so stop! Instead give yourself the love and support you need knowing you did the best you could in that moment. Learn from the experience, forgive yourself and move on. We all do things we wish we had done differently at times in our lives. When we just let it go knowing that next time we can make a different choice and change our actions, our soul benefits the most. Here are some effective phrases that make a difference.

Instead of saying "I should _____, I have _____, or I need to _____," Say, "I could _____, I can _____, I choose _____, I want to _____, I'd like to _____, I would love to _____, I'm going to _____, I will be _____ or It's time for me to _____."

Instead of saying, "No problem," say, "You are welcome" or "My pleasure." Instead of saying, "I forgot," say, "I did not remember." Instead of saying, "I should have, could have etc.," say, "I wish I had . . . next time I will." Instead of saying, "I do not have the money," say, "I choose not to spend money on that right now" or "I choose not to do that."

NOURISHMENT FOR YOUR SOUL: Your words are very powerful. Choose words that reflect what you desire to experience.

FOOD FOR THOUGHT: I speak words of truth and love to myself and others.

Making Loving Choices

"The choices you make are the results you create."

When making loving choices here are some questions to reflect upon so that you make choices which will serve you while creating the outcome you desire to experience.

- 💜 Will this choice give me the outcome that reflects what I desire to experience?
- 💜 Is this choice in alignment with my life's purpose?
- 💜 How does my body feel when I think about making this choice?
- 💜 Will this choice enhance my life in the direction I desire to go?

NOURISHMENT FOR YOUR SOUL: There are always two options when making choices: 1) follow your heart 2) follow someone else's heart. By following your heart, you choose to move forward in a way that feels good to you. By making choices that reflect the wisdom within, you experience the rewards of these choices. Making wise choices creates success, a feeling of peace, comfort and contentment. By following your heart, you choose to use your own power, and it is reflected in your experiences.

FOOD FOR THOUGHT: I make choices that reflect my heart's desires and truths within my soul. I make choices that are honorable for me. The choices I make create the outcome I desire to experience.

Take Loving Actions

We've all taken actions in our life we wish we could take back. When this happens, you can ask the angels to erase all effects that action had on everyone involved through all existence of time, and forgive yourself, knowing you did the best that you could in that moment.

- ♥ Reflect upon what changes you can make next time that would create the outcome you desire to experience. When you take action and it doesn't give you the outcome you desire, reflect upon the thoughts and feelings that brought you to take this action.

- ♥ Reflect and respond with love rather than react. Although your goal is to stay centered in your natural state of love, we all get caught up in our emotions from time to time. Instead of allowing yourself to be overcome by the emotions and react, you can take a moment to reflect and get centered before you respond. It takes strength to say, "Let me take a moment to think about it." or "I will get back to you." But it will be a moment worth taking. This gives you the opportunity to respond rather than react out of any fear-based illusions. Responses are more powerful than reactions. When you respond with love, you are acting from your own power. When you react out of fear, you are allowing outside sources to control you.

FOUR STEPS FOR RESPONDING WITH LOVE

1. Stop and take four deep breaths.
2. Call on your angels for assistance. Ask your angels to help you see the situation from a higher perspective, and to guide your actions so that they reflect love.
3. Reflect upon what your lesson is.
4. Respond with loving intentions and watch the miracles happen!

NOURISHMENT FOR YOUR SOUL: Make this a ritual that you perform in every situation which requires action. The reason this works is when you stop to breathe, you breathe in spirit and it changes your fear-based emotions to love. When you are in your natural state of love, you are able to see things from a higher perspective and beyond that moment, giving you the capacity to take the best course of action which enriches your experience and benefits those involved.

FOOD FOR THOUGHT: I take time to reflect and respond with love. I take loving actions.

♥ Take actions that create unity. Here are some questions to reflect upon to determine actions which will serve you and others. Is this action going to create unity or separation? How will I feel taking this action? Is this something I desire to do? Why am I taking this action? How will this action benefit myself or others?

♥ Sometimes we are afraid to make the "wrong" decision, so we do not take any action. This can lead to procrastination which is fear-based stagnant energy. When we procrastinate, we make a choice to stay right where we are at. Some procrastinate and hope the situation will go away. This is really a state of denial and only makes a situation worse and the lesson keeps coming back as a different experience. It is best to face the situation so the lesson can be learned and move on. Procrastination does have its place in life. Thomas Kinkade says it perfectly. He states, "Procrastinate undesirable behavior and put it off forever and it never gets done." This quote shines light on procrastination and how it can serve us.

NOURISHMENT FOR YOUR SOUL: Be kind and gentle to yourself. Take the blessing from the lesson and know that you have the opportunity to make a different choice next time.

FOOD FOR THOUGHT: My actions reflect the truths within my soul and create unity.

CHAPTER 8
Creating Loving, Fulfilling Relationships

Now that you have developed a healthy loving relationship with yourself, it is time to take that to the next level and create loving, fulfilling relationships with others. This includes attracting a soul mate and creating a divine love partnership. When you show up as the love that you are, and express that love, you attract loving experiences, opportunities and relationships into your life and you experience the greatest blessings life has to offer. When you love yourself, it is then you can truly love others.

Relationships are such an important part of our lives. Although there are many different types of relationships such as family, friends, acquaintances, partners, and so on, our foundation for all of these begins with our relationship with ourself. If we desire changes to occur in relationships, we must begin with ourself. Since our relationships with others merely reflect our underlying beliefs, we can change our relationships by changing our beliefs about the relationship and the person. When we do this, our relationship will shift to reflect these beliefs or we will attract new people who mirror our new beliefs. We can not change what others do, but we can change the way we respond to them. It's not appropriate to ask the angels to change a person, but we can ask for the characteristics we desire in a relationship to be present. One of two things will occur. Either the relationship will shift to reflect those changes or the relationship will gently end so what we desire can come into our life.

We all want to experience loving, harmonious and fulfilling relationships in our lives. In order to create loving and fulfilling relationships, we must open our hearts and minds to the concept of unconditional love. In order to experience unconditional love in relationships, we must first be and give the love that we desire to experience. As we express the love that we are, we will attract people who reflect that love into our lives. It brings us great joy to share our lives with people with whom we resonate and truly enjoy spending time with. Creating loving and fulfilling relationships gives us all the opportunity to experience love at its best—acceptance, respect, compassion, forgiveness and gratitude—the blessings unconditional love brings.

Recipe for Loving Relationships

Be the model of love you desire to experience in your relationships and that is what you will attract and experience."

- ♥ **Commitment:** It takes commitment, time and energy from both people to create a healthy, balanced, fulfilling relationship. It takes both people to be present in the relationship on all levels.

- ♥ **Honesty/Trust:** Honesty is always the best policy. When we are honest, we build trust in relationships. Honesty and trust are like the glue that bonds two people together, creating a solid foundation for the relationship.

- ♥ **Communication:** Open, loving communication is essential in a healthy relationship as it increases the intimacy and creates the dynamics for success.

- ♥ **Nurture:** All relationships require nurturing to keep them growing, thriving and alive. Part of nurturing is taking time for each other, sharing thoughts, feelings, dreams, desires, having fun together, enjoying each other's company, planning, praying, meditating and manifesting together.

- ♥ **Compromise:** Healthy relationships require compromising with both people being true to themselves, stating their truth and blending those truths. This creates a win-win situation for everyone. When we blend our differences it creates balance in the relationship. No person or relationship is perfect all the time, but it can be as fulfilling as we make it to be. What's important is that the relationship is fulfilling for both people involved. All relationships have their challenges and blessings and are a work in progress. What creates the success of a relationship is our ability to overcome the challenges, blend our differences, and embrace the gifts.

- ♥ **Freedom:** It is essential to be free to be ourself in relationships and allow others to be themselves. If we find ourself in a relationship that does not allow us to be ourself, or doesn't support us in fulfilling our desires and dreams, we are probably not in a relationship that will allow us to expand and grow. Everyone grows at their own pace and is on their individual path. However, it is essential that there is common ground and the respect and support of one another in fulfilling our individual endeavors as we work together to create the life we desire. Although we each have our own path, we can still stay connected with one another along the way.

- 💜 **Release Judgments:** Judgments are thoughts, feelings, expectations and opinions projected onto another. We are human and from time to time we get caught up in placing judgments. Many times it is in an attempt to help others as we can see things more clearly when we are not standing in their shoes. We do not always know why people make the choices they make or what they've been through, nor do we know what lessons are important for them to learn. Therefore, it is essential for us to refrain from placing our judgment on them. Everyone must decide for themselves what is right for them. What is right for them may not be right for you and vice versa. Respect others for the choices they make. Allow them the freedom to make their own choices without judgment. When we place judgment we subscribe to their energy. When we do this it lowers our vibration to meet their vibration. When we detach from their drama and stay centered in our natural state of love, we simply observe the situation without absorbing the energy. At times we find ourself being judgmental, we can stop, forgive ourself and send loving thoughts to that person. When we release judgments of ourself and others, our relationships will be more loving and fulfilling.

- 💜 **Choose Not to Participate in Gossip:** Do not repeat anything you hear about another person that you wouldn't want said about you. Many times, after a story has been shared with several different people and each person adds their own perception, it has lost its truth. Gossip just brings negative energy back to you and lowers your vibration. When you gossip, your subconscious mind doesn't know the difference between you talking about yourself or another person, therefore, with repetition, it creates a belief and begins to create that situation in your life. Remember, the thoughts you think and words you speak are very powerful, so choose them wisely. When someone says something about you that is untrue, say to them, "That is not true." Think to yourself, that is not truth for me. Let it go and affirm your truth. If it is not true, it shouldn't bother you. If it does bother you, reflect upon why. If there is some truth to it and it is not something you desire, then you have the power within you to change it. If someone approaches you with gossip, you can say, "Thank you for sharing" and send love to the person being gossiped about. This will stop gossip in its tracks when you do not participate in discussing it further. This raises the vibration for all.

♥ **Honor Differences:** Thank goodness we are not all the same. The world would be a boring place if we all thought the same, acted the same, liked all the same things, etc. Diversity is a blessing as that is what makes us unique and an individual expression of God. Honoring each others differences can bring great blessings when we are open-minded, and accept, respect and appreciate the diversity we each bring into this world.

♥ **Be Responsible:** In healthy relationships, it is essential to take responsibility for your own lessons, experiences and life, and allow other people to take responsibility for theirs. When you take responsibility for your own life, you let go of the need to blame others, situations or circumstances for what you are experiencing. Instead, use your own power to create the life you desire to live by the way you choose to use your energy through the thoughts you think, words you speak and actions you take. When you allow others to take responsibility for their own experiences and life, you empower them. When you let go of feeling responsible for the actions of others or their feelings and experiences, you are able to detach from them and respond with love. You will feel much more at peace as a result. When you try to "fix" things for them, you enable them and it does not serve either of you. In order to allow other people to take responsibility for their experiences and situations, you must detach with compassion.

♥ **Compassionate Detachment:** This means detaching from the situation or experience, yet being supportive by offering advice, encouragement, suggestions, and wisdom with no expectations of how they choose to use it. When we detach, we let go of the energy attached to the experiences of others and accept their choices. This prevents us from trying to make people be who we desire them to be or make choices we think are best for them. Instead, accept them for who they are. When we detach with compassion, we detach from the situation, not the person. We support them but we do not allow ourselves to absorb their energy. Instead, we tend to our own feelings about it. Doing this allows them to take responsibility and make changes for themselves when they are ready and will prevent us from being disappointed if it doesn't happen the way we expect it to. Sometimes when we are close to someone and they are going through a challenging time, we can feel their pain and it affects us and the relationship. The greatest gift we can give in this situation is to detach with compassion. This is a lesson that is easier said than done when it involves someone we are close to and love so much, but once it is recognized it brings much peace. By asking the angels for help, I assure you it will have a better outcome than we can imagine and happen with grace and ease.

NOURISHMENT FOR YOUR SOUL: Relationships do not have to be a struggle. Inviting the angels into your relationship is very powerful and creates an amazing connection! When you invite the angels into your life, you experience the blessings of unconditional love.

FOOD FOR THOUGHT: In order to create the relationships you desire to experience, you must first be willing to give that which you desire to receive.

Resolve Conflicts with Love

"The only way to get the best of an argument is to avoid it."
—DALE CARNEGIE

If there is conflict in your relationships, then there is something within you that triggers that conflict and needs healing. There is an energy attached to that person or situation that needs to be addressed. Conflict is simply a message to you. When you view it as a message without judgment, it is then you can detach and understand what this message means. It gives you the opportunity to see what your part is, what their part is, and how the situation can be resolved. When you resolve conflict with love, everybody wins. When conflict shows up in your life, know it is a reflection of a conflict within you, and you can change it if you so desire by facing it head on and going within. When you resolve conflict within, you will experience peace in your outer experiences. Here are some effective ways to resolve conflict with love.

- ♥ Visualize the situation already healed.
- ♥ Ask for angelic assistance.
- ♥ Do *Bridge of Love Visualization*. You can also use this visualization to resolve conflict within yourself by visualizing yourself in place of the other person.
- ♥ Release the need to be "right." What is right for you may not be right for someone else and vice versa. Be open to seeing the oth-

ers view point, but stand your ground in what you believe. Each person can have their own opinion and both be right. There are no right or wrong answers, only the individual's perception of the circumstance. Sometimes the best solution is to agree to disagree, then everyone wins.

NOURISHMENT FOR YOUR SOUL: *"If you have a choice to be right or to be kind, choose to be kind."* —Dale Carnegie

FOOD FOR THOUGHT: I see all relationships through eyes of love.

BRIDGE OF LOVE VISUALIZATION

This visualization is designed to send loving thoughts and energy to anyone you are having conflict with as it clears the space and shifts the energy, building a bridge of love.

- Invite in your angels by saying, "Dear Angels and Archangel Uriel, please assist me in releasing anything unloving relating to this person and open my heart to giving and receiving love to him/her."
- Visualize standing in front of the person you are having a conflict with.
- Take a moment to feel the love you have for yourself.
- Expand this love to this person by visualizing a ray of pink light going from your heart to theirs.
- Take a moment to think loving thoughts about this person by allowing your mind to focus on the good in this person.
- Affirm: I open my heart and mind to giving and receiving love to and from you. All of my relationships are harmonious and loving. I chose to build bridges of love in all of my relationships. And so it is!

NOTE: This visualization is found on *Your Journey to Love Daily Practice* CD included with this book.

EXERCISE: WRITING CONFLICT OUT OF YOUR LIFE

When you are having a conflict with another person or holding onto anger, resentment or feeling hurt, writing is a powerful method to release from your body the emotions that bind you to that person or situation, without offending the other person. When you release the emotions, peace and harmony will follow. You will be amazed at how the conflict resolves itself or how calm you will feel. The lines of communication will open up with ease so you can discuss it with them.

1. Write a letter to that person and say anything you want to say in that letter, knowing you are not going to give it to that person. Express to the person how you felt with what they did.
2. After you have finished your letter, burn it or tear it up and throw it away. Ask the angels to transform the energy into love.
3. Make a list of all the good that you see in that person and focus on those things.
4. Give gratitude for the lessons and gifts that person has brought to the relationship and to your life.

When doing this exercise you may need to write several letters from time to time until the energy is released and the situation is resolved. Then you will be able to respond to the situation with love.

NOURISHMENT FOR YOUR SOUL: When you focus on the good in others it gives them the opportunity to express this good in your presence.

FOOD FOR THOUGHT: As I express my feelings in writing, I release them from my body with grace and ease. I see the good in all people and situations.

PRAYER FOR RESOLVING CONFLICTS WITH LOVE

Dear Angels, and Archangel Uriel,

Please show me the truth in this situation. Assist me in seeing it from a higher perspective. Help me stay centered in my true self and to come from a place of love with all my communications. Assist me in releasing any anger, resentment and judgment I have so I will feel peace. Assist me in recognizing and taking responsibility for my lessons, and allow the other person to take responsibility for their part. Assist me in discerning where I end and other person begins, releasing any energy that I have taken on from the other person, and help me detach from their experience. Assist me in seeing that person as a divine child of God and see the light they are and the blessings they bring. Assist me in forgiving myself and the other person, opening my heart and mind to giving and receiving love to and from this person. Guide me to see, respond and resolve this situation with love, and create an outcome that is for the highest good of all concerned. Thank you for making this so!

NOURISHMENT FOR YOUR SOUL: If you want to resolve conflicts in relationships and outer experiences, you must resolve the conflict from within. This prevents you from attracting and experiencing those situations.

FOOD FOR THOUGHT: I resolve conflicts with love and angelic assistance.

EXERCISE: ENVELOPE OF LOVE

This is a great way to resolve conflict with love and clear the path for forgiveness.

1. Put a picture or the name of anyone with whom you are having a conflict or would like to forgive in an envelope, then seal it.

2. Put the envelope somewhere it will not be disturbed and place a rose quartz, which represents love, on top of the envelope. I like to place the envelope on the windowsill as this shines light on the situation and keeps the energy of the rose quartz clear as the sun shines on it.
3. Ask your angels to heal the relationship and watch miraculous solutions appear!

NOURISHMENT FOR YOUR SOUL: Forgiveness brings you freedom so you do not have to experience that issue or situation in that relationship, and also clears it for future relationships.

FOOD FOR THOUGHT: All of my relationships are harmonized. I AM in divine relationships. I view all relationships from a higher perspective.

Sometimes we experience challenges in relationships due to past-life karma. Karma is simply the natural law of cause and effect. Karma is not about punishment—that is a man-made belief created by society as a means of control. Before incarnating into this lifetime, we made agreements, known as soul contracts with other souls to balance and heal this karma. Karma can be recognized when re-occurring patterns or themes present themselves in your life. These opportunities provide situations for your soul to evolve. The following prayer will assist in healing and balancing karma from past-life relationships.

PRAYER FOR HEALING AND BALANCING PAST-LIFE KARMA

Dear God, Angels and Archangel Raziel,

I ask that you remove the energetic ties that bind me and (person's name) to the pain of the past. Please help us to heal the past with love, creating harmonious relations in the present. Thank you for making this so!

Then visualize the person involved and say, "I forgive you for all past experiences in all lifetimes. I send you love and release you from the ties that bind us to the past. You are free. Please forgive me for all past experiences in all lifetimes. Please send me love and release me from the ties that bind us to the past. I am free. Let's begin anew and share a harmonious relationship in this lifetime that honors our soul contracts.

How to Respond in Loving Ways to the Negative Behaviors of Others

"You can not solve the problem with the same kind of thinking that created the problem" —ALBERT EINSTEIN

We cannot change the way other people choose to live their life, however, we can change the way we allow it to affect us and how we respond to them. This can empower them to be the love that they are. When people exhibit unhealthy behaviors, they are hurting inside. What they need most is love. I believe God is in each and every one of us and that people themselves are not "bad." However, due to the illusions of fear they use their energy in unhealthy ways. If we respond with anger, this just creates more violence in our world. We can help them the most by choosing not to play a part in their behavior by judging or getting angry in return, but instead respond to them with love. When we respond with love, we reflect back to them their true self. When we do this, we are being a model of God's love, and this reflects how we feel about ourself. When we respond with love it feeds the fire with love, increasing the vibration and shifting the energy. As we do

CREATING LOVING, FULFILLING RELATIONSHIPS

this, we create a peaceful planet where all of us can live by changing the vibration to love. Here are ways we can do this.

- 💜 **Be a model of the love you want to see in the world.** If you want to see love and peace in your outer world, you must be and express love and peace yourself. Then the outer world will reflect this change.

- 💜 **Respond with love.** You always have the choice to fuel the fire with fear or feed the fire with love. As you feed the fire with love the fear will subside. This shifts the energy and makes room for healing to take place with a better outcome.

- 💜 **Choose not to participate.** When you choose not to participate in another's energy, you are not judging them, you are simply choosing a different experience for yourself. You have a choice of what energy you interact with. You can set boundaries around what you are willing to accept and experience. You do this by activating your choice of free will.

- 💜 **Resist arguing.** Once you have spoken your truth, just let it go and say, "I'm not going to respond to this anymore, I am finished." Do not allow anyone to continue pushing you until they get what they want. Stand your ground.

- 💜 **Stop constant complaining.** When someone is continuously complaining about everything but doesn't do anything to make it better, this is dumping. By participating in this you are putting energy into enabling them to be a victim. Instead, empower them by choosing not to participate in this pattern which keeps them stuck; help them move beyond it. When you have had enough, let them know. You can say, "I'm sorry you are going through this." Offer them suggestions. Love yourself enough to remove yourself from the situation if possible. You can say, "It's time for me to go." or "I have an appointment." This is always true as we have appointments with ourself to tend to our own life. Let them know you are there for them but this is theirs to take care of and it's time for them to do something about it rather than complain. Simply state you are choosing not to listen to it anymore. This is different from being a sounding board for someone who just needs to vent or wants suggestions so they can create a better situation for themselves.

♥ **Return to sender with love.** When you return to sender with love you are choosing not to be the target and are setting the intention for the energy to be returned to them in a loving way so they can tend to it themselves.

NOURISHMENT FOR YOUR SOUL: When people are behaving in a negative way, send them love; it changes the vibration. Be the fuel that feeds the fire of love!

FOOD FOR THOUGHT: I AM the fuel that feeds the fire of love just by being the love that I AM. I attract and surround myself with positive, loving people and situations.

MIRRORS OF LOVE VISUALIZATION

This visualization is perfect to use when you are around people that are sending out negative energy, situations where there is conflict or where you feel like you are being psychically attacked. This will help to transform the energy.

- Visualize a full mirrored shield all around your body going from head to toe.

- Repeat after me, "Dear Angels, I ask that all lower energy be reflected back to sender with love. Thank you!"
- Affirm: I AM surrounded and protected by mirrors that transform harsh energy and return to sender with love. I attract only loving experiences, opportunities and relationships into my life now. And so it is!

NOTE: This visualization is found on *Your Journey to Love Daily Practice* CD included with this book.

Unhealthy Relationships

I share this information with you so you may discern if you are in a healthy relationship which is nurturing your soul's growth. Many times people stay in relationships because they think if they love someone enough they can "fix" them or they will change. The truth of the matter is, if you cannot accept someone for who they are and what they do now, do not stay in that relationship. They will only change if they are ready and willing, and they must do it for themselves, not for you. Do not fall in love with a person's potential or you will be disappointed when the relationship does not work. Sometimes people stay in relationships for financial reasons. In truth, all the money in the world can't fill in for the ingredients missing in a relationship. Sometimes people stay in relationships because of the fear of being alone or not being loved by another. In truth, if you are in a relationship that is not healthy, you need to let go of that relationship in order to attract the relationship you do desire to come into your life. When you are between relationships, it is helpful to get comfortable being alone without actually being lonely. Enjoy the time that you have to yourself and do the inner work that is needed for you to attract the type of partner you desire.

Sometimes people stay in relationships for the sake of their children. Although this seems like it would be beneficial for the children, it really creates a situation where everyone loses. Your children will feel the stress and tension of a relationship that is not working and they will lose out on seeing the best in both parents. We are models for our children, so we want to model healthy relationships to them so they will know that kind of relationship is out there for them and to not settle for less. What is best for children is to have a loving, healthy, stable environment. If that cannot be accomplished in the current relationship and you have done everything possible to make it work, then it's better for all to move on.

Happiness comes from within ourselves not from others. We must first be happy with ourselves before we can be happy in other relationships. Sometimes people look for fulfillment from others and they become dependent on them to make them happy or take care of them. They blame others for their mishaps or unpleasant situations, however, the bottom line is you are responsible for and create your own life. This is why it is important for us to look within to find happiness rather than expect someone else to bring it to us. By taking responsibility for yourself and your life, you can find happiness within which is where happiness resides and thrives. When we depend on someone else to bring us happiness, we become co-dependant rather than taking the responsibility for our own life. As a result we often feel disappointed. Although relationships bring us great happiness, they are not our source of happiness as this begins within. This is part of being self-sufficient. Self-sufficient means to be independent, and free from needing or expecting someone else to do what you can do for yourself. This is different from helping someone out or working as a team, with each person doing their part. I'm referring to someone who doesn't take responsibility for themselves and wants, expects and depends on you to make everything okay for them. In healthy relationships we are with that person by choice, not because we "have" to be with them.

If you find yourself in a situation in which someone is co-dependent on you in an unhealthy way, be a model by the way you live your life. Guide the other person to independence by showing them to go within to have these needs met instead of looking to you or other sources. At first they may be angry or hurt because it takes them out of their comfort zone. It really is the best gift you can give them, and in the long run they will appreciate it. You help them by not rescuing them and doing things for them that they must do for themselves.

Give them the tools, information, advice, inspiration, and example, but allow them to take the initiative to make it happen. You are not responsible for their life and you cannot create it for them. They must do it on their own. A good rule of thumb to follow is if someone continuously depends on you to do something they can and should be doing themselves, it is essential that you speak up.

Misconceptions About Love

I'd like to address some mis-conceptions about love that occur in our society so you can determine for yourself if you are in a healthy relationship or not.

- ♥ Love is not control. For example, if a person says, "If you do _____ then I will love you," or "If you loved me you would _____." That is not real love. People pleasing is doing things to please others to be loved and accepted but you are miserable in the process. This is not healthy. It is wonderful to do things for others you want to do, things that you do willingly with an open heart. However, to feel forced or pressured to do things interferes with your choice of free will. This is control.

♥ Love is not manipulation. If someone verbally attacks you accusing that you should do _____ because they did _____, or gave you _____, do not fall for it. This is not good relations; this is manipulation.

♥ Love is not punishment. If a person mis-treats you and says, "You deserve it because you did _____," that is punishment not love.

♥ If someone truly loves you they do not intentionally or deliberately try to hurt or abuse you. You do not deserve to be abused in any way—verbally, sexually, physically or emotionally. If you find yourself in this kind of situation, call on your angels for assistance and love yourself enough to walk away and get help. This is not healthy for anyone. You do not have to accept abuse to be loved. You do have a choice . . . Choose to say good-bye. You deserve to be loved!

♥ None of us are victims of life, circumstances or any individual. We are powerful beings who can change our life if we so desire. When you feel like a victim that is a message that you are giving your power away and not standing up for yourself. Instead, be the powerful light that you are and say, "No, I will not allow you to do this to me." Your relationships with others begin with yourself. Others will treat you the way you believe you deserve to be treated. If you desire your relationships to change, change the beliefs you have about yourself and you will attract new people into your life who reflect those beliefs.

NOURISHMENT FOR YOUR SOUL: When you recognize you have a choice, it keeps you in your power. You are a powerful being who has a choice in what you experience. Choose to say no to these fear-based, unhealthy relationships and say yes to love!

FOOD FOR THOUGHT: All of my relationships are healthy, harmonious and loving. I AM surrounded by people who love me. I see my past as a learning experience without judgment and I create new and loving experiences for myself.

Holding On or Letting Go

Throughout your lifetime there will be people who come and go in your life. You will come in contact with others on this earth plane who will present you with opportunities to grow and evolve. Remember, you have chosen these people prior to your incarnation. These people reflect lessons and opportunities for your soul to grow. When you have grown as much as you can grow with that person or have outgrown the relationship, your soul decides it is time for you to move on. So when relationships end, do not look at them as failures. Instead, see them as opportunities for growth and reflect upon the lessons you've learned as well as the gifts they have given you. These relationships have been a part of shaping who you are today. It actually takes great strength to have the courage to end a relationship, rather than stay in a space that does not feel good or serve you and neither of you are able to grow any longer.

Relationships go through shifts and changes. Oftentimes they need a little fine-tuning to reflect your growth. When you are in a relationship and one person is growing rapidly but the other is not, it is essential that you can express yourself during this time and share your experiences with the other person so you can stay connected. This also opens the door and allows them to grow along with you if they choose. In any relationship we either grow together or grow apart. We all grow at different levels and at different speeds depending on our awareness and willingness to live out our life's purpose. Due to the law of free will, God presents opportunities and experiences for our soul's growth, but we must be willing to become aware, accept the opportunity and take the necessary steps to make that happen. When we choose not to participate in God's divine plan, we are not living in a state of love and light, but rather darkness and fear. Relationships may dissolve because you have outgrown each other or because as you grow, your interests and priorities change and the similarities you once shared are no longer present. This is all a part of life and the best thing to do is recognize when to let go and when to hang on.

♥ Reflect upon the following questions to determine whether to hold on or let go of a relationship. Is this a healthy situation? Does this relationship allow me to grow? Does it support where I desire to go? Am I free to be myself in this relationship? Am I in love with this person? Can I accept this person the way they are? Do I feel safe in this relationship? Is there an equal amount of giving and receiving by both of us? Are both of us willing to do what it takes to make this relationship work?

♥ Communicate with your inner child and see how she/he feels about this relationship. This will also help you identify hurt, resentment or buried anger related to this person or past relationships which is blocking the flow of love between the two of you.

♥ Do a creating boundaries exercise by writing inside a heart all that you desire in a mate or partner. One of two things will happen. The relationship will shift and those desires will be present in the relationship, or the relationship will gently end, making room for a new relationship which supports your desires.

♥ Invite in your angels for assistance.

♥ If this is a relationship you desire to stay in, do *Resolving Conflict Exercises*, *Divine Love Partnership Meditation* and *Divine Love Exercises* to invoke in the energy of divine love, strengthen the connection, and take your relationship to a deeper level.

NOURISHMENT FOR YOUR SOUL: When relationships end, instead of holding onto judgments, anger and resentments, reflect upon the blessings that relationship brought and give gratitude for what you shared. When you do this, you are freeing yourself from that relationship. This helps to clear the energy between you and the other person and it opens you up to attract the good qualities you desire in a relationship because that is what you will be focusing on.

FOOD FOR THOUGHT: I follow the wisdom within and I know when to hold on and when to let go. I allow this process to occur with grace and ease.

Soul Mates

A soul mate is someone whom you have been with in a previous lifetime(s). Soul mates are not always romantic relationships. They can be a relative, friend, someone you pass on the street who you feel a connection to, or even a pet. You may feel a deep love for a soul mate but not be in love with them. This is familial love. The more lifetimes you have shared with a person, the more intensity you will feel. You also feel a deeper connection to the soul mates who have been a husband or a wife in previous lifetimes. You come in contact with many soul mates throughout your lifetime. Sometimes soul mates stay part of your life and sometimes you come in contact with a soul mate to learn certain lessons, to be a catalyst, or because there was a soul contract to complete and then you go your separate ways because you have chosen different paths in this lifetime. Relationships with soul mates are not always all peaches and cream and can be a rough road when there is unfinished business or karmic lessons. However, these relationships can be very fulfilling when you are with the right person at the right time. Some soul mates you have a stronger connection to than others. These are people who are part of your soul group or soul family that you recognize as kindred spirits. When you come in contact with people from your soul family, you feel as if you have known them forever or experience a deja-vu feeling. You feel this deep connection because your soul carries into this lifetime the previous memories shared therefore, their essence is part of your soul and your heart feels it. These kinds of relationships are precious gifts. Sometimes we experience soul communications with members of our soul family.

Soul Communications

Soul communications are telepathic communications that touch us on a deeper level. Their purpose is to give us support and help us to move forward in our life as part of our soul's contract. These communications come out of the blue and are an example of our inner connectedness. Sometimes we are aware of them, sometimes not. As your psychic abilities develop and your awareness expands you will become more attuned to these communications. This recipe will help you to recognize, understand and know where these soul communications are coming from.

CREATING LOVING, FULFILLING RELATIONSHIPS

💜 When these soul communications occur, the person they are relating to or coming from will instantly come to your mind.

💜 Sometimes you may be going about your day and out of the blue you'll get a thought or a feeling about a member of your soul group. When you get this intuition, even though on a conscious level you may not know what is occurring in that person's life because you are connecting on a deeper soul level, ask for guidance and take the action you are guided to take.

💜 Sometimes you may hear something and recognize that sounds like something a member of your soul family would say to you.

💜 Sometimes members of your soul family will come to you in your dreams and when you wake up you feel like you've had a conversation with them.

NOURISHMENT FOR YOUR SOUL: When you think of other's, know they are thinking of you too. Send them love. Thank them for being a part of your soul's journey.

FOOD FOR THOUGHT: I AM grateful to my soul family for touching my heart and being a part of my life.

MESSAGES OF LOVE:

Question: "Dear Angels, please tell me more about the meaning of soul family." Here is the message I received.

> *There are some things in life the mind cannot consciously understand on a physical level but touch you on a deeper soul level, which opens you up to greater love and experiences. Your "soul family" who you feel a similarity to, are people you come in contact with who play a large part in reflecting to you lessons of your soul. This is what people call*

kindred spirits. Although the familiar essence is there, it doesn't always mean you will keep a physical connection to them. Although you may not interact on a physical level, you are telepathically interacting with them to assist them on their journey and vice versa. Just follow your heart and do not get caught up in what the physical situation appears to be. Just know they are touching you as you are touching them. This is a strong connection that helps each of you evolve. It is best to give gratitude on a soul level as the physical may not recognize the gift, although those who are highly aware feel a more powerful surge from time to time. Many times, on a human level, you want these to be a physical connection because your soul family makes you feel closer to your source, what you refer to as "home." Many times the inspiration comes from your soul family pushing you to go within for the motivation to ignite your own power. They are showing you the power that resides within yourself. Your soul family is not always your immediate family or birth family. Some people have more physical contact with members of their soul family on the earth plane depending on their mission and choice of free will.

EXERCISE: SOUL MATE CONNECTIONS

This exercise will assist you in understanding the contract with the soul mates you come in contact with in this lifetime.

1. Find a comfortable place in which you will not be interrupted. Bring your journal and a pen with you as you may want to record what you retrieve.
2. Take a few deep breaths and relax.
3. Invite in your angels and guides to assist you.
4. Visualize the person you are inquiring about.
5. Ask your angels what the purpose of your uniting in this lifetime is.

6. Ask them to show you other lifetimes you have been with this person and what your relationship was.
7. Record the information that you receive and reflect upon this wisdom to guide you.

Divine Love Relationships

DIVINE LOVE

Two hearts beating as one . . .

One heart,

One mind,

One soul,

One Love—Divine!

—The Angels

Divine Love is what we all dream about and desire. It seems as though everyone is looking for the "one" person who will make their life complete, make them whole, make them happy and so on. Sometimes in life we go from relationship to relationship searching for this "one" person. The truth of the matter is that this divine love begins with the relationship we have with ourself. Divine love occurs within you when your masculine and feminine energy merge. When we are able to love ourself unconditionally, it is then we will experience this deeper love in our relationships with others. The way the universal law works is that we must be willing to give that which we desire to receive and experience. Therefore, when you are the love you desire to experience, that love emanates from you and you will attract it into your life. If you are in a relationship which does not support that foundation, then the relationship will gently end and someone new will come into your life who will reflect the love that you are being, giving and desire to experience. The following recipes will empower you to go within and manifest a relationship that reflects what's in your heart. Once you attract a soul mate relationship, your relationship can evolve into a divine love partnership when both people choose this endeavor and are committed to it. Regardless of whether you are in a soul mate relationship or divine love partnership, what's most important is that the quality of the relationship you are in reflects the desires of each person so that it is fulfilling and empowering for both of you.

Attracting a Romantic Soul Mate

You are given many opportunities to experience a loving, joyful, harmonious, and romantic relationship with a soul mate. In order for this to occur, both people must be willing and ready. If you have had a relationship with a soul mate and the relationship did not work out, know there are other possibilities out there. Focus on your desires for a soul mate partner and you will attract one. This recipe will guide you in manifesting from within and attracting a romantic soul mate.

- ♥ Ask your angels for assistance and be sure to ask them to bring you a soul mate relationship that is harmonious and loving.

- ♥ Make a list inside a heart of the characteristics you desire in the relationship with your mate. Be sure to list things like spiritually aligned, like-minded, physically, mentally and emotionally available. At the bottom of the heart write, "Anything else that is for the highest good of both of us." That way if you left out any important details, they will be present.

- ♥ Create affirmations that reflect what you desire to experience in this relationship. Tape them and listen to them every night before you go to bed or write them down and review them every day.

- ♥ Make room in your life for him/her by visualizing yourself holding hands with your partner (as a soul) and doing things you enjoy together. Before going to bed, visualize the two of you snuggling together.

- ♥ Create space in your home for your soul mate. Be sure to bring the masculine and feminine energy into your bedroom.

- ♥ Give gratitude for this relationship being present in your life now.

- ♥ Call on Archangel Chamuel to bring the two of you together in the physical realm.

- ♥ Play *Harp Magic* or *Angels Gift* as it invokes the angelic energy and magnifies your manifestations.

- ♥ Treat yourself the way you desire to be treated. Take yourself out on a date, go to a movie or out to dinner or a play. Make a list of ways to love yourself. Put on some soft music and do some free-flowing dancing or body movement; this opens up the flow. Visualize dancing with your partner.

- ♥ Do *Attracting a Soul Mate Meditation* daily.

NOURISHMENT FOR YOUR SOUL: All of these activities set the intention and create the energy for the relationship to manifest in your life.

FOOD FOR THOUGHT: I AM now in a harmonious, loving, passionate, intimate, divine soul mate relationship and we are enjoying life together.

ANGELIC TOOLS:
- ♥ *Angelic Reflections II: Tides of Abundance* CD by Bonnie Ann Lewis (*Attracting a Soul Mate Meditation*)
- ♥ *The Romance Angels* audio by Doreen Virtue

ATTRACTING A SOUL MATE MEDITATION

This meditation is designed to unite you and your soul mate and open you up to attract one another in the physical. It will prepare both of you to come together and enjoy a loving, joyous, harmonious, fulfilling relationship.

- I invite you to close your eyes, focus on the music and just relax.

- Take three or four deep breaths. As you breathe in breathe in love. As you breathe out breathe out any fears you may have about attracting a soul mate.

- Repeat after me, "Dear Angels and Archangel Chamual, please help me release any fears that are blocking me from attracting a soul mate into my life. I AM ready for my divine life partner to come forth in my life now. Please assist the process of bringing us together so we may walk hand in hand and heart to heart through life."

- Visualize your soul as a flame of white light within the center of your BEing.

- With your intention, allow the light of your soul to extend out of you toward your new partner, as you continue to breathe deeply.

- With each breath, visualize the light of your partner's soul moving toward you and the space between you getting smaller and smaller, bringing the two of you closer and closer together.

- As you take your next breath, the two of you will merge as one.

- Now I invite you to send love to your soul mate wherever they may be at this time, knowing they are on their way to you and the two of you will meet in the physical very soon.

- Feel the love the two of you already share.

- Affirm: My heart is now open to giving and receiving love to and from you. I AM walking hand in hand and heart to heart with my life partner. And so it is!

- Thank your angels and Archangel Chamual for already making this so.

May you and your life partner have a happy, joyous celebration as you unite in the physical and walk hand in hand and heart to heart enjoying your life together!

Namaste'

NOTE: This meditation is found on my
Angelic Reflections II: Tides of Abundance CD

DIVINE PARTNERSHIP
Celebrating the divine union and expression of the masculine and feminine.

Creating a Divine Love Partnership

MARRIAGE TAKES THREE

I once thought marriage,
Took two to make a go,
But now I am convinced
It takes the Lord also.
And not one marriage fails,
Where Christ is asked to enter,
As lovers come together,
With Jesus as the center.
But marriage seldom thrives,
And homes are incomplete,
'Til He is welcomed there,
To help avoid defeat.
In homes where Christ is first,
It's obvious to see,
Those unions really work,
For marriage still takes three.

—*Abbey Press*

A Divine love partnership is a deep spiritual romantic relationship with a soul mate. It represents a bond that forms between two people when you invoke in the energy of unconditional love into your relationship and merge together on all levels of your existence. This strengthens the relationship and takes it to a deeper level. You can experience this divine love when you are in a soul mate relationship which supports the desire and intention of both involved by asking for angelic assistance. This partnership evolves when you are with a soul mate and both of you have reached a higher level of awareness in which you desire to experience a deeper form of love allowing spirit to be the center of your relationship. To create a divine love partnership, you must learn life lessons, and follow divine guidance to manifest this in your life.

Each relationship we have had in the past contributed to and prepared us for this divine love relationship. This began with the relationship we had with our parents. Therefore, we must heal the conflicts from those relationships in order to be open to this kind of love. We do this by healing the child within. I'm not saying that all of these things need to occur before you can be in a loving relationship. I'm simply describing the process that occurs in creating and experiencing deeper, more meaningful relationships. Many times we work through these steps in relationships as that is part of our learning and evolving process. Sometimes in one relationship we'll have physical attraction, without a strong soul connection, while other times, there is a strong soul connection without the physical attraction. It is possible and essential to have all of these with one person and experience divine love. In a divine love relationship, all of the essential ingredients are present. You will have the physical attraction, the passion, the intimacy, and feel connected on all levels of your existence. You will both be physically and emotionally available to commit to the relationship. You will have similar interests, goals, intentions, and values. All the necessary components to experience a relationship that is satisfying, fulfilling and empowering for both of you exist. This creates a solid foundation that supports a divine love partnership which reflects the passions and desires of each of you.

In a divine love partnership you feel deeply connected to one another beyond what words can explain. There is a synergy (synchronistic energy) that happens and your life is enriched with love and light.

You will love to spend time with this person as being in their presence brings a sense of infinite love, support, security, passion, intimacy and joy between the two of you as you bring out the best in one another. Honesty and trust are present and communication flows easily. You will find that when you communicate, your communications compliment the other. This is a reflection of spirit speaking through both of you. You will learn similar lessons but not necessarily at the same time or in the same manner. This type of relationship has such a strong bond that often times you feel what the other person is feeling and know what they are thinking or need.

In sharing a divine love partnership there is a commitment in which each person shows up as the loving being they are. Each of you mirror to one another the lessons you came here to learn in a loving way. A safe space is present so that each of you can grow and heal at your own pace from anything that is blocking you from being your true self or fulfilling your life's mission. It reflects your strengths so that you can accomplish what you came here to do. It teaches you to be honest with yourself and others and to live with integrity, taking responsibility for your own experiences and lessons, and allowing the other person to be accountable for theirs. You feel as though you can get through and accomplish anything together. This doesn't mean everything will be perfect all the time and you won't have disagreements or challenges. It just means that you truly love one another unconditionally and have the desire and passion that it takes to overcome any obstacles that are in the way of this divine love expressing itself. This creates a win-win situation for all involved.

Divine Love Partnerships are meant to take you to a greater understanding and advancement, learning soul lessons at a rapid pace. They often have a higher purpose related to being of service and helping the world. When you unite with your soul mate, the two of you will follow a divinely guided path in which you will walk hand in hand and heart to heart through life, being of service together. This nurtures the growth of your individual soul's while working together for the greater good of humanity, making this world a better place. You do this by manifesting your desired life together where each of you fulfill your life's purpose, blending your gifts and talents to compliment one another and be of service. Although divine love relationships are not very common in our society at this time, I believe with the evolution of humanity as people become more aware of these concepts, more people will attract a soul mate in which they will experience this divine love, and the relationship will support a partnership that will reflect the love they share. As two souls merge, their energy becomes one and emanates this divine love out into the universe, bringing balance to our planet.

The following recipes will guide you in taking your soul mate relationship to a deeper level and create a divine love partnership. A divine love partnership is very rewarding as it magnifies the love that you feel, and enriches your life experience tremendously. When you unite with a soul mate, experience divine love and create a divine love partnership, it is truly the most amazing, fulfilling experience and presents the greatest blessings!

NOURISHMENT FOR YOUR SOUL: May you experience the true blessings of unconditional love as your soul mate relationship evolves to a deeper, spiritual, divine love partnership with assistance from the angelic realm.

FOOD FOR THOUGHT: I AM in a divine love relationship now. I AM walking hand in hand and heart to heart with my life partner now.

ANGELIC TOOLS:

♥ *Angelic Reflections II: Tides of Abundance CD* by Bonnie Ann Lewis (*Divine Love Partnership* Meditation)

Prayer for a Divine Love Partnership

Dear Angels, Archangels and Ascended Masters Devi, Ishtar, Krishna, Oonagh, Aengus, Aphrodite, Guinevere and Isolt, please:

Surround us in your divine white light. Wrap your arms around us so that we may feel the warmth of your embrace. We invite you into our relationship to assist us in creating a divine love partnership.

Assist us in seeing beyond the illusions the light within each other's soul.

Guide us to overcome the challenges we encounter with love so we may experience a loving, harmonious relationship and respond to one another with love. We ask that you guide us in building a solid foundation based on love.

Assist us in overlooking the idiosyncrasies of our personalities so we may focus on our true characteristics, reflecting to one another our greatest qualities so we may both shine.

Guide us both in expressing ourselves truthfully so we may experience true intimacy.

Guide us both so we may be awake to who we are and what we came here to do, so that we may serve humanity and assist in creating heaven here on earth.

Open our hearts and minds to giving and receiving love to and from one another.

Guide us in manifesting our desires and dreams together so that we may experience an abundant life.

Assist us in agreeing upon a common ground so that we may both benefit from each situation. Help us to stay heart to heart when we do not see eye to eye, always meeting in the middle when there is adversity.

Guide us in giving each other the space to learn and grow at our own pace and still remain connected.

Provide us with the financial abundance and independence so that we may both do what we love for a living.

Assist us so that we can be the best parents we can in guiding and supporting our children to grow and bloom with love, and to succeed.

Assist both of us so we may be healthy in body, mind and spirit so that we may enjoy a life of longevity, abundance and happiness.

Help us to always feel and remember the love and passion which brought us together.

Guide us to learn our lessons with love so we may experience the blessings love brings. We ask for your assistance in keeping the lines of communication open so that we may resolve conflict with love and ease.

We ask for your assistance so we may love each other as deeply as you love us so that we may experience the blessings of true love.

Guide us to pray, play, work, exercise, learn, grow, love, and enjoy each other and life. We ask for your presence to be the center of our relationship at all times. We ask you to guide us as we walk hand in hand and heart to heart, supporting each other along the way.

For these are our true desires. Thank you for making this so!

Nurturing a Divine Love Relationship

TOGETHERNESS

No matter what comes your way,
Everything will be okay,
Because you have one another,
And will weather it together.

—*The Angels*

It is very easy to get caught up in the activities of everyday life, children, job, finances, etc. It is essential to make time for each other to nurture the relationship, stay connected, keep communication open, keep the intimacy and passion alive and just enjoy each other's company, free from the distraction of the outside world. This will keep you connected as you interact with the outside world. The following recipe will guide your way.

- 💜 **Invite the angels into your relationship.** When disagreement or conflict occurs, ask angels to intervene, to help you see with compassion the other person's point of view and help you resolve conflict with love.

- 💜 **Make a date** night or lunch date regularly.

- 💜 **Pray together.** When situations or challenges arise, pray together and ask for guidance for what to do. This creates positive results for the highest good of all concerned.

- 💜 **Spend time out in nature together.** This helps relieve stress and will open you both up to greater communication.

- ♥ **Take time to connect,** communicate, and share your feelings, thoughts and dreams.

- ♥ **Surprise each other** once in a while. This keeps the romance alive.

- ♥ **Do little things for one another** because you know it will make life easier for them or bring them joy.

- ♥ **Take responsibility for your own feelings** rather than blame your partner.

- ♥ **Make love a priority** throughout your day, not just in the bedroom.

- ♥ **Make your bedroom into a sanctuary of love** that reflects what you both desire to experience in the relationship.

- ♥ **Manifest your life together.**

- ♥ **Take time to participate in activities you both like to do together.** Have fun and laugh as laughter opens the heart.

- ♥ **Meditate together.** The Divine Love Partnership Meditation invokes in the energy of divine love into your relationship, strengthening the relationship and taking it to a deeper level.

- ♥ **Seek guidance together.** When you are faced with making a decision, communicate with the angels together by using any oracle cards by Doreen Virtue.

- ♥ **Give gratitude for each other** and the blessings your relationship brings.

- ♥ **Create a safe and nurturing space** for the other person to express themselves freely.

- ♥ **Respect your differences.** Accept each other for who you are. Compliment each other's strengths and support one another as you overcome your so-called shortcomings.

- ♥ **Establish some rituals** that you do together on a daily basis.

NOURISHMENT FOR YOUR SOUL: When you nurture your relationship it keeps you connected and sets the intentions for what you desire to experience in your relationship. This is powerful!

FOOD FOR THOUGHT: We nurture our relationship and experience the blessings of love, passion, intimacy and joy that it brings.

DIVINE LOVE PARTNERSHIP MEDITATION

Divine Love is the deepest form of romantic love one can experience. When you feel this love within yourself, it will be reflected in your relationship with your partner. This meditation is designed to strengthen the bond between you and your partner, and create a deeper connection on all levels of your existence. It will open you up to giving and receiving unconditional love to and from one another, and release any fears that are blocking you from creating and experiencing a divine love partnership. This exercise is very powerful when done together with your partner holding hands.

- I invite you to close your eyes and just relax.

- Repeat after me, "Dear Angels, please assist me in releasing any blockages that are in the way of me experiencing a divine love relationship. I invite you to guide this relationship so my mate and I can experience a divine love partnership."

- Take four deep breaths. As you breathe in breathe in love, as you breathe out let go of any fears, resentments, anger or conflicts you may have relating to your relationship with your mate.

- Visualize your flame of white light within the center of your BEing glowing like a candle. See the flame of white light that exists within your partner glowing like a candle.

- Visualize these candles moving toward one another. As they meet in the middle the two of you will merge as one, expanding and illuminating into a brighter flame.

- Visualize a ray of pink light going from your heart to your partner's heart.

- Take a few moments to think about when you and your partner first met and reflect upon what attracted you to your partner in the first place.

- Pause.

- Feel the love, passion, intimacy and romance the two of you share and the joy that brings.

- Pause.

- Visualize you and your partner walking hand in hand enjoying your life, knowing whatever challenges that cross your path, you will weather together. Whatever dreams you have you will support one another and achieve together and whatever successes you experience, you will celebrate together.

- Affirm: My heart and mind are open to giving and receiving unconditional love. I give and receive respect, acceptance, compassion, forgiveness, and gratitude easily and effortlessly. I AM in a divine love relationship now. And so it is!

- Divine love has now been activated within your relationship with your partner. May this bring both of you peace and harmony as you go forth to nurture this relationship, which will enrich both of your lives.

May you always enjoy the blessings your Divine Love Partnership brings!

Namaste'

NOTE: This meditation is found on my
Angelic Reflections II: Tides of Abundance CD

Divine Love Exercises

These divine exercises are designed to take your relationship to a deeper Level. They will ensure open communication, increase your intimacy and keep the passion alive in your relationship. Use as you feel guided. When doing these exercises, it is best for each of you to do them individually and then share with one another. These short and sweet exercises are great to incorporate into a date night.

EXERCISE #1: BLENDING AND BALANCE

Make a list of opposites present in your relationship. Share the list with one another. Discuss how the two of you are going to blend these differences.

NOURISHMENT FOR YOUR SOUL: This will bring to your awareness where the blending and balance needs to occur so the two of you can work on this together, creating a harmonious relationship.

FOOD FOR THOUGHT: We blend our differences and experience balance and harmony in our relationship.

EXERCISE #2: PASSION AND PLAY

Each of you make a list of what you like to do for fun. Include your desires, hobbies, interests and then share with one another. This is a fun exercise that gives you the passion to pursue these interests together. You may be amazed how much the two of you have in common.

NOURISHMENT FOR YOUR SOUL: In divine love relationships it is essential that there are many common values, morals, and interests, for it is these commonalities that will pull you through when conflict occurs. This exercise will help you to focus on these blessings and keep them active in your life.

FOOD FOR THOUGHT: We enjoy and embrace the commonalities present in our relationship.

EXERCISE #3: VISION AND CREATION

Both of you make a list of what you desire in the relationship, then share your list with each other. Set a plan in motion for bringing these desires into the relationship. Here are some creative ways you can do this together: prayer, visioning, affirming, and imagery.

NOURISHMENT FOR YOUR SOUL: When you utilize these creative ways to bring your desires into your relationship, you open up your channels of creativity, your sacral chakra, which also increases your sexual desires.

FOOD FOR THOUGHT: We create our relationship together and experience the dreams and desires of both of us.

EXERCISE #4: BLESSINGS AND GRATITUDE

Both of you make a list of the blessings you see in the relationship and share with one another. You can continue to add to this as more come to mind.

NOURISHMENT FOR YOUR SOUL: Place this list where the two of you can visit and reflect upon it daily so you can enjoy the blessings on a regular basis. The more you reflect on your blessings, the more the blessings will come!

FOOD FOR THOUGHT: We reflect upon, give thanks for, and embrace the blessings our relationship brings us.

EXERCISE #5: CREATING YOUR DIVINE SPACE

Make your bedroom a sacred space which reflects what the two of you desire to experience in the relationship. When doing this, surround yourselves with things that make you feel good and that represent the love that the two of you share. Here are some suggestions: place pictures of the two of you; imagery that you've created together; *Divine Partnership* art by Eva Sakmar-Sullivan; bring in the colors of red, pink, purple, fuchsia and orange in your room decor. This will help to bring in the energy that you both desire. You can put the special cards that you have given to each other on the wall and reflect upon their message. You can also place rose quartz under your bed to bring in the energy of love.

NOURISHMENT FOR YOUR SOUL: When you are in your bedroom you want to feel a sense of peace, love, passion, intimacy and joy. You want to set the scene for openness and connection. To increase the intimacy, ask your angels to help the two of you connect on all levels of your existence.

FOOD FOR THOUGHT: Our intimate space reflects the love, passion, intimacy and joy present in our relationship.

EXERCISE #6: REFLECTIONS

Both of you make a list of the characteristics you love or admire about each other or what attracted you to your partner. Share this with one another.

NOURISHMENT FOR YOUR SOUL: This exercise helps you to focus on the strengths within each of you and reflect upon what brought you together in the first place. This makes both of you feel good and appreciated and it re-ignites the spark that drew you to one another. As you reflect on the good within each other, you will experience that in your relationship.

FOOD FOR THOUGHT: We reflect upon the love within each of us, and express it to one another.

EXERCISE #7: CREATING A PATH OF SERVICE TOGETHER

This exercise will assist you in creating a partnership where you will combine your gifts and talents in being of service together.

♥ **Pray together.** Join hands and ask for angelic assistance by saying the following prayer:

Dear God, Angels, Archangels and Ascended Masters,

We ask you to reflect to us our gifts and talents that compliment one another and guide the way for us as we combine these gifts and talents to be of service. We thank you for making this so!

♥ **Combine your gifts and talents.** Both of you reflect upon your gifts and talents that you'd like to bring to this partnership. Make a list of the aspects of this career of service you would like to do and the gifts you have to contribute. Share them with one another and come up with an action plan to move in that direction.

♥ **Manifest it together.**
1. Set your intentions by writing your desires for this path of service inside a heart.
2. Create and recite affirmations that reflect the desires of both of you.

3. Visualize together by joining hands and each of you doing your own visualizations. Share with one another.
4. Create an imagery board that reflects the career you've created together. Visit it often.
5. Light a candle and say the following prayer:

   Dear God, Angels, Archangels and Ascended Masters,

   Here are our desires for our path of service together. We ask for your love, support and guidance in bringing these dreams to life. We thank you for making this so!

6. Both of you take at least one guided action step each day toward bringing these dreams to life.
7. Give gratitude for this already being so. Enjoy your journey as it all unfolds.

NOURISHMENT FOR YOUR SOUL: Remember to relax and play along the way!

FOOD FOR THOUGHT: I AM now being of service with my divine love partner. We give thanks for the opportunity to be of service together.

About the time I was manifesting what I refer to as a divine love relationship, I had read about the music of Peter Sterling in *Healing with the Fairies* by Doreen Virtue. I felt an instant connection and I knew I was to have that music, so I contacted him right away. He was kind enough to ship his CD's to me overnight and I received *Harp Magic* and *Angels Gift* just in time to take with me to the Hawaiian Healing Retreat I was attending that Doreen Virtue was holding in Kona. After Peter's music came into my life, some amazing things began to happen. I began receiving visions and messages. Although at the time I did not consciously understand what they all meant, I intuitively knew these were regarding my soul mate. This is the first time I had experienced such strong, deep feelings and emotions about someone I hadn't physically met.

During this time, many poems about love and this relationship came through me. When I was in California taking my ATP® Training, I felt a masculine energy in my aura on my right side. The energy felt very elemental. I felt this presence especially when I would walk along the beach in the mornings. The day I left to fly back home to Texas, I cried and felt like I was leaving part of my heart behind. Although at the time I didn't understand what these feelings were all about, after meeting John and finding out he was born and living in California at that time it all made sense. I kept hearing the name Lewis but it sounded like *Lu-ise*. I later came to understand, I was hearing the name of my soul mate that I was connecting with and would be coming into my life. As we all know, my last name is now Lewis and my husband John has that elemental energy.

Prior to our connecting in Dallas, John had a meeting with one of the practitioners at the Church of Religious Science that he attended in California where he lived, and she had told him that he would be meeting someone who was his soul mate but that right now she was going through some tough times. The month I arrived in Dallas to heal from my medical condition, he was transferred to Dallas for a job. It was a year later before we met. When we met, he lived in an apartment that overlooked a pond with swans! When I brought him to Austin for the first time to visit he loved it and immediately felt like it was home. When we moved into our new home, we came across a picture of Dallas all lit up that he had taken several years earlier when he was in Dallas on business. Little did he know being drawn to taking that picture had a greater meaning, and that he would later be transferred to Dallas and meet me, his soul mate!

During the Hawaiian Healing Retreat, I had the opportunity to swim with the dolphins and it filled me with such a sense of love, peace and joy. What an amazing experience! Also during the healing retreat, I received guidance to take the ANGEL THERAPY PRACTITIONER® certification course that Doreen Virtue was teaching the following February. As I waited, I read most of Doreen Virtue's books, and shared them with my mom and sister, Lynn. They lived in Michigan so we would talk on the phone about the books and share our experiences. Then Lynn and I were guided to do planetary healings together with assistance from the angels, archangels and dolphins. One day during one of our healing sessions Lynn and I were guided to do a healing on a person who had been in a car accident. At the time, we did not know who this person was. We just followed the angels' guidance and were grateful for the opportunity to help someone. During this time I saw visions of a white car and this person in a hospital where we conducted the healing with the help of Archangel Michael and Archangel Raphael. We were guided to send healing energy to him but mainly focus on his head. After the healing I saw visions that the person was fine and had purchased a new white car. After I met John, I found out it was him! During the accident he suffered with a large deep wound to his head, and his face was badly bruised. The car he had been driving during the accident was white and the new car he purchased was also white.

When I was manifesting this relationship, I did my imagery and set my intentions for what I desired in a relationship in the center of a heart. At the bottom I added the words, anything else that would be for the highest good of both of us. My husband and I laugh about this since cooking is not one of my favorite things to do. Although I do cook when the children are with us, lucky for me, he likes to eat salad everyday for lunch and dinner. This is an example of an item I did not have on my list that benefits both of us! It is amazing our similarities and differences that compliment one another. John has a Master's in Business Administration, but also holds a Bachelors Degree in Psychology. Our passion to help others, similar interests in activities and like mindedness are blessings of our relationship. I knew what I desired in a relationship but had never experienced all of it with one person. In each relationship I had a piece of it. When I married my husband, I got the whole package!

I later came to understand, that along with Doreen Virtue's teachings, Peter's music opened me up to these experiences and this love. *Harp Magic* magnified what I was manifesting and amplified my vibration to attract what I desired into my life, and *Angels Gift* invoked the angels who guided the way in bringing us together. My husband's favorite CD of Peter's is *Heart and Soul*. Whenever I play it he say's, "I just love this music." We noticed later that Peter recorded it in Ojai California and that is where my husband lived before moving to Dallas. It is so amazing to see that interconnectedness that weaves the web of creation within our lives! It brings great joy to re-unite with kindred spirits.

I was blessed with the opportunity to meet Peter Sterling in person for the first time during my ATP® training, and what a blessing that was. Hearing his heavenly music in a live performance was absolutely beautiful and breathtaking! My first experience as an ANGEL THERAPY PRACTITIONER®, was the Whole Life Expo in San Francisco, California. Initially I was going to attend the expo for a specific lecture. Then I was guided to be an exhibitor and do readings, so I did. I flew to San Francisco with two suitcases full of

Doreen Virtue's products, two tables and my belongings. After I had signed up, I found out that Peter Sterling was also going to be there. I shared a booth with another ATP® and of all the booths in that hall, our booth was located 10 feet from where Peter was playing the harp! I was busy doing readings the whole weekend while listening to Peter's beautiful, divine music. This was one of the most miraculous experiences in my life aside from the birth of my two precious children and meeting my husband. I experienced for the first time how utilizing my talents and gifts helped so many people. I felt very blessed and touched.

Since that time, Peter's music has been such a part of my personal and professional life, and I feel so blessed that our paths have crossed. His music plays in our home, often all day long, creating a loving, peaceful, calming and joy-filled environment. I play it during my classes, workshops and private sessions. What I noticed is that it always takes my students where they need to be to retrieve the information they desire or receive the healing they require. It assists me in being a clear channel for the angels' messages. I listen to it when I'm writing, relaxing, meditating or just want to feel the loving essence of the angels. All of the meditations on my *Angelic Reflection* CD's and the Daily Practice CD included with this book have been blessed with Peter's heavenly harp music. Peter has many CD's available and each one has touched my heart and soul in its own unique way. His music is truly the speech of angels and is simply magical. Anyone who listens to this celestial music will be touched beyond words! To experience the blessings of Peter's *Harp Magic*, visit his website at www.harpmagic.com.

I'd like to wrap up this topic with a verse from a song that my husband and I love as it reflects the meaning of love and sets a divine example for all of us.

tice, I want to assure you they are in a beautiful space. It is a new beginning for them rather than an ending. They want us to go on with our life here on earth. We will unite with them again. Sometimes our departed loved ones will come into our lives once again during this lifetime by incarnating through other relationships that enter our life such as through grand children, nieces, nephews, etc. When this occurs, we will recognize their essence. Sometimes our departed loved ones express through people in our life to let us know they are with us. For example, someone may say a phrase that our departed loved one always said or they may show an expression or mannerism that resembles our loved one. When this happens, this is our loved one letting us know they are still with us and sending their love. Sometimes our departed loved ones will become spirit guides to us. In order for this to occur, they go through much training in the afterlife to prepare them for this endeavor.

When we lose a loved one due to what we perceive as a tragedy, our humanness tends to go into the thoughts about what happened to our loved ones, so we feel pain for their sufferings and our loss. The angels assure us that these loved ones do not suffer as their soul leaves their physical body before the incident occurs. The incident is just the way the physical body chose to leave the earth plane. Here are a few examples where I have observed this. It may bring you much peace when you experience the loss of a loved one, whether it is because of a physical condition or what appears to be a painful incident or tragedy.

During an angel reading with one of my clients, her departed son came through. My client was in distress over the way her son had died as it was tragic and appeared he had suffered. The message from the angels for my client was that her son had not suffered as he had already left his body prior to the incident. This brought much peace to my client and eased the pain and grief she was experiencing. My mother-in-law was in the latter stages of Alzheimer's when she fell and hit her head and slipped into a coma. While in the coma, she appeared to be struggling to breathe and my husband and I were concerned she was slowly suffocating. I asked if she was suffering and the angels assured us she was not suffering as she had already left her body. What we were observing was the process in which her physical body was shutting down. The cause of death is really irrelevant and is not to blame for a person's death, for when a soul chooses to leave this earth plane it also chooses how the physical body makes its exit. In my lifetime, I have experienced the transition of two people who I was close to, my mom and my mother-in-law. I share these experiences with you in hopes they will bring you peace and comfort when someone you love leaves this earth plane.

When my mom made her transition it was very sudden. She was only 58 years old. The week before I was talking to her on the phone and she was telling me about this back pain she was having, and was going to the doctors to find out what was going on. I was scheduled to go to California to meet my future mother-in-law for the first time but was going to cancel my trip. However, my mom insisted that I go. My mom lived in Michigan and I lived in Texas. While I was in California, my mom had some tests and they found she had cancer throughout her body and there was no treatment that would help her. The doctors gave her six months to live, but three days later she chose to leave the earth plane. I knew she chose to leave because she did not want to be a burden to anyone and she did not want to suffer. I honor her for that. Although I miss her physical presence, I'm comforted by the fact that she is in a better place, free from pain, and I feel her presence with me.

Three days before she passed I was talking to her on the phone and she told me what the doctors had said. I was crying and asking questions about treatment possibilities and she simply said, "Do not worry, everything is going to be just fine." She was very calm. The next day my family said she was laughing, visiting and seemed like herself. The following day she was in a lot of discomfort and my Dad drove her to the hospital where my sister worked because that was where she could receive the best care. As they were driving, I spoke with her for a few minutes on the phone and she said she had to go now. I could tell she was drifting in and out of consciousness. That night my sister called me and said she was getting worse and she had gone into a comatose state. I took the first flight out I could. I arrived at the airport at 9:00 p.m. and she had passed at 6:00 p.m. I was upset because I felt I was not there for my mom. I was mad at myself and felt guilty that I had gone on this trip to California because if I had not gone, I would have been there for her. I asked the angels why I didn't know it was her time to go. They told me it was not meant for me to know or be there. They said to see the physical death happen at that time in my life would have been very painful for me. I was still recovering from my NDE. Mothers have a sense of knowing what is best for their children. My mom's whole life was us children and my dad. I knew she held on as long as she did for me. One month prior to her leaving the earth plane, she met my future husband and told my sister she knew I would be fine. I know this allowed her to leave peacefully. Although she has left this physical plane, she is still very much alive to me and I feel her presence with me. Having the ability to communicate with her is such a blessing. Looking back, I see where there were indications that she was ready to make her transition, in which I did not recognize at the time. I later came to realize that I had been there for her. I helped her remotely for while I was on the plane, I sent the angels and love to her. This brought me much peace. I've come to understand death is between each individual soul and God. As humans we sometimes feel guilty for what we have or have not done when a loved one makes their transition. When it is time for a soul to leave this earth plane there is nothing we can do to prevent that from occurring. However, we can send them love and angels to assist their process. If it is a situation where it is not their time to go, their angels will intervene.

Little did I know a year later my mother-in-law, whom I had only met that one time, would be moving from California to Texas and I, along with my husband, would be helping take care of her. She was first in an assisted living facility and then later transferred to a full medical care home. She was in her mid 80's and she had been diagnosed with Alzheimer's. My husband and I felt blessed to be with her during these final years of her life. I had only known her for a short time but we had been through so much together. We went through all stages of this disease with her. I knew she was preparing for her transition, and I recognized that during this time, she was flipping back and forth between her physical existence and the spiritual realm, and that as her condition worsened, she spent more and more time out of her body. Although much of what she said did not make sense to anyone, I understood some of the things she was saying having the awareness of the spirit world. She seemed to be at peace when I would talk with her. She would always say, "You know?" I would reply, "Yes, I understand." She would smile.

When she made her transition it was an amazing healing experience for all of us. I asked the angels how I could help in this situation and they told me I was to assist her in her journey to the afterlife, and be a bridge between my husband and her so he could understand what was occurring. This would help him be at peace with her passing. During the last few days of her life, she went into a coma. As she was crossing over to the afterlife, I called in all the angels and continued sending her love. I was given visions of what was occurring which I shared with my husband. This really brought much comfort for him. I saw her spirit going through the tunnel and then the angels showed me a vision of her at a resting place. The day after her funeral service, they showed me another vision of her in a beautiful garden filled with flowers having tea with her mother. My husband said this vision spoke to his heart as he was very close to his grandmother when she was on the earth plane. As I prepared what I was going to say during the service, I asked the angels to help me speak from my heart and guide my words so they would ease the feelings of pain and sorrow for those left behind. Here is what I shared.

> *I'd like to take this time to celebrate the life that Jean has shared with us. Although I have only known her for a short time, we have been through a lot together. I feel blessed for the opportunity to share these last three years of her life. She is truly a woman of great strength. I'd like to share with you some of my fondest memories with her. When she first came to Austin, John was still working in Dallas. So many times I would call Jean and ask her if she would like to go for dessert or run errands with me. She would get so excited because she loved to go. Sometimes she would be in her pajamas and say "oh, just give me a few minutes; I'll get dressed," and when I'd go to pick her up, she always had her lipstick, her earrings and her pins on. She was always so full of life and love. Her most treasured gift to me is her son John. I am forever grateful for her bringing him into this world and blessed to share my life with him. Although we will all miss her physical presence, her spirit lives within all our hearts. Know this is not an ending for Jean, but a new beginning. She is surrounded by many angels and her loved ones who have gone before her. I will always remember Jean for her playful essence and the love that she gave to all. She has truly touched my heart.*

I have included the remembrance prayer from her service. Feel free to use it as is or adjust it to reflect your heart.

A REMEMBRANCE PRAYER

Dear (loved ones name),

We will always remember the beautiful light you shine on this earth and the love that you have shared with all of us. We will hold this love in our hearts forever. We are all better people . . . for you have touched our lives. We love you.

Here are some ways in which you can stay connected to your loved ones who have left this earth plane. May it bring you much peace to feel their presence as you communicate with them.

EXERCISE: COMMUNICATING WITH DEPARTED LOVED ONES

AUTOMATIC WRITING METHOD

1. At the top of a piece of paper write the name of your loved one and below it the question(s) you want to ask.
2. Invite in your angels by saying, "Dear Angels and Archangel Michael, please surround me in your divine white light. Please assist me in connecting with (your departed loved one's name) so that I may communicate clearly."
3. Relax. Take three or four deep breaths and quiet your mind.
4. Then repeat that person's name three times or more if necessary until you receive a sign they are present. You may hear their name, you may feel them, you may smell their perfume or cologne, you may see them, or you may just know they are there.
5. Once you are aware of their presence, begin your questions, one at a time.
6. Ask the first question. Be still until the answer begins coming and write down everything you receive.

7. Go back and read what you received.
8. If you have further questions, proceed with asking those.
9. Continue with the rest of the questions in this same manner.
10. When you feel you are finished, send love to that person for connecting with you and sharing their advice, and thank your angels for their assistance.

TELEPATHIC METHOD

1. Invite in your angels by saying, "Dear Angels and Archangel Michael, please surround me in your divine white light. Please assist me in connecting with (your departed loved one's name) so that I may communicate clearly."
2. Relax. Take three or four deep breaths and quiet your mind.
3. Then repeat in your mind your loved ones name or think about this person until you become aware of their presence.
4. Begin communicating with them mentally by thinking of the question you want to ask.
5. Be still and listen and their response will follow.
6. Continue with the rest of your questions.
7. When you are finished, send them love and thank the angels for their assistance.

PICTURE METHOD

You can communicate with your departed loved ones by focusing on their picture and utilizing the telepathic or automatic methods. The picture can help you connect more quickly as you feel more connected when seeing them in physical form. Most of the time we have great success with these methods, however, there are occasions when that person is not available at that time for whatever reason. When this occurs, the angels usually tell me or show me a symbol like a closed curtain or door. I do not question why, I just honor it and try another time.

NOURISHMENT FOR YOUR SOUL: Take the information that comes from departed loved ones as advice, just as if they are talking to you on earth. They are not angels, so they do not know your life's purpose. Some do become our spirit guides but they must go through training in the afterlife to do this.

FOOD FOR THOUGHT: Your loved ones are always with you. They are just in energy form now instead of physical form.

IN LOVING MEMORY

May the angels' remind you your loved one is safe in their embrace.
May you know they are in a beautiful space.
May their loving presence be forever in your heart . . .
May you always be reminded of
The love, life, laughter and joy he/she brought to your life . . .
May you always remember to
Celebrate the life and precious memories
you shared with him/her . . .
May you stay connected to your loved one for they are always near.

—Bonnie Ann Lewis

CHAPTER 9
Getting to the Heart of the Matter

RAINBOWS

With these recipes come love,
Light, comfort and hope,
For brighter days ahead.
Know beyond the rain,
There is always a rainbow shining bright.
Follow the light and
You'll see its glow and beauty.

—*Bonnie Ann Lewis*

In order to get to the heart of the matter one must look beyond the illusions to the truth. Illusions are created by fear that stems from old beliefs of society such as lack of love, scarcity and judgments. Fear manifests in many forms. The result of these fear-based beliefs is unloving behaviors such as gossip, manipulation, control, envy, jealousy, competition, criticism, peer pressure, rejection, anger, resentments, stress and violence; addictions to mood-altering substances such as drugs, nicotine, alcohol, and foods that contain sugar, chocolate, caffeine, processed foods and artificial colorings, all of which take us out of our natural state of love. These chemicals affect our body in many ways and create imbalances and dis-ease in our lives.

When we are entwined in the illusions of the human experience, we use more energy and thus feel drained, tired, depressed or irritable. When we are not in our natural state of being, we are in a state of fear which causes our heart to close. Many times we do this to block out the pain or to protect ourselves from getting hurt. Although this can be a useful tool to get us through traumatic times, it is meant to be temporary, but sometimes people keep the barrier up and it blocks their connection. When our heart closes, we lose our capacity to give and receive love to ourselves and others. These illusions are man-made. They are not part of who we are, they are merely part of our human experience at this time on earth. As humans we all experience some of these illusions so there should be no shame or embarrassment with the experience. We need not place judgment upon ourselves for these human conditions, but instead recognize and move beyond them. While it is important to look at these shadows, it is essential not to dwell on them.

It is essential to get to the core of what is going on within instead of just treating the symptoms for true healing to take place. We have previously discussed how our body gives us messages that reflect to us unfulfilled emotional needs. Unfilled emotional needs can manifest into physical conditions, addictions and unhealthy behaviors. This section of the book will provide you with the recipes to naturally fill these emotional needs from the inside out by getting to the core of the issue. As you get to the heart of the matter, healing of your inner child takes place.

Healing the Child Within

A FREE SPIRIT

Allow yourself to dream . . . for it expands your mind.
Allow yourself to love . . . for it opens your heart.
Allow yourself to experience . . . for that is what life is all about.
Allow your heart to open . . . for it helps your soul to grow.
Allow yourself to live with an open heart and mind . . .
for that creates your experiences.
Allow yourself to choose whatever your heart desires . . .
for that is the key to true happiness and success.
Allow yourself to experience the richness of life . . .
for it is your birthright to live abundantly.

—*Bonnie Ann Lewis*

Your inner child is the emotional part of yourself that matures and evolves. This occurs in a healthy progression as you grow in physical years when the needs of your inner child are met. The basic needs of your inner child are love, nurturing, support, safety, security, praise, attention, opportunity to play, to be creative, and to express.

Sometimes events happen in your life and your inner child closes down, or sometimes it does not develop as your physical body grows due to trauma or painful experiences. Therefore, you may be an adult in physical years but may still be in a childhood or teen stage emotionally. When the needs of your inner child are not met, you feel a lack of love. As you nurture your inner child by giving it the love that it needs, healing takes place and you return to your natural state of love. Then you are emotionally available to give and receive love in relationships while being of service to others.

HEALING OF THE INNER CHILD

Connecting With Your Inner Child

Connecting with your inner child is the first step to healing the child within. You can connect with your inner child by communicating with him or her. This can bring to your awareness what emotional needs are not being met and areas that require more love. When you get to the heart of the matter, your inner child heals and matures. The following exercises will guide you through this process.

EXERCISE: COMMUNICATING WITH YOUR INNER CHILD THROUGH INTUITIVE WRITING

1. Write down on a piece of paper or in your journal the questions you'd like to ask your inner child.
2. Relax. Take three or four deep breaths and quiet your mind.
3. Ask the angels to help you connect with the child within.
4. Ask your inner child to come forward and communicate with you.
5. Visualize what the child within you looks like.
6. Ask your inner child the questions you have for him/her one at a time. Then as your response comes forward, write down everything you receive with your non-dominant hand. Respond with your dominant hand.
7. Continue communicating until you feel finished.
8. Ask this child for a symbol so that you can recognize and connect with him/her.
9. Thank your inner child for communicating with you.
10. Thank your angels for their assistance.

Here are some suggested questions to ask your inner child:

1. How old are you?
2. What is your name?
3. What do you need from me?
4. How can I help you?
5. What are your desires?
6. Why are you feeling _____?
7. How do you feel about this situation or person?
8. Why are you hurting?
9. What does this behavior, addiction, or situation give you?
10. How can I fill that void in a healthy way?

EXERCISE: DRAWING YOUR INNER CHILD

This exercise will connect you with your inner child so you can draw what your inner child looks like. This gets your creativity flowing and helps you to feel more connected to yourself.

1. Close your eyes. Take three or four deep breaths.
2. Visualize your flame of divine white light, your spark from God, in the center of your BE-ing.
3. Now go a little deeper with that and as you stare into this flame, see it transform into an image of a child. This is your inner child.
4. Focus in on what this child looks like for a few moments and when you are ready, open your eyes and draw this child.

NOURISHMENT FOR YOUR SOUL: Allow your creativity to come alive as you bring this child to life. Be creative and allow whatever comes to be a part of your drawing. When you are finished, send love to this child and place him/her where you can visit often.

FOOD FOR THOUGHT: I honor and acknowledge the child within me.

Nurturing Your Inner Child

To nurture your inner child, reflect upon those things you loved to do as a child and do them. This will ignite the passion, playfulness, creativity, and innocence that exists within you. When you allow your inner child to come out and play, you will feel a sense of freedom. There are infinite ways to bring out that inner child. Here are a few suggestions to trigger the memories of your playful self.

- Put on music and dance. You can dance with a partner or just do a free-flowing waltz. This opens up the flow of energy.
- Swing on a swing at the park.
- Do any kind of artistic endeavors that speak to your heart.
- Do some creative writing or journaling.
- Paint or draw.
- Listen to and create affirmations.
- Play with oracle cards.
- Sit beside a river or pool and dangle your feet in the water.
- Go to the beach and build sand castles.
- Spend time out in nature.

NOURISHMENT FOR YOUR SOUL: I AM no longer that child who must protect myself from my feelings, others, life, fear and the world. I AM free to be me!

FOOD FOR THOUGHT: I AM now a healthy, happy adult, creating my own positive, loving experiences; and I AM safe and free to express and be myself.

ANGELIC TOOLS:

- 💜 *Forgiveness and Loving the Inner Child* audio by Louise L. Hay
- 💜 *Angel Therapy* by Doreen Virtue
- 💜 *Affirmations for the Inner Child* book by Rokelle Lerner
- 💜 *Songs for the Inner Child* CD by Shaina Noll
- 💜 *Magical Unicorn* or *Dolphin and Mermaid Oracle Cards* by Doreen Virtue
- 💜 *Rhythms of Life* music CD by Jodi Lovoi

The following recipes are to be used in conjunction with, not in place of necessary healthcare.

Healing Food Addictions and Cravings from Within

Food cravings and addictions stem from unfulfilled emotional needs. They are messages from our body letting us know what areas of our life need attention and more love. We can heal these addictions and cravings by going within. Our relationship with food is not just about what we eat, it is also affected by the thoughts, beliefs and feelings attached to it. If every time you eat something you feel guilty or are afraid of what it will do to your body, then it is time to re-evaluate what you are eating and the way you feel about food. Food is meant to provide our body with nourishment, "fuel" required to survive and thrive, not as a comfort that fills an emotional void or blocks out pain. Foods that contain chemicals such as caffeine, alcohol, processed foods, sugar, and colorings in them are addictive. The more you eat them, the more your body will crave them. When you eat healthy foods and feel good about what you eat, your body will feel good too. This recipe will assist you in creating a healthy relationship with food to promote your vibrant health and well-being.

- 💜 Ask your angels to help you have a taste for healthy foods.
- 💜 Look up the food that you are craving in the book, *Constant Cravings* by Doreen Virtue.
- 💜 Recite the affirmation given in the book for at least 30 days. This changes your belief system.
- 💜 When you stop consuming foods that contain addictive chemicals, your body will stop craving them.
- 💜 Praise yourself each time you choose a healthy snack.
- 💜 Be kind and gentle and forgive yourself anytime you give into your craving, then set the intention to choose healthy foods next time.
- 💜 Listen to the messages your body is giving you. For example, if you are craving caffeine this is an indication you are tired and need more energy. Instead of filling your body with these stimulants, take time to give it the rest it requires so you can feel refreshed, rejuvenated and recharged naturally. If you are craving chocolate or sugar, this is an indication you desire more love in your life. Instead of using food as a substitute for love, give yourself the love and attention you desire and deserve.

NOURISHMENT FOR YOUR SOUL: Occasionally allow yourself to have the food you are craving in small amounts as a treat rather than use it as a replacement for love. As you change your belief system, your cravings for foods that are not complimentary to your body will subside.

FOOD FOR THOUGHT: Everything I eat brings me vibrant health and energy.

ANGELIC TOOLS:

❤ *Constant Cravings* by Doreen Virtue (this book is out of print but can be found on Amazon through affiliated book outlets)

❤ *Healing Your Appetite* by Doreen Virtue

Healing Physical Conditions from Within

"The doctor of the future will give no medicine, but will interest her or his patients in the care of the human frame, in a proper diet, and in the cause and prevention of disease." —THOMAS A. EDISON

From a metaphysical perspective, physical conditions are not hereditary. However, the belief that created the condition can be passed from one person to another or from generation to generation. Physical conditions manifest from unconscious beliefs. When you address the belief that creates the condition you will not experience it. Some conditions can stem from our genetic make-up. As we change our beliefs, it changes our stem cell structure, which heals it on a cellular level. Instead of worrying about catching what others had or have, surround yourself in a shield of white light. This increases your vibration and protects you from absorbing the energy of that condition. If you believe you will have a physical condition because your parent or other family member did, put energy into changing the thought patterns that create that condition. When you disengage from the belief associated with the condition, it will not be a part of your experience. Others can help and guide us in our healing process. However, we are the only ones who can heal ourselves. All healing begins within, therefore, as we heal on a spiritual level we will then see the healing of our physical body take place.

Physical conditions may make us feel frustrated, angry or limited. One must detach and see it as merely a message from our body telling us a part of ourselves that needs more love. When we view physical conditions as a punishment, curse or something someone else gave us, this keeps us feeling like a victim and in a state of fear. Fear adds fuel to the fire; love heals. When we view it as a message without judgments, detach from it and see it for what it is, we can then give our body what it needs and desires for healing to take place.

Sometimes we unconsciously create physical conditions to protect ourselves from others or to prevent us from being present and experiencing life fully. We may also feel we are being driven by outer influences and might feel threatened. This may come from having an unhealthy childhood. Therefore, we may have taken on the belief that life is painful, change is scary, and we do not deserve good. Sometimes if we feel overwhelmed with life we put limits on ourself to not experience it fully. This creates beliefs such as, if I limit myself, no one else can put more expectations on me, or if I can't do something, no one can push me to do that which I do not want to do. If I am hurt, no one else can hurt me, or if I do not have time, I do not have to do it. The list goes on. We use these limited beliefs as excuses to say no. These situations keep us feeling like a victim rather than taking responsibility for our own life and being empowered so that we can say, "No, that is not right for me." or "No, I will not do that." We are powerful beings who can change any situation we desire and choose to change.

Although we are moving into a time where medical professionals are becoming more aware of the connection between the mind, body and spirit, at this time traditional medicine focuses on treating the symptoms rather than the body as a whole and getting to the source of the dis-ease. They are forced to come up with some diagnosis or label for insurance purposes and then are quick to give you drugs to "fix" it. Sometimes the side effects of the drugs create other problems. Traditional medicine has its place. There are some instances in life when medication is necessary, is a gift and can assist us in our healing process. However, to depend on drugs for the rest of your life is not always necessary or the best answer. When you go to the doctor and receive a diagnosis, I encourage you to get to the truth of what's really going on within your body rather than subscribing to that label and accepting that as the way it is. Instead, use the symptoms as a guide for the message your body is giving you. When you get to the core of what's creating the dis-ease, it can heal itself naturally without putting chemicals into your body.

If you receive a diagnosis or treatment recommendation that doesn't feel right to you, go for a second opinion before making a decision about your healing process. The bottom line is, it is your body and it is essential you are comfortable with the healing process which is best for your body. My prayer is that this part of the book will teach you to tune into your body and not allow the labels that are given from traditional medicine to become your truth, but rather use them as a guide to heal your body so that you can be in your natural state of love and enjoy your life!

It has been my experience that combining traditional medical advice and technologies with alternative therapies is very powerful and beneficial to the whole person while the healing process occurs. My vision is for the traditional medical professionals and alternative professionals to work together in unity. I believe combining the expertise and wisdom from both of these will contribute to a more empowering, natural and successful method of healing for all. I'd also like to see the insurance companies include health education and alternative therapies as a covered benefit choice for I believe this promotes a healthier well-being and will contribute to reducing the overall medical expenses incurred in our society. This recipe will guide you in creating vibrant health and well-being.

- ♥ Call on Archangel Raphael for his assistance with your healing process.

- ♥ Get to the core. Discern what the message your body is giving you by looking it up in *You Can Heal Your Life*, by Louise L. Hay. Ask your angels for more specifics on how it relates to you. Here is an example: I have never been prone to getting headaches, however, while I was adding my personal experiences to this book, I was experiencing headaches and felt overwhelmed due to the emotions that were still attached to past trauma. Also, as a child I was told that anything that went on in our house was to stay in our house and was to be kept private. At some level, I bought into this belief. Therefore, I had fear around speaking my truth. I looked up headache in *You Can Heal Your Life* and asked for clarity on how it was related to my specific situation. The angels told me that it was about feeling love for what I was doing rather than fear. So I began affirming: I love who I am and what I do and the headaches went away. Sometimes it is necessary to piece together aspects of your symptoms to get to the root of the cause. Here are a few examples. If you are healing from a fractured bone, you would look up fracture, the side of body it is on, and the bone involved and recite all the affirmations related to those. If you are healing from another condition, you would look up the parts of the body that are affected by that condition and recite all of those affirmations.

- ♥ Affirm to create a new thought pattern and ask the angels to make it so.

- ♥ Do not identify with the "label" or the condition. Instead, use it as a guide to heal from within and you will have great success!

- ♥ Call on your angels and ask them to release the energy from you that created this condition, and ask that they take away the physical condition or discomfort you are experiencing now. Thank them.

- ♥ Thank your body for the message and think loving thoughts about the area of your body being affected. Send love in the form of pink light or green healing light to those areas in your body where you are feeling discomfort.

- ♥ Visualize it already healed. If you fracture or break a bone, visualize the bone bonded back together. If you sprain a muscle, send love to that muscle.

- ♥ Seek out medical doctors and healthcare professionals who are open to alternative therapies and treatment that reflect your philosophy. Osteopaths, Naturopaths and Holistic Practitioners are some good ones to consult.

- ♥ Ask your angels to guide you to the medical professionals who can assist you in your healing process and recommend the necessary treatment for you. Ask that they be present with you at all your doctor appointments and assist you in seeing the truth in the situation.

- ♥ Ask that only loving hands touch you and bless everyone involved. If you are having a procedure done, ask the angels to guide the procedure and work through those who are involved so it is performed in a divine way.

- ♥ If a loved one has or had a condition you are concerned about getting, look up the condition and begin reciting the affirmation

- Ask your angels to assist your body to be receptive to the treatment you choose for yourself. Ask that whatever treatment you choose serves your body in a divine way.

- Do *Colors of the Rainbow Meditation* daily until the discomfort or the dis-ease subsides. When you experience pain in your physical body, that is an indication there is lower energy stuck in that area and needs releasing. *Colors of the Rainbow* will assist in releasing and transforming this energy. This is a powerful self-healing meditation.

NOURISHMENT FOR YOUR SOUL: For over-the-counter remedies, use as much all natural, homeopathic, herbal, alternative therapies as possible.

FOOD FOR THOUGHT: I AM vibrantly healthy and full of life.

ANGELIC TOOLS:
- *You Can Heal Your Life* and *Love Your Body* by Louise L. Hay
- *Angelic Reflections I: Awakening* CD by Bonnie Ann Lewis (*Colors of Rainbow Meditation*)
- *Angel Medicine* by Doreen Virtue

COLORS OF THE RAINBOW

This meditation is designed to relieve physical conditions and discomfort through color therapy and activate rainbow light so you may feel vibrantly healthy, revitalized and full of life.

- I invite you to repeat after me, "Dear Angels, Archangel Raphael and Archangel Michael, I ask you to assist me with my healing process."

- I invite you to close your eyes. Focus on the music, allowing your mind to clear and your body to relax.
- Take three or four deep breaths. As you breathe in, breathe in love. As breathe out, let go of any stress you may be feeling in your body.
- Visualize an open healing bed with a white fluffy blanket, a crystal clear dome, and buttons on the side that represent different colors.
- Visualize yourself laying inside this cozy bed, feeling the white blanket embracing you like your angels' wings.
- At this time tune into where you feel discomfort, distress, or see darkness in your body.
- With your intention, you can let this energy go by pushing the black release button on the side of this amazing healing bed.
- As you push this button, you will feel this machine gently removing all energy attached to this dis-ease by lifting it up from your body to the crystal dome where the energy is transformed.
- Pause.
- Now I invite you to press another button that will dispense the color of energy your body intuitively knows it needs to heal those areas.
- Breathe in deeply, allowing your body to take in this energy that is shining down from the dome, filling those spaces where the darkness has left.
- Pause.
- Continue pushing any other buttons to change the color your body desires to take in, breathing deeply as this healing color shines down upon you replenishing these areas.
- Pause.
- Visualize a ray of rainbow light emanating down from the dome of this healing bed and breathe deeply, allowing your mind, body, and spirit to absorb this healing energy.
- Pause.
- Affirm: I AM vibrantly healthy and full of life.
- Your body is now filled with vibrant energy and you are now revitalized and full of life!

- Thank the angels and archangels for helping you transform your fear into love.

May you take this rainbow energy with you and experience vibrant health and vitality always. Rainbows of love to you!

NOTE: This meditation is found on my *Angelic Reflections I: Awakening* CD

Several years ago one of my healing options involved major surgery. Due to the severity of this condition, and the benefits my body would receive by removing certain body parts, I chose to have the surgery done as part of my healing process. Prior to the surgery, I went within and recognized the beliefs that had created the condition I was experiencing. I set the intention that the parts of my body that are necessary for hormonal balance be healthy and remain. I began reciting affirmations, sending love as pink light and blessing those parts of my body that were affected. I thanked them for being a part of me and supporting my body and the birth of my children.

In preparation for this surgery, I used the Healing Physical Conditions from Within recipe and I was guided to wonderful, open minded doctors which led to an amazing healing experience. Prior to my surgery, I talked to my surgeon and told him I did not want to be given any pain medication in recovery as I am very sensitive to chemicals. I discussed with him that I was working with Dr. Ehrin Parker, an Osteopath that practices integrative medicine and she was guiding me on pre-op and post-op nutritional and herbal supplements that would prepare my body for the surgery, reduce the pain that can occur and promote a quicker healing process. I informed him about the supplements I was taking. He was fine with all of that and confirmed it wouldn't interfere with the traditional practices being used.

The day after my surgery, I was lying in bed in my private hospital room. I had my headphones on listening to *Angel's Gift* by Peter Sterling, crystals placed all over my body and I was doing a healing meditation. While I was doing this, my doctor came in to see me. I said, "Hi, I'm meditating." He just smiled. I chuckled to myself as I imagined what was going through his mind. That afternoon I was walking around and I went outside and sat on a bench with my husband to enjoy the sunshine and fresh, warm air. My doctor was amazed I was even out of bed. The day I came home from the hospital, I went to see Lynda Shannon my acupuncturist for a treatment. When I went to see my doctor for a follow up check, he was amazed at what a quick recovery I had and was surprised that I did not exhibit any of the usual symptoms or side effects most women have after this type of surgery. He said to me, "I do not know what you did but whatever it was, it worked! All of the healing that I did, allowed me to keep the parts of my body necessary for it to function on its own without synthetic hormone treatments. It also prevented me from feeling as though I'd lost parts of my soul, which sometimes occurs when people have body parts removed. I am grateful for Dr. Parker's expertise that supported my desire to use as much natural healing remedies to support my body. I am blessed that the surgeon who performed my surgery honored my healing process. This is an example of combining traditional medicine with alternative therapies and the angels guiding me to the perfect doctors that would support my natural healing process. There are some wonderful, open-minded health care professionals out there and you can ask the angels to guide you to the people who can assist you in your natural healing process.

Healing Addictions from Within

Addictions take us out of our natural state of love. They make us feel disconnected. They can take precedence over our lives. When we get to the source of the addiction, it is then we can begin to heal it from within and it no longer controls our lives. This recipe will help you create healthy habits.

- ♥ Identify the behavior or addiction.
- ♥ Let go of classifying yourself as having a problem or something being wrong with you. Instead focus upon changing the behavior and affirming you are perfect, whole and complete. You do not need to be fixed, you just need to recognize the truth within yourself.
- ♥ Explore why you do it and what it gives you by going within. Reflect upon and discover the unconscious belief so you can fill that void with a more desirable behavior.
- ♥ Determine what else you can replace it with that will give you the same gain, but constructive, healthy and enjoyable.
- ♥ Create and recite affirmations that reflect new thought patterns and beliefs.
- ♥ Visualize yourself already free from these. When you can resolve something or create something in your mind, it will happen in your physical experience.
- ♥ Call on your angels and ask them to help you to feel loved and fill that void with love. Release the energy attached to that addiction to help you participate in healthy behaviors.
- ♥ Join a support group or work with an individual therapist to help you work through the emotions attached to the addiction.

NOURISHMENT FOR YOUR SOUL: You have the willingness and courage it takes to overcome any addiction.

FOOD FOR THOUGHT: I feed my addictions with love. I AM perfect, whole and complete.

Healing Fear-based Behaviors that Affect Society

We all deserve and have the ability to create all that we desire to experience in our lives. This is our birthright. This includes who we desire to be, items we desire to acquire, things we desire to do, and relationships we desire to share, as long as it is with good intention and love and not at the expense of others. There is enough to go around in this universe of everything we all require and desire. We just need to be reminded how to re-connect to the infinite source of the universe where abundance is available to all of us, choose this for ourselves and be open to receiving these gifts. When we realize there is enough to go around for everyone, we release the need for greed, jealousy, envy, competition, manipulation, aggression and deception that many feel they need to use to get what they want. These behaviors are nothing more than errors in our thinking. They are all learned behaviors. They are not part of who we are. The underlying catalyst is fear.

Here are some examples of the most common behaviors that are affecting our society and blocking the flow of unconditional love. We've all experienced some of these in our life at one time or another as they are part of the human experience at this time. These behaviors come from fear, old beliefs and unfulfilled emotional needs. When we look on the brighter side of these feelings and bring them to the light, we can heal them by giving our body love to fulfill these emotional needs. I invite you to explore these ideas and see how they relate to your life. As you heal any of these behaviors that apply to you from within, you will contribute to creating a brighter, peaceful and more loving environment for all! This recipe will guide you in creating healthy behaviors.

- **Jealousy/Envy:** comes from the belief that someone has something you want and cannot have. In truth, you can have anything you desire. A better use of your energy is to put it into manifesting that desire into your life experience.

- **Competition:** comes from the lack of self-confidence and the belief that you need to be better or have more than another to be worthy. In truth, we are all equal and material gains are not the source of our self-worth. There will always be someone who has a bigger house, more expensive car and so on. What's important is that you are happy with what you have and purchase items that reflect your desires. Accumulating material possessions to impress or out-do others does not serve your soul.

Healthy competition such as in a contest, game or sports is different. This is where people are working toward achieving a similar goal in which they set for themselves or their team. Healthy competition is when everyone supports one another as they all do their best to achieve that goal. When you are secure and believe in yourself, you have no desire to compete against others because you know winning or losing is not what is important. It's the relationships, lessons and blessings that come out of the experience that are important. Be and do the best you can and feel good about your performance regardless of what the outcome is. Enjoy the experience, and be happy for yourself and those who achieve their goals. The true meaning of winning is feeling good about your accomplishments and yourself, not to be better than another.

- ♥ **Greed:** comes from the belief that there is not enough to go around. In truth, there is plenty for all of us, we just need to open our minds to receive it.

- ♥ **Judgments:** come from the belief that you need to be "right" or "perfect." Judgment occurs when you do not understand a situation or person. As humans those things we do not understand, we fear. When you judge, you put energy (your opinion, anger, blame, criticism etc.) into the situation. You do not know what other people have been through in their life or what their lessons or purposes are, so it is not appropriate to judge what's right or wrong for others. When you release your judgment, it allows others the freedom to make choices about what feels right to them, and also allows them the freedom to be themselves. Certainly you can give advice from your own experiences. However, it is important for you to respect their decisions, actions and choices. In truth, when we come to a place of understanding, compassion and neutrality, judgment no longer exists.

NOURISHMENT FOR YOUR SOUL: You always have the choice to see through eyes of love from a higher perspective, and have compassion, send love and angels rather than judge. That is what is needed and helps others the most.

FOOD FOR THOUGHT: *"If you judge people, you have no time to love them."* —Mother Teresa

- ♥ **Blame:** You are responsible for your own lessons, experience and life. When you understand this truth, you lose the desire to blame someone else. Blame is a losing game. Responsibility is power and everyone wins.

♥ **Control/Manipulation:** comes from the belief that you have to manipulate others by making them feel guilty or pressuring them so they do what you want them to do. This interferes with others choice of free will. In truth, when you allow others to make their own choices for what is right for them, you honor their choice of free will. As they express their individuality, that creates a better outcome for all.

♥ **Aggression:** comes from the belief that you need to be mean to get what you want. In truth, it is love that will bring you what you want and take you where you desire to go.

♥ **Perfectionism:** comes from the belief that you must be perfect to be loved and accepted. In truth, we are all perfect, whole and complete. Life is not about perfection, it is about progression.

♥ **Rejection:** comes from the feeling you are separate. The truth is, you are one with spirit and are an individual expression of all that God is. With rejection comes the desire to be loved, accepted and fit in. When you love, honor and accept yourself, then you will attract others who will love, honor and accept you too.

♥ **Anger:** Anger is merely a message from your body that it is time to change something, that something is not right or serving you, that some constructive action must take place, that something needs to be done differently, or there is a part of you that needs more love. Anger can stem from underlying fear or repressed feelings. It is an outward expression of fear. Anger appears when one feels threatened, restricted or their boundaries invaded. It disconnects you from your natural state of love. Anger needs an avenue of expression or it will eat away at you, and create emotional and physical conditions. Many often feel guilty or embarrassed for feeling angry. We all get angry sometimes, that is part of our humanness and there need not be any shame attached to this. Sometimes we have a good reason to feel angry. It is essential that we do not internalize it or direct it toward someone else but instead release it constructively.

Releasing Anger in Healthy Ways

When we address our anger, we control it rather than it controlling us. When we learn healthy ways to release or redirect it, it has served its purpose.

- ♥ When you are feeling angry, write down everything you can think of that contributes to why you feel angry in that moment. Here are some questions to reflect upon: What am I angry about? What triggered this anger? Who am I angry with? What part did I play in it?
- ♥ Ask your angels for assistance by saying, "Dear God, angels and archangels, please assist me in releasing this anger that I am feeling with grace and ease. Archangel Uriel, please help me see this situation from a higher perspective so I can forgive all involved and release the energy attached to it. Thank you."
- ♥ Write your feelings in your journal to release the emotions attached to the experience.
- ♥ Do physical exercise.

- ♥ Go out in nature and breathe deeply. As you breath in, breathe in love. As you breath out, let the anger go.
- ♥ Hugging a tree can help you to release emotions. As you wrap your arms around the tree, ask it to remove from your body, mind, conscious and unconscious, any energy that is not of love and does not serve you. Visualize the tree absorbing any lower energy or darkness from your body, knowing as it absorbs this energy it is transformed instantly by the healing energy of mother earth. Then ask the tree to replenish those spaces with nourishing energy and visualize a ray of blue light filling your body. Feel the calmness that exists within you now. Thank the tree for its assistance.
- ♥ Take time out, meditate, listen to peaceful music.
- ♥ Participate in any kind of creative activity such as art, drawing, music, playing a musical instrument, writing, or singing to shift the energy.
- ♥ Allow yourself to feel that anger for a moment. Notice where you feel the tension in your body and then let it go by putting a rose quartz up to your heart and breathing deeply.
- ♥ Affirm peaceful, loving affirmations as this shifts the energy.
- ♥ Read anything uplifting or inspirational.
- ♥ Participate in any activity that brings you joy.

NOURISHMENT FOR YOUR SOUL: Anger is merely an illusion of the truth. When you become aware of and acknowledge anger it looses its power. When you are feeling angry, stop, breathe, reflect upon why, release the anger, replace with positive energy, and respond with love when you are centered and have more clarity.

FOOD FOR THOUGHT: I understand the source of my anger and release it with grace and ease. I express anger in healthy ways and everyone benefits.

Anger can also be a clue about your life purpose. It may be letting you know about something you came here to change. Many times it can be a blessing in disguise as the opposite of anger is passion. You receive the greatest blessing when you get to the core of the anger and transform it into passion. This shifts the energy and your experience bringing much peace and tranquility. When you recognize what the core of the anger is, it has served its function and will subside. Any situation that lights your fire or pushes your buttons is a situation in which you are not yet capable of loving unconditionally. When you are angry about something, you can choose to shift your focus to "How can I help?" or "What can I do to make this situation better?"

EXERCISE: FROM ANGER TO PASSION

When you reflect upon why you are angry and recognize what you could do differently to make the situation better, you may become aware of where your passions lie and can create a better experience for yourself.

1. Ask Archangel Uriel and Archangel Michael for their assistance.
2. Reflect upon the following questions: What can I do to turn this anger into passion? How can I be of service in this situation? What organization, volunteer work or career could I do that would contribute to creating a better situation?
3. Make a list of the steps you can take to direct your energy toward those endeavors.
4. Enjoy putting your energy into a cause that speaks to your heart.

Here is an example. Perhaps you see garbage along the beach and it triggers anger in you because people are not respecting our beautiful earth. Instead of getting caught up in the anger, put energy into picking up the garbage. This shifts your energy because you feel good about being of service in creating a beautiful earth. This reflects your passion to help the environment.

NOURISHMENT FOR YOUR SOUL: Underneath anger lies hidden passions to be discovered. When you look beyond the anger and get to the truth of it, passion comes to life!

FOOD FOR THOUGHT: I transform anger to passion with grace and ease.

EXERCISE: RELEASING UNDESIRABLE CHARACTERISTICS

Before you release characteristics that are not complimentary to you, accept them and love them, then thank them for being a messenger and they will become harmonized within you. A great sense of satisfaction comes when you face your uncomfortable emotions and transform them into joyful experiences. It is important to let go of the old in order to make room for the new. So as you release that which no longer serves you it is essential to replace it with what you desire. This exercise is helpful in releasing behaviors, habits, and characteristics that are undesirable to you. Your releasing hand is your dominant hand, the hand you write with. Your receiving hand is your non-dominant hand.

1. Write down what you desire to release with your dominant hand. Example: I release _____ with love, joy, grace and ease.
2. With your non-dominant hand, write down the qualities you desire to exhibit beginning with I AM.
3. Use these as affirmations to create the unique you!
4. Recite them often and enjoy the blessings that come your way.

NOURISHMENT FOR YOUR SOUL: Releasing is a natural rhythm of life and when we get into the routine of letting go of those things that no longer serve us, we make room for the new to come into our lives. This is true in all aspects of our life.

FOOD FOR THOUGHT: I release that which no longer serves me with grace and ease.

Transforming Fear into Love

Fear can make you feel sad.
Love will make you feel glad.
Fear can stop you in your tracks,
Love will keep you turning back,
To what means the most to you.
Fear can destroy tomorrow,
What you created today.
Fear is nothing more than an illusion . . . It is not real.
It can numb you so you do not feel.
Love will always make that heal.
Fear is a reflection of the mind,
Let it go and you will find,
Within your heart, the energy,
Of a different kind—LOVE.
For beyond fear,
Is the DIVINE!

—*The Angels*

FEAR

Fear is not part of who we are, it is the human interpretation of the illusions of life on earth. Fear has its place. It can be an instinctive message from our body that something is not right for us or warn us for our safety. However, it can also be the very thing that prevents us from being the love that we are and moving forward in our life. It prevents us from making changes, causes us to make excuses, and creates blockages in achieving our desires. Fear can surface as memories from painful past experiences. Worry and concern about the future also creates fear. Although they are not truth for us, they come up to show us areas that require more love and attention. Fear dissolves when love is present. The choice is yours. You can choose love or fear and that choice shapes your experiences. When we let go of fear, we open our heart to feel the presence of love in all areas of our lives; we love all that we are and all that we do. Anytime you begin to worry, thank God and the angels for taking care of that situation divinely for you. This shifts your consciousness from fear to love. It's like reprogramming your mind. In order to create a healthy, fulfilling, lifestyle, we must close the doors to fear and open our hearts and minds to love.

NOURISHMENT FOR YOUR SOUL: *"Fear is a reflection of the mind, not of the heart, for the heart's only reality is love. Focus on the love in your heart, and the fear in your mind will subside."* —Bonnie Ann Lewis

FOOD FOR THOUGHT: My heart and mind are open to love.

ANGELIC TOOLS:
- ♥ *Let LOVE Be* by Bonnie Ann Lewis
- ♥ *Overcoming Fears* audio by Louise L. Hay

EXERCISE: RECOGNIZE, RELEASE AND RE-CREATE FEAR

Recognition Therapy: helps you to release fears, resentments, anger and judgments of self and others. When you recognize and acknowledge them without judgment, and do not internalize them, it brings them to the light so they lose their power. It is important to release fear on all levels—mental, emotional, spiritual and physical. These exercises will guide you through that process.

Releasing Prayer

Dear Angels, Please assist me with my releasing process. I choose to release not relive this experience. I Ask you to clear the energy associated with the past and transform it into light. I thank you for helping me release this with love, grace and ease. Amen.

Recognize: (mental clearing)

1. On a piece of paper, record all your fears and why you are fearful.
2. Write down the worst that could happen if this were to occur.

Release: (emotional)

As you release the energy and the emotional attachment associated with the fear, you no longer attract that experience. To release the energy:

1. Reflect upon how you will feel if that happens.
2. Allow the fears to come forward, feel their energy, and when you are ready, let them go.
3. Visualize, feel and imagine yourself surrounded with love.

Re-create: (mental)

1. On a new sheet of paper, create an affirmation to transform each fear into love.

2. Affirm: I release all fear into the light with joy and ease. All of my fears are healed with love. I create joyful loving experiences for myself. I release the past with grace and ease. As I release the past, new experiences flow into my life.

Releasing Ceremony: (spiritual, physical)
1. Ask for angelic assistance by saying, "Dear Angels, and Archangel Michael, please assist me in releasing the fears within my body, being, and thought forms (conscious and unconscious), and replace them with love. Please help me to feel safe, secure and loved throughout this process."
2. Thank your fears for coming forward to the light and reflecting to you where you need healing. Say, "Thank you for coming forward. I now choose love."
3. Tear up and throw away or burn your list of fears.
4. Thank all spiritual beings who helped you in this process.
5. Thank yourself for doing the work.

Release & Rejuvenation (physical)
1. Light a candle and take a soothing detox bath with mineral bath salts or detox clay powder.
2. Listen to or recite your new affirmations out loud while in the bath.
3. As the water goes down the drain visualize all the lower energy going with it.
4. Rejuvenate by spraying spritzer around your body or applying some essential oils of your choice.

NOURISHMENT FOR YOUR SOUL: It is fear that blocks you from moving forward and accomplishing your goals. When you remove these blockages, it is then you will move forward rapidly and joyfully.

FOOD FOR THOUGHT: I release all fear to the light for transformation with grace and ease.

ANGELIC TOOLS:
- Mineral Bath Salts by Soleil's Influence
- Detox Clay Powder
- Spirit spritzer of your choice by Soleil's Influence

Releasing Fears from Past Traumas

MEMORIES

Memories are merely reflections of the past,
Sometimes things trigger these memories.
If it warms your heart . . . Keep it.
If it does not . . . Let it go.
For memories are from the past,
Visions are of the future,
The gift is in being present,
Focus on the now.

—*The Angels*

Memories are merely thoughts from past experiences in this lifetime or previous lifetimes. They can be either loving or fearful memories. We've all had past experiences that have instilled fear in us. As part of the awakening process, we must heal these painful experiences so they no longer affect us the way they previously did. I believe the true purpose of these experiences is not for us to give up, but to move beyond the limitations the fear created. We can do this by taking the lessons and the love and leaving the pain behind. The angels said, "*You can choose to entertain these fears or you can let them go. For in your heart you know what is real and what is not."* Our past experiences contribute to our ability to see clearly what is happening in this moment and they can affect the way we perceive a situation. We must detach from undesirable experiences and see them from a new perspective to create a positive experience.

The purpose of the past is not to dwell on it, "beat" yourself up over it, or blame yourself or others. Instead, it is to learn from the lessons, to take what blessings that experience brought and let the rest go. Sometimes this involves forgiveness of self or others. When you stay stuck in the past, it causes you to be stagnant and prevents you from being open to new experiences, opportunities and lessons. It encompasses your energy and does not make room for the new to enter. Releasing the past is a natural part of life. When we release the past, we then make room for all the good to enter. Things that may need to be released are judgments, the beliefs of others we inherited as a child, resentments, anger, etc.

After my NDE, I went through a period in which I was experiencing many fearful thoughts associated with the trauma that I experienced. Although I knew these fears did not relate to the present, I still felt the emotional attachment to them. Karen Hutchins explained to me that our mind stores happy and painful memories of past experiences in the part of our brain called the amygdala. She began educating me about the amygdala in layman's terms and explained that from time to time, certain things trigger these memories and bring up the feelings associated with those experiences. On my drive home I was reflecting on our conversation. I had a sense of knowing that I could release the pain from these memories, by transforming the fears to love and that would heal my amygdala. So when I arrived home I looked up the amygdala on the internet so I could see what it looks like. I called on Archangel Michael and Archangel Raphael and asked for their assistance in healing my amygdala. As a result this technique was born!

EXERCISE: AMYGDALA HEALING TECHNIQUE

1. Find a place where you will not be interrupted.
2. Visualize your amygdala. It may be helpful to look it up on the internet or in a medical journal so you can see what it looks like.
3. Scan your amygdala with your spiritual vision for any darkness which represents fear.
4. Call on Archangel Michael and Archangel Raphael to assist you in your clearing process by saying, "Please remove from my amygdala the painful memories of the past and replace them with divine love. Please help me to keep only the lessons and the love from that experience."
5. Then release the pain associated with those past memories by stating, "I choose to release all traces of painful memories that have gathered in my amygdala. I choose to entertain only the love and the lessons from these experiences, and let the rest go."
6. Visualize Archangel Michael vacuuming out this darkness with his tube of white light. As this fear enters the tube of white light it is immediately transformed into divine energy.
7. Then ask Archangel Raphael to replace those spaces with his divine healing energy.
8. Visualize your amygdala filling with Archangel Raphael's vibrant emerald green light and then pink light which represents love.
9. Affirm: My amygdala is filled with thoughts and memories of love.
10. Thank Archangel Michael and Raphael for their assistance.

NOURISHMENT FOR YOUR SOUL: After using this technique for some time, I began hearing the words in my mind, "I can see clearly now that the pain is gone." (This is a phrase from the song "I Can See Clearly" by Johnny Nash).This was my sign it had worked. I was truly amazed at how simple and effective this technique is. From this technique, it came to me that if we could heal a part of our brain, then we could use this technique on any part of our body. So I encourage you to utilize this technique on any part of your body that is not in harmony or balance with your well-being, adjusting the wording where necessary to reflect the specific part of your body you are working with.

FOOD FOR THOUGHT: I release the patterns in me that created the fear from past experiences. I move forward with love in my heart. I can see clearly now the pain is gone.

MESSAGES OF LOVE:

During the time I was hearing "I can see clearly now that the pain is gone." I also heard this message from the angels.

> *This is a symbol of the soul recognizing on a conscious level that when you get out of the emotional rut and let the pain of the past go, it is then you see the light and clarity comes. When one is in pain it is difficult to see beyond it. This is not a time to present the lesson. This is a time to give compassion. As a person moves beyond the pain they are in a state to receive wisdom from the lesson, not until then. Be the band-aid to protect the wound while healing by giving love and compassion. Be the ancient wisdom for the soul after the wound has healed by being the messenger of love that you are, for this helps the soul to grow. It already knows and needs only to remember.*

CHAPTER 10
Freedom

BE FREE

Choose only those things that make your heart sing with joy,

For your heart is the doorway to your soul.

When you follow your heart your soul will grow,

For it is love and light that make you whole.

It's pain, struggle and fear that pays the toll.

Love is the ticket to freedom for the soul.

—*The Angels*

The true meaning of freedom is moving beyond the veils of illusion, being free from the fears that prevent you from being the powerful being you are and experiencing all that you desire in your life. When you remove these illusions and live in your natural state of love, you will then experience the freedom to be and express your true self, freedom to love and be loved, freedom from fear, unhealthy behaviors and patterns as well as physical limitations, freedom from outer influences of society, freedom from judgments of self and others, freedom to do what your heart desires, financial freedom to pay for all that is required and desired to fulfill your life's mission and be supported by the universe. The only thing preventing you from freedom is your own beliefs, fears and limitations you have placed upon yourself. Freedom is a state of mind. When you remove the obstacles from your mind it will be removed in your physical experience. Obstacles are gifts that give you the desire, the strength, the stamina, the drive, the motivation, and the courage to move past them and reach your goals, dreams and desires. When obstacles are removed from your life the outcome is freedom. Freedom brings peace, tranquility and serenity, love, peace, unity and abundance.

NOURISHMENT FOR YOUR SOUL: When love is the foundation of your life, the creation of your life is simple.

FOOD FOR THOUGHT: I AM free to be me and spread my wings so I can soar above the apparent challenges in my life.

Emotional Freedom

Emotional freedom comes from releasing the ties that bind you to old beliefs and experiences. The ties that bind are created by fear. When we replace them with love, it is then we are free. Living and loving everyday, learning your lessons with love and opening your heart and mind to loving experiences, opportunities and relationships will bring emotional freedom.

Living and Loving Everyday

"Enjoy the day, no matter what comes your way!"

The thoughts you think when you awaken in the morning will create the theme for your day. These thoughts go out into the universe and attract experiences that reflect them.

- ♥ Change thoughts of fear to love by beginning your day with a positive thought when you first wake up in the morning and the universe will magnify it. For example, if you wake up in the morning feeling tired and you do not feel like getting out of bed, choose to recreate those thoughts by reinforcing with positive words or affirmations such as, "I am energetic and choose to embrace this new day with excitement and optimism."

- ♥ Before you go to bed, say to yourself, "Tonight I will have a restful sleep and upon awakening I will feel recharged, rejuvenated and energetic as I welcome this new day." Soon you will see that you will begin to wake up feeling energetic and ready to go. We all know that when we feel good, we feel we can accomplish our desires and handle anything that crosses our path, and we encounter pleasant experiences.

- ♥ Love all that you are, all that you do, where you are and what you are doing today. Know it is a stepping stone to where you desire to be and enjoy the process of getting there. Put love into everything that you do. When doing something you do not enjoy or want to do, imagine for a moment you are doing something different and feel the vibration of that thought. Allow these feelings to remain as you complete your task at hand. This will help you shift your focus to enjoy what you are doing in the moment. When you make this part of your belief system it comes into form.

- ♥ Reflect often upon the blessings each experience has for you.

💙 Find creative ways to utilize or incorporate your talents and gifts where you are today.

NOURISHMENT FOR YOUR SOUL: Live life to the fullest and enjoy the good that comes your way. *"Only good will come your way, when you choose love every day."* —Bonnie Ann Lewis

FOOD FOR THOUGHT: I love all that I AM and all that I do.

I'm going to share with you an example of this in my life. My desire was to open a healing center, become an ANGEL THERAPY PRACTITIONER®, Spiritual Teacher and Published Author, so I could be of service. I was working in a dental office, but really wanted to be at home with my children instead of putting them in daycare. I felt burned out, drained and even a little resentful because prior to having my children, I planned to be a stay-at-home mom thinking I had retired from dentistry for good. However, due to a divorce, this is what I needed to do at the time to support myself and my children financially while I was creating my life anew. Although it was not what I wanted to be doing, I made a conscious effort to change my thoughts and shift my perception about my job.

I asked the angels to help me feel energetic and motivated and to help me have a positive mindset while working at my job at the dental office. I reminded myself that this was a stepping stone to where I was going and I chose to do this because it supported me while I was manifesting my desired life. I made a list and reflected on the blessings that job brought me, and found creative ways to utilize and incorporate my talents and gifts into my present life circumstances. I began feeling grateful for that job in which God had chosen to be the channel for my financial abundance at that time. I began doing affirmations while I worked. I would send healing energy to my patients, and ask the angels to assist us when doing dental procedures. I would ask the angels to help my patients heal quickly from that procedure. I saw so many miracles happen! I continued following my angels' guidance and taking steps to manifest my life. Within a year, I was out of the dental office and I had opened the Swan Self-Awareness Centre!

This was a big lesson for me to love what I was doing even though I wanted to be doing something else. I knew I had to learn to be happy and peaceful in the now in order to create and experience that in the future, otherwise happiness and peace would always be one step ahead of me. Just by changing my thoughts to, "I choose to be here right now," rather than, " I have to be here right now," and giving gratitude for the blessings this situation offered, changed my whole experience!

Learning Lessons with Love

"When we respond to life with love, life loves us back."

THE GIFT

Always look for the positive,
For that is the gift in each experience.
Let the fear and pain go,
Keeping only the lessons and the love,
For this is what helps your soul to grow.

—*The Angels*

We came here to participate in life, to have experiences so our soul can evolve. But when these experiences become painful, many turn to unhealthy behaviors to escape, withdraw, and take the pain away. We can change these painful experiences by changing our perception of them. This gives us the opportunity to take the lessons and love and leave the rest, by seeing the blessings in every situation. Sometimes it is tempting to just stay stuck or to blame outside sources. However, it's important to retreat from time to time, to go within, for that is where the truth lies for you. Then take that truth to create your own experiences by applying it to your life. This is participating in life with joy. You can ask your angels to help you open your heart and mind to all experiences and see the blessings. Each experience has a gift to offer. Find out what the gift is by reflecting upon what you gained from that experience, or how it served you or another. Being grateful allows your soul to grow the most. Regardless of what you do, you will learn the lessons you came here to learn. In order to learn lessons, you do not have to experience fear, struggle and pain. You can choose to learn these lessons with love, grace and ease. When you do this, you open your heart and mind to loving experiences and opportunities.

- ♥ Ask your angels to help your lessons be presented with love, grace and ease, and to help you be open and receptive to whatever each experience has for you, so you can see the blessings in that situation.

- ♥ Take only the lessons and the love from each situation and let the fear, pain and struggle go by choosing to see the positive in that experience and embracing the joy that it brings.

- ♥ Each morning when you wake up, thank God for this beautiful day, and ask that it be filled with experiences and opportunities for you to grow in love. Give thanks for all that the universe provides for you and all the good in your life.

NOURISHMENT FOR YOUR SOUL: As you embrace the gifts by taking only the lessons and the love the experience brought, you become enlightened.

FOOD FOR THOUGHT: I take only the lessons and the love from all of my experiences, and enjoy my life. All of my experiences bring greater enlightenment.

Opening Your Heart and Mind to Loving Experiences, Opportunities and Relationships

"When we do things with an open heart, it presents the greatest blessings."

BLESSINGS

Open your eyes to a bright new day,
Then good things will come your way,
As blessings from your heart.

—*The Angels*

As you open your heart and mind, you open yourself up to new opportunities, experiences and relationships. As this occurs, you receive the gifts the universe has for you or that you desire and so deserve.

- 💜 Forgive yourself and others.
- 💜 Let go of the old so you can welcome the new.
- 💜 See the blessings in all people, all things, all experiences, and most of all yourself.
- 💜 Be aware of the opportunities that are presented to you each day and take guided action even though you do not know the outcome or see the big picture.
- 💜 Take time to quiet your mind so you can listen to your heart.
- 💜 When unpleasant things occur in your life, you can choose to perceive them as opportunities for growth rather than misfortunes.

♥ Do *Bubble of Love Visualization*.

NOURISHMENT FOR YOUR SOUL: Each experience is an opportunity for growth. When you enjoy and accept each moment, you open yourself up to more good opportunities and experiences. When you live with an open heart, prosperity flows in infinite ways.

FOOD FOR THOUGHT: As I release the past with ease, I welcome the new with an open mind, open heart and open arms. I see all experiences, opportunities and relationships clearly through eyes of love. I create fulfilling experiences for myself. My life is filled with loving experiences, opportunities and relationships. I open my heart and mind to receive God's infinite blessings.

BUBBLE OF LOVE VISUALIZATION

This visualization is designed to encompass you in the energy of love so that you can experience loving experiences throughout your day.

- Visualize yourself surrounded in a bubble of pink light. Breathe in love and feel the warmth of love around you.
- Take a moment to feel the love you have for yourself.
- Now expand this love to your family, co-workers, community and out into the world.
- Ask your angels to assist you so that only love is given and received.
- Affirm: I AM safe, secure, loved and loving. I give and receive love with grace and ease. And so it is!

NOTE: This visualization is on *Your Journey to Love Daily Practices* CD included with this book.

Creating Financial Freedom

Many feel strapped by the financial ties that bind them. In our society we have been conditioned to live paycheck to paycheck and beyond our means. Oftentimes when we receive salary increases, instead of paying off what we already have, we go out and buy bigger homes, more expensive cars and purchase more material items which just increases the amount of debt we incur. The concept of paying off cars, homes and being debt free and financially independent is beyond the consciousness of many. If you have lived this way in the past, forgive yourself for today is a new day and you can choose to change your financial practices right now to contribute to an abundant economy. I'm here to share with you that anything is possible when we ask for angelic assistance, and there are infinite possibilities if we just open our minds and hearts to these concepts. There is nothing wrong with wanting more or something better. The key is to work smarter, not harder, and manifest these from within rather than going into debt. In order to create financial freedom in your life, it is essential to observe your relationship with money, create beliefs that reflect your truth about money and create financial practices that reflect your beliefs and support your desire for prosperous living.

Your Relationship with Money

For many, bills and debt seem a threat or burden. The more you are fearful and angry about lack of money, the more energy you put into that lack. Therefore, that is what you attract in your life. If you are angry at yourself for spending money when you did not have it to spend and have created debt as a result, it is important to forgive yourself and realize you did the best you could at that time with the knowledge you had. Now you have the opportunity to make different choices and you will have more profitable experiences.

It is important to look at what the bills in your life represent. I'd like to define the difference between bills and debt. Bills are what we pay on a monthly basis in return for a service or item such as utilities, cell phones, mortgages and cars. Debt is what we incur when we borrow money and live beyond our means, such as carrying large amounts on credit cards when we do not have the money to cover it and can only make minimum payments. This also includes buying houses or cars that are beyond what your budget will support and having monthly payments that are too high for your budget at this time. Instead of allowing money to control you, be the controller of it by the thoughts you think, choices you make and actions you take. Although you will always have bills in your life that have to be paid on a regular basis, you can reduce these by becoming debt free.

I'd like to explore an idea with you. We all have an abundant supply of money available to us at all times. Let's take the concept of "bills" out of our vocabulary and see them as an exchange for the gifts we receive for the services or items we have in our lives. Let's view "debt" as borrowed gifts, knowing the universe will provide for us to return them. This shifts the energy from burden to blessing which changes our beliefs from lack to abundance, opening us up to receive the money to pay for these. When we develop a healthy relationship with money, our cash flow will increase and our financial situation will improve.

NOURISHMENT FOR YOUR SOUL: I'm sure you've heard the metaphor "Money doesn't grow on trees." While this is true, I'd like to share an idea with you. Money does not grow on trees, however, the amount of money you have will grow when you plant the seeds of prosperity in your mind!

FOOD FOR THOUGHT: My prosperous thoughts create infinite returns.

Creating Prosperity and Abundance Consciousness

"Prosperity is the freedom to do what you want whenever you want. It is no amount of money." —JOHN RANDOLPH PRICE

Abundance and prosperity are more than just money. True prosperity means to live abundantly with love in all areas of your life. Prosperity has many facets: vibrant health; loving, fulfilling relationships and experiences; financial abundance; resources; wisdom; guidance and direction to fulfill your desires and achieve your dreams as you fulfill your life's mission. We have addressed living a prosperous life throughout this book. For the purpose of this chapter, we are going to focus on financial Prosperity.

Money is simply the physical exchange of energy. All the money we can imagine is available to us when we expand our mind to receive it. In order to bring an abundance of prosperity into your life, you must create it in your consciousness before it can come to physical form. This is due to the law of free will to choose. You must believe you deserve prosperity and already have it in order to receive it. This is due to the law of magnetism. You must take guided action to bring it to into physical form due to the law of cause and effect.

The lack of money comes from our belief system created by past programming of society's beliefs and fears. We can change this situation by reprogramming our thoughts to represent abundance, prosperity and a knowingness that life will support us in whatever we choose to do. Love and gratitude create prosperity consciousness; fear creates poverty consciousness. When you shift out of poverty consciousness into prosperity consciousness, you open the doors to financial freedom. You then become free from accumulating debt to accommodate your desires. Instead, you create from within, trust and allow the universe to fulfill your desire. It is your divine right to be supported by the universe in all ways and live an abundant, prosperous life just for your asking. All the money you require and desire is already available to you. You must first believe this is so and then it will flow to you. Allow the universe to bring the prosperity from any source or any channel it chooses. Do not limit yourself by trying to figure out where it is going to come from. Just know and believe it will come and focus on having plenty. When you open your mind to infinite possibilities, prosperity follows. You can live a richer life by changing your consciousness to reflect the financial abundance you desire to experience.

GIVING AND RECEIVING

As we know, giving and receiving are natural rhythms of life. Therefore, it is essential to balance our giving and receiving by giving with an open heart and allowing ourselves to receive with gratitude. Although giving and receiving involves more than just money, it is essential for us to achieve a healthy balance in our financial giving and receiving as well. This keeps us in the flow of financial abundance.

Tithing has been a long time tradition in many religions. When I was a child, I thought it was odd you had to pay to go to church. As a young adult I felt obligated to do this. As I matured, I came to understand the concept of giving and receiving and realized that the true meaning of tithing is about giving back and supporting the teachings of that organization where you are spiritually fed. Now, I give with an open heart as this reflects my gratitude for the blessings I receive. The same is true with anything in our lives.

GRATITUDE PRAYERS FOR PROSPERITY

These prayers can assist you in remaining in a state of gratitude, which creates prosperity and abundance consciousness.

Giving Affirmation: *Thank you angels for providing me with the abundance of cash to pay for all of my needs and desires. And so it is!* (I recommend reciting this whenever you spend money for you are affirming abundance is already present in your life and the gratitude you have for this truth.)

Receiving Affirmation: *I bless this money and ask that it be multiplied infinitely for both or all of us. And so it is!* (I recommend reciting this anytime there is an exchange of money for services, teachings or products.)

Gratitude Affirmations: *Thank you for the abundance I receive for utilizing my gifts and talents being of service. Thank you for the divine experiences, opportunities and relationships present in my life now.* (I recommend reciting this anytime there is an exchange of energy for a service you provide.)

NOURISHMENT FOR YOUR SOUL: Abundance gives you the freedom to do and acquire all that your heart desires!

FOOD FOR THOUGHT: I give and receive money with gratitude and balance. My life is filled with an abundance of love, vibrant health, wealth and prosperous opportunities and experiences. An abundance of good flows to me continuously.

ANGELIC TOOLS:

 Angelic Reflections II: Tides of Abundance CD by Bonnie Ann Lewis

---

TIDES OF ABUNDANCE MEDITATION

This meditation is designed to assist in the manifestation of your dreams and desires.

- I invite you to close your eyes and breathe deeply.
- Focus on your breath and as you breathe in, breathe in love. As you breathe out, let go of any concerns or fears you may have about receiving abundance.
- Now I invite you to follow me on a beautiful journey as we take a walk along the beach.
- Imagine yourself strolling along the ocean shores with the wind gently blowing your hair.
- Breathe in the smell of the fresh salt water that cleanses your mind, body and soul with each breath you take.
- Feel your feet sinking into the warm sand as the sound of the ocean waves splashing the shore fills your ears, bringing you a sense of peace and serenity.
- As you take your next step, pause for a moment and look down at your feet. A piece of shell catches your eye. You bend down to pick it up and to your surprise it is a shell shaped like the feather of an angels' wing. You stop for a moment to admire the shell.
- Pause.

- As you continue your stroll along the beach, you hear an angelic voice that says, "Use this to write in the sand." After taking a few more steps you bend down and with your shell you draw a heart in the sand.

- Inside the heart you write down a dream or something you desire to experience in your life. As you complete the writing in that heart, affirm whatever your dream or desire is and state, "And so it is!" Then say, "Thank you universe for making this so."

- Then you continue walking down the beach drawing more hearts in the sand to reflect all of your desires and dreams, affirming and giving gratitude for each one as you go.

- Pause.

- Now turn and face the ocean and extend your hands up in the air and say, "Tides, please come in and take my desires and dreams and bring them back to me to experience in my life." Affirm: I AM ready to receive these blessings. Visualize the tides coming in and taking your dreams out to the universe and manifesting them into form, then bringing them back to you with the new tide as experience.

- See these desires present in your life now. Allow yourself to feel the joy these blessings bring.

- Pause.

- Take a moment to send love and gratitude to the ocean for being a conduit for bringing your dreams and desires to life.

Now I invite you to bring yourself back into your body and into this room and when you are ready, open your eyes and record anything you would like to capture from this experience.

May abundance always be present in your life and may all of your dreams and desires be delivered to you on angels' wings.

Angel Blessings to you!

NOTE: This meditation is found on my
Angelic Reflections II: Tides of Abundance CD

Prosperous Financial Practices

I invite you to apply these angelic principles to your life and watch your finances flourish! The following recipe will guide your way to financial freedom.

- ♥ Make a list of thoughts that come up when you think about money and people that have money. This will show you the beliefs that you have about money and will help you to determine what beliefs to change. Communicate with your inner child to discover what fears you have relating to receiving an abundant supply of money, and what is necessary to heal those issues.

- ♥ Make a list of all your bills and the payoff amount of your debts. Write down what that bill or debt gives you. Go through each bill on your list and visualize it paid in full. You can visualize the balance on that debt zero or visualize writing a check for the full amount and stamped paid in full. Give thanks to the universe for the service or product that you received in exchange for money.

- ♥ Be grateful for the bills that you have and the continuous flow of money to pay them, as they are the exchange for what you have in your life in this moment. When writing out bills, give thanks for the abundance of money to pay for all of your debts and bills in full. View debts as borrowed gifts to shift the energy.

- ♥ Create prosperity consciousness by using affirmations to transform your thoughts and beliefs from poverty to prosperity. (I recommend taping the affirmations from the *Har-Money* Prosperity Cards by Heidi Baer, and listening to them every night before you go to bed.) By creating what you desire in your mind, you are putting it out into the universe for it to be supplied for you. But, you need to be willing to follow whatever is needed to reach your desire, one step at a time. If you are in a situation in which you feel you cannot do something due to a lack of money, it is helpful to figure out what steps you can take toward that goal in which money is not required. When you take each step, one at a time, when you get to the step that requires money, they money will be there. The reason for this is it teaches you to take the steps you need to build a solid foundation. Otherwise you would just go and do whatever was fulfilling for you in that moment. When it is for your highest good and is divine timing to do something, and you ask for the money, it is always there. This is a guideline to follow when you feel frustrated because you want to do something but do not have the money. When this happens, ask the universe what steps you need to take first or what is blocking you from being in the flow and receiving this support.

- ♥ Live within your physical means and continue to create in your mind what you require and desire and more will flow your way. When you live within your means your means has room to expand, but when you are living beyond your means, you are always expanded and trying to catch up. This leaves no room to create the space for more expansion.

- ♥ To keep your finances in balance, allow your income to increase before you increase your expenses.

- ♥ Visualize your bank account carrying an infinite balance.

- ♥ Focus on what you desire rather than the money for it. This takes your focus off lack of money and puts energy into your desire.

- ♥ Pay cash as often as you can. Each payday, take out a certain amount of cash to spend for groceries and miscellaneous things. This plants the seeds in your mind that you have plenty of money as you see it continuously circulate in your life. For me, there is something about having the cash that gives the feeling of plentifulness.

- ♥ Use credit cards for convenience or unexpected purchases rather than a source of income and pay off credit card balances every month. When you only pay the minimum payment on your balance, you accrue interest charges that create even more debt. While there are times in our life where having the option to borrow money is a blessing, it is essential to set your intentions to pay it off. When you use your credit card, say the giving affirmation and affirm you already have the money to pay this in full. Thank the universe.

- ♥ Create an infinite budget using the exercise in this book.

- ♥ Use the *Overflowing Prosperity Meditation.*

NOURISHMENT FOR YOUR SOUL: As you set your intentions for these situations to occur in your life, you will be amazed at how often they are achieved.

FOOD FOR THOUGHT: I AM financially independent. An overflow of money constantly circulates in my life. I have an abundance of money to pay for the needs and desires of myself and my family with plenty to spare and to share. Money flows to me in avalanches of abundance. My cash flow greatly exceeds my expenses.

ANGELIC TOOLS:
- ♥ *Har-Money* prosperity cards by Heidi Baer
- ♥ *The Abundance Book* by John Randolph Price

- *Creating True Prosperity* by Shakti Gawain
- *Money is My Friend* by Phil Laut
- *Creating Money* by Sanaya Roman
- *Angelic Reflections II: Tides of Abundance* CD by Bonnie Ann Lewis (*Overflowing Prosperity Meditation*)

OVERFLOWING PROSPERITY MEDITATION

This meditation is designed to assist you in accessing your spiritual bank account. It will open you up to the flow of prosperity that already exists within you, and create prosperity consciousness so you will attract it in your physical experience. Your spiritual bank account is continuously replenished as you withdraw from it. This infinite supply of financial prosperity is available to you always. You just need to remember to tap into it as part of your daily practice. Anytime you require money enter this space in your mind and take out the amount of money that you desire.

- I invite you to close your eyes. Focus on the music, allowing your mind to clear and just relax.
- Take three or four deep breaths. As you breathe in, breathe in love, which is the source from which your money flows.
- As you breathe out, release any financial worries or concerns, any beliefs of lack and any fears you may have about giving and receiving money.
- Let's begin your journey to your spiritual bank account!
- In front of you is a door with a heart, and inside the heart is the symbol for money. This symbol gives you direct access to your spiritual bank account. Whenever you visualize this symbol, it will take you directly to this space.
- Now open that door and enter.
- Inside you will find a space filled with light, love and the money for all that you require and desire to fulfill your life's mission and enjoy your life.
- As you look around you will see shelves and shelves of cash.

- Take out the cash for what you require and desire, knowing that as you withdraw from this account it is always replenished simultaneously.

- Now hold the cash in the palm of your hands. Bring it up to your heart and visualize whatever you took the money out for already present in your life now.

- Allow yourself to feel the gratitude that exists within you for these gifts and universal generosity.

- Affirm: I AM an open channel in which prosperity flows. I release money with joy and it returns to me multiplied in miraculous ways. I create all that I require and desire in my mind and I take guided action that leads me to attracting overflowing prosperity to my life experience. My income far exceeds my expenses. I now have an abundance of cash to pay for all of my needs and desires with plenty to spare and to share. And so it is! Thank you universe for the cash to pay for all of my needs and desires and the overflowing prosperity present in my life now.

May your life always be overflowing with prosperity!

Blessings to you always!

> NOTE: This meditation is found on my
> *Angelic Reflections II: Tides of Abundance* CD

EXERCISE: CREATING YOUR INFINITE BUDGET

Since money is energy, it is meant to be an exchange for the services you provide. It is the process of giving and receiving with the universe. When you create a budget you are telling the universe what you want so it can provide for you. When you make a budget it is important to include your needs as well as your desires. It's helpful to create a money journal that reflects your infinite budget. Include why you want the money and what you will do with it. You can also create some affirmations as well.

CREATING YOUR YEARLY INCOME

1. Reflect upon and make a list of your goals and your money requirements for the forthcoming year.
2. Set a goal for the income you desire to receive that year.
3. Give thanks as if it is already provided.
4. Follow with the monthly budget exercise.

CREATING A MONTHLY BUDGET

1. Create a budget in your mind for all that you require and desire. Remember this budget is infinite. This budget is a continuous flow of energy from you to the universe and the universe to you.
2. Write down all your needs and desires that require money, the amount desired and the date you need it by.
3. Next to each one write an affirmation that states this need or desire is already present in your life.
4. Go through each need and desire and visualize these already present in your life. Feel the pleasure they bring.
5. Thank the universe for supplying all the money for your needs and desires in advance.

NOURISHMENT FOR YOUR SOUL: By doing this on a monthly basis, you will learn how to manifest more quickly as you are continuously creating prosperity a month in advance! When you are ready, the money is already present. Your spiritual bank account is always full. As you retrieve from it, it is replenished instantly.

FOOD FOR THOUGHT: I release money with joy and it returns to me multiplied in miraculous ways. I create all that I require and desire in my mind, and spirit brings it to life in my physical experience. I have an abundance of money after paying for all my needs and desires. I now have financial security, freedom and independence. And so it is! Thank you universe!

This experience I share with you is an example of financial freedom and angelic assistance. When I was writing this book, I began receiving visions of my husband and I traveling and teaching these principles. I have always had a passion for traveling and have known for a long time it was to be a part of my life's mission. During one of my conversations with the angels I said I was willing to travel and teach these principles but I wanted my husband to be a part of the package and I wanted it to accommodate my children's schedules so I could still be here for them as they are the most important part of my life's purpose. Since we share them with their dad, this allows us the freedom to travel in moderation, and still have our time with them. The angels assured me they were working on it and that a lot was going on behind the scenes which would unfold in due time. I'm excited to see how the angels work their magic to answer these prayers!

Since opening the Swan Self-Awareness Centre, I have been taking care of the business aspects including finances, my website, advertising, marketing, etc. along with conducting private sessions, teaching, writing and raising my children. As I was self-publishing this book, I decided I was ready to delegate some of these business duties to other people so I could focus my time and energy on writing, teaching, being of service, and my family, as these are my passions and where my gifts lie. I asked the angels for assistance with this endeavor and we are beginning to see this come to fruition. My husband and I had already discussed him taking over the financial aspects. However, at the time he was frequently working seven days a week twelve to fourteen hours a day as a manager in technology. While he was making a lot of money, his quality of life was being sacrificed. He desired to spend more time together and do other things he enjoys, was burned out and wanted to make a career change, doing something he was more passionate about. He was afraid to make this change due to the financial responsibilities we had. He said he would feel much better making this change if we reduced our expenses by paying off our debts. So with the help of the angels and the principles in this book, I guided my husband in manifesting a new career for himself and the financial support to do this. Doors of opportunity opened up for John to make the career change that he desired when the company that he worked for downsized their management and he got laid off. Often times when people lose their jobs, they go into fear and feel like a victim of circumstances. In truth, these experiences are the universe opening the doors for something better. He recognized this as a blessing for it gave him the opportunity to make the career change he desired. Although he was a little apprehensive about this change which involved several months without working while he took some training, he followed his passions and the angels' guidance. By the time this career change presented itself, the money came through various channels and we paid off our credit cards, cars and our mortgage!

In the midst of all of this, I was in the process of bringing my angelic tools to life. Although we had previously manifested the money and put it aside to self-publish this book and my CD's, we were concerned about investing that money into my angelic tools when we did not know what was going to happen with my husband's career. I asked for clarity from the angels on whether I should continue to bring my angelic gifts forward at this time or wait until my husband was secure in his new career. The angelic guidance I received was to continue moving forward and trust. That my husband would only be out of work for a few months to do his training and then opportunities would open up for him. John was concerned with the state of the economy and was hearing about people getting laid off and how hard it was to find a job. He was fearful. He had been continuously employed since he graduated from college. This career change was a big step for him. I gave him this message from the angels: *"The economy is not your support, God is. Focus on that which you desire as what you believe will occur, will shape your experience. Do not get wrapped up in the drama of society."*

He took a leap of faith and kept his focus on his desires while doing what he needed to do to get where he wanted to be, although there were days he had his doubts, wondering what the outcome would be. When he would have these moments, he kept replacing those thoughts with a wonderful affirmation Louise Hay says, "Only good comes to me now." He continued to have faith knowing the angels would come through. Then he would continue focusing on his desires while thanking the angels for taking care of the details. And it paid off!

Just as the angels promised, opportunities opened up for him. While he was in the midst of taking his training, he already had contract opportunities awaiting him when he was finished. While engaging in his contract work, a permanent position combining his previous expertise, his new skills that reflect the training he took, and what he is passionate about opened up for him. He has now taken over the financial aspects of the Swan Self-Awareness Centre, which is truly his forte'—thank you angels! This career change allows him the flexibility to travel with me when that time comes, and best of all, we get to spend more time together as a family enjoying life! As you can see, I followed the angels' guidance and continued to move forward bringing this book to life. I had already gone through my career change and with my husband's love and support have achieved this dream. I feel blessed that I had the opportunity to give back to him as I supported and guided him through his career change.

REFLECTION

FREEDOM

Freedom is my birthright . . . a gift of my natural state of love

I now have the freedom to:
Be and express the love that I am.
Choose my experiences and create my life.
Experience love in all that I do.
Do what I love for a living.
Have my desires fulfilled and prosper.
Live abundantly with financial freedom.
To be loving and loved.
Attract all I require and desire to fulfill my life's mission.
Be supported by the universe in all my endeavors.
It is love that sets me free and brings me peace.
I am free!

—Bonnie Ann Lewis

PART III
Creating with Love

INTEGRATING MALE/FEMALE
Celebrates the masculine and feminine in perfect balance.

CHAPTER 11
Co-creating

"Life is yours to create, create it with love."

We are the creator of our own lives and co-creators of this universe with our source—God/Angels/Spirit. Co-creating is working with this source to manifest our desires. Love is the energy of creation. Since angels are messengers of love and light sent from God, they can assist us in creating our life. As we let love be the foundation of our lives we manifest an abundance of good and all that we require and desire to fulfill our life's mission. As we do this for ourselves, we contribute to the well-being of our planet. Co-creating is allowing spirit to guide us, taking the action steps necessary to make it happen, and allowing life to unfold with grace and ease. All that is required is for us to "tune into" the truth of who we are, our oneness with God and the angels. When you create with love you will experience the divine gifts that love brings which includes: peace, unity, abundance and freedom, and in the process you will be contributing to creating a world of love and peace. This is co-creation.

Creation occurs when our spiritual self and our physical self work together to bring our desires and dreams to life. Our physical self is our masculine side, the action, doing, giving and will to focus our mind. Our spiritual self is our feminine side, our intuition, imagination, creative flow, Be-ing, our spirit, passion, desire and receiving. In the spiritual dimension, only thoughts exist and in the physical realm, it takes both thoughts and actions to come to form. Therefore, the process of creation takes both our spiritual nature and our physical existence to bring our desires to fruition in our earth experience. We all deserve to be, experience and acquire all that we truly desire. Our desires are God talking to us and are a part of our life mission. Since we know our thoughts, words and actions create our experiences, we can use this as a guide to create our life.

Creating is a natural rhythm of life, therefore you have the power within to create all that your heart desires. In order to do this, you must look within and connect to your natural state of love in which everything begins and exists, and choose what you desire to create. In part I you looked within and tapped into your desires, passions, gifts and talents. In part II you removed the illusions that were blocking you from receiving these desires. Now in part III you are ready to put into action the principles to bring your desires into physical form naturally through manifestation. This section will allow your creativity to flow as you utilize your natural resources and honor the natural rhythms of life to bring your desires to fruition. Creating your life and all your desires is an exciting and creative process. We are going to focus on creating the following: all that you desire to be, the items you desire to acquire, the relationships you desire to share, the things you desire to do and experience, your divine life, career, and sacred space. The following recipes will guide you step-by-step in creating your life with the assistance of the angelic realm. It is time to begin!

Steps for Creating

"When you create with love, you love your desires into being!"

You will be putting the treasures of your soul into action to create your desires. When you utilize the treasures of your soul to create, your heart and head are working together. What that means is your thoughts, words, feelings, and actions are all in unison with each other, so when you say something, you believe it, feel it to be true, and take the steps to make it happen. This speeds up the fruition of your manifestations. As your awareness increases you begin manifesting much quicker than before. It begins with your thoughts creating the belief and expanding your mind, and making space for the dream or desire to become a part of your experience.

In creating your life, it is essential to let go of limiting beliefs as they block the flow of receiving your desires. Instead of thinking about all the reasons why that won't happen or you can't accomplish it due to a lack of money, time etc., put your energy into focusing your thoughts on your desire and taking the steps you can take toward that goal to make it happen. When you re-focus your attention it opens you up to receive your desires. Take the steps that you can take now. Each step will lead you to the next. When you take the steps you can take in the moment, you open up the channels to provide whatever it is you need next to move forward. The reason for this is to teach you to do what presents itself each day so that you can build a solid foundation for your project or endeavor. Be patient and aware of what is going on around you. Whatever you focus your attention on and put your time and energy into will come to form. If this is something you truly desire you can make it happen!

This recipe will guide you in using the treasures of your soul and work within the natural rhythms of the universe to bring your desires and dreams into your life experience. These principles can be applied to any area of your life to achieve what you desire to experience. I utilize these principles personally and in my Angel Therapy® Practice with great success.

1. **Decide what you desire.** Through meditation and prayer you can get clear on your intentions. An intention is a desire you want to bring into your life. When you are clear to the universe, the universe is clear to you. This is similar to picking out the seeds you desire to plant.

2. **Set your intentions.** On a piece of paper draw a circle or a heart. At the top of your paper write the topic of your desire. Fill in your circle or heart with all your desires and dreams for that endeavor. This is similar to planting the seeds.

3. **Pray/Ask for angelic assistance.** Light a candle and ask God and your angels to guide you in bringing your dreams to life by saying, "Dear God and Angels, these are my desires. I ask you to bring this or something better to me. Please guide me to take the necessary action to bring these desires to fruition. Please bring these to me in a way that is for the highest good of myself and all concerned. Thank you!" You must ask for what you want and then be open and receptive to receiving it. You only need to ask once. It is best to ask for assistance and allow the universe to bring it to you in whatever way is for the highest good for yourself and all concerned.

4. **Surrender and release.** Allow spirit to enter. Detach from the outcome and expectations of how you think it "should" be as this blocks the flow. When you let go, you open yourself up to receive. Do your part by nurturing and taking guided action and allow the angels to work their magic. The outcome will be better than you imagined!

Continue to nurture the seeds you planted with the following activities.

5. **Take guided action.** Take the steps you are guided to take with courage and confidence, knowing they will lead you where you desire to go. One of the biggest misconceptions people have about manifesting is that they think by praying or visualizing their dreams will come knocking on their door as if by magic. The truth of the matter is that you need to do your part to make things happen. When you take guided action, doors of opportunities open, and the magic does occur.

6. **Create affirmations** that reflect your desires and recite them often so they become part of your belief system. State them as if what you desire already exists in your life. You are creating it in your mind and expanding your consciousness to receive it.

7. **Visualize** your desires in your mind's eye. See them in your life now.

8. **Add feeling.** Feel the excitement of your desire already present in your life and feel the joy it brings.

9. **Creative writing** is very powerful. Write a story about your desires and dreams in first or third person as if it already exists or is happening now. First person is as if you are writing the story yourself. Third person is as if someone else is telling a story about your life.

10. **Create an imagery** as this brings your desires to life in your physical eyes. This is a powerful tool to help you focus on and bring in the energy of your dreams and desires so they can become a part of your life experience. The more real you make it in your mind, the sooner it will manifest because when you believe it is yours, it comes into your life!

11. **Give thanks.** Have faith and trust the universe is putting into alignment your desires. Allow things to happen in divine timing and enjoy the process and blessings you receive along the way!

12. **Celebrate** every day knowing your seeds are now sprouting. Continue spreading gratitude as you go. Soon they will bloom and you will enjoy the fruits of your labors of love!

NOURISHMENT FOR YOUR SOUL: Any time you begin to worry, or try to figure out how, or fear it will not happen or what the results will be, redirect your thoughts by affirming: Thank you God and angels for taking care of the details in this situation. Remember to enjoy the process of creating by being grateful for each step along the way.

FOOD FOR THOUGHT: I align my male and female self and co-create with ease and grace, blending heaven and earth. I AM manifesting my dreams and desires at Godspeed.

ANGELIC TOOLS:

♥ *Angelic Reflections II: Tides of Abundance* CD by Bonnie Ann Lewis

Monthly Manifesting Exercises

The full moon is a time to release that which no longer serves you and to let go of those things you no longer desire to have in your life. The new moon is a time to focus on what you desire to bring into your earthly experience. You can look on the calendar to see in advance when the new moon and full moon occur each month. Mark the day and set your intentions to participate in this powerful manifesting process.

EXERCISE: FULL MOON—RELEASE

During a full moon is the time for releasing. This is a great time to clean out cupboards, closets, drawers, garage, etc. and give those items away or have a garage sale so someone in need can use them. When we release what no longer serves us, we make space for what we do desire to come into our life.

1. Make a list of the things in your life you desire to let go of or that no longer serve you. Remember to include judgments of self and others, old patterns, fears, guilt, shame, burdens, physical conditions, challenges, relationships, etc.
2. When you are finished take that piece of paper and burn it. (You can use a fireplace, chiminea or you can just tear it up and throw it away.)
3. Say a prayer, "Dear God and Angels, these are things that I choose to let go of for they no longer serve me. I give them to you and ask that they be transformed into divine energy and returned to the universe with love."
4. Give thanks to God, your angels and yourself.

NOURISHMENT FOR YOUR SOUL: This exercise may bring up emotions for you. You may feel like crying. If so, let the tears flow as this is a way for your body to release. You may feel relieved and feel like dancing or singing. Know that whatever you feel is part of your releasing process.

FOOD FOR THOUGHT: I release and I let go with ease. I AM free and open to receive!

EXERCISE: NEW MOON—FOCUS ON DESIRES

During a new moon is a time for focusing on your desires.

1. Write inside of a circle or heart what it is you desire to experience in your life.
2. Light a candle and say a prayer of your choice or you can use this prayer, "Dear God and Angels, these are my desires and dreams. I give them to you to make happen. Please guide me to take the necessary steps to bring them to life. Please support me in all of these endeavors."
3. Give thanks for it already being so.
4. Nurture your desires and dreams utilizing the treasures of your soul. This brings them to fruition more rapidly.

NOURISHMENT FOR YOUR SOUL: Your desires may take more than one full moon cycle to come to fruition. Remember there is a lot going on behind the scenes, and sometimes certain steps need to be taken before others so things can fall into place and form a solid foundation for your manifestations. Look for the signs that develop with each cycle which brings you closer to your desire. Give thanks.

FOOD FOR THOUGHT: All of my desires and dreams are present in my life now. Thank you God!

Supporting Your Manifestation Process

Here are some things you can do to help move the energy in your desired direction.

- Surround yourself with like-minded people.
- Take classes and workshops that reflect your interests.
- Read books related to what your desires are.
- Join support groups or gatherings that peak your interests.
- Focus on your desires.
- Share your dreams with people who will support, encourage and inspire you along the way. Refrain from sharing them with people who do not support your ideas as this creates thoughts of fear and slows down your manifestation process.

NOURISHMENT FOR YOUR SOUL: When you do these exercises and activities on a regular basis, you will be creating your life one month at a time, therefore making your desires a part of your everyday life!

FOOD FOR THOUGHT: I joyfully manifest my desires into my life every day.

Creating Manifesting Tools to Map Your Progress

Creating tools to help map your manifestation progress is a great idea as they provide insight for the stage your manifestations are presently in. You can look back and see what you have accomplished and you can give gratitude as this affirms it is already present in your life now. Be sure to review often as this will help you to keep the energy moving in the direction of your desires and dreams. If things are not coming to fruition, it may be a situation of divine timing when something else must fall into place before it can happen, or maybe action needs to occur or it may not be for highest good of all concerned. If it is a true desire, be persistent and keep your eye on your goal. Ask your angels for guidance and direction.

- ♥ **Manifesting board:** What I did for a manifesting board was to purchase a large bulletin board and put it up on the wall in my office. I place on it symbols, pictures, words and affirmations of what I desire to experience in my life. At the bottom I add a gratitude affirmation that states, "I give thanks to the universe for supporting me in all ways with all of my endeavors and gifting me with all my needs and desires now." I visit it often and it inspires me to keep moving forward to achieve these desires and dreams.

- ♥ **Gratitude board:** A dry erase board works great for this because you can change it and add to it easily. This helps you to reflect upon the blessings in your life on a regular basis. The more you give gratitude for your blessings, the more blessings flow to you.

- ♥ **Boxes:** Manifesting boxes are a great tool to use for your manifesting. You can use any type of box and decorate it to your taste, or you can use a wooden or ceramic box that has a special meaning to you. Write down your desires and place them inside the box. Remember to visit and reflect upon them often. Each time you write an intention, you are making a wish to the universe. My husband gave me a knick-knack shelf that has three drawers on it and I labeled one desires and dreams, another one gratitude, and the other one healing. Then I write on slips of paper what I desire and place them in each box. From time to time I sit down and go through each one and it is amazing how much I accomplish and what manifests in my life.

NOURISHMENT FOR YOUR SOUL: You can be as creative or simple as you would like. The importance is in the intention and practice, not so much in the method itself.

FOOD FOR THOUGHT: I use my creative abilities and enjoy watching my dreams come to life!

♥ **Imagery** is a divine tool in which you create a visual image that reflects what your desires are. The purpose is to bring your dreams into your physical reality so it can manifest into form. You can create your imagery on poster board, foam board or on construction paper. You can use photos, pictures, sayings, quotes, words from magazines, words you write, stickers, markers, stamps, or whatever you desire. Be as creative or as simple as you'd like. Anything goes!

When adding words to your pages, use affirmations as if your desire is already present in your life such as: I AM _____, I now have _____, I AM now _____, _____ is present in my life now, I now experience _____, I AM enjoying _____, my relationships are _____, in all of my relationships I experience _____, and so on. Once you have created your imagery it is beneficial to do the following.

- Visit it often.
- Put them up on a wall or make them into a book which you review frequently. (A book of construction paper works good for this. I prefer the Academy Book of Colors by Mead. You can find this at office supply or craft supply stores).
- Make a list of what you can do now to accomplish your desires and take action on those things.

- Give gratitude for them being present in your life now.

NOURISHMENT FOR YOUR SOUL: When you get out of your own way and allow the angels to assist you, your dreams and desires will manifest more quickly.

Imagery Ideas: Here are some ideas for imagery pages, however, your possibilities are infinite. You can create imagery pages for anything you can imagine or desire!

Vibrant health • Wealth/Prosperity/Financial abundance
Relationships/Love (family, friends or romantic) • Career, New job
All you desire to become • Travel • Spiritual growth • Self-esteem
Creativity • Activities you desire to do • Pet • Addition to family
Material items such as new home, car, etc.

NOURISHMENT FOR YOUR SOUL: Anything you can imagine or desire, you can create. Allow your creativity to come alive for it will bring your dreams to life! Enjoy the beauty of your dreams. Celebrate your riches!

FOOD FOR THOUGHT: I bring forth the dreams and desires from my mind into my life by creating beautiful imagery.

MERCURY RETROGRADE AND MANIFESTING

According to astrologists, Mercury Retrograde is a time in which the planet Mercury appears to move backwards, affecting the global energy. This happens two–three times a year, and lasts for about three weeks each time. Mercury Retrograde is something to be aware of but not go into fear about. Sometimes mercury in retrograde causes delays in our manifestations. Mercury retrograde is not a negative thing, we just need to learn to flow with the energy which is all about reviewing the past, reflecting, re-doing, re-thinking, and re-processing. When Mercury is in retrograde it gives us the opportunity to reflect upon past experiences, lessons or situations so we can complete what hasn't been finished so we can move on. Some things that may occur during this time period are mis-communications, delays, detours, changes of plans, or technical issues. It has been said not to sign legal documents, contracts or start a new project that hasn't already been set in motion. Instead it is a time to finish up things we've previously started. There is a website that talks in depth about this and a calendar of when this occurs: www.astroprofile.com. I always mark my calendar so I am aware of these dates so I can assure a smooth passage through this time. What the angels taught me is to ask them to remove any effects that Mercury Retrograde may have on my project or situation. It is amazing how things continue on their merry way with grace and ease when we ask for angelic assistance!

NECTAR OF DIVINE ESSENCE
Celebrating that our creativity is truly divine.

CHAPTER 12
Creating Your Divine Life

LIFE'S RECIPE

Living a fulfilling life of success and inner happiness is
being aware of your current recipe and knowing how to
adjust it to create what you desire to experience.

You have the natural resources inside of you to create your life.
You just need to remember your birthright,
utilize the treasures of your soul,
And flow with the natural rhythms of life to create a life that
reflects all that your heart desires and the truths of your soul.

Your recipe for living is made up of your thoughts,
beliefs, feelings, words and actions. It is fueled with
passion from your desires and dreams.

When you blend it together with angelic guidance and assistance,
Add a touch of faith and trust, season with an abundance of
love, spreading gratitude as you go, you will surely have
a heavenly experience!

—*Bonnie Ann Lewis*

Your divine life is for you to create in whatever way speaks to your heart. When you have a desire for something, create it in your mind and follow the steps one at a time to bring it to form. It will manifest. When you are involved in a project and you have mentally created it and are doing it out of love and desire, the universe will support and provide whatever is needed to manifest it. You will find that you will meet the people you need to meet, and the information and knowledge you need will come to you as you follow through in this project. The money that will give you the freedom to do whatever you require and desire for your dreams to fly will also show up. I encourage you to fill your life with all that your heart desires and watch your dreams come to life!

Living on Purpose

"The future belongs to those who believe in the beauty of their dreams!"
—ELEANOR ROOSEVELT

Living on purpose means that you are being and expressing the love that you are, and living your life with integrity, according to your desires and spiritual truths. Your mission is what you came here to do in service to others, and at the same time contributes to the evolution of your soul. Sometimes we unconsciously fill our lives with "stuff" to help us feel fulfilled and happy. This gives us instant gratification but leaves us feeling empty. We also participate in activities that keep us busy doing but may not nurture our purpose; these are delay tactics. Instead, focus on that which reflects the truths within your soul. Your life's purpose always involves things that you love or have a passion for, and manifests through your creative expression. Creative expression is how you choose to bring your gifts and talents to the world to be of service. You've probably heard the saying, "Do what you love and the money will follow." This means when you do what you love, the universe will support you in all ways.

In Part I of this book you retrieved your gifts, talents and passions and in this chapter you will learn how to incorporate these into your life so that you can align more with your life's purpose. When you become aware of your life's purpose, it will be beneficial not only to you but to those around you. The more you move forward with your life's work, the more information becomes available to you and more doors of opportunity will open for you. This is a message to begin moving in that direction with the manifesting process.

When I first remembered my life's purpose, I felt passionate and wanted to do it all right away. The angels said to just take one day at a time and focus on what presents itself each day, and they would guide my way. When you do this you will accomplish your desires and achieve your dreams. With each step I took, more guidance, opportunities and clarity opened up for me. To this day it still amazes me how the angels guide me step by step in achieving my dreams, and how they gently ease me into each facet of my life's purpose preventing me from feeling overwhelmed. These experiences have shown me the magic of the angels in action with all the synchronicities, and how life unfolds with grace and ease when we invite the angels, archangels and ascended masters into our life.

NOURISHMENT FOR YOUR SOUL: When you are in your natural state of love fulfilling your life's purpose, it is then you experience the joys of true happiness and experience abundance in all areas of your life.

MESSAGES OF LOVE:

Question: During my awakening I became aware of the many facets of my life's mission. Although it all felt very right to me and I was excited, I felt a little overwhelmed with how I was going to accomplish all of it and where to begin. I also felt a sense of urgency, but with it came much fear. My question to the angels was "How am I going to accomplish all of this?"

Dear Child,

Focus on the love in your heart instead of the fears in your mind. Continue to manifest, and focus on your desires. Doors will open and you will connect with those necessary for your desires to come to fruition. Be clear on your intentions, continue to ask for guidance, be open and receptive. We will guide you each step of the way. Be aware of the messages that come and follow the guidance to assure a solid foundation. This is not about hurrying up, it is about moving forward one step at a time, and going with the flow. All is well. You are moving along your path rather quickly. All is in divine order as you know, and certain things must fall into place before other things come to fruition. All will occur in divine timing. Stay close to us in heart and mind. We will guide your way.

Question: What am I to focus on first?

Focus on that which you feel passionate about. Go through doors that are open. Go with the flow and all will evolve in divine timing. You are a child of God, an angel upon this earth; you are connected to God/Source/Spirit. You are receiving and in the flow of divine guidance and ancient wisdom. Continue on in love. Remember balance is important as well. If you need to slow down ask for this to occur. When you feel tired . . . rest. Much info comes to and through you. For you are a clear channel and connected in heart and mind. Pull from this knowledge for forward movement. Go forward in peace and love. Nameste'

Simplifying Your Life

Our society has created such an imbalance on our planet earth due to the fast-paced lifestyles many are living. Always on the go, in a hurry, with a to-do list a mile long, deadlines to meet, appointments to go to and so on and so forth. Many are on the run all the time, eating fast food and not providing their physical body the proper nourishment it requires to thrive. They are doing too much without having the time to just be, rejuvenate, and recharge so they are feeling burned out. They are over-working to pay for all the material things they desire and they lose the quality of life because they have all these material blessings with no time to enjoy them or no time to spend with their loved ones. Multi-tasking has become a way of life for many. This kind of lifestyle creates stress.

It's time to get back to the basics of life and focus on what's really important. There needs to be a balance so that you do work that is fulfilling to you and supports you in the physical but also incorporates your spiritual practices so you can live a balanced life and enjoy your journey. Being honest with yourself, living according to your inner guidance, getting rid of the "shoulds," de-stressing your life, living in the now, and setting the intention for a divine day, will all contribute to simplifying your life so that you may experience a healthy, harmonious, balanced lifestyle which reflects your desires.

Getting Rid of the "Shoulds"

"Out with the 'shoulds' and in with the good."

"Shoulds" are those things you do during that day out of obligation. These "shoulds" can fill your life and sometimes distract you from your life's purpose. Are you too busy with day to day obligations that you do not have time in this moment to do the things that you enjoy or desire to do? Are you setting aside joy for another day for example, saying, "I'll do this when . . . ?" If so, it is time to prioritize. You experience joy in the present, not in the past or the future. When you do things that bring you joy and are fulfilling, you are being guided from your higher self in ways that are relevant to your life's purpose. When you are doing things out of obligation, you are being ruled by your ego. It is important to distinguish what and why you are doing things so that you can do activities that bring you joy in the moment and are relevant to your life's purpose.

You may be thinking, "I have so much to do already how am I going to manage adding one more thing to my day?" When you set your intention for what you desire to do each day and incorporate these activities a little at a time, you'll be amazed at how much you get accomplished and the joy you will feel by following your heart's desire! You will also see how much time during the day is spent on things that are not so important. Once you release these "shoulds" from your day, you will make room to do the things you desire to do that reflect the truth within your soul.

Getting rid of the "shoulds" means having to say no sometimes, delegating to others and asking for help. It also means not taking the responsibilities of everyone else on your shoulders, but allowing other people to do things for themselves. When you first begin to make this shift, you may find others get upset because they are used to you doing your share and their share. However, with consistency and persistence they will begin to adjust to this change. If they need direction, you can teach them how to do it which will empower them. They will in turn feel good about their accomplishments.

EXERCISE: OUT WITH THE "SHOULDS," IN WITH THE GOOD

1. Make a list of your daily activities.
2. Go through your list and put a "C" next to the ones you choose to do because you enjoy them. (these are things you want to keep in your life).
3. Then go through and put an "O" next to the ones you do out of obligation or to please someone else. (these are ones you want to eliminate from your day).
4. Finally, go through and put an "N" next to the ones that are necessary at this time.

This will be your guide as to which activities to let go of and which ones to incorporate into your day. The ones that are necessary for you to do right now, choose to do them with love instead of out of obligation. Focus on what the blessing is in doing that activity and how it serves you and those involved.

NOURISHMENT FOR YOUR SOUL: When you "have" to do something it is a chore. When you choose to do something it is a choice. It changes your perception and your experience.

FOOD FOR THOUGHT: I chose to do those things that feed my soul or help others.

Living in the Now and De-Stressing

IN THE MOMENT

The purpose of the past is to learn from the lessons,
To take from those experiences the blessings.
The purpose of the future is to give you the opportunity,
To create what you desire.
The purpose of the now is to live and enjoy life fully,
For the gifts lie in the present!

—*Bonnie Ann Lewis*

Living in the now is to be fully present with what you are doing. It means to focus on and give your full attention to the activity or the person you are experiencing it with without being pre-occupied with the next thing you are going to do on your list. When we do not live in the now, we are either in the past or the future and we never truly embrace what our current experiences offer. When we stay stuck in the past or are afraid of the future, this creates stress. Stress takes us out of our natural state of love and takes a toll on our body. It creates imbalances and affects our body, mind and spirit. We do not always have control over what goes on around us, however, we can change the way we allow it to affect us. This reduces the impact stress has on our body. Even good things can create stress in our lives when we worry about the details and outcome. When we live in the now, we trust in life's natural processes and know only good will come to us. The following recipe will guide you in living in the now.

❤ Limit your multi-tasking. Although multi-tasking can be beneficial in certain instances, other times it defeats the purpose. When we multi-task we are not in the moment and our attention is not entirely focused on what we are doing. This creates a feeling of being pulled in many directions and results in stress or unfulfilling experiences.

❤ Enjoy each day for what it is while nurturing your visions and dreams for tomorrow. As you live in the now you are consciously creating your future. In truth, the power is in the present, the present is all that exists, and your future is yet to be created. Therefore, embrace the gifts that are always in the present moment. As we stay centered in our natural state of love and live in the present moment, it helps us de-stress and we have more peaceful experiences.

❤ Do that which your heart desires today. If you are always waiting for things to get better or to do what you desire tomorrow, you will be living in the future instead of the now and your dreams will always be one step ahead of you.

NOURISHMENT FOR YOUR SOUL: Alan Cohen shares some words of wisdom in the August, 2000 issue of *PhenomeNEWS* about living in the moment and being in the present that I will share with you. He states, "Anything that is worth doing, is worth doing with a whole heart, mind and body. We get into trouble not because we do things that are wrong but because we approach our activities with divided intentions. Our body is doing one thing and our heart is elsewhere. This means to be fully in the present with whatever you are doing. When you are at school, keep your attention on school, when you are with a friend, really be with that friend, when you are doing a certain activity, focus on that activity."

FOOD FOR THOUGHT: I AM living in the now and enjoying each moment to the fullest, embracing the gifts of the present and creating my bright future. *"Create the life you will love to live while enjoying each moment for what it is."* —Bonnie Ann Lewis

Setting the Scene for a Divine Day

A DIVINE DAY

Take time for love . . . for it feeds your soul.
Take time to pray . . . for it's your opportunity to ask for assistance.
Take time to meditate . . . for it quiets your
mind so you can hear your heart.
Take time to rest . . . for it recharges your energy.
Take time to eat healthy foods . . . for it nourishes your body
and gives you the energy to accomplish your desires.
Take time to play . . . for it frees the child within.
Take time for your career . . . for it gives you
the opportunity to be of service.
Take time for you . . . for it restores your soul.
Take time for your loved ones . . . for they are life's greatest gifts.

Take time to exercise . . . for it relieves stress and clears your mind.
Take time to give . . . for it brings much joy.
Take time to receive . . . for it brings you blessings and joy to others.
Take time to hold on . . . to what's important to you.
Take time to let go . . . for it releases what no longer serves you.

Take time to be creative . . . for it frees your spirit.
Take time to listen to your heart . . . for it will guide your way.
Take time to be . . . for it strengthens your connection to spirit.
Take time to laugh . . . for it opens your heart.
Take time to cry . . . for it releases tension.
Take time to listen . . . for it brings great wisdom.
Take time to talk . . . for it allows you to express who you are.
Take time to seek advice . . . for it heals your heart.
Take time to go within . . . for it brings the
truth forth with greater awareness.
Take time to be in nature . . . for you will feel
energized and a sense of freedom.
Take time for spiritual practices and physical
activities . . . for it keeps you in balance.
Take time to love . . . for it makes your heart sing, makes life
worth living, and is the greatest blessing you give and receive.
Take time to enjoy life . . . for that is your purpose,
To be and share the love that you are and enjoy your journey!

—Bonnie Ann Lewis

The Art of Balance and Harmony

Life truly is a balancing act. There are many areas of your life to incorporate balance such as balance between your male and female self, work and play, spiritual practices and physical activities, giving and receiving, time for self, time with loved ones, and so on. Creating balance in your life may require re-arranging your priorities. Although you may strive for continuous balance, you go in and out of balance from time to time due to your earthly experiences. This is a natural part of life. The key is to be in balance as much as possible and live a balanced lifestyle to create a healthy well-being for yourself. As you learn and choose to live your life in balance, you help to create balance on the planet. To live in balance is to blend all aspects of yourself on the physical, mental, emotional and spiritual level, using your natural resources and going with the natural rhythms of the universe.

When your life is balanced, you will experience harmony, desirable experiences, abundance, prosperity and fulfillment. You will feel motivated, energetic, joyful, refreshed and rejuvenated. You will feel vibrantly healthy and full of life on all levels. When you experience inner peace, balance and harmony, this creates synchronicity in your life and things just flow. This is God in action expressing through you. You will be able to live up to your greatest potentials and live a fulfilling life that brings inner happiness and success, for love is the source of all of these and everything good. To establish a balance that works for you, tune into your body each day for what it needs by following your inner knowing, your feelings, and your heart. Your desires for these will help you determine the proper balance for you. You will receive the greatest benefits when you establish a lifestyle that helps you incorporate these essentials in a way that enables you to create balance and harmony.

Love • Prayer • Meditation • Exercise • Eat healthy • Rest • Play Career • Time for yourself and others • Spend time out in nature Inspiration (such as angelic music or positive food for your brain)

NOURISHMENT FOR YOUR SOUL: When all aspects of yourself function together it creates balance and you experience harmony.

When you are in your natural state of being, you are in balance, centered and your mental, physical, emotional and spiritual needs are met. Your desires are then fulfilled and harmony follows.

FOOD FOR THOUGHT: I AM living a balanced life. *"Balance is learning when to hold on and when to let go."* —Keith Urban

Daily Rituals

Since we are spiritual beings in a physical body, it is important to nurture both aspects of ourselves and include our spiritual practices as part of our daily living. When we create daily rituals, we set the intention for these things to occur throughout our day. I have created these guidelines to make it simple for you to incorporate these activities into your day. Although we all lead busy lives, these spiritual practices can easily be incorporated to create balance in our lives. In the beginning it may seem like a lot to do, but most of these practices only take a few minutes. As you incorporate them into your routine they become a way of life. The investment that you make will truly enrich your life!

The most important thing to remember is that you enjoy doing these daily practices. You will have days in which all of these practices do not fit into your day, as life happens. That's okay. Be gentle with yourself and choose the ones you feel are most important that day. I'm sharing a sample of how I incorporate my spiritual practices into my daily rituals for you to use as a guide. Adjust it to serve you and fit your lifestyle.

UPON AWAKENING

All of the following practices only take about 30 minutes of your time. It is time well spent as it sets the scene for your day.

- 💜 Morning prayers and blessing to the universe. (2 minutes)
- 💜 Daily practices on CD included with this book. (15 minutes)
- 💜 *Chakra Power Meditation* on *Angelic Reflections I: Awakening* CD (10 minutes)
- 💜 Mirror Exercises. (1 minute)
- 💜 Set your intentions for the day by making your divine activities list. (5 minutes)
- 💜 Connect with your angels in whatever way you choose. Any of Doreen Virtue's oracle cards are great for this. (however long you choose)

NOURISHMENT FOR YOUR SOUL: It's time for you to wake up and let your light shine!

FOOD FOR THOUGHT: "*I awake in the morning and sit up in bed allowing loving thoughts for the day to unfold in my head.*" —Bonnie Ann Lewis

ANGELIC TOOLS:
- 💜 *Your Journey to Love Daily Practices* CD (included with this book)
- 💜 *Angelic Reflections I: Awakening* CD by Bonnie Ann Lewis
- 💜 *Daily Guidance from Your Angels Oracle Cards* or any other Oracle Cards by Doreen Virtue

SETTING YOUR INTENTIONS

YOUR LIFE

Imagine your life as you dream it to be.
Visualize your life as you desire to see.
Feel the love and joy that surrounds you now.
Let the universe take care of the how.
Know this is the life you are meant to live.
Gratitude for these blessings is what you can give.

—*The Angels*

Setting your intentions on a daily basis keeps you in the flow of those things occurring. Utilize these intentions during the day as your guide for creating what you desire to experience.

- ♥ Focus on what you desire to occur, experience or accomplish today.

- ♥ Write out on your intentions sheet your desired activities. You can also write these on a dry erase board or type them into your computer. Use the method that works best for you.

- ♥ Review them at the end of the day and give thanks for what you achieved. The things not achieved that day add to the next day if it is still important to you. Continue doing so until you achieve it.

- ♥ Stay true to your goals despite obstacles.

I have created a daily intention form on my computer and I print out a dozen at a time on recycled paper so they are easily available to set my intentions every day. Here is an example for you to use.

EXERCISE: MY DAILY INTENTIONS

My days are filled with divine activities that
reflect the desires and truths within my soul.

Thank you universe for supporting me in all my endeavors.

NOURISHMENT FOR YOUR SOUL: I have found that creating a daily schedule has set the intention and helped me to create balance in my life as well as incorporate my life's work into my days. It also helps me to focus on what is most important. When you create a schedule, allow room for spirit to enter. Be flexible and allow things to flow but stay true to your intentions. As you do this you will see how much you accomplish and how often you succeed.

FOOD FOR THOUGHT: I set my intentions for the day using them as a guide for creating and experiencing a divine day. My day is filled with divine activities.

THROUGHOUT YOUR DAY

The following can be easily incorporated throughout your day.

- Remember to communicate with your angels throughout your day. This will allow them to assist you and create a more peaceful day for you. You will be amazed at how smooth, synchronistic and divine your day will be!
- Listen to angelic music as this raises your vibration and helps you to stay centered in your natural state of love. I play Peter Sterling's angelic music in my home and office all day long and I listen to *Let LOVE Be* or other inspirational music in the car when running errands.
- Listen to or review affirmations. Most of the time I listen to these before taking a rest or going to bed, however, you can listen to them while driving in the car or review them during your lunch break.
- Sit in quiet meditation. Anytime you can fit this into your day is good! I like to do this in the middle of the day after lunch as I find it refreshes and rejuvenates me for the rest of my day. For those of you who work outside of the home, just taking 10 minutes or so when you can to be

outside and breathe deeply is helpful. Perhaps this could be done during your lunch break. When outside, take a few deep breaths, allowing your mind to clear and your body to relax. That breath of fresh air will revitalize and rejuvenate you, allowing you to open to the voice of spirit. This can have the same effect as quiet meditation. Since there are guided meditations throughout this book, below I am sharing with you how to practice quiet meditation.

QUIET MEDITATION

Quiet meditation relaxes your body, relieves stress, and opens you to receiving divine guidance. Spending at least 10–20 minutes a day in quiet meditation is beneficial to your well-being.

- Before you begin, ask your angels to guide your meditation and take you to a place where you feel safe, secure and loved where you can just be. Affirm: I am safe, peaceful and tranquil.
- Upon entering meditation, breathe deeply and visualize your spark of white light, then see it expanding throughout your body and aura. Be still and open.
- Just be and enjoy the solitude without trying to force things to happen. Any time you have a busy mind, shift your thoughts to the word love and continue breathing deeply. This directs you back to centre. Often times when we quiet our mind, the angels' messages do flow in. Just allow yourself to be in that moment and flow with the experience knowing whatever occurs is perfect for you.

NOURISHMENT FOR YOUR SOUL: Meditation is a tool to quiet your mind so you can hear your heart. Taking time to be or walking out in nature and breathing deeply for 10–20 minutes can constitute for quiet meditation.

FOOD FOR THOUGHT: I take time every day to quiet my mind and listen to my heart.

BEFORE GOING TO BED

All of the following practices only take about 30 minutes of your time. It is time well spent as it relaxes you so you can have a peaceful sleep. Short and sweet as it's time for sleep!

- Send blessings to the universe prayer. (1minute)
- Reflect upon blessings from the day and give gratitude. (1–2 minutes)
- Send love to your body and affirm: I love all that I am and all that I do. (1 minute)
- Invite your angels into your dreams. Ask them to take you into a deep sleep and help you to wake up feeling refreshed, rejuvenated, recharged and full of life, for each day is a new beginning. (1 minute)
- Listen to or review affirmations. (10 minutes)
- Do the Chakra Clearing evening meditation by Doreen Virtue. This meditation helps you to release everything from your day and have a peaceful sleep. (20 minutes)

NOURISHMENT FOR YOUR SOUL: Sometimes I alternate listening to chakra clearing and affirmations depending on how tired I am when I get to bed. If you fall asleep listening to your affirmations or chakra clearing that is okay, because it will still go into your subconscious mind and is beneficial to you.

FOOD FOR THOUGHT: I AM consistent and enjoy my daily rituals. I create each day to reflect what is in my heart. My days are harmonious and peaceful.

ANGELIC TOOLS:

 Chakra Clearing audio by Doreen Virtue

Daily Prayers

Saying daily prayers is essential to incorporate into your day as this is your way of asking God and your angels to assist you in your life. Daily prayers set the scene for your day. The following prayer will help you to stay centered in your natural state of love and remind you to ask for angelic assistance every day. Feel free to use as is or adjust it to reflect your desires and truths.

PRAYER OF LOVING INTENTIONS

Dear God, Angels, Archangels and Ascended Masters,

I ask that you assist me in releasing any anger, resentment, fear or judgment so I can stay centered in my natural state of love. Please guide my thoughts, actions and words to reflect love throughout this day so I may attract loving experiences today. Please assist me in showing up as the love that I am and guide my true self to shine through in all that I do. I ask that you guide me to participate in divine activities today that are for the highest good of myself and all concerned, and reflect the truth within my soul. Help me to be in the moment and feel love, passion and joy in all that I do. I ask that you assist me in quieting my mind so I may hear my heart and your messages clearly. I ask that you assist me in staying grounded on this earth plane while being an open channel for your love. Thank you for making this so!

Here are some other prayers you may want to incorporate into your daily prayer time. You can write these prayers down on a large index card, punch a hole in them and connect them together with a binder ring. This keeps them handy and makes it easy to recite them, or keep this book on your bedside table where it is at your fingertips.

PRAYER FOR PROTECTION

"The light of God surrounds me,
The love of God enfolds me,
The power of God protects me,
The presence of God directs me,
Wherever I am, God is, and all is well!"

—Unity Church

GRATITUDE PRAYER

Thank you God for this beautiful day. I ask that this day be filled with experiences and opportunities for me to grow in love. I give thanks for all that the universe provides for me and all the good in my life.

BLESSINGS TO THE UNIVERSE

Good Day Universe. *I send love, peace, joy, thanks and prosperity to the universe in all directions.*

Good Night Universe. *Thank you for today's blessings and for supporting me with all of my endeavors. Thank you for the divine opportunities, experiences and relationships present in my life now.*

NOURISHMENT FOR YOUR SOUL: These prayers and blessings keep you in a state of gratitude, and keep a healthy balance in giving and receiving with the universe.

FOOD FOR THOUGHT: I make prayers a part of my daily practice.

EXERCISE: BOOK OF YOUR LIFE

You are the author in the book of your life with God writing the foreword. I'd like you to take a moment to think about your life in relation to a book. Imagine you are writing your own book of life. Writing a story about what you desire to experience in your life is a very powerful technique. It sets your intentions into motion and guides you to focus on that which you desire.

1. Take some time to reflect upon the truths within you and write a story about your desired life as if it already exists now.
2. Write it in either first or third person. Be sure to include all that you desire to be, all that you desire to do and experience, relationships you desire to share, the state of your existence, and anything else you can imagine. Paint a beautiful masterpiece of your life with words. Your possibilities are infinite!
3. When you write your story, be specific about your desires, but, leave the details of how it will happen to God and your angels so that they can put the magic into it.
4. After you write your story, light a candle as this represents the light of God. Take your story in your hands, visualize it all encompassed in white light and say the following prayer: "Dear God and Angels, This is what I desire to experience. Please guide me in manifesting these into my life experience."

5. Release it and let it go. You can do this by visualizing your story as a ball of white light lifting from your hands, going out into the universe and coming back to you as experience. This brings it full circle.
6. Thank your angels in advance, for you know your prayers have been heard and answered and this is already so.
7. Affirm: And so it is!
8. Continue nurturing the story of your life using the treasures of your soul. You will be amazed at the results for it will turn out better than you ever imagined!

NOURISHMENT FOR YOUR SOUL: This exercise is very powerful as it inspires you to focus on the life you desire and fulfills you as it comes to life in all senses of your being.

FOOD FOR THOUGHT: I have painted a beautiful masterpiece for my life with my words and I AM now experiencing my dreams!

ANGELIC TOOLS:

♥ *Angelic Reflections III: Life Reflections* CD by Bonnie Ann Lewis

---

LIFE REFLECTIONS

This meditation is designed to guide you in looking through the window of your future so you can create the life you desire to live to reflect your spiritual truths. I'm going to take you on an amazing journey where you will gather much wisdom as you see your life unfolding before your eyes . . . on angels' wings!

I recommend you find a peaceful place in which you feel safe and comfortable and will not be interrupted. Be sure to have some water and your journal by your side as you will be collecting a lot of information throughout this journey that you will want to record and remember. It is essential to continue breathing deeply throughout this meditation as this opens you up to the flow of the wisdom that resides within. After each step you will be given time to record what you receive. If you require more time, pause the CD until you are ready to move forward. May this angelic wisdom serve as a guide in living and creating a life you will love! Each time you do this meditation you will receive more wisdom and clarity regarding your life's path.

- Before we begin this journey, I invite you to call on all your spiritual team of helpers by repeating after me mentally, "Dear Angels, Archangels, Ascended masters, any other beings of light and Spirit Guides, please assist me in this meditation. Please show me a movie of my life so I can see my life's journey clearly and guide me as I reflect upon this journey to bring forth the wisdom so I may walk it with grace and ease."

- In addition to seeing the details of your life's journey, you may also hear, feel or just know information. Trust whatever comes through is truth for you.

- I invite you to close your eyes and take four deep breaths. As you breathe in, breathe in love, truth and clarity. As you breathe out, release any blockages that are in the way of you seeing your life's journey clearly.

- Visualize your third eye in the middle of your forehead. With your intention open your eyelid completely and see a ray of white light with sparkles of purple light stimulating and activating your third eye, so you may see the truth of your life's journey.

- Affirm: It is safe for me to see my past, present, and future clearly so I may create my life as I desire it to be. I see my life's path and future clearly with my spiritual vision.

- Let's begin.

- You are now standing inside your home looking out a large window where you see a white garden gate with an arch above it filled with beautiful pink, red and yellow flowers.

- Now I invite you to enter this gate. As you walk through the gate into a beautiful garden, you will smell the sweet fragrances of these beautiful flowers and feel the sun shining down upon you.

- Continue walking through the garden, taking in the beauty of nature and the blessings it brings. Continue breathing deeply, allowing yourself to feel centered and at peace.

- As you continue walking through the garden, you will approach a canopy of trees.

CREATING YOUR DIVINE LIFE

- As you continue on your journey you will see the sunlight shining down through the canopy of trees that is above your head.

- Follow this path to where your path of light meets the horizon where heaven and earth are one. Turn around and take a refreshingly deep breath. Reflect upon where you've been, where you are now, and where you are going.

- Take a few minutes to review the highlights, events, accomplishments, activities and people in your life.

- I'm going to be silent for several minutes while you reflect upon your life and record anything you'd like to capture from this experience.

- Once again close your eyes and take a few deep breaths, inhaling through your nose and exhaling out your mouth.

- At this time bring your attention back to the canopy of trees. As you walk through this canopy of trees, it will lead you along your path of life and you will see many roads and trails that branch off in different directions. Allow your angels to guide you to where you are to go.

- As you walk this path, follow the signs before you and collect clues and information about your life's journey. Pay close attention to the details and what crosses your path.

- The first sign you come to is marked Spiritual Team. This road is Purple with sparkles of white light and will show you your spiritual team that is here to guide you through life. As you walk this road, breathe in this white and purple light and say, "Dear Members of My Spiritual Team, please show me who you are."

- Once again close your eyes and take a few deep breaths, inhaling through your nose and exhaling out your mouth.

- Now you will merge back into the canopy of trees and continue walking until you reach the second sign marked Animals. This trail is Brown and will show you your power animal and totem animals that are here to assist you in your life. Your power animal came in at birth and will be with you throughout your life. It assists you with being in your own power.

- As you walk this trail breathe in this brown energy and say, "Dear Power Animal, show me who you are."

- Now say, "Dear Totem Animals, please show me who you are." These are animals that are around you that come and go and that you can call on to assist you in your life.

- Once again close your eyes and take a few deep breaths, inhaling through your nose and exhaling out your mouth.

- Now merge back into the canopy of trees and continue walking until you reach the third sign marked, Gifts, Talents and Healing Abilities. This road is Gold and will show you the gifts, talents and healing abilities you brought into this life or that you will master in this lifetime. As you walk this trail breathe in this vibrant Gold energy and say, "Dear Spiritual Team, please show me the gifts, talents and healing abilities I have brought into this life time."

- "What gifts, talents and healing abilities am I to focus on and master in this lifetime?"

- Once again close your eyes and take a few deep breaths, inhaling through your nose and exhaling out your mouth.

- Now merge into the canopy of trees and continue walking until you reach the fourth sign marked Life Lessons. This road will bring you information regarding the lessons you came to learn in this lifetime, the challenges that may come up for you and give you guidance on how to learn these lessons with love. This road of life lessons is Turquoise. As you walk this road, breathe in this vibrant turquoise energy and say, "Dear Spiritual Team, please show me what my primary lessons are that I came to learn in this lifetime."

- "What challenges may I encounter?"

- "How may I learn these lessons with love, grace and ease?"

- Once again close your eyes and take a few deep breaths, inhaling through your nose and exhaling out your mouth.

- Now merge back into the canopy of trees and continue walking until you reach the fifth sign marked Health. This road is Orange and will show you any physical challenges that may come up for you in this lifetime, and give you guidance on how to overcome them. As you walk this road breathe in the vibrant orange energy and say, "Dear Spiritual Team please show me what major physical conditions I am to watch out for."

- "What am I to do to heal these?"

- Once again close your eyes and take a few deep breaths, inhaling through your nose and exhaling out your mouth.

- Now merge back into the canopy of trees and continue walking until you reach the sixth sign marked Nourishment. This trail is Green and will show you the foods you need to nourish your body and the types of foods that are not complimentary to your body. As you walk this trail, breathe in the freshness of this vibrant green light and tune into your body and say, "Please show me the foods that are most nourishing to you."

- Once again tune into your body and say "Please show me the foods that are not complimentary to you."

- Once again close your eyes and take a few deep breaths, inhaling through your nose and exhaling out your mouth.

- Now merge back into the canopy of trees and continue walking until you reach the seventh sign marked Crystals. This trail is mixed with colors of the rainbow. It will show you what crystals will help to support you mentally, physically, emotionally and spiritually along your journey. As you walk this trail breathe in the rainbow energy and with your intentions see with your spiritual vision the crystals that would be beneficial for you to have in your environment.

- Once again close your eyes and take a few deep breaths, inhaling through your nose and exhaling out your mouth.

- In front of you is a white bench. I invite you to sit or lie down on this bench and rest for a few moments. Look up at the sky and see the light shine down upon you and just relax. Focus on the music, allowing your mind to clear and take you wherever it desires to go. Take a moment to drink some water.

- At this time close your eyes and take a few deep breaths, inhaling through your nose and exhaling out your mouth.

- Now merge back into the canopy of trees and continue walking until you reach the eighth sign marked Relationships. This road is Pink and will show you the primary relationships you will share in this lifetime. As you walk this road, breathe in this beautiful pink energy and say, "Dear Spiritual Team, please show me the primary relationships I will share in this lifetime. Show me my partners, marriage(s), children, grandchildren and friends."

- Once again close your eyes and take a few deep breaths, inhaling through your nose and exhaling out your mouth.

- Now merge back into the canopy of trees and continue walking until you reach the ninth sign marked Helpful People. This trail is Yellow and will show you the helpful people that will come into your life to light your path and pave your way. As you walk this path, breathe deeply and take in this beautiful yellow light and say, "Dear Spiritual Team, please show me the helpful people that will enter my life and light my path."

- Once again close your eyes and take a few deep breaths, inhaling through your nose and exhaling out your mouth.

- Now merge back into the canopy of trees and continue walking until you reach the tenth sign marked Creative Expression. This road is Light Blue and will show you your creative channels of expression. As you walk this road breathe in this calming blue energy. In front of you is a tree of creativity. It has green leaves and is filled with orange balls. Each ball represents a creative channel of expression. Pick from the tree as many orange balls as you feel guided to take. Hold each ball in your hand and tune into what that creative channel is for you.

- Once again close your eyes and take a few deep breaths, inhaling through your nose and exhaling out your mouth.

- Now merge back into the canopy of trees and continue walking until you reach the eleventh sign marked Career/Jobs. This road is Red and will show you how you can share your passions and be of service and what job or career would be most beneficial for you to be in. As you walk this trail breathe in this vibrant red light and say, "Dear Spiritual Team, please show me the jobs and careers that are most reflective of my passions and life's purpose."

- Once again close your eyes and take a few deep breaths, inhaling through your nose and exhaling out your mouth.

- Now merge back into the canopy of trees and continue walking until you reach the twelfth sign marked Home. This road is Pink and Green. It will show you the areas in which you are attracted to on the globe, the ideal place(s) for you to call home, and what your homes look like. As you walk this trail, breathe in these pink and green colors and say, "Dear Spiritual Team, show me areas of the earth that I am energetically aligned with."

- "Please show me the places in which I am to live."

- "Show me what my homes look like."

- Once again close your eyes and take a few deep breaths, inhaling through your nose and exhaling out your mouth.

- Merge back into the canopy of trees where the light is shining down upon you. You are now back at the beginning of the canopy of trees.

- At this time take yourself back to the garden of flowers. Take your shoes off and feel the cool soft grass beneath your feet as you walk through the arched gate and back into your home.
- Send love to yourself. You have retrieved much information on your journey. May you take this information and use it as your personal guide in creating and living your life.
- May you feel illuminated with the light of God around you and through you as you journey through life with grace, ease and love.

Reflections of love to you!

NOTE: This meditation is found on my *Angelic Reflections III: Life Reflections* CD

Creating Your Sacred Space

THE HOUSE OF LOVE

I dwell in the house of Love;
My dwelling place is filled with peace and eternal calm.
Love attends me in my home of the Soul, and
Joy awaits upon me in the "Secret Place of the Most High."
My house is built for me by the hand of Love, and
I shall never leave this Home of the Spirit, for it is always present.
I shall abide in this home forevermore.
My home is a house of love.

—*Dr. Ernest Holmes from The Science of Mind Textbook*

Our homes are a reflection of who we are. They are where everything begins. When creating our sacred space, we want to bring into our environment that which reflects who we are and what we desire to experience. Feng Shui is a method used for creating balance and harmony in your life through the placement of objects. As these objects are placed in certain areas of your home, office, etc. it increases the flow of energy to bring into your life that which you desire. Feng means wind which represents heaven and Shui means water which represents earth, creating a balance between heaven and earth. I used the book, *The Western Guide to Feng Shui* by Terah Kathryn Collins and I took a Feng Shui class from Stacy Davenport which was a tremendous help. Stacy Davenport is a Feng Shui Master and Teacher in Austin, Texas. To learn more visit www.stacydavenport.com. I combined Feng Shui principles and angelic guidance in our home and the Swan Self-Awareness Centre so I consider them to be angelically Feng Shui'd! I also had a consultation from Stacy to fine-tune the energy as our life shifted into new endeavors. So many people who come into our home say they feel so much love here as well as the presence of the angels. What's most important to remember is that what is in your home feels good to you as the power is in the intention.

- ♥ Surround yourself with beings of light by displaying pictures, posters or statues of them in your environment. This reminds you to ask for help and it invokes their energy into your environment. What I like to do is use the *Archangel and the Ascended Masters* Oracle Cards by Doreen Virtue, and place them on the window sill of the room or in the area which I desire to bring in their energy. I have the artwork included in this book throughout our home. A few of my favorite places to find photos of these beings of light are www.sacredimages-ami.com and www.stardolphin.com.

- ♥ Surround yourself with things you love.

- ♥ Create an altar in your home of items that have special meaning to you or that represent the energy you desire to create.

- ♥ Use Feng Shui principles to bring balance into your home. The purpose of Feng Shui is to place objects in your home in certain areas to direct the flow of energy throughout, creating balance, love, peace, harmony and prosperity. This helps the energy in your home support who you are, what you are doing, and where you want to go since everything begins at home. Home is the foundation for your life.

- ♥ Bring in pictures of helpful people, photos or figurines of animals and pieces of crystals, and place them in specific areas to enhance the vibration according to the Bagua layout in *The Western Guide to Feng Shui*.

- ♥ Use colors that bring in energy you desire in each space of your home in accordance to the colors recommended for that specific area of your home. Color stimulates movement, helps you feel alive, motivated, relaxed and peaceful.

NOURISHMENT FOR YOUR SOUL: There are many inexpensive ways to do this. Be creative and have fun!

FOOD FOR THOUGHT: My home is a reflection of who I am and what I desire to experience.

ANGELIC TOOLS:
- ♥ *The Western Guide to Feng Shui* by Terah Kathryn Collins

Creating Your Divine Career or Job

Your career or job is what you do to be of service and in exchange you receive money and support for your time and energy. There are many people who are in jobs that do not feed their soul, leaving them unhappy and unfulfilled. Oftentimes people end up in jobs because they knew someone, that's what was available at the time, or it was just a means to pay the bills. However, you will prosper more when you do something you feel passionate about to support you in your life. Maybe growing up you had dreams of the perfect career or job for yourself and someone told you that you could not make a living doing that so you needed to get a "real" job? Perhaps you've been in a career a long time, are bored, burned out and would like to try something else? When you feel this way, know this is your soul letting you know this job has served its purpose and it is time to move on. There is someone else out there that would love your job; that job is for them. It takes a lot of courage and a leap of faith to change careers so you can do what you desire to do, but the benefits are infinite. It changes your whole sense of well-being. It truly feeds your soul when you are doing what you love for a living.

Once you decide what you want and set your intentions, you can move forward in that direction one step at a time. Ask the universe for assistance and then take the steps to make it happen. As your life comes into alignment with your truth, your job or career will also shift. Before you know it, you will be doing what you love. In order to attract a job you love, you must love the job you presently have. You do this by giving gratitude for the blessings it brings so when you go on to your next job you will attract the good aspects of that job. Instead of searching for a job, go within and create it. Take the steps you are guided to take. Allow your job to come to you on angels' wings. The following recipes will guide you in the direction of doing what your heart desires, enjoying yourself, feeling fulfilled and accomplishing your life's purpose.

EXERCISE: DESIGNING YOUR CAREER OR JOB FROM WITHIN

In this exercise we will be utilizing the creative affirmative writing process. It is truly amazing how powerful this exercise is.

1. Imagine you have an infinite amount of money and time. What would your ideal job or career consist of?
2. On a piece of paper, make a list of what activities you would like your ideal job to consist of. To determine this, focus on your passions, gifts, talents and desires.
3. Then in paragraph form write a job description that reflects the job of your dreams, as if it were an ad requesting someone with all your skills.
4. Light a candle. Hold your job description in your hands. Say the following prayer, "Dear Universe, here are my desires for my perfect job (or career). Please bring it to me now. I am ready and I claim this now. Please help me so this job provides the financial abundance to support myself and my family. Thank you!"
5. Ask your angels for assistance on what action steps you can do to manifest this job. Take guided action.
6. Reflect upon this job description often to keep the energy moving in that direction.
7. Affirm and give gratitude for this job already being present in your life now.

NOURISHMENT FOR YOUR SOUL: A job without love is "work." When you put love into it, it becomes service. As we serve, we experience joy and receive an abundance of good in return. Love yourself and put love into everything you do.

FOOD FOR THOUGHT: As I create my job description from within, the universe meets my requests. I AM now doing what I love and I AM supported abundantly by the universe. I AM grateful.

Sharing Your Gifts and Talents with the World

SHINE

The beautiful you always shines through,
Touching many along the way,
Being the light in their day,
So they may see,
What its like to be free
From fear, struggle and pain.
When you let it go there is much to gain.
This opens the heart and mind,
Reaching people of every kind.
The love you give so freely,
Helps others shine!

—*The Angels*

When you are sharing your gifts and talents with the world, you are expressing yourself with love and letting your light shine. As you express yourself with love, you are:

- ❤ Bringing forth the love within to the physical world, expanding God's love to all.
- ❤ Allowing God to express through you by being a channel, vessel or instrument for God's infinite love.
- ❤ God in action, being a messenger and model for love.
- ❤ Bringing heaven to earth.

NOURISHMENT FOR YOUR SOUL: As you give, share or serve you also receive. As you teach you learn. When you share your gifts and talents you are making this world a brighter place.

FOOD FOR THOUGHT: I AM a clear channel for God's love and light and I AM shining bright.

MESSAGES OF LOVE:

This was a message I received from Jesus when I was dealing with fears about sharing my gifts and talents with the world.

> *You are meant to do great work on a much broader scale. It is time to release your fears and expand your exposure. You have all of the tools and information to do this. Stand your ground in your teachings. Remember you are one with spirit and me. You are filled with and surrounded by infinite wisdom. Fear no more and know your truth, walking in my footsteps teaching love. Dear Child, go in peace.*

This was a message I received when I was upset about a comment from someone else's opinion.

> *Dear Child,*
>
> *Do not lower your light because it is too bright for someone else. Recognize their opinion is their business not yours. Regardless of the opin-*

ions of others, allow your light to shine. As you shine your light, you inspire other's to do the same.

Focus on Service

We are spiritual beings in physical bodies here to serve as co-creators and expand God's love through our service to others. We do this by spreading God's love in all that we are and all that we do.

- ♥ Being of service is the ability to set yourself aside and be in a place of neutrality to help others. Utilizing your intuitive abilities in service is to be a clear channel for this divine love, light and wisdom to come through you for the good of humanity. People will be attracted to you for your wisdom and insights.
- ♥ Service means to do things with love, with an open heart, and in return the universe gives back in infinite ways.
- ♥ God gave you gifts and talents to be of service and be supported in life so you can do what you came here to do and fulfill your mission with love, joy, grace and ease.
- ♥ You have something that you can share with the world, to make someone else's load a little lighter or day a little brighter, and make this world a better place.
- ♥ When you focus on service, you will attract those who will benefit from the blessings you have to offer.

NOURISHMENT FOR YOUR SOUL: As I focus on service the universe supports me in all ways.

FOOD FOR THOUGHT: I AM now being of service utilizing my gifts and talents. I make a powerful loving impact on this world.

ANGELIC TOOLS:

♥ *Heart and Soul* Music CD by Peter Sterling

EXERCISE: WHAT'S IN MY HEART?

1. Take a piece of paper and draw a big heart.
2. Take three or four deep breaths and ask yourself the following questions: "What's in my heart? What am I passionate about? What are my dreams for myself? What are my dreams for the world? What do I have in my heart to share with the world?"
3. Inside the heart, record whatever comes to you from your heart.
4. This will be a guide for you to follow the passions of your heart.

NOURISHMENT FOR YOUR SOUL: When you allow your heart to lead you, you will always know the way.

FOOD FOR THOUGHT: I AM aware of, and follow the passions of my heart.

EXERCISE: EXPRESSING YOUR DESIRES

Now that you've discovered your desires, dreams and passions, reflect upon how to express them by asking your angels for clarity on how you can share your gifts and talents with the world. You can use the automatic writing exercise, *Going Within* to communicate with your angels to receive this information. Here are some questions to ask: "What are my hidden gifts and talents? How can I utilize these gifts in my service? How do they relate to my life's purpose?"

NOURISHMENT FOR YOUR SOUL: We all have gifts and life experiences worth sharing that can assist and guide others along their path.

FOOD FOR THOUGHT: I AM expressing my true desires. The universe supports me in all of my endeavors.

PROCESS . . . PRACTICE . . . PRESENT

In order to share your gifts and talents with the world, you must first create a solid foundation for yourself and others, and the following steps must occur.

1. **Process:** It is important when you receive information that you take the time to process it so that you understand it, then you will be able to clearly share the information with others.
2. **Practice:** by applying it to your own life.
3. **Present:** by sharing it with others and to the world.

NOURISHMENT FOR YOUR SOUL: By utilizing these steps, you will evolve and be able to deliver the messages clearly and thoroughly. Life experiences add passion for you and serve others better, for you are a model they can really relate to and be touched by your life experiences.

FOOD FOR THOUGHT: I share my life experiences with others to light their path and assist them in their growth.

MESSAGES OF LOVE:

> *Dear Child of the Light,*
>
> *You are a divine teacher of ancient wisdom. It's time for you to move forward and polish your teachings. Practice them as well. The childhood fears needed to come forth to increase your light body. The things you asked for are compassion and the release of judgments and fear. Your prayers have been answered. The NDE has brought you to greater enlightenment. It has opened your heart. This has also been a process*

of releasing the fear about your life's purpose and speaking your truth. One is first the student. This you have done. Now it's time to teach. See yourself through eyes of love and just be that beautiful light that you are. Do not allow others to stand in your way. Remember to pace yourself and play.

Marketing From Your Heart

While I was in the process of self-publishing this book, many wanted to know if I had a marketing plan. While this is a common concern for those self-publishing, I had a sense of knowing the angels would guide my way. Traditional marketing can be time consuming, expensive and may not have the outcome you expect. It is not always necessary to invest a large amount of money in advertising to be successful, unless you are guided to do so. For me, my marketing plan is simple. The angels are my marketing team. I have received many visions and guidance for my marketing endeavors. The following recipe will guide you in sharing your gifts and talents with the world by marketing from your heart.

❤ Ask for angelic assistance. You can call on Archangel Gabriel to help you with your marketing endeavors and materials such as designing your website, business cards, brochures, promotional items, as well as people who can assist you in this area.

❤ Keep a journal of the guidance you receive and use as a guide for your marketing plan. Your angels will give you divine ideas specific to your desires and the gifts you have to offer.

❤ Follow the angels guidance by taking action steps.

❤ Recite the prayers in this recipe.

♥ Do *Marketing Within* Exercise.

NOURISHMENT FOR YOUR SOUL: As you set your intentions and follow the angels' guidance, you will be amazed at how you attract those who will benefit from your services and teachings as well as how your products reach who they are meant to reach.

FOOD FOR THOUGHT: I share my gifts and talents with the world by marketing from my heart.

PRAYER FOR SHARING YOUR GIFTS AND TALENTS

Dear God, Angels, Archangels and Ascended Masters,

Please help me to release any fear associated with fulfilling my life's purpose. Please help me to be an instrument of your love. Please open my heart and my mind to reflect your love. Please give me the courage and confidence to be my true self, share my gifts with the world, and fulfill my life's mission. Please provide me with all that I require and desire in order to do this. Thank you for supporting me in all my endeavors. Amen.

PRAYER FOR INTENTIONS TO BE OF SERVICE

Dear God, Angels, Archangels and Ascended Masters,

I choose to be an open channel for your divine love and messages. Please guide and bring me the opportunities to utilize my gifts and talents to be of service. I ask you to bring to me those people who are open to and will benefit from the wisdom I have to share. Thank you for making this so!

CREATING YOUR DIVINE LIFE

A TEACHER'S PRAYER

Dear God, Angels, Archangels and Ascended Masters,

Please join together those people who are meant to assist one another on their journey. I request your presence here today and ask you to fill this room with love and light. I ask that all who gather here touch one another, be blessed with your love and guidance and receive whatever serves their soul's growth. Please speak through me and bring forth the words that will open the hearts and minds of all. Thank you for making this so!

SACRED BLESSING FOR YOUR PRODUCTS

After my angelic tools came back from being manufactured, I blessed all of them with love and sent gratitude energetically to all who participated in bringing them to life. I have included the prayer that I use. Feel free to use it as is or adjust it to reflect your intentions.

1. Place your finished products in front of you or stand in front of them with your arms open wide. If you'd like you can also light a candle as this brings in the light of God.
2. Invoke love into all of these gifts by visualizing pink light going from your heart to them.
3. Recite the following prayer:

Dear God, Angels, Archangels and Ascended Masters,

I ask that you infuse these divine gifts with love as they go out into the world to empower and enrich the lives of all they touch. I ask that these divine tools reach those who will benefit from them and be open to their messages and healing energy. May each person these gifts touch be blessed with infinite love and peace. May they embrace this love and pass it on, contributing to the creation of heaven here on earth. I send love and gratitude to all who participated in bringing these angelic tools to life, including those who did behind the scenes work that we may not be aware of and often go without recognition. I thank you for your guidance and direction with these endeavors. Amen.

4. Visualize them going out into the world on angels' wings.

EXERCISE: MARKETING WITHIN

We all have dreams and desires for our business. The question that exists for many is how do we achieve these aspirations? We are all creators of our own life with God/Angels/Spirit. You have the power within to create all that your heart desires. Everything begins with you. Marketing Within presents the angelic principles to bring your business desires and dreams to life from the inside out. This exercise will assist you in attracting whatever you require and desire for your business to succeed and flourish!

1. **Meditate and Get Clear on What You Desire.** When you are clear to the universe, the universe is clear to you.
2. **Set Your Intentions:** Draw a heart on a piece of paper. Put the name of your business on top of the heart. Fill your heart with all your desires and dreams for your business. Be sure to include:

- The physical space you desire for your business in a divine location.
- The necessary connections such as helpful people, clients, patients, students, customers, resources, suppliers (whatever you need) that will benefit from your services, teachings, and products.
- Open doors of opportunity for your business to thrive.

- Financial means to accomplish your goals and dreams for your business, with plenty to spare and share. Ask that your business supports itself financially and prospers.
- Describe the type of people with whom you desire to work and do business with.
- Anyone or anything else that is for the highest good of yourself and all concerned.

3. **Prayer:** Light a candle and ask the universe to support you in all ways by saying, "Dear Universe, these are my dreams and desires for my business. I give them to you to bring to fruition. Thank you!"
4. **Ask for Guidance** and take action on the necessary steps to bring these desires to life. Take these steps with courage and confidence knowing they will lead you where you desire to go.
5. **Create Affirmations that Reflect Your Desires.** Examples: My business is constantly growing. My prosperity is constantly increasing. I bless my customers, clients, students, and all the people I interact with, with love and gratitude. (These affirmations came from the website of Louise L. Hay. They spoke to my heart so I'm passing them along.)
6. **Visualization:** Put love around and within your establishment. See in your mind's eye your business as you'd like it to be, and feel the joy that brings. Affirm: And so it is!
7. **Create an Imagery or Vision Board** and visit it often. This is a powerful tool to help you focus on and bring in the energy of your dreams and desires for your business so they can become a part of your life experience.
8. **Gratitude:** Give thanks, have faith and trust the universe will put into alignment your desires. Enjoy the blessings you receive!

NOURISHMENT FOR YOUR SOUL: The most important principle to remember is to focus on service and your business will flourish!

FOOD FOR THOUGHT: My business is a reflection of my desires and is prospering in infinite ways!

Action Steps for Your Life's Mission

"Go confidently in the direction of your dreams. Live the life you have imagined." —HENRY DAVID THOREAU

Once you know what your life's purpose is, you can begin to take the steps to shift your life in the direction of your dreams. Creating an action plan will help you stay focused, on track, and continuously moving in your desired direction.

- ♥ Ask for guidance and direction from your angels. Check in regularly to ensure a successful outcome.
- ♥ Create an action plan by making a list of action steps.
- ♥ Take at least one step each day toward your desires.
- ♥ Release any fears you may have about fulfilling your life's mission. As you release the fear, you open yourself up to attract what you require and desire to succeed.

NOURISHMENT FOR YOUR SOUL: As you release the fear that comes up regarding your life's purpose, you will be ready to move forward with the next step. Each step you take will bring you closer and closer to achieving these aspirations.

FOOD FOR THOUGHT: I take the action steps with confidence and courage toward fulfilling my life's mission.

EXERCISE: RELEASING FEARS ABOUT YOUR LIFE'S PURPOSE

1. Make a list of fears relating to fulfilling your life's purpose.
2. Write down what's the worst that could happen if that fear was to occur.
3. Allow the fear to come forward and when you are ready, let it go.
4. Ask Archangel Michael to help you release all energy attached to any of these fears and transform them into love.
5. Visualize the fear in a ball in the palm of your hand. Blow it into the universe for the angels to transform.
6. Affirm: I choose to release all fear with ease.
7. Then create an affirmation to reflect a new thought pattern about what you desire.

WALKING WITH JESUS

I had just put the polishing touches on this book after the editing process. As I was taking a walk, I was reflecting upon all that I had accomplished and the amazing way this book came together. I was feeling gratitude for all the love and support I received from all on earth and also in spirit. My thoughts shifted to wondering if I was ready for this next step of my life's purpose when my book is complete—getting out in the world! Although I have great passion about doing this, I felt butterflies in my stomach. The first thought that came to my mind was—transformation! A Few moments later I felt Jesus' presence beside me. Then I felt his hand take mine and a sense of peace came over me. I heard, *"Dear Child, You are not alone. I am here with you and will guide your way. You have much love in your heart to share with the world that will help and guide many. Continue to walk in faith, one step at a time. You are ready and have everything you require to reach the world and succeed. Bless you for walking this lighted path with grace and love. It's time to celebrate!"*

In my heart I knew this was true, as I had begun to feel the energy encompassing this expansive transformation during the birth of this book. I had been receiving visions of this and had already begun the manifestation process. I had been reciting my affirmations, and had already created my imagery boards to reflect these visions, dreams and desires. I thanked Jesus for guiding and visiting me. My conversation with Jesus inspired me to focus on celebrating the birth of this book. As I continued my walk, I began to visualize myself surrounded by all the wonderful people I have to share my life with, and those who have been a part of this divine endeavor and my journey to love. I felt such deep gratitude and a feeling of excitement came over me. I started visualizing my dreams and desires for this divine celebration. When I returned home, I shared with my husband my visit from Jesus and my dreams for celebrating the birth of this book. I felt gratitude for his love and support and having him to share my excitement and life with.

Universal Support

THE UNIVERSE

The universe is a vast place,
Where you serve and play
With the angels and the guides,
And see the truth of what's inside.
For they teach and guide
You to show your beautiful face
To the world!
It allows you to go at your own pace,
For it's your heart that holds the space

> For you to grow in love,
> And create all that you are dreaming of.
> To expand your mind to reflect your heart,
> Giving you a place to start,
> Living your dreams, desires and goals,
> For these are the truths within your soul.
>
> —*Bonnie Ann Lewis*

Many have inherited the belief that if they do what they love, they won't be able to make a living. In truth, when you are doing what you love, and living your life on purpose, you will feel fulfilled and will attract abundance in all areas of your life. The universe will support you in all your endeavors in all ways. All you must do is remember to ask! The universe supports you by providing all your needs and desires to fulfill your life's mission. There are infinite ways in which the universe supports you, but here are a few to bring to your awareness. I encourage you to go within and add your own requests on how the universe can support you. You can also create some affirmations to reflect your requests.

- ♥ Financial Abundance
- ♥ Resources
- ♥ Opportunities
- ♥ Physical space you desire for your business.
- ♥ Helpful people including: clients, students, customers, suppliers
- ♥ Teachers, classes, books, tools, schools
- ♥ Wisdom, knowledge, guidance, direction
- ♥ Courage, inspiration, empowerment
- ♥ Creativity, motivation, and focus
- ♥ Spiritual, physical, mental and emotional support

NOURISHMENT FOR YOUR SOUL: God is your source not outer influences. Everything begins within. The universe is your friend not your enemy. The universe provides for you all that you require and desire, however, you must ask and be open to receiving. The universe can only give to you that which you believe is yours.

FOOD FOR THOUGHT: I AM supported by the universe in all my endeavors as I fulfill my life's mission.

MESSAGES OF LOVE:

> *You deserve to receive abundance for sharing your gifts and talents. You must believe you deserve to receive. This is a natural process of life, giving and receiving. If you keep giving but do not allow yourself to receive, you will feel drained. You can be financially independent through your service to humanity. Focus on being supported by the universe, have faith, trust all is in divine order. Focus on what is in front of you each day, we will guide thy way. To receive, open up your arms and visualize yourself receiving and accepting with gratitude the gifts you've asked for.*

UNIVERSAL SUPPORT SACRED CEREMONY PRAYER

This prayer is intended to open you up to receiving universal support and can be recited for all your endeavors. You will recognize this throughout the book.

- 💜 Before doing this prayer, set your intentions for your desires by writing your desires in either a circle or a heart. This creates boundaries around what you desire to experience.

CREATING YOUR DIVINE LIFE

- ♥ Light a candle and place your boundary sheet in front of the candle. This represents the light of God and shines light on the situation or endeavor.
- ♥ Ask the universe to support you in all ways by saying: "Dear Universe, these are my dreams and desires. I give them to you to bring them to life. Please guide me to take action on the necessary steps to bring these desires to fruition." (It is best to ask for assistance and allow the universe to bring it to you in whatever way is for the highest good for yourself and all concerned.)
- ♥ Visualize all of these desires and dreams coming together forming a ball of white light. See this ball of white light in the palm of your hands, then blow it out into the universe.
- ♥ Affirm: The universe supports me in all my endeavors. And so it is!
- ♥ Thank the universe for making this so.

NOURISHMENT FOR YOUR SOUL: Take the action steps with courage and confidence knowing they will lead you where you desire to go.

FOOD FOR THOUGHT: I AM connected to the infinite source of the universe. The universe provides me with the money and means in advance to meet all of my needs and desires. I now have an abundance of money to pay for all that I require and desire to fulfill my life's mission. I AM open and receptive to receiving universal support in all my endeavors. I AM grateful!

I'd like to share some examples of universal support in my life so you can see the angels in action and the miracles that occur. When I began manifesting my divine career, I had no idea how it would work out. I just asked for angelic assistance, took one day at a time and followed the angels' guidance. When I got out of my own way, it all fell into place with grace and ease. I was guided to the people I needed to connect with and the money was there for me to accomplish these endeavors. When I was bringing my angelic tools to life, the angels, archangels and ascended masters guided, orchestrated and directed all of the divine endeavors I embarked upon. It was truly amazing how they guided me step by step. As I took each step, the next step presented itself or an opportunity opened up for me. I feel so grateful and blessed to have these heavenly helpers in my life!

When I was preparing to record my *Angelic Reflection* Meditations, it was my dream to incorporate Peter Sterling's heavenly *Harp Magic* since his music has been so much a part of these meditations from the beginning. I was listening to his music when I channeled the meditation and had his music playing when I presented them in my classes and workshops. I saw how his music touched others and the magic that occurred as it took them where they needed to be for healing and retrieving the wisdom from within. Although I wasn't even sure this was possible, I followed the angels' guidance and contacted him. To my surprise, this dream came to life! We are all blessed Peter's divine music is part of these meditations. The angels guided me on the specific music to use for each meditation and the way it all came together was simply magical! Each day I went to the studio, I called in all the spiritual beings that were assisting us on these angelic endeavors. My producer George Coyne was amazed at how these meditations came together with such synchronicity.

The recording process consists of the following steps: Recording the vocals, editing, adding music and then the final mix. One day as we were adding music to one of the meditations, we had to loop the music as the meditation was longer than the musical piece. In doing this we ran into a little glitch. My producer George was working on it for some time and it just was not falling into place. Mentally I asked the angels for confirmation that this was the music we were to use. I

CREATING YOUR DIVINE LIFE

heard a "*Yes*." Then, George said, "Maybe we should try some different music." I said, "The angels are telling me this is the music to use." So verbally I said, "Dear Angels, Archangel Michael and Archangel Sandalphon, please help us so this music falls into place with grace and ease." About 30 seconds later it all came together! George looked at me with big eyes and an expression of amazement on his face. I said, "That's how it works when we ask for angelic assistance!" Throughout the process we only encountered a few challenges. However, the angels came to our rescue. Time and time again we saw the angels in action while bringing these divine gifts to life!

Since these meditations are part of the book, I was bringing them to life simultaneously. The angels guided me when to stop writing and focus on recording the meditation CD's. When I was close to completing this book, I received guidance to self-publish and it seemed like everywhere I turned I was seeing information about self-publishing. So I asked the angels for their assistance in guiding my way and providing the financial means for me to do this. Shortly after asking the angels for guidance, I received an email from a woman named Carolyn Porter who was looking for angel stories for a book she was writing. She had gotten my email address from the Angel Therapy® website. I emailed back that I did not have a story at this time as I was writing a similar book myself. I was guided to visit her website and to my surprise she had self-published all of her own books and teaches a class that provides a manual she had written for self-publishing. I purchased the manual *Write, Design, and Self-Publish Your Book* and had some private sessions about publishing over the phone as she lives in Georgia and I in Texas.

Several months later I received a call from Carolyn and she said she was coming to Austin to visit and could she come see my healing center since she was getting ready to open a healing center in Georgia.

She came and I shared all of my knowledge with her. Carolyn also teaches a training for public speaking which I knew instantly I was to take. I told her I would like to take the next one she was having. At the time she did not have one scheduled so we coordinated our schedules, she began marketing it and the class formed. It was a wonderful opportunity for me to overcome the fear I had about public speaking in a safe, nurturing environment with like-minded, heart-centered people. It was very empowering and helped me feel more comfortable about speaking my truth. When I took my speaker training, since I was coming from out of town, Carolyn offered for me to stay at her home. I have been touched by her hospitality and generosity. Come to find out Carolyn lived in Austin many years ago. Our connection was so perfect. She was coming from where I am going (writing books and speaking) to where I was (having a healing center). When I first met Carolyn I felt an instant connection, like I had known her for years. This is another example of a soul connection. Since then Carolyn and I have become friends and she has guided me through the process of bringing this book to life!

Since Carolyn has published many books herself, she is very knowledgeable about the process and knows many tips for how the book industry works. She had done all the research, footwork, price comparisons, etc., along her self-publishing journey, saving me from having to do all that—thank you God! She gave me recommendations for designers and printers. I asked the angels for guidance on which to choose that would be for the highest good for this endeavor and all concerned, received my quotes and went with those. Due to her expertise, she paved my way and the process was very simple. Carolyn also edited this book. This was a great blessing to have someone do the editing that was like-minded and understands the content. Her expertise, guidance and genuine essence has been a Godsend! With this being my first book, there was much to learn and many decisions to make. When I was consulting with the representative from the company that was going to be printing this book, he said he would send me a sample of a book to show me certain aspects of the color printing process. When I received it in the mail and opened it up, to my surprise it was Carolyn's book, *Angel Love,* and the representative had no idea of our connection! Thanks to Carolyn's expertise and direction and the assistance from the angels, self-publishing was a very smooth process for me. In addition to Carolyn's services and teachings, I am blessed with her friendship and I am truly grateful. For more information regarding Carolyn's services, gifts, talents and books, you can visit www.drcarolynporter.com or www.wheremiracleshappen.com.

Even after working with the angelic realm all these years, I am continually amazed at the miracles that happen with their presence in my life. Some find it a challenge to believe life can be this simple and come together with such grace and ease. This is the magic that occurs when we invite the angels into our lives and the blessings we receive for being open to and following their guidance. There will always be challenges in life. However, when we ask for assistance and allow our friends in high places to help us through these challenges, we have more pleasant experiences and better outcomes. Although it took a lot of time and energy bringing forth my angelic tools, it has brought me great joy and I have had so much fun in the process! I have re-connected with some wonderful people and shared many angelic experiences that have touched my heart and soul. I am forever grateful for the assistance from my friends in high places for making this happen!

HEAVEN ON EARTH

Our life is filled with so much light and love,
That shines down upon us from the higher power above.
With the creating of heaven here on earth,
We can all strive for what we deserve.
For these gifts from God are our birthrights,
We are all one with the universe.
You will go much farther in life,
When you walk in love,
Bathing in the blessings,
God sends from above.
On angels' wings you will fly,
Not struggling with the when, how or why.
By asking and trusting and letting go,
Taking steps, moving with the flow.
For God sends his love on angels' wings,
And helps take care of everything,
You require and desire to fulfill your mission,
For love is who you are.

—*Bonnie Ann Lewis*

CONCLUSION
Creating Heaven on Earth

*"The angels can help us create a world of love,
light and peace, beginning with oneself."*

Heaven is within each of us. It is a state of divine consciousness rather than a location. Our world is created by the energy each and every one of us puts out there. In addition to our thoughts creating our personal experiences, they also contribute to creating the universal, global, collective consciousness. No matter where we are or what we are doing, we can always contribute to creating a world of love and peace just by showing up and being the love that we are, and putting love into everything we do. The more love we spread, the more love that comes to us. We as humans are the bridge between heaven and earth. As we create love and peace in our own life, it is projected out into our world.

Action Steps for Creating Heaven on Earth

*"Our greatest tool for changing the world is our capacity to change
our mind about the world."* —COURSE IN MIRACLES

Many people feel they do not have anything to contribute to making the world a better place. I'd like to show you that there are many things each of us can do right now to contribute to making this world a better place, right from where we are. No special tools, skills or money are needed, just an open heart and open mind. You are unique and important in the creation of our new earth. We need your love and light. You have unique talents that represent who you are, your purpose here and the part you are to play in the creation of heaven on earth. We are so glad that you are here sharing your love and shining your light, making this world a brighter place. When you set the intention for yourself and send it out into the universe, it reaches all of life. You can always choose to be the light that someone else could use today when darkness falls upon them. Here are some ways.

- ❤ When you see an accident, do not put energy into trying to figure out what happened. Instead, send love and angels to all those involved.
- ❤ When you hear disturbing, negative news, or about violent acts, automatically send love and angels to all who are involved. Ask the angels to heal the negativity for the people involved and our world.
- ❤ When you see someone hurting, send them love and help if you can.
- ❤ When you see a hurt animal, send healing energy. Call on the fairies to help the animal and ask what you can do to help. They will guide you.
- ❤ If you hear of someone who is dying, surround them in love and ask the angels to help them feel safe, secure and loved as they cross over. Ask that it be a peaceful experience for them. Send love and angels to their family and friends.
- ❤ When someone is having an unpleasant experience, give them a smile or words of encouragement.

- ♥ When you hear about someone being ill, send them love and picture them well in your mind.
- ♥ When you see someone struggling to achieve a goal, picture in your mind they are already achieving this goal.
- ♥ Use earth-friendly cleaning supplies and personal toiletries.
- ♥ Recycle as much as possible to keep our environment clean and lessen the amount of garbage going into the landfill. Anytime you are out walking or hiking, take a garbage bag and pick up trash along the way. Use recycled or reusable bags when shopping. Make your home and the environment as green as possible. See books under angelic tools that can guide you with this.
- ♥ Change to online billpay and electronic statements as much as possible to reduce the amount of paper used. Use downloadable flyers and brochures on your website and magnets for business cards. This saves our trees!
- ♥ When economical increases occur, instead of going into the fear, ask your angels to show you the way to increase your cash flow and provide you with the money so you can continue to purchase your needs, desires, and thrive.
- ♥ For those of you who watch the news and read the paper, choose to be aware of what's going on in the world without getting wrapped up in the drama that is being presented by the media.
- ♥ Each morning when you wake up, send love out into the universe. This reaches all people, animals, nature, water, trees, forests, lakes, oceans, flowers, etc. You can also send it to specific places on the planet that you feel guided to assist. Doing the following activation will send love to the earth, reaching all of its inhabitants.
- ♥ Support the soldiers, policeman, firemen, EMS, etc. by sending them love and Archangel Michael for protection.

💜 Surround the schools that our children go to with the white light of protection. Ask Archangels Michael, Metatron and Mother Mary to be present there and keep our children safe and grow and bloom with love.

NOURISHMENT FOR YOUR SOUL: Anything you do with loving intentions contributes to creating heaven here on earth. *"Inner peace creates world peace."* —Wayne Dyer

FOOD FOR THOUGHT: I AM a divine center where love and peace reside and projects out into the world.

ANGELIC TOOLS:
💜 *Green Made Easy* by Chris Prelitz
💜 *The Green Book* by Elizabeth Rogers and Thomas M. McDonough
💜 *True Green Home* by Kim McKay and Jenny Bonnin

EARTH LOVE ACTIVATION

This activation places a shield of protection around our planet and increases the love and light that is dispersed throughout our earth, raising the vibration. By adding this activation to your daily rituals you are contributing to creating a world of love and peace.

- I invite you to visualize the earth in the palm of your hands.
- Open your heart and allow the love within to flow as a stream of pink light encompassing the earth.
- Now visualize a circle of angels surrounding our planet, shining their love and light upon it.
- Affirm: Our world is filled with love, light and peace. And so it is!

NOTE: This activation is on *Your Journey to Love Daily Practices* CD included with this book.

An Abundant Earth

There are many people experiencing fear and turmoil in their life due to these unique economic times. Although there are many shifts and changes in the economy and atmosphere as our planet transforms into an abundant earth, it is essential that we stay centered in our natural state of love, for this contributes to a positive outcome for all.

These changes are just a reflection of the illusions of fear being presented to us for transformation so we can all experience heaven here on earth. As we pour love into all of these situations, the transformation happens with grace and ease. From the visions and messages I have received from the angels, I know these shifts and changes are leading us in a good direction, and we will create and experience divine results by being and expressing the love that we are.

We can all contribute to an abundant earth by changing our way of living, financial practices, assisting those less fortunate and taking care of our planet earth. By doing this, we create a healthier way of life for our children and future generations. My vision is to see everyone have a home to live in, food to eat, clothes to wear and all their needs and desires met. This will create more balance on our planet and a world of love and peace. As we all come together and do our part by living a healthier lifestyle, helping those in need, (I'm referring to those who really need help, not those who do not choose to help themselves.) and take care of our planet, an abundant earth is created! Here are some ways to contribute to an abundant earth.

- ♥ Live within your means while manifesting from within, and take guided action, knowing God will provide all that you need and desire. This creates abundance rather than poverty consciousness.

- ♥ Call in more angels and archangels to assist our planetary transformation. Ask them to create an outcome that is for the highest good of all concerned.

- ♥ Refrain from getting caught up in the drama that is occurring around you, and caused by fear. This will only create more fear. Instead, send love and peace to our planet and all of its inhabitants. Affirm that love, peace and abundance exist on our planet and in all our lives now.

- ♥ Assist or donate to organizations, charities or programs that speak to your heart. If you desire to help those less fortunate, ask the angels to supply you with the money and means to assist these causes. This makes you a steward for the money to benefit others or a philanthropist.

- ♥ Many complain about having to pay taxes. Instead of being resentful for having to pay these, consider this an investment you make to contribute to the well-being of our planet and an exchange for how the government helps us all. Send love, angels and gratitude to the people in our government systems. Affirm that all is being done for the highest good of all concerned.

NOURISHMENT FOR YOUR SOUL: We are all making a difference in the world by sharing our knowledge, courage, resources and love. Together we are creating heaven on earth and our possibilities are endless!

FOOD FOR THOUGHT: Our world is filled with love, peace and an abundance of good for all.

EARTH BALANCE AND PLANETARY HEALING
Celebrating our Divine Heritage.

Earth Balance and Planetary Healing

Much of our society is a reflection of a very masculine approach to living. At this time, we are experiencing a transformation on the planet that is bringing in more feminine energy to create a more nurturing way of living for all and creating balance and harmony on our planet. As a result of this global shift we as a society are letting go of the old fear-based energy and ushering in the energy of unconditional love. This recipe shares some angelic wisdom that will ensure a positive impact on our planet. These acts of love will expedite this transformational process so we can all experience heaven here on earth.

♥ In our society we view the global happenings as disasters because they affect all of humanity and our planet, and we see the people involved as victims. In truth, these happenings are a reflection of the energy being projected out into our world, and the people involved are not victims but on a soul level have chosen to be a part of that experience to open the hearts of all. When these happenings occur and there are deaths, those souls chose to exit the earth at that time. Although our hearts go out to all of those involved in these tragic situations, it is most beneficial to all and for our own well-being to forgive those involved rather than seeking revenge. As we do this, it creates harmony on our planet rather than discord and gives us peace of mind. In order to prevent these tragedies from happening, we must all close the doors to fear and violence and open our hearts to love and peace. Fighting and war are not the path to world peace and freedom—Unconditional love is. We must stop the wars and acts of violence which are affecting our planet and our people. As we come back to our natural state of love, these disasters will subside and we can all live in peace and harmony.

♥ At this time, negative things are occurring in the world around us and there is violence being projected from the media that reflects what's going on in the world which instills fear. While the purpose of the media is to inform us of what's happening in the world, all the gruesome and heart-wrenching details trigger fear in people. This causes people to respond in anger and seek revenge which contributes to the violence in our world. Instead if these details were omitted and the focus is on what we can all do to help, it will lessen the fear in people, open their hearts and have a powerful loving impact on this world. As the media reflects more of the positive and good things happening in our world that will contribute to creating a more peaceful, loving world for us all. To experience love and peace on our planet, we must all be the love that we are and set examples of this love in our television shows, movies, media, video games, and so on. As love is projected from our society, our world will mirror this love.

♥ When we hear about these acts of violence and worry or get angry about them, we are feeding that lower vibration of energy which just creates more fear and violence. Instead, focusing our energy on seeing the situation healed shifts the energy, is more powerful and creates outcomes that benefit us all. It is important for us to be aware of what is happening in the world without getting wrapped up in the human drama or putting more fear-based energy into it. We can do the most good by staying centered in our natural state of love in the midst of the chaos, and send out love and angels. The angels can help on a global level creating miracles greater than we can even imagine.

♥ There are many changes in the weather happening right now. These acts of nature are a reflection of the energy being projected out into our world and the result of the way our planet is being treated. The best way we can make a difference is for all of us to send love to these areas that are being affected by these natural disasters instead of going into fear and putting energy into what is occurring. When we send love it can lessen the impact it has on everyone. Loving thoughts are powerful! We can also call in more angels, lend a hand, offer assistance or provide supplies to those who have been affected by these situations. Caring for our planet will lessen these natural disasters.

NOURISHMENT FOR YOUR SOUL: Fighting and war are not the answer to freedom. Unconditional Love, Cooperation, compromise and community are. As we all send out love into the world, peace and harmony will prevail.

FOOD FOR THOUGHT: I participate in acts of love to create planetary healing and earth balance.

ANGELIC TOOLS:
♥ *Angelic Reflections IV: Universal Love* by Bonnie Ann Lewis

---

UNIVERSAL LOVE MEDITATION

This meditation is designed to connect you with the love, light and peace that resides within so you can embrace it and expand this love throughout the universe, sharing with all of life. As you do this you contribute to creating heaven here on earth. It is designed to open you up to giving and receiving universal love, and creating balance on our planet earth. It will shift any lower vibrations of energy bringing love and peace to our new earth and all its inhabitants, thus creating heaven here on earth. This powerful meditation sets the scene for the creation of our new earth . . . on angels' wings!

- Let's invite in the wonderful beings of light that are available to assist us by repeating after me, "Dear Angels and Archangels, please surround me in your divine white light and guide me through this meditation. Thank you!"

- I invite you to follow me on a magical journey of love so you may embrace the universal love that is available to you and already present in your life now, for love is the magic of life!

- Along this journey you will be contributing to the creation of heaven here on earth.

- Before we begin, I invite you to join me in a short visualization as this sets the intention, creates the space, and opens the flow for universal love.

- At this time, I invite you to stand or sit upright with your hands stretched out to your side with your palms facing up.

- Take a long deep breath. As you breathe in count to four. Hold your breath for four counts and then release it slowly, counting to four once again.

- Now see a ray of pink light coming from the heavens into your non-dominant hand. (this is the opposite hand in which you write with) Feel it flowing through your heart going out your dominant hand, (the hand you do write with) and flowing back into the universe.

- Affirm: I give and receive love in balance to and from the universe and all its inhabitants.

- At this time, we will begin our journey.

- I invite you to get comfortable in your chair, relax your body and take three or four deep breaths.

- With each inhale, breathe in love from the universe, and with each exhale send love back out into the universe.

- Now bring your focus to your heart, the part of yourself that gives and receives love.

- Feel the warmth of love that is present within you.

- As you continue breathing deeply, breathe in the energy of unconditional love, allowing acceptance, respect, compassion, forgiveness and gratitude to be ever-present in your thoughts, words and actions.

- As you exhale, let go of any judgments about yourself or others, knowing they will be transformed as they are released to our loving angels for purification.
- Now visualize hugging all of the people you've interacted with, had conflict or challenges with today, and send pink light from your heart to theirs.
- Bring your attention to a circle of people in front of you.
- As you join hands with these people, you will become a part of humanity's circle of love that surrounds the globe.
- In the center of the globe is a heart that represents all of humanity.
- With your intention, open your heart and send love to this heart, knowing it will reach all and be returned to you simultaneously.
- Now I invite you to take another deep breath, allowing yourself to receive this infinite flow of unconditional love coming from everyone and the entire universe back to you.
- Feel the powerful effect giving and receiving love has on us all.
- As you take your next deep breath, you will be standing in the middle of a forest. I invite you to send love to all the animals in the forest, the trees, plants and flowers, knowing as you send this love through the forest it reaches all of the wild life and all of nature. You are now encompassed by the forest of love and the animals, trees, plants, flowers and fairies thank you for your love.
- As you take another deep breath, you will find yourself standing in front of the big, beautiful ocean.
- Take several dips into this water, allowing it to cleanse your mind, body and spirit.
- As you bathe in God's love, open your arms to the universe and send love throughout the ocean, knowing as you send this love it reaches all of the sea life, the rivers and the lakes.
- You are now standing in the ocean of love and the sea dwellers thank you for your love.
- Now I invite you to send love to the four directions of the universe. With your first breath inhale love, and as you exhale direct this love to the north. With your second breath inhale love, and as you exhale di-

rect this love to the south. On your third breath inhale love, and as you exhale, direct this love to the west. As you take one more deep breath, inhale love, and as you exhale direct this love to the east.

- At this time, I invite you to send peace and love to where there is war and to any specific places on the planet you feel guided to assist.

- Send love into the atmosphere to balance the energy, creating a calmness in the acts of nature.

- Send love to the mountains and the deserts . . . where there are floods see sunshine absorbing the water . . . where there is drought see rain.

- Send love throughout the earth reaching the crops that nourish our bodies.

- Send love and gratitude to mother earth and to the heavens.

- Once again expand this love you feel within toward the heart in the center of the earth, reaching the whole universe and all its inhabitants.

- Let's affirm: I AM a loving being of light I have a powerful loving impact on this world just being myself. Our world is filled with love, light, peace, unity, abundance and freedom. We give thanks for this truth. And so it is!

- Thank your angels and the archangels for their love and support and the opportunity to experience the magic of love.

- We bless you and thank you for doing your part in creating heaven here on earth.

May you feel the universal love that is forever flowing in your life and embrace the blessings that it brings!

Namaste'

NOTE: This meditation is found on my *Angelic Reflections IV: Universal Love* CD

Best of Both Worlds

Many people believe that in order to "be spiritual" or live a spiritual life, they can not have material possessions or wealth. This is a myth, for in truth we already are spiritual beings and we are here on earth to evolve through experience, while enjoying life. That includes having material possessions. While it is essential not to base our happiness and self-worth on these material possessions, it is equally important to have the material items and financial support we require and desire to accomplish our life's mission, while making it an enjoyable experience. By putting into perspective our material items, they become something that makes our life easier and more enjoyable rather than a collection of stuff for the purpose of material gains as life does have a greater meaning and purpose.

- ♥ The key to having the best of both worlds is to lead a spiritual life and experience the material blessings earth life offers.
- ♥ The spiritual aspect provides us with inner happiness which is reflected in our outer experience.
- ♥ The material blessings are here to meet our needs and for us to enjoy our experience.
- ♥ Since we are spiritual beings in a physical body having a human experience, we must learn to be connected to both realms simultaneously, balancing the spiritual and the physical energies. When we unite our spiritual nature with our earth experience, we experience balance and harmony.
- ♥ As we honor both our humanness and divinity we will experience the best of both worlds.

NOURISHMENT FOR YOUR SOUL: The true meaning of the best of both worlds is creating and experiencing heaven here on earth.

FOOD FOR THOUGHT: My life is filled with an abundance of spiritual gifts and I AM enjoying and grateful for the material blessings present in my life now.

Do you desire to experience heaven here on earth? I believe this can happen and it all begins with each of us. Through our own healing, expressions and manifestations we each contribute to the creation, changes and well-being of our planet earth. We are blessed with an abundance of divine light beings to assist us in creating a world of love and peace. The key to living a fulfilling and abundant life is to live in divine consciousness. The energy of divine consciousness is unconditional love. When we live our life in the vibration of love, we reach our greatest potential, and we experience the best of both worlds by having a spiritual experience and enjoying the material blessings earth life offers. The recipes in this book have been shared to guide your way in experiencing heaven on earth in your life. Now I'd like to share with you my vision of what heaven on earth can be if we all believe and do our part to make it happen. Every dream has wings and together we can bring these dreams to life!

HEAVEN ON EARTH MEDITATION

This meditation is designed to create a vision for our new earth and guide us all to do our part in creating heaven here on earth.

- Close your eyes, take a few deep breaths. I invite you to entertain a divine idea with me as I take you on a journey of experiencing heaven on earth.

- Before we begin this journey, I invite you to leave behind anything that does not serve you anymore.

CREATING HEAVEN ON EARTH

- Invite in your angels by saying, "Dear Angels, please assist me in releasing anything that is preventing me from experiencing heaven on earth now."

- At this time allow any old beliefs, conscious or unconscious, from this lifetime or past life times, related to lack, poverty, fear, violence, disease, judgments or conflicts, to come forth so they may be released with grace and ease. Just allow them to come forward without judgment, knowing you are letting them go.

- Pause.

- Now bring your focus to a bridge that lies in front of you.

- I invite you to walk across this bridge, breathing deeply as you go, and with each exhale continue letting these illusions go with ease. Know as they go out into the universe they are transformed instantly by the white light of your angels.

- Pause.

- Visualize your angels' wings dusting off any remains of these illusions that are not a part of who you are.

- You have just crossed over the bridge of love that connects you to all of life and you are now free to receive the blessings of heaven here on earth.

- Open your heart and mind and imagine what a world of love looks like to you.

- Bring these images to life by setting the intention for a world where everyone is living in the vibration of love, where everyone is loving and loved unconditionally, accepted, respected, compassionate, forgiven, and grateful, and free to be and express themselves as the love they are.

- A world where each and every one of us are utilizing our natural gifts and talents, being of service and enjoying the material blessings life offers experiencing fulfillment in our selves, careers and relationships, where everyone is vibrantly healthy and full of life.

- A world where everyone is living in truth and integrity, experiencing all that their heart desires, where harmony and balance is present.

- Visualize a world where everyone has plenty of food to eat, a home to live in, and clothing to wear. A world where everyone nurtures the environment and only clean air and water exist. Where our animals are safe and free, a world where there is love, peace, unity, freedom, co-operation, commitment, community, and an abundance of good for all!

- Be in this world where only love exists. Allow yourself to feel this world of love and the comfort, peace and joy it brings.

- Visualize our world lit up with bright white lights that represent each of us. Know our world of love is being created here and now because we are all sharing our love and shining our light to make it happen.

- Take yourself to that place where we are all one. Feel the powerful effect love has on all of life. Embrace this love and take it wherever you go, for in truth it is present in your life and in our world now!

- Affirm: I AM love. Our world is filled with love. I give gratitude for this love and the blessings it brings as love is the magic of life!

- For this is heaven on earth!

May you hold this vision and allow the loving presence you feel within to be sent out into the universe as we all create and experience heaven here on earth! Love and Peace to you!

> NOTE: This meditation is found on my *Angelic Reflections II: Tides of Abundance* CD

GUARDIAN OF THE EARTH RAINBOW
Celebrating humanity taking its place in the universe.

PART IV

Gifts of Love

BLESSINGS AND CONGRATULATIONS!

Love makes the world go around
And we must first begin with ourselves.
This you have done by reading and
Participating in this divine guide for living.

Thank you for your attention and
Congratulations on the completion of your
Angelically guided journey to love.

This is an investment you have made in yourself
That will be infinitely valuable throughout your life.

Your success is my inspiration.
I am honored to be a part of your journey.

Remember . . . every step you take
Is part of your journey.
Enjoy the beauty of your dreams,
Celebrate your riches.
Always remember the beautiful,
Powerful being you are,
For you are a gift to this world!

Let your powerful light shine and enjoy your journey!

May your life always be filled with loving experiences, opportunities and relationships as you embrace the blessings love brings!

Blessings to you always,
—Bonnie

ARCHANGEL URIEL
Archangel of Creativity.

YOUR JOURNEY TO LOVE

Angelic Exercises

PART I: AWAKENING TO LOVE

Who am I? 66
Discovering Your Beliefs 77
Overcoming Obstacles. 139
Doorways of Opportunities. 140
Finding Your Soul Colors and Creating a Portrait 163
Going Within 202
Escorting Earthbound Spirits to Light. 231
Exploring Your Desires 244
Character Desires. 245
I Desire to Experience. 246
I Desire to Acquire. 247
Expanding Your Desires:
Discovering Your Gifts, Talents and Life's Mission 249
Inner Happiness. 253
Success 254
Re-creating Dreams. 259
Relationship Reflections 264
Experiences Reflections 268

PART II: THE POWER OF LOVE

Forgiving Self. 280
Forgiving Others 281
Count Your Blessings. 284
What I Love About Me. 287
Creating Boundaries 290
A Love Letter to You 294
Self-Recognition. 294
Writing Conflict Out of Your Life. 313

Envelope of Love 314
Soul Mate Connections 328
Divine Love Exercises 345
Communicating with Your Departed Loved Ones 361
Communicating with Your Inner Child 368
Drawing Your Inner Child 369
From Anger to Passion 389
Releasing Undesirable Characteristics 390
Recognize, Release and Re-creating Fears 393
Amygdala Healing Technique 397
Creating Your Infinite Budget 418

PART III: CREATING WITH LOVE

Full Moon—Releasing 433
New Moon—Desires 434
Out with the "Shoulds," In with the Good 447
My Daily Intentions 456
Book of Your Life 462
Designing Your Career or Job from Within 473
What's in My Heart? 477
Expressing Your Desires 477
Marketing Within 482
Releasing Fears About Life's Purpose 485

PART IV: GIFTS OF LOVE

Messages of Love Art Meditation 524

Angelic Tools by Bonnie Ann Lewis

The *Angelic Reflections* Series is a compilation of the meditations presented throughout this book.

- ♥ *Angelic Reflections I: Awakening*
- ♥ *Angelic Reflections II : Tides of Abundance*
- ♥ *Angelic Reflections III: Life Reflections*
- ♥ *Angelic Reflections IV: Universal Love*

 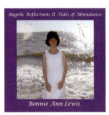  

Let LOVE Be: An affirmative, angelic song for creating divine consciousness, and attracting love, peace, unity, abundance and freedom into your life.

You can purchase these angelic gifts at www.swanselfawarenesscentre.com or www.bonnieannlewis.com. A portion of the proceeds from these angelic tools will be gratefully donated to support various charities.

Connections

The following are links to helpful people and places to purchase the products referred to throughout this book:

Jill Anderson, Graphic + Web Designer: www.JillLynnDesign.com

Ascension Mastery International: www.sacredimages-ami.com

Bill Bastas, Photographic Craftsman: www.bastas.com

Beth Carpenter: healthyhelp4u.com

George Coyne: www.parrottracksstudio.com

Stacy Davenport: www.stacydavenport.com

Floyd Domino: www.floyddomino.com

Karen Drucker: www.karendrucker.com

Hay House Publishing: www.hayhouse.com

Karen Hutchins: www.cicada-recovery-services.com

Jodi Lovoi: www.rhythmsoflife.com

Dr. Ehrin Parker: www.ehrinparker.com

Dr. Carolyn Porter: www.drcarolynporter.com

Eva M. Sakmar-Sullivan, Visionary Art: www.stardolphin.com

Lynda Shannon: www.vancechiro.com

Nature's Treasures: www.naturestreasurestx.com

Peter Sterling: www.harpmagic.com

Soliel's Influence: www.energywithin.net

Doreen Virtue: www.angeltherapy.com

Alpha Zelle: www.alphazelle.com

Four Colour Print Group: www.fourcolour.com

Your Journey to Love Cover Art

This artwork is a reflection of a vision I received from the angels. It symbolizes unconditional, universal love and is intended to usher in the energy of our new earth. The flower of unconditional love has five heart-shaped petals connected in the center of the circle of life with the energy of love. Each petal represents an aspect of unconditional love and is an art within itself. As you let love be the foundation of your life, you will experience the blessings unconditional love brings—love, peace, unity, abundance, and freedom. As we all activate, embrace and express this unconditional love, heaven on earth is created! This art work is designed to be used as a meditation tool to bring you messages of love.

RECEIVING MESSAGES OF LOVE ART MEDITATION

1. Find a cozy space where you will not be interrupted and take your journal and a pen.
2. Invite in your angels by saying, "Dear Angels, please bring me the messages of love you have for me. Please bring them in a way that I can understand them. Thank you!"
3. Place this book or a printed image of this artwork in front of you. Place your hands over it to feel the energy.
4. Close your eyes. Focus on love, and breathe deeply until you feel a sense of peace and relaxation.
5. Open your eyes and focus on the picture.

6. Allow the messages of love to flow. As soon as they begin flowing, write down everything you receive. Your messages may come as a feeling or sensation, voice, vision, thought or a sense of knowing.
7. Thank your angels and send blessings and gratitude to the artwork for being a conduit for these divine messages.

May these messages of love warm your heart and enrich your life!

Divine Inspirations

These divine movies and presentations have crossed my path and touched my life so I'm passing them along. We are very blessed to have these divine examples that nurture our souls' so we may all create and experience heaven here on earth.

- *You Can Heal Your Life: The Movie* by Louise Hay
- *Conversations with God* by Neale Donald Walsh
- *How to Know God* by Deepak Chopra
- *Mother Teresa: The Movie*
- *Ambition to Meaning* by Wayne Dyer
- *There's a Spiritual Solution to Every Problem* by Wayne Dyer
- *Everyday Grace* by Marianne Williamson

Afterword

When the angelic wisdom began coming forth for this book, although it felt so right in my soul, and I could feel the desire, passion and excitement in my heart as I thought about helping others my ego would question, "What credentials do you have to write this book?" I continued on . . . When I began communicating with the angels, the voice of the ego was still there. I heard the angels say, *"Your personal experiences are your credentials."* Although at the time I didn't understand the extent of what that meant. I continued on . . . As I got closer to completing this divine endeavor, there were times the voice of the ego became stronger and more persistent. I continued on . . .

From the beginning I knew this book was the foundation for all my teachings. However, I am truly amazed that it has evolved into this divine guide for living and how it all came together! Although I had my fears and doubts along the way, I'm so glad I followed my heart, divine guidance and continued on. As it turned out, over the course of writing this book, I was guided to take the training and education and received my professional credentials along the way. When I took my ATP® training I received guidance from an Angel Therapy® staff member to journal my journey, which I did. Those journals have been a Godsend in bringing this book to life. I am greatly honored to be the creative channel for this endeavor.

I encourage anyone who feels they have something to share or the passion to write but do not know where to begin or have the credentials to do it anyway. We are all here to learn and grow through and with each other. Personal experience is the greatest credential you can have because when you've walked that path, you have the wisdom, knowledge and compassion to help others. If it feels right in your heart and soul, follow it. You will be divinely guided and supported by the universe. You will always be at the right place at the right time, doing the right things, meeting the right people and receiving the information you require and desire to accomplish your endeavor.

This book has truly been a labor of love. It has been a process of letting go, trust and walking in faith. The passion to help others burned bright inside of me, but I had no idea of the time, energy and persistence this endeavor would entail. There were days I wondered if I would ever finish it and wanted to just give up. But with the loving guidance, direction and support from the angels, archangels and ascended masters, and more persistence than I ever imagined I had in me, I have given birth to this dream! I truly believe writing is a work of art in which we allow the love of God to express through us. I have come to love the writing process and seeing how it all unfolds, creating a beautiful masterpiece of reflections of the heart. The gift for me lies in the healing that occurred along the way, and the joy it brings to empower others. My prayer is that this divine guide blesses all it touches. My passion for writing this book came from my desire to help others. At the time I channeled the information I did not recognize the value and impact it would have on my own life. Again, I am so blessed and grateful for the blessings this experience has brought!

Love and Light to you,
Bonnie

About the Author

Bonnie Ann Lewis is an ANGEL THERAPY PRACTITIONER®, Professional Spiritual Teacher, and Medium (certified by Doreen Virtue). She is also the Founder of the Swan Self-Awareness Centre in Austin, Texas, and is blessed to be one of the youth teachers at Center for Spiritual Living Central Texas.

Bonnie is a messenger of love and a guiding light. Her passion is to create a world of love and peace by opening the hearts and minds of all by educating them about the powerful beings they are. She believes we can all contribute to making this world a better place beginning with oneself, and together we can make it happen! Her passions come alive and shine through in her gifts of writing, teaching, angelic guidance coaching and angelic tools.

Her vision is that we all live the life God intended for us to live—a fulfilling life of love, peace, unity, abundance and freedom. These are our birthright and the blessings of experiencing heaven here on earth.

Mrs. Lewis shares her home in Austin, Texas with her beloved husband John, two precious children, Rebecca and Joshua, and two pet guinea pigs, Rachel and Shiloh. Her other passions include, hiking, cycling, rollerblading, spending time in nature, relaxing by the ocean in their home-away-from-home in Port Aransas, Texas, creative projects, painting, music, traveling, and reading.

For more about Bonnie and the angelic gifts she brings to this world, visit www.swanselfawarenesscentre.com or www.bonnieannlewis.com. You can also contact her at bonnielewis@swanselfawarenesscentre.com.

To be inspired, empowered and enlightened, we invite you to join Bonnie for any of her angelic presentations, workshops or events.

Your Journey to Love Daily Practices

Blessed with the heavenly harp music of Peter Sterling

Here are some short and sweet meditative visualizations, activations and invocations to include in your daily practice. These simple yet powerful practices are placed throughout this book. I have listed them here and included them on the CD with this book to make it easy for you to incorporate them into your daily rituals. The time that you take will be an investment that will enhance your well-being and enrich your life!

1. **Introduction:** Because we are spiritual beings in a physical body, it is essential for us to maintain our spiritual self as well as our physical body to ensure a healthy well-being. *The Daily Practice* CD included with this book will make it simple to include these short and sweet meditative visualizations, activations and invocations into your daily rituals. These powerful practices will embrace your body, warm your heart, nourish your soul, inspire your mind, and enrich your life! (0:42)

2. **Activating Your Light Body Invocation** expands and activates your light body by releasing lower energy, invoking more light into your body, raising your vibration. The more light you contain within you, the higher your vibration is and the more loving experiences you will attract. (1:42)

3. **Shields of Love Activation** protects you from taking on energy of lower vibration and the emotions of others. It's best to do this exercise first thing in the morning and then repeat throughout

your day as needed. If you do not have this CD available to you throughout your day, just call in your angels and ask them to activate your shields of love and focus on this activation. As you do so it will replay in your mind, setting the intention for this to occur and you will have re-activate your shields of love! (1:40)

4. **Centering Visualization** is designed to help you stay centered in your natural state of love even when there is chaos around you. It will also help to balance the masculine and feminine energy within you. You can do this in whatever position is comfortable for you. (1:14)

5. **Bubble of Love Visualization** is designed to encompass you in the energy of love so that you can enjoy loving experiences throughout your day. (1:19)

6. **Bridge of Love** is designed to send loving thoughts and energy to anyone you are having conflict with as it clears the space and shifts the energy, building a bridge of love. You can also use this visualization to resolve conflict within yourself by visualizing yourself in place of the other person. (1:46)

7. **Releasing Visualization** is designed to release any lower energy you have absorbed and clear your energy field so you attract higher vibrations of energy. This can be done instantly anytime you feel yourself picking up lower energy or another's emotions. Follow with the Shields of Love Activation. (1:49)

8. **Mirrors of Love Visualization** is perfect to use when you are around people that are sending out negative energy, situations where there is harsh energy or where you feel like you are being psychically attacked. This will help to transform the energy. (0:58)

9. **Rainbows of Love Activation** is designed to activate the rainbow light that your body needs to be vibrantly healthy and full of life. It will keep you energized, re-vitalized and filled with universal energy. I recommend doing this outdoors or visualize yourself outside. (1:33)

10. **Earth Love Activation** places a shield of protection around our planet and increases the love and light that is dispersed throughout our earth, raising the vibration. By adding this activation to your daily rituals you are contributing to creating a world of love and peace. (0:47)

11. **Grounding Visualization** helps to keep you grounded, creating a balance between heaven and earth. I recommend doing this outdoors or visualize yourself outside. (1:34)

12. **Blessings:** May you have a glorious day filled with love, peace and joy! Namaste' (0:07)

Throughout your day you can re-activate any of these practices by focusing on them and setting the intention for that to occur. When you think about them, your mind replays the entire practice and will re-activate the energy.

Messages of Love

YOUR JOURNEY TO LOVE

MESSAGES OF LOVE

YOUR JOURNEY TO LOVE